A SHORT HISTORY of  Quebec

PREFACE

The first edition of this book originated in 1984 with the authors' perception that Quebec history as represented in English-language literature had a traditional, political orientation that neglected important elements in Quebec society. Emphasizing socio-economic relations, we reshaped the periodization of Quebec history and within this framework, integrated recent research.

The aftermath of the October 1992 referendum which rejected the Charlottetown constitutional accord both within and outside Quebec represents a propitious time to publish a second edition of our *Short History of Quebec*. The referendum debate gave immediacy to the historical themes central to this book: Quebec as a distinct society—dare one call it "the national question"?—with its implications for language, culture, and civil law; the status of women and of aboriginal self-government; institutions and the place of Quebec in the federal political and judicial structure; provincial powers; equalization, regional development, and the issue of the free movement of goods, capital, and persons across provincial boundaries.

Many in Canada are deeply frustrated with Quebec's insistence on the primacy of French language and collective rights, and with what is perceived as its violation of the principles of tolerance and liberal democracy. Witness the warm reception given to the works of Mordecai Richler (1992) and David Bercuson and Barry Cooper (1991). For their part, Quebecers seem increasingly comfortable with a vision of the provincial government as their "national" and potentially sovereign government. This apparent disintegration of the historic unity of the St. Lawrence political and ideological system adds a timeliness to this book which insists on the historicity of these questions.

Important sections have been rewritten for this edition, especially those dealing with the recent past, Our periodization has been refined, particularly in dividing the period from the 1930s. We have increased the number of illustrations, improved and updated the bibliography, and have tried to simplify language and terms.

Three colleagues—Bettina Bradbury, Robert Sweeny, and Pierre Tousignant—read all or parts of the first edition and their comments helped us shape elements of our interpretation, periodization, and presentation. Jack Little, Peter Gossage, Donald B. Smith, and Jacques Ferland contributed important comments for reshaping this edition. While their suggestions led to important improvements, they have no responsibility for the final text. Our editor, Camilla Jenkins, has been draconian in reminding us that an important element in the historian's craft is writing in language that is simple and straightforward.

INTRODUCTION

Writing a short and readable synthesis of the history of Quebec imposes difficult choices. Not wanting to write in as comprehensive a fashion as Paul-André Linteau, René Durocher, Jean-Claude Robert, and François Ricard in their two-volume history of contemporary Quebec, we defined certain themes that give unity to our interpretation of the Quebec past. In her work, *The Dream of Nation: A Social and Intellectual History of Quebec* (1983), Susan Trofimenkoff emphasizes ideology and the experience of women. Our work is complementary to hers; we have interpreted Quebec history in a socio-economic framework based on a re-evaluation of the traditional periodization.

Our geographical frame is the province as defined in 1912 and confirmed by the Privy Council in 1927: from Ungava Bay and Hudson Bay to the Appalachians, and from the Ottawa Valley to Labrador (Figure 1). Although we do not neglect the relationship of Quebec to larger Canadian and North American realities, our perspective is Quebec and its people. Francophones outside Quebec are not treated systematically.

At the same time, we avoid treating Quebec as a monolithic whole and have been careful to highlight regional, class, and ethnic diversity; life in the Gaspé

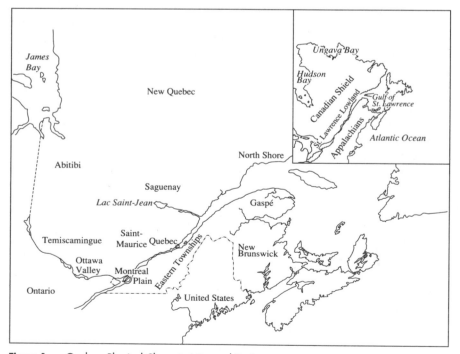

Figure 1   Quebec: Physical Characteristics and Regions

and on the Montreal plain, for example, has always been very different. Variations in dialect, economy, and social structure differentiate the francophone populations of the Saguenay, the Eastern Townships, and the Ottawa Valley. At the same time, the worker in the snowmobile factory in Valcourt is separated by profound class differences from members of the Bombardier family, although they share a similar cultural heritage. Ethnic differences and the particular structure of capitalism have increasingly set Montreal apart from the other regions of the province.

New approaches in social history, with their emphasis on long-term evolution in social and economic relations, have incited historians to reflect on periodization—a particularly apt exercise at this juncture when the historical context surrounding native land claims, Bill 178, and free trade is regularly distorted. Can the "distinct society" issue be discussed without reference to the Quebec Act of 1774, the Rebellions of 1837–1838, or the history of francophone rights outside Quebec?

Without denying the importance of political events such as the Conquest or Confederation, we have subordinated them to a socio-economic framework that explains them in a broader perspective. Our periodization is much closer to that of Gilles Paquet and Jean-Pierre Wallot (1982). Although we agree with their concept of process, our time periods are different and we relate our periodization closely to the passage of Quebec through distinct modes of production and exchange. Property and other forms of economic power, the law, social structure, institutions, and gender are central to our focus.

Until the 1650s, native peoples had the demographic superiority, power, and cohesion to remain dominant and European trading networks remained reliant on prehistoric native exchange systems. The preindustrial period, from the 1650s to the 1810s, was first characterized by a rapid decline in native strength. By the late seventeenth century, a rapidly maturing colonial preindustrial society based on a peasant economy and commercial capitalism had been established. Europeans had gained control of the trading areas and the seigneurial, legal, religious, and administrative institutions took shape.

We join Robert Sweeny (1986), Joanne Burgess (1987), and Serge Courville and Normand Séguin (1989) in seeing the end of the Napoleonic Wars as the benchmark from which we can discern fundamental changes in forms of production and social, capitalist, and political relations. Transition to industrial capitalism in the period from the 1810s to the 1880s was admittedly uneven and the persistence of preindustrial characteristics in some sectors of the economy and in some regions must not be discounted. Early industrialization was complex; wage labour was often introduced, or the scale of production changed, before new technology arrived. Immigration and urbanization were important characteristics of the period. The end of the Napoleonic Wars marked the beginning of a change in

British attitudes towards their Canadian colonies, a process that culminated in responsible government, federalism, and Confederation. By mid-century the form of the modern state can be discerned in institutions like schools, in the land registry system, colonization roads, the dismantling of seigneurialism, and in the establishment of the Civil Code of 1866. The period before 1837 saw an important rise of nationalism among the francophone professional class as well as a renaissance of the Roman Catholic church.

The half-century from the 1880s—when the National Policy and completion of the Canadian Pacific Railway symbolized the formation of a pan-Canadian state—to the 1930s can be characterized as the period of monopoly capitalism. Quebec had been the traditional manufacturing centre of Canada, and with its abundant natural resources it became important in mining, electricity, and pulp-and-paper. Capital in these and other industrial sectors was concentrated in the hands of anglophones; francophones turned to regional and co-operative sources of capital. In the period, the Roman Catholic church reached its social and political zenith.

Monopoly capitalism had particular consequences for women. Catholic ideology and Victorian ideals forced bourgeois women to channel their energies into home, family, and philanthropic activities, while women from the popular classes often served as cheap factory labour in addition to their domestic and childrearing responsibilities.

The crisis of capitalism in the 1930s led people to question the role of the state and the nature of capitalist society. The years between the Depression and the 1960s were transitional and it is appropriate to deal with them as a distinct period. The reforms proposed by Catholic intellectuals such as Lionel Groulx, Georges-Henri Lévesque, and members of the Ecole sociale populaire ranged from corporatism to statism and included independence. In the years after 1929, diminishing demand for Quebec's raw materials, farm products, and manufactured goods was reflected in massive unemployment and poverty. The incapacity of Catholic agencies to deal financially with these needs undermined the power of the church and forced the state to intervene. Provincial government expenditures in health, social services, and education rose from $60 million in 1933 to nearly $600 million in 1959.

The Second World War also triggered modernization of the political and economic structures: women received the provincial vote; education was made compulsory for children under fourteen; Hydro-Quebec was established; and important labour legislation was enacted.

Contemporary Quebec—the 1960s to the present—emerged from this period of depression, war, and reconstruction. With a growing sense of their collectivity, Quebecers reordered their society, granting a larger role to the state in the economy, health, and education. The nationalization of electricity was broadened, education became secular and democratic, and universal health care was implemented. In the same period, nationalism became a stronger force. Francophones questioned their place in the Canadian federal state, and language assumed a new centrality in politics.

A demographic transition was complete by the end of the 1960s as the birth rate declined to one of the lowest in industrial countries. The integration of immigrants into the francophone sector therefore gave a new importance to the language question. The language debate stimulated francophone nationalism and culminated in the adoption of Bill 101 in 1977. Divorce rates rose dramatically after the federal divorce law of 1968, and single parent families, usually headed by women, became more common. Women pressed for a redefinition of their position in Quebec society, both in the workplace and with respect to issues such as abortion and birth control. In public life, women gained limited power in the civil service, the courts, unions, and the cabinet.

The decline of manufacturing in favour of the tertiary sector and Montreal's slipping importance in the pan-Canadian economy (already evident in the 1930s when its stock exchange was superseded by Toronto's) was symbolized by the transfer of many head offices to Toronto. The process was most notable in the financial sector.

In addition to the importance we give to socio-economic processes, we have emphasized class, gender, and groups largely invisible in traditional histories of Quebec. From their place at centre stage in the first chapters, we try to follow the passage of native peoples through the subsequent periods.

Women have been absent from elite history because until recently they did not formally participate in politics, the professions, or the army. When we use parish, notarial, or judicial records to look at population, work, the family, and social relations, however, a different view emerges. Servants, for example, were the largest group of paid workers in eighteenth- and nineteenth-century urban Quebec, and most of these were women. Although domestics represented 22.4 percent of Montreal's active labour force in 1825, the liberal professions, which shaped our political history and memory, were filled by just 2 percent of the active population. Consideration of women's experience is fundamental to our periodization and socio-economic perspective. Nonetheless, the debate over whether women's history should be separated from traditional history presents an ongoing organizational dilemma.

Not all aspects of Quebec history can be treated in a brief work. For some important issues, such as proto-industrialization, research remains preliminary and viable conclusions cannot be presented. We see this book's vocation then as twofold. It gives an overview of the main elements of Quebec history and, at the same time, addresses important interpretative questions. It is our modest wish that this book will serve to reinforce the maxim that "all history has to be looked at again."

A word about using the book and about further reading: each chapter has a bibliographical note that directs the reader to general works on the subjects and period treated in the chapter. This is supplemented by a larger and more comprehensive general reference list at the end of the book.

The changing political reality of Quebec poses problems of terminology. In the period of New France, for example, the French inhabitants of the St. Lawrence Valley were called "Canadiens"; in British North America they were known as "new subjects," "Canadiens," and "Lower Canadians." After Confederation, "French Canadian" was commonly used and more recently "Québécois." Although they are neologisms, we use the terms "francophone" and "anglophone" to distinguish between the two main cultural communities of Quebec. Contemporary designations are more correct in an historical perspective and are occasionally used in the text, but they are not without ambiguity to readers. The English-speaking population of Quebec is heterogeneous and, here too, the terms English, Scot, Irish, and American are used to understand particular events. The term anglophone is used when members of these different English-speaking communities acted in a common fashion.

The variety of currencies and units of measurement poses problems as well. French *livres* were commonly used until the mid-nineteenth century, overlapping with various British currencies after the Conquest. With the introduction of banking institutions in the 1820s, the dollar rose in importance and was formally adopted in 1862, when six livres equalled one dollar and £1 Halifax equalled four dollars. Throughout the text, the currency used reflects that of the document. The metric system has been adopted throughout.

Native Peoples and the Beginnings of New France to 1650

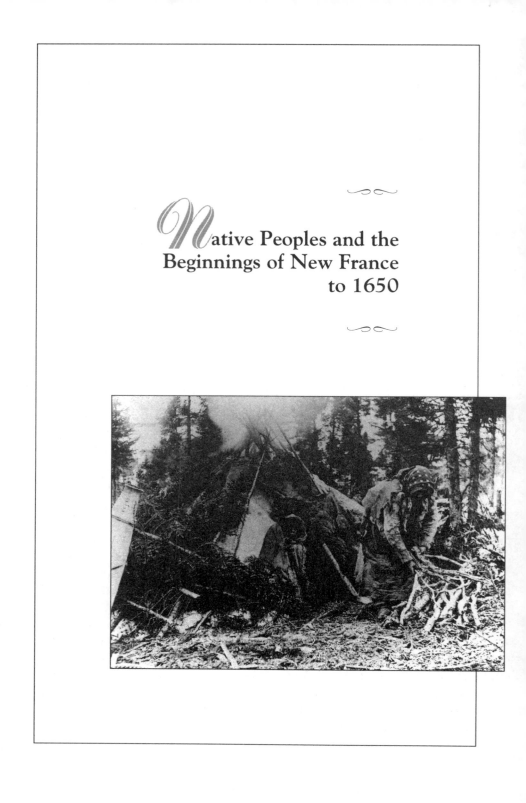

*T*he history of early Canada has been coloured by the writings of European travellers and missionaries eager to promote settlement or Christianity. From this eurocentric perspective, native peoples were never more than a backdrop to the heroics surrounding the establishment of European communities in North America. Early Canadian history should, however, centre on the original inhabitants. Several millenia before the arrival of Europeans, native peoples were coping with both the harsh North American environment and evolving intertribal relations. Until the mid-seventeenth century, Europeans were a small minority on the continent, who had to adjust to native ways of conducting trade and war. It is the recent work of archeologists more than of historians, that has led to a better appreciation of native history and its centrality in understanding early New France (Trigger, 1985).

The interpretion of the pre-1663 period as the "Heroic Age" of French colonization is a good example. Even anthropologists such as Bruce Trigger, who has studied this era from a native peoples' viewpoint, have been unable or unwilling to break with this traditional benchmark. Yet 1663, when the French crown assumed direct control of the colony, was essentially a political point of reference with little significance for the colony's developing economic and social structures and with even less importance for native peoples. Indians played a decisive economic role in enabling a French colony to take shape along the St. Lawrence. If we accept their importance, then the first major turning point of the postcontact era is the demographic and economic upheaval created by the dispersal of the Huron in 1650.

PRECONTACT NATIVE SOCIETY

Native oral traditions invariably maintain that a Creator placed humans on earth in North America at the beginning of time. Archeological evidence indicates that the ancestors of the native peoples were hunters who crossed the Bering Strait from Asia some 40 000 years ago and spread through North and South America. After the retreat of the glaciers more than 10 000 years ago, hunters moving into eastern Canada followed herds of caribou and other game. About 3000 years ago the climate stabilized, creating an environment in which population could increase and spread across Quebec. The food supply came from fish, migrating birds, and mammals such as moose, deer, and caribou. This meat diet was supplemented by wild berries and nuts. Fish, fowl, and vegetation were scarce in winter and survival depended on ideal weather conditions and heavy snows, which slowed down the prey. Population was therefore limited by seasonal fluctuations in the meat supply (Clermont, 1974).

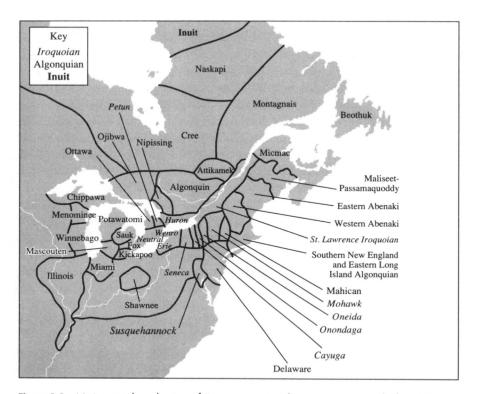

Key
Iroquoian
Algonquian
Inuit

Inuit

Naskapi

Petun

Ojibwa
Nipissing
Ottawa

Cree

Montagnais

Beothuk

Micmac

Attikamek

Algonquin

Maliseet-
Passamaquoddy

Eastern Abenaki

Western Abenaki

Chippawa
Menominee
Potawatomi
Huron

Winnebago
Sauk
Fox
Neutral
Wenro
Erie

Mascouten
Kickapoo

Miami

Seneca

Illinois

Shawnee

Susquehannock

St. Lawrence Iroquoian

Southern New England
and Eastern Long
Island Algonquian

Mahican

Mohawk

Oneida

Onondaga

Cayuga

Delaware

Figure 1.1 Native people at the time of European contact: language groups and tribes. It is important not to confuse the Iroquoian speakers with the Iroquois Confederacy. The Confederacy was one group of Iroquoian speakers, made up of the Mohawk, Oneida, Onondaga, Cayuga, and Seneca tribes.

Plant cultivation developed in South and Central America about 9000 years ago. These practices spread northward and by about 1000 A.D. most peoples in southern Ontario and Quebec had begun to raise corn, beans, and squash. In these societies, summer food surpluses fed the population during the winter, and broke the link between population growth and limited seasonal resources. On the Canadian Shield, however, soil and climate conditions prevented the development of horticulture and although corn was obtained through trade, the population of this region remained sparser than farther south.

By the time of European contact in the sixteenth century, the North American population was divided into complex band, tribal, cultural, and linguistic subgroups. The northeastern quarter of the continent contained three separate language stocks: Algonquian, Iroquoian, and Inuit (Figure 1.1). Within these three groups there were many different dialects. Language did not necessarily correspond with economic and cultural delineations. Most Algonquians in Canada were semi-nomadic hunters, for example, but those living along the present-day New England seaboard practised horticultural subsistence similar to the Iroquoian peoples of the lower Great Lakes.

The precontact period was one of great cultural development, in which villages became larger, warfare more widespread, political structures more complex, and funeral rites more elaborate, while pottery design took on distinctive regional characteristics (Trigger, 1985: 100–8). During this period most of the peoples of the Northeast adopted the behavioural patterns that were observed by the early European travellers, such as funerary ceremony and political organization into confederacies. It must be remembered, however, that native societies were undergoing constant change, which was accelerated by the coming of Europeans.

While the exact size of the precontact population cannot be determined—even estimates for well-studied tribes such as the Huron vary by 50 percent—it is clear that North America was not a virgin land at the beginning of the fifteenth century. The Algonquian-speaking peoples in central and eastern Canada numbered some 70 000 and another 100 000 lived in New England. About 100 000 Iroquoians lived around Chesapeake Bay, the lower Great Lakes, and along the upper St. Lawrence Valley. The Inuit, inhabitants of the Canadian Arctic, numbered perhaps 25 000, of whom 3000 lived in northern Quebec and Labrador.

These native peoples can be divided into two broad categories of subsistence, determined by local environment and resources: the semi-nomadic hunters of the Arctic, the Canadian Shield, and the Appalachians; and the sedentary horticulturalists of the St. Lawrence lowlands. The subsistence pattern of semi-nomadic peoples was dictated by a sharply defined seasonal cycle. During the winter, the population divided into small bands which moved into the interior in search of moose, caribou, deer, and bear. When conditions made it difficult to capture these larger mammals, beaver and otter were hunted. It is estimated that a hunter in Quebec had to kill twenty to thirty beaver, seven moose or caribou, and a bear for his family to survive through a winter (Clermont, 1974).

Early European observers echoed Jesuit Pierre Biard's observation that "If the weather then is favourable, they live in great abundance; but if it is against them, they are greatly to be pitied and often die of starvation" (1615). In the spring, individual bands returned from their winter hunting grounds in the interior and formed larger groups at propitious sites near lakes, rivers, or the Atlantic, where they lived on fish and shellfish, migratory birds, fruits, nuts, and small game. "Free from anxiety about their food" (Thwaites, 1896–1901, 3: 79–81) they bartered with neighbouring bands and had time for social activities. Warfare was not an important part of these people's existence; if it occurred, it was carried on during the summer months.

Figure 1.2 A Cree woman arranging firewood outside her tent. Illustrations of native peoples from the early historical period are highly stylized and often contain many inaccuracies, but more recent pictures can be helpful in reconstructing traditional life. This photograph, taken by Hudson's Bay Company Trader, A. A. Chesterfield, in the Ungava District at the beginning of the twentieth century, shows a Cree caribou-skin lodge and, on the left, a toboggan. The woman and child are both clad in caribou skins and, apart from a cloth handkerchief tied around the woman's head, show little European influence.

The technology of semi-nomadic peoples was utilitarian. Since transportation was so important to their subsistence, their birch-bark canoes were superior to those of sedentary tribes and their moccasins, beaver robes, snowshoes, and long, narrow toboggans enabled them to travel warmly and easily through snow and forests. Other aspects of their material culture were less developed: apart from birch-bark bowls and hunting and fishing gear, they had few utensils. Knives and arrowheads were made of stone, and needles and harpoon heads of bone and antler. Their conical lodges (Figure 1.2), covered with bark in the summer and skins in the winter, were easy to dismantle, transport, and reconstruct. With a radius of only two to three metres and inhabited by up to a dozen people, these lodges were used for sleeping and for shelter on the coldest days; most activities took place outside. A fire in the centre of the lodge served for both cooking and heating. Although some smoke escaped through a hole in the top of the lodge, these dwellings were stuffy and caused severe eye infections.

The Iroquoian tribes were sedentary, living in palisaded villages joined by networks of trails. Longhouses (Figure 1.3), the main structures in their villages, were

Figure 1.3 An Iroquoian longhouse at Lanoraie. This artist's conception of an Iroquoian longhouse near Montreal is based on archeological evidence found at the site. The only important interior division in a longhouse was the grain storage area at one end.

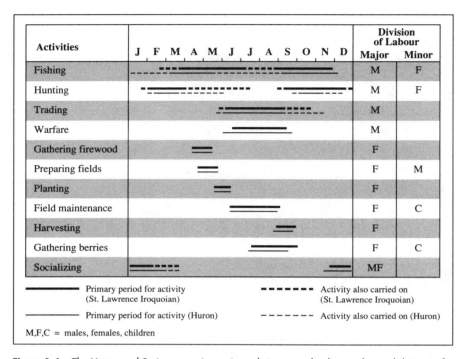

| Activities | J F M A M J J A S O N D | Division of Labour | |
		Major	Minor
Fishing		M	F
Hunting		M	F
Trading		M	
Warfare		M	
Gathering firewood		F	
Preparing fields		F	M
Planting		F	
Field maintenance		F	C
Harvesting		F	
Gathering berries		F	C
Socializing		MF	

————————— Primary period for activity (St. Lawrence Iroquoian)　　　－ － － － － － Activity also carried on (St. Lawrence Iroquoian)

————————— Primary period for activity (Huron)　　　－ － － － － － Activity also carried on (Huron)

M,F,C = males, females, children

Figure 1.4 The Huron and St. Lawrence Iroquoian subsistence calendars and sexual division of labour. Iroquoians in general had the same subsistence patterns, with minor variations caused by environmental differences. The life cycle of the various species of fish and game determined a fairly rigid calendar in which men left the village from mid-winter to late autumn. Hunting was a more important activity for the St. Lawrence Iroquoians than for the Hurons, and their fishing was concentrated over longer periods during the spring and autumn. This left less time for winter socializing (Chapedelaine 1989: 120–21).

twenty to thirty metres long, and six or seven metres wide. Constructed of wooden supports that were tied together and covered in bark, the longhouse had few interior divisions. Each longhouse had four or five fireplaces, around which several related families worked, played, ate, and slept. Raised platforms along each side provided storage and sleeping space. Villages had populations of about 1500 and occupied the same site for about fifteen years, or until the surrounding soil or the firewood supply was exhausted.

Iroquoian life also followed a seasonal pattern (Figure 1.4), although horticulture freed them from the winter survival crises of their semi-nomadic neighbours. Iroquoian women worked in village fields growing corn, beans, squash, sunflowers (for seeds and oil), and tobacco. Women's work also included collecting firewood, making pottery, cooking, and raising children. Men cleared new fields and prepared new village sites. Although meat formed only a small part of the Iroquoian diet, the men hunted beaver and Virginia deer in February and in the autumn. Fish was the major source of protein for Hurons and St. Lawrence Iroquoians and spawning-season fishing expeditions drew men away from their villages for several months each year. Trade and warfare were other good-weather activities that depopulated Iroquoian villages of their males. The population socialized and practised crafts primarily in the winter, when the community was together.

In addition to many of the tools and goods of their more peripatetic neighbours, the Iroquoians produced horticultural tools such as hoes, axes adapted to clearing fields, and pestles to grind corn into flour. Since sagamite—a soup made of corn flour and fish—was a staple in the Iroquoian diet, pottery cooking bowls were an essential part of Iroquoian craftwork. These people were also skilled at making reed baskets and mats and hemp fishing nets.

For all native peoples, the family was the basic social unit and its structure depended on subsistence patterns. Among hunters, families were patriarchal, centring around a male head who was respected for his skill. Family life in horticultural communities centred around female members, who raised the crops essential for survival. This structure was reflected in the organization of their longhouses, which were inhabited by matrilineally related families, often a woman and her daughters or a group of sisters. All native peoples had incest taboos, and partners were chosen from outside the kinship group.

Marriage had political and social significance. In Algonquian tribes it cemented bonds between different groups sharing adjacent territories; in Iroquoian villages it reinforced the sense of community by uniting members of the different clans that made up the village. In contrast to European societies of the time, young people chose partners without parental interference. In Indian societies couples were normally monogamous, although important Algonquian chiefs might have two or three wives as symbols of their power. Although divorce was accepted, it rarely occurred among couples with children.

Political organization centred around the tribe. In hunting societies, the tribe was usually a loose association of bands which met briefly in the summer; in these circumstances unity was more cultural than political. Summer gatherings were the occasion for barter, storytelling, games, and the opportunity for young people to meet and court. Political discussions generally concerned external relations, and band chiefs prepared war parties when the occasion arose. Since hunters exploited vast, sparsely inhabited territories and had little contact with their neighbours, however, conflicts were minimal and warfare was not an important activity.

Iroquoian society, with its farming, villages, and larger population, required more organization and sense of community to function. In every village each clan had a civil chief, who was responsible for order, religious ceremonies, trade, and the changing of the village site, as well as a war chief, who determined war and defence strategy. These leaders were chosen by clan matrons from among suitable candidates in their own families. Chiefs from each village met occasionally in tribal or league councils to decide on matters of common interest and joint war parties. Women were not allowed to speak in village or tribal councils.

Conflict in horticultural societies was endemic because the denser population increased tensions within the tribe and at the same time added to external competition for both land and game. As well, when horticulture was adopted, male activities such as hunting and fishing were overshadowed, leading men to seek prestige through military feats. Warfare strengthened community solidarity by focusing aggression on an outside party, mainly through the ritualistic torture of male prisoners. Captives were brought into the village and symbolically adopted into the family of a recently killed tribesman before being subjected to a long ceremony during which the whole community—men, women, and children—spent hours mutilating the victim before opening the body and eating the vital organs. The prisoner was expected to show his bravery by singing his war song and by threatening his tormentors. Women and children captives were rarely tortured, but were adopted and assimilated.

Although differences in subsistence patterns influenced social organization, all Indian societies shared similar concepts of acceptable behaviour, believed that the supernatural influenced daily life, and divided labour along sexual lines.

As well as hunting, fishing, trading, and warring, men produced spears, bows and arrows, snowshoes, and canoes. In Iroquoian tribes, men cleared land for new village sites: small trees could be chopped down with stone axes but bigger trees had to be felled by stripping their bark and burning the base.

In addition to having and raising children, women prepared food and hides, made clothes, collected firewood and berries, and smoked meat and fish. Their other tasks depended on the main subsistence activity of the people involved. Among horticulturalists, women, aided by children, did all the tasks associated with raising the crops. They also produced pottery, baskets, and mats. Whenever a band moved its camp, women in hunting societies often carried the heaviest loads so that the men would be free to pursue game en route.

Although early European observers often described native women as drudges with little control over their own lives, the women were in fact remarkably autonomous and enjoyed complete freedom to organize their tasks (Leacock, 1986). Mary Jemison, an Englishwoman adopted by the Delaware, observed that Indian women's labour was comparable to that of white women, the main difference being that "we [native women] had no master to oversee or drive us, so that we could work as leisurely as we pleased" (Axtell, 1985: 324). In contrast, explorers and missionaries, failing to recognize the importance of hunting since in Europe it was considered a leisure activity reserved for the nobility, described Indian men as lazy. The Europeans based their opinions on observations in the villages; they did not identify the men's contribution to horticulture and rarely followed them in their subsistence activities.

Native peoples valued individual freedom, disliked coercion, and expected people to show each other politeness and respect. Social control depended on community norms such as generosity, self-sacrifice for one's family, and stoic acceptance of adversity. Social control was generally enforced by relatives, with family members responsible for their kin's transgressions. To avoid being involved in feuds with fellow tribespeople or allies, families paid reparations that depended on both the seriousness of the crime and the sex and status of the victim. In cases of murder, for example, a slain Huron chief would command greater compensation than someone of lesser importance, and the compensation for a women (forty beaver robes on average) was greater than for a man (thirty beaver robes) (Trigger, 1976, I: 60).

Chiefs governed largely through respect. Since they could not order people to act against their will, there were consultations and attempts to reach consensus. Only in the most rare and dramatic forms of deviant behaviour (witchcraft, murder, and treason) did councils execute tribespeople (Trigger, 1963).

Indian society was based on communal sharing rather than private accumulation. European concepts of property were unknown and this absence of familiar norms allowed the French to disregard native claims to territory. Hunting bands had specific territories which they exploited rationally in a cycle determined by the seasonal availability of fish and game. Although Europeans perceived them as roaming the woods, they followed predetermined routes which took them to the regions best suited to their particular subsistence activities. Horticulturalists shared communal fields and well-defined hunting territories and fishing camps. Hospitality and helping the needy were considered great virtues and those who accumulated wealth were expected to be generous in providing the less fortunate with food, clothing, and other necessities. Prestige was acquired more by donation than by accumulation.

This principle can be seen in trade relations: goods were exchanged in the form of presents, often of equal value. Trade had social as well as economic connotations and barter was usually accompanied by feasts, games, speeches, and the smoking of peace pipes. Trade in precious commodities such as copper from north of Lake Superior or wampum (beads made of polished shells and used to decorate clothing or to make armbands and necklaces) from Long Island pre-dated European contact by hundreds of years.

By the fifteenth century, trade in the Northeast increasingly centred on the exchange of agricultural surplus from sedentary tribes for meat and fur surpluses from hunters. The Huron, for example, traded corn and tobacco for pelts with their northern neighbours, the Nipissing and Ottawa. These native trading systems later formed the framework for the rapid expansion of the fur trade.

Since all native peoples believed that most aspects of nature—sun, moon, rain, and disease, for example—as well as some fabricated objects such as fishing nets were animate, religion permeated daily life and the supernatural was considered to be responsive to human behaviour. Hunters contacted the spirit of their prey to ensure success and they disposed of inedible parts according to a strict code so that the animal's kin would not be offended. The bones of a bear, for example, were carefully buried rather than being thrown to the dogs. Gifts were made to the spirit of the rain to ensure good harvests and to the spirit of the river for safe voyages.

Because their spirituality commanded genuine respect for the welfare of other life forms, native people are often seen as the first environmentalists. In order to explain their willingness to destroy the balance in nature and to hunt animals to extinction in the fur trade, historian Calvin Martin argues that diseases afflicting native peoples in the early seventeenth century were blamed on animal spirits. As disease spread, the Indians came to believe that the animal world had broken its contract with the human world. This freed hunters from their obligation to kill only sufficient prey for subsistence (Martin, 1978). Martin's thesis is sharply contested by historians who argue that more prosaic considerations motivated Indian behaviour (Krech, 1981). Although Martin's thesis is based on flimsy and controversial evidence, it does draw attention to native ideology as an important factor in shaping the early history of Quebec.

Dreams were an especially important medium for contacting the spirit world. In all tribes, shamans—healers and seers—interpreted dreams to learn of prospects for successful hunts or war parties. Although shamans relied on a wide variety of herbal remedies for many ailments, some illness was thought to originate with spirits, in which case shamans contacted the spirit to appease it or drive it from the body.

As in other cultures, myths helped to explain the mysteries of the universe. Native myths undoubtedly formed a coherent philosophy, but only fragments are available because missionaries recorded only stories that closely resembled biblical or western mythological traditions. The Huron creation myth of Aataentsic, for example, in which a woman fell from heaven and landed on the back of a turtle floating on the primeval sea, was considered to be a distortion of the biblical flood. Thus the lens of Christian interpretation makes it difficult to reconstruct native ideology and weigh its influence on behaviour.

Native peoples believed that the soul is immortal and they gave great attention to funeral ceremony. On a person's death, the soul left the body and travelled to a land in the West. Native peoples often buried weapons, bowls, clothes, and pipes with the dead, believing that the spirits of these personal effects helped the soul face the world of the dead. In some regions of the Northeast, funeral ceremonial practice peaked in the early years after European contact.

When Hurons changed village sites they re-interred everyone who had died since the village last moved, in a common grave or ossuary. In the reburial—or Feast of the Dead—ceremonies, relatives cleaned any remaining tissue from the skeletons, wrapped the bones in new beaver robes, and presented bowls, pipes, knives, tobacco, and wampum to ensure the happiness of the spirits of deceased family members in the land of the dead. Common burial sites and ceremonies reinforced tribal unity and alliances with neighbouring groups at a time when solidarity was needed to face the challenges of European cultural imperialism and increased warfare. Grave offerings were also a means of redistributing wealth. This was of particular importance after European contact because wealth generated in the fur trade threatened the egalitarian basis of Huron society (Ramsden, 1981).

With emphasis on relative egalitarianism, generosity, individual freedom, and consensus, native cultures had very different values from European merchants, for whom wealth and the accumulation of goods were central. These differences had an important effect on the relations between Indians and European intruders.

THE COMING OF THE EUROPEANS

Despite the Viking expeditions around 1000 A.D., over the centuries North American societies had developed in isolation from other world cultures. Contact with Europe followed the voyages of John Cabot (1497) and the Corte-Real brothers (1500–1502), when fishermen from western Europe rushed to exploit the cod fishery on the Grand Banks off Newfoundland. By 1580, more than 400 Portuguese, Spanish, and French ships, manned by nearly 10 000 sailors, were crossing the Atlantic to Newfoundland each year. In shipping volume, the cod fishery was Europe's most important trans-Atlantic commerce, far outstripping the gold and silver trade that linked Spanish America and Seville (Turgeon, 1986). The development of the Newfoundland fishery signalled the beginning of North America's integration into European merchant capitalism.

Fishing practice was divided into the green and dry fisheries (Figures 1.5 and 1.6). In the green fishery, the cod was cleaned and salted on board ship. Ships engaged in this fishery landed only briefly in Newfoundland and the continent to replenish water and firewood supplies. With its huge salt requirements, the green fishery was dominated by ports in southwestern France where salt was cheap and plentiful. Cod processed this way was worth less on European markets but ships could make two trans-Atlantic trips a year.

In the dry fishery, fishermen established coastal bases from which they fished the inshore waters in small boats. The fishermen brought the cod ashore, cleaned and laid it out on drying flakes, and saved the livers separately in barrels.

Figures 1.5 and 1.6 The cod fishery. These two illustrations depict the green and dry fisheries. The dry fishery demanded greater organization and seasonal occupation of the shoreline, and it had the greatest impact on native peoples. It provided them with opportunities to obtain European metal wares, but it also disrupted their seasonal migrations and barred some groups from their traditional summer fishing stations. This forced them to live in the interior, where food was less abundant.

Figure 1.7 Natives in the whaling industry. The first important contact between Quebec native peoples and Europeans occurred in the Gulf of St. Lawrence. Native skills and labour were of particular significance in the whaling industry. Contact in this region did not dramatically disrupt the traditional subsistence pattern of the native peoples. Rather it enriched them; they received metal tools in payment for their labour, in exchange for furs, and by salvaging wrecks.

Although the dry fishery was more labour intensive and required spending two to three months a year in Newfoundland, it produced a higher quality and higher-priced cod. Cod was caught not only for food but also for the oil that could be extracted from the livers. Cod oil and whale oil were the main machine lubricant and lamp fuel used at that time.

Whaling was also an important activity off the coast of Labrador and in the Gulf of St. Lawrence from the mid-sixteenth century on. Whaling required more capital than cod fishing did, in order to equip larger vessels of 200 to 300 tons with crews of 50 seamen. Whalers also needed shore bases with lodgings and elaborate equipment such as ovens to render oil from blubber. These bases offered native peoples both employment (Figure 1.7) and the opportunity of scavenging for discarded metal wares.

The economic importance of the fishery should not be underestimated. Until the end of the French regime in 1760, France imported far more cod than fur and the fishery employed many more seamen and ships than all other French colonial trade combined. The fishery not only had a profound impact on Europe, but it also brought the native peoples of Newfoundland and the Gulf of St. Lawrence into sustained contact with the European world. From the beginning, the two groups exchanged presents, which provided natives with metal tools and utensils in return for meat, fish, and furs. Diffused throughout the Northeast along native trade routes, European articles stimulated and reinforced trading and political alliances and prepared native populations for the fur trade.

The growth of the Newfoundland fishery was only one manifestation of the expansion of Europe, which became the dominant world economy in the period from 1460 to 1620. European population growth, the expanding production of commodities, and the availability of bullion in the form of Mexican gold and Peruvian silver stimulated the development of merchant capitalism (Davis, 1973).

While Spain and Portugal were establishing overseas empires, French enterprise was left to private trading companies exploiting the Newfoundland fishery and the Brazil coast. The French crown did sponsor the voyages of Giovanni da Verrazano (1524), Jacques Cartier (1534, 1535–1536, 1541–1542), and Jean-François de la Rocque sieur de Roberval (1542–1543) in an attempt to find a short route to the Spice Islands of Southeast Asia but, apart from establishing a French claim to important parts of what is today Canada, these trips achieved little. Settlements founded by Cartier and Roberval in 1541–1543 failed because they lacked an economic foundation and because the native population was hostile to them. Religious conflict in France in the second half of the sixteenth century precluded further French government involvement in North America.

THE EMERGENCE OF THE FUR TRADE

The fishery integrated North America into a European-dominated economic system and introduced natives to European wares. Quantities were limited, however, and direct contact between natives and Europeans was largely restricted to areas along the Atlantic seaboard.

Exchanges between Indians and Europeans took on new dimensions with the gradual development of the European market for furs, particularly beaver. The long barbs at the tip of each hair in the beaver's soft underpelt made it ideal for felt. Although the felt-making technique, which transformed animal fur into a soft, supple, water-resistant material, had been known to European hatters since the Middle Ages, felt became a rare commodity when the European beaver became extinct. North American beaver supplies stimulated European felt production and brought the wide-brimmed hat into fashion. The wide-brimmed hat first became popular with the Parisian bourgeoisie during the Ligue (the religious wars at the end of the sixteenth century). It rapidly gained the favour of the aristocracy and bourgeoisie throughout France. By the 1630s it was standard military dress and had reached all classes of male society. Fur became the second export staple of the Canadian economy.

Development of the fur trade in the last quarter of the sixteenth century coincided with a major demographic change in the St. Lawrence Valley. In the 1540s, the explorers Cartier and Roberval had visited the important native villages of Stadacona and Hochelaga. Later in the century, for reasons that remain obscure to historians and archeologists, the St. Lawrence Iroquoians were driven from their lands or annihilated. They may have been destroyed by tribes from farther west seeking direct access to European trade, or they may have been decimated by European diseases brought by Cartier, Roberval, and the French settlers. On the basis of Hochelagan pottery found in late prehistoric Huron sites, other archeologists speculate that the St. Lawrence Iroquoians were adopted by the Huron (Pendergast and Trigger, 1972). Whatever the cause, their disappearance meant that the French, unlike the British colonists farther south, did not encounter a large, well-established, sedentary local native population when they settled the St. Lawrence Valley early in the seventeenth century.

The fur trade depended on the labour of native peoples and on their centuries-old trading network. As already noted, each hunting family used some thirty beaver annually for food and producing robes. After being worn for a year, the pelts that made up the robes shed their long guard hairs, exposing the short hairs required for the felting process. Several hundred thousand used pelts, known as *castor gras d'hiver*, would have been available annually in the St. Lawrence–Great Lakes region at the end of the sixteenth century, and they were in great demand by Europeans.

By 1575, the demand for furs was rapidly increasing and European merchants were being drawn up the St. Lawrence, where they tried to obtain regional monopolies. Anxious to establish its claim over the territory, the French crown gave out charters with trade monopolies, but the merchants were unable to tap the St. Lawrence region fully. Until 1626, annual fur exports from Canada rarely exceeded 9000 to 12 000 pelts, and in that record year only 22 000 pelts were exported. Samuel de Champlain established a fort and a warehouse at Quebec in 1608 and these, along with his personal contact with native chiefs, consolidated trade in the hands of one group of merchants by 1615. Nonetheless, the volume of furs that depended on Indian suppliers did not increase significantly.

During the first half of the seventeenth century, French merchants never effectively regulated the supply of furs. They entered alliances on native peoples' terms and never had the military force to impose their own objectives. Along the St. Lawrence, the fur supply depended on the Montagnais, who traded the product of their own hunt and controlled access to the hunting bands of the interior. Once they had the European trade goods they wanted, they had little incentive to increase the volume of trade.

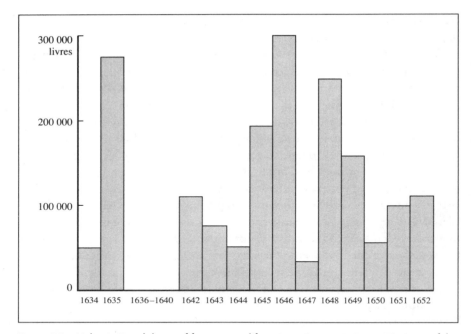

Figure 1.8 Value in French livres of furs exported from New France, 1634–1652. Some of the fluctuations in volume were due to warfare between French native allies and the tribes of the Iroquois Confederacy, particularly the Mohawk. When Champlain first visited the St. Lawrence in 1603, he found the Montagnais and Algonquin warring with the Mohawk. As part of his alliance with these tribes and with the Huron Confederacy, he participated in battles against the Iroquois on Lake Champlain (1609), at the mouth of the Richelieu (1610), and south of Lake Ontario (1615).

Along the Ottawa River and in the Great Lakes region, the situation was more complex. The Algonquin tribe was forced by its powerful Huron neighbours to share French trade, but this alliance created a formidable barrier blocking direct French access to other tribes. The Hurons did not hunt beaver themselves but used their extensive trade network with more remote tribes to exchange corn and European goods for furs. Thus, even though many natives of the Great Lakes region were becoming familiar with European technology, the French were unable to trade directly with them or to increase the number of pelts.

Since trade statistics from the early seventeenth century are incomplete we have only a partial picture of exports (Figure 1.8). It is clear, however, that the trade was very unstable and it is unlikely that the monopoly holders made any net profit (Campeau, 1975; Trudel, 1966–1983, vol. 3). In the best years after 1632, the value of furs shipped to France reached 300 000 livres, falling to under 50 000 livres in disastrous years. These variations underline the precarious nature of an economy that depended on native populations, who did not respond to increased demand in the same way as Europeans.

In 1614, the establishment of a Dutch trading post at Fort Orange (Albany, New York) provided the Iroquois with an alternative source of European goods, and warfare subsided for the next twenty years. After 1640, however, when the Dutch began to supply them with firearms, the Mohawk found it easier to raid fur convoys en route to Trois-Rivières than to hunt for pelts.

In the 1630s, disease added yet another variable to this system. With no immunity, natives, particularly the children and elderly, rapidly fell victim to diseases such as smallpox and influenza and villages were decimated. Tribes in the French alliance were particularly vulnerable since they were in constant contact with missionaries and interpreters, whereas the Dutch rarely visited the Iroquois. The Montagnais and Algonquins along the St. Lawrence suffered from measles or smallpox in 1634 and died in large numbers. Between 1636 and 1639, the Hurons were afflicted by a series of epidemics, and population declined from about 25 000 to about 10 000. Disease actually helped Jesuit missionaries increase the number of conversions because it undermined the prestige of shamans, but at the same time the epidemics were as important as warfare in reducing the supply of pelts by killing off hunters and traders.

Decimated by disease, divided by missionary propaganda, and unable to obtain firearms unless they turned their backs on traditional customs such as feasts that maintained village solidarity, the tribes of the French alliance fell victim to the numerically and militarily superior Iroquois. The Iroquoian-speaking tribes of the lower Great Lakes—the Wenro, the Huron, the Petun, the Neutral, and the Erie—were adopted by the victorious Iroquois to make up for losses suffered through disease and warfare. At the same time, Mohawk war parties raided the Algonquin and Montagnais hunters throughout the interior of Quebec, despoiling them of their beaver pelts.

This destruction completely disrupted the French trading system and was a crucial turning point in Canadian history. Along the St. Lawrence Valley, the native population declined so dramatically that the French were in a majority by 1650 (Figure 1.9). Without native allies to collect and transport furs to the warehouses at Trois-Rivières and Quebec, the French were forced to take over these tasks themselves. These circumstances marked the end of a commercial system entirely dependent on native labour and trading networks, and the beginning of French territorial expansion by the coureur de bois supported by an agricultural community.

The structure of the early fur trade and its economic uncertainty had retarded settlement. Because native peoples did not have European-style institutions of government and religion and did not live in permanent agricultural communities, European nations did not acknowledge their territorial claims. Thus, when the

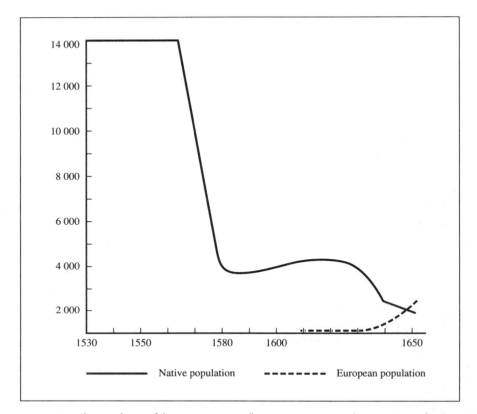

Figure 1.9 The population of the St. Lawrence Valley, 1530–1650. Population estimates for the period of early Contact are at best approximate because of the lack of data. The trends are clear, however. The population of the St. Lawrence Valley dropped drastically between 1550 and 1580, as 8000 to 10 000 St. Lawrence Iroquoians disappeared from the area between Lake Ontario and Quebec City. Although nomadic Montagnais and Algonquins moved into the area at the beginning of the seventeenth century, they were decimated by disease after 1634 and then attacked by the Iroquois after 1641. By 1650, the Algonquins and Montagnais had started to retreat into the interior.

.crown granted trade monopolies, it also granted vast tracts of land and insisted that the companies settle the region. There was little economic need for European settlement, however, since trade depended on native peoples trapping and transporting furs to a warehouse on the St. Lawrence. Here, a few Europeans could guard the fort, prepare bales of pelts for shipment to Europe, and maintain relations with the native peoples. In this economic system there was little demand for the labour or agricultural produce of settlers. French emigrants preferred the Carribean, where tobacco and, later, sugar plantations held the promise of bettering one's social and economic status. The failure of French settlement policies in the St. Lawrence region therefore owes less to any antagonism of merchants towards settlers than to the dependence on a native rather than a European labour force.

The formation of the Company of One Hundred Associates in 1627 changed settlement patterns very little. The company's charter required it to settle 4000 immigrants within fifteen years, but the loss of the first two fleets to English pirates brought it to the verge of bankruptcy. It is therefore unfair to criticize it for failing to meet its obligations. In promoting missionary activity, the company did manage to attract a small agricultural population. Many immigrants who settled in Canada in the period 1632–1650 came as servants indentured either to the Jesuits, Ursulines, or Hospital Sisters, or to the model Christian community established at Montreal in 1642 by the *Société de Notre-Dame pour la conversion des sauvages*. They stayed because the priests and nuns required their labour and agricultural surpluses rather than because of involvement in the fur trade.

Many people did not stay: indeed, in the period 1632–1650, almost three-quarters of all immigrants on a three-year indenture returned to France after their contract expired. After 1650, the expansion of the fur trade created a demand for European canoeists and for agricultural surpluses. More than half of all immigrants therefore remained in the colony, despite the increase in Iroquois raids. The amount of land granted to settlers after 1650 also reflects the greater number of permanent residents. In the nineteen years before the 1650 dispersal of the Hurons, just under 6000 hectares had been ceded to settlers, but in the following five years over 15 000 hectares were granted. With these new economic conditions, the population of the colony grew from 1206 in 1650 to 2690 in 1660 (Dickinson, 1986a).

⌒⌒⌒

CULTURAL INTERACTION

Europeans and their trade transformed the life of native peoples. They quickly adopted such European commodities as copper kettles, metal tools and weapons, textiles, and foodstuffs such as bread and alcohol. For their part, European settlers used native products such as the birch-bark canoe, snowshoes, moccasins, and toboggans. Native crops, such as corn and tobacco were also adopted, although most settlers continued to prefer European grains.

Attitudes, languages, and standards of behaviour are more difficult than material goods to transfer from one culture to another. Native peoples had a world view suited to their environment and way of life, and because of the importance they gave to individual freedom and tolerance, they did not impose their values on others. It is very difficult to determine native attitudes to European customs since

European interpretations always cloud the recorded reactions. It appears that to native people some European behaviour was repugnant (for example, blowing one's nose into a handkerchief), whereas other practices were thought simply foolish (building large homes that could not be moved easily). The overall impression is that natives never thought themselves in any way inferior to Europeans (Jaenen, 1976a).

Europeans, in contrast, wanted complete control over both the territory and its inhabitants. Judging other cultures by European norms, they saw themselves and Christianity as superior; and they considered native peoples to be barbarians and even agents of the devil. Since native peoples did not have European forms of government, religion, or economic organization, the Europeans dismissed them as having no culture at all. The French wish to force Christianity and European culture on native populations is illustrated by the seventeenth-century French monk Emery de La Croix: "They must be shown the road to humanity and true honour, so that they no longer live like brutes. Reason and justice must prevail, and not violence which is suitable only for beasts" (Dickason, 1984: 39).

From the arrival of the first missionary in 1615 until the end of the French regime in 1760, religious orders tried to impose Christianity on the native peoples (Figure 1.10). At first, natives rejected the missionaries because they tried to destroy native ways of life. When European diseases ravaged the tribes, they blamed the Jesuits at first (Trigger, 1976). Given the native belief that disease had spiritual causes, however, epidemics finally served the Jesuits' cause, since people turned to the Jesuits when shamans failed to find cures.

At first, French policy was designed to assimilate native populations by teaching them French and settling semi-nomadic tribes in agricultural communities. This proved unrealistic, however, and by 1640 the Jesuits had abandoned plans to educate young Indians in seminaries based on European models and to settle the Montagnais on reserves. Once they showed greater acceptance of native culture and made the decision to live with bands in their own environment, the Jesuits had success with tribes such as the Attikameks and the Hurons. They were also helped by fur trading company policies such as the sale of firearms to converts only. Even so, only a minority of native peoples became Catholics, and many converts continued to live much as before. Conversion to Christianity meant that converts could no longer participate in the social life of their communities. As Jérôme Lalemant, superior of the Huron mission, noted in 1645:

> The greatest opposition that we meet consists in the fact that their remedies for diseases; their greatest amusements when in good health; their fishing, their hunting, and their trading; the success of their crops, of their wars, and of their councils, almost all abound in diabolical ceremonies. To be a Christian one must deprive himself not only of pastimes, and of the dearest pleasures of life, but even of the most necessary things. (Thwaites, 1896–1901, 28: 53)

Figure 1.10 "France bringing the Faith to the Savages." This painting by Récollet Brother Luc shows France, personified as the queen mother, Anne of Austria, bringing Christianity to the native people of North America. The ideology that motivates this painting is clear: France was bringing salvation to an inferior people who knelt in gratitude before one of the main financial sponsors of early missionary work. For the artist, it was not important to realistically depict Indians, their housing, or the landscape. This painting, which hangs in Quebec's Ursuline convent, was used to teach native peoples to respect their European benefactors. Religious imagery such as the picture held by the queen was an important means for missionaries to present the mysteries of Christianity.

Considering the importance of dreams, feasts, and the family in native life, it is hardly surprising that the natives did not want to be converted. Nevertheless, an increasing number of Hurons were baptized during the 1640s, and by the time of their dispersion the majority were Christian (Campeau, 1987).

The Europeans' conviction that they were culturally superior enabled them to adopt features of native life without losing their identity. The coureurs de bois might wear native dress and travel by canoe or on snowshoes; they might even marry Indian women. Yet they remained resolutely Christian, and most ultimately re-integrated into colonial life. Native ideas and values never made a serious impression on the European population in the St. Lawrence Valley.

Warfare was the final major area of contact between the two cultures. Traditional histories of New France emphasize the heroism of the early settlers in defending themselves from fierce warriors. Native peoples' practice of guerrilla warfare and torture shocked European observers. Despite a few severe attacks, though, warfare directed against Europeans during this period was less widespread and bloody than is usually portrayed. Most Iroquois hostility was directed at native allies, not at the French. Indeed, Iroquois representatives continually asked for French neutrality.

For the half century from 1608 to 1666, just over 200 settlers were killed by the Iroquois and of these a quarter died because of the strategic errors of their commanders (Dollard des Ormeaux, for example, was killed along with fifteen companions in 1660. He had shut himself up in a crumbling palisade with no source of water and no avenue of escape. Duplessis-Kerbodot, governor of Trois-Rivières, is another example. He waded into a swamp to attack Iroquois hiding behind trees on the edge.) Warfare was a general threat only between 1650–1653 and 1660–1661; most other years were relatively peaceful. There were important regional differences: Montreal was often threatened in the first two decades after its founding in 1642, but Trois-Rivières witnessed intense warfare only between 1651 and 1653. Iroquois war parties attacked the Quebec City region, where most colonists lived, only after 1650 and most deaths occurred in 1661. Nor were captives always burned at the stake; well over half were either freed or they escaped, and some chose to live with their captors (Dickinson, 1982a; Axtell, 1985).

CONCLUSION

The coming of the Europeans had a profound impact on native society that ran the gamut from technological advances to epidemics, alcohol abuse, and the destruction of traditional values. Through trade, the native peoples would be progressively integrated into the Atlantic economy. This process was uneven across Quebec. Natives in the St. Lawrence lowlands experienced severe dislocation; elsewhere the impact was less disruptive. The white intruders, on the other hand, spent the first half of the seventeenth century becoming acclimatized to the North American environment. Although they absorbed useful elements of native material culture, French setters established a colonial society with European political and religious institutions.

The dispersal of the sedentary tribes of southern Ontario and the dramatic decline in the semi-nomadic populations of the interior of Quebec marked the end of that period of Canadian history dominated by native labour and trading systems. By 1650, the French dominated the St. Lawrence Valley. Economic opportunity for the Europeans, which had been limited by reliance on native labour, grew as colonists began supplying foodstuffs to nomadic tribes and transporting pelts themselves.

FURTHER READING

OVERVIEW
The best overview of native peoples of the Northeast can be found in Bruce Trigger, ed., *Handbook of North American Indians*, Volume 15. Those interested in prehistory should consult J.V. Wright's *Quebec Prehistory* and *Ontario Prehistory: An Eleven Thousand Year Archaeological Outline*. On the disappearance of the St. Lawrence Iroquoians, readers should consult James Pendergast and Bruce Trigger, *Cartier's Hochelaga and the Dawson Site*. A concise history of this period from an Indian point of view is provided by Bruce Trigger in *Indians and the "Heroic Age" of New France*. For a more detailed analysis of this period, readers should refer to Bruce Trigger, *Natives and Newcomers: Canada's "Heroic Age" Reconsidered*.

INDIVIDUAL TRIBES
Some of the best studies of individual tribes concern the Huron. Conrad Heidenreich's *Huronia: A History and Geography of the Huron Indians, 1600–1650* and Bruce Trigger's *The Children of Aataentsic: A History of the Huron People to 1660* give detailed accounts of these people. On the problems faced during the winter, readers can consult Norman Clermont, "L'hiver et les indiens nomades du Québec à la fin de la préhistoire." Eleanor Leacock presents an interesting assessment of Montagnais women's status in her "Montagnais Women and the Jesuit Program for Colonization."

RELIGION
On the importance of religion in native societies and Calvin Martin's controversial thesis, see his *Keepers of the Game: Indian–Animal Relationships and the Fur Trade* and Shepard Krech III, *Indians, Animals and the Fur Trade*, which groups several essays on this thesis.

EARLY FRENCH SETTLEMENT

The most complete coverage of French activities in North America during this period can be found in Marcel Trudel's *The Beginnings of New France, 1524–1663*, which is an abridged version of his monumental four-volume *Histoire de la Nouvelle-France*. Olive Dickason's *The Myth of the Savage and the Beginnings of French Colonialism in the Americas* gives an excellent view of French attitudes toward the native peoples. John Dickinson's "Les Amérindiens et les débuts de la Nouvelle-France" evaluates the impact of native peoples on the early settlement of Canada.

$\mathscr{P}$reindustrial Quebec, 1650s–1810s

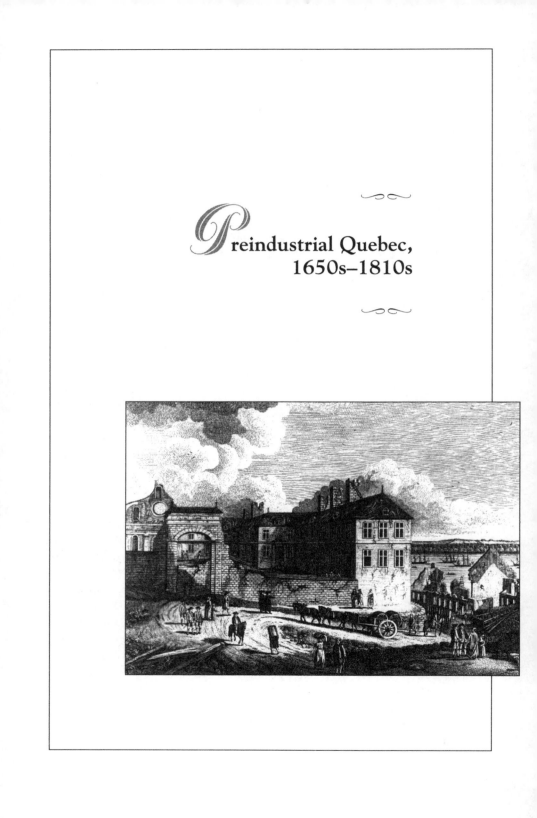

he disappearance of Huron intermediaries from the fur trade in New France by 1650 created new economic opportunities. French immigrants began to be attracted to two distinct sectors: the fur trade and agriculture. There was the work of collecting and transporting furs to Montreal and Quebec, and of supplying foodstuffs to coureurs de bois and semi-nomadic hunters. The expansion of farming marked the birth of what is best described as a preindustrial society. The forms of work, production, and institutions persisted through the Conquest, with British authorities largely leaving essential structures in place. Fundamental change in the socio-economic structure of Lower Canadian society occurred a half century after the 1760 Conquest.

Preindustrial society under both the French and British regimes had three cornerstones: the family, agriculture, and a rigid, hierarchical social structure. The family, rather than the individual, was at the centre of social and economic relations; legal systems defined and emphasized the rights and obligations of the family unit. The male head under French law, for example, was responsible for the actions of his wife and children. If they were wronged, only he could initiate legal procedures.

The economic backbone of this society was the peasant household. Peasant is the appropriate term since the rural inhabitants in New France were small-scale agricultural producers who controlled their own land and whose production was centred on the family unit. Much of the capital in the preindustrial world was invested in agriculture: in land, in farm buildings, in livestock, and in farm implements (Davis, 1973: 231–33). Although most of what the peasantry produced was consumed in the home or bartered within the local economy, farm households were important markets for commodities produced by local artisans or imported by merchants. More important, peasant surpluses supported the elite, particularly the seigneurs and the religious hierarchy.

The state promoted a paternalistic concept of society, ostensibly protecting the weak but in reality ensuring respect for the privileges of the aristocracy. The state's principal goal was to maintain order. Military expenditures far surpassed civil expenditures, which were largely devoted to the salaries of administrative and judicial officials. State revenues came from crown subsidies, seigneurial dues, land sales, and customs duties. They were not sufficient to allow the state to invest heavily in public works, however, and until 1815, road construction relied solely on the corvée, the unpaid labour of the popular classes: peasants, day labourers, and artisans. With strong ties to the monarchy, established churches aided the state in upholding order; the Judaeo-Christian version of morality was the basis for criminal codes and for education. In return, the state used its power to back the authority of religious officials, establishing parishes, enforcing the tithe, and maintaining order at church ceremonies.

Across the period, French and British officials imposed structures that are best described as "ancien régime." The governments of both France and Britain were monarchies strongly supported by their respective aristocracies. In this system, birth and nepotism were fundamental in determining status and professional advancement in the church, military, and government. The French crown named members from this elite to govern the colony and they determined law, policy, and taxation to the benefit of their social class. After the Conquest, British authorities, despite pressure from newly arrived merchants from Britain, largely respected the ancien-régime structures of authority, an established church, and the system of seigneurial property.

Before and after the Conquest, the mass of colonists had little influence over how they were governed and this continued even after creation of the first elected assembly in 1791. This did not mean, however, that the power of crown and aristocracy was unchecked. The lack of a police force in rural areas, for example, meant that government ordinances were often ignored. Riots, charivaris, and threats against government officials, judges, or others in authority were other forms of popular resistance.

Despite the primacy of agriculture, trade was an important force. Merchants derived their profits through the exchange of commodities. They exported staples such as fish, fur, wheat, and timber and encouraged the consumption of imported goods. The peasantry used its agricultural surplus to pay for these imports, and thereby became increasingly integrated into a market economy.

While most merchants needed only modest amounts of capital, the scale of their enterprises grew across the preindustrial period. Most capital was tied up in stocks of raw materials or finished products in warehouses, ships, or canoes. The requirement for liquid assets was even smaller, since most trade was financed by credit. For large ventures, several merchants might join together to reduce risk but the duration of the partnership was often limited and, in French law, could not survive the death of one of the partners. In such partnerships, each individual remained personally responsible for the debts of the association. In business dealings outside their region, merchants relied on personal contacts and good will built up by preceding generations (often with members of their extended family) for information, credit, the enforcement of contracts, and the collection of debts.

Despite the formation of large trading companies, such as the Company of One Hundred Associates, to exploit monopolies granted by the crown, there is no evidence of modern capitalism in the preindustrial era. Large companies never established accounting procedures that reflected an understanding of capital. Their main goal was to gain a monopoly and their activities were often decentralized. If anything, the companies reflected the desire of the state to direct and control economic policy (De Vries, 1976: 133).

Most artisans produced their goods working in family shops with their own tools, and therefore required only small amounts of capital. In such a system, only exceptionally large work sites such as ironworks required a significant fixed investment. Much of this production was for the agricultural community, although the aristocracy and the church encouraged luxury trades such as sculpting and silversmithing. In Europe, town guilds gave masters control over competition, prices, and quality, but in the colony market conditions were more important in regulating artisanal production. Also, European industrial expansion in the seventeenth and eighteenth centuries was fuelled by cottage industries: the production of goods by members of the peasantry who did not have enough land to support themselves by agriculture alone. In the colony, abundant land precluded the development of a large pool of rural industrial labour during the preindustrial period.

Class relations were rigidly defined and enforced by the state. The popular classes—the peasantry and artisans—were expected to know their place and to show suitable deference to their superiors. Upward social mobility was rare since educational institutions catered only to the bourgeoisie and the aristocracy, and family contacts were needed to enter trade and the professions. Peasant accumulation of wealth, when it existed, was channelled into land and the needs of the farm.

Most bourgeois in Europe reinvested their capital in business, although many aspired to the nobility and therefore put money into military, judicial, and administrative offices, dowries, and seigneurial land (De Vries, 1976: 214). The aristocracy was expected by social custom to spend its wealth ostentatiously by building fine houses, following fashion trends, and employing large numbers of domestic servants. As a result, it tended not to invest in trade and industry. In the colonial context, however, the local aristocracy behaved in a different fashion. Its military functions implicated it in the fur trade and gave it a similar economic outlook to that of the bourgeoisie during the French regime.

SEIGNEURIALISM

The seigneury was a form of property that regulated social and economic relations between seigneur and censitaire, the individual who paid seigneurial dues on a land concession. Theoretically, the seigneur granted land to all prospective settlers and provided a grist mill. The mill was only built once population warranted the investment and, as population pressure on the land increased, seigneurs withheld lands and charged higher rents. Peasants were obliged to pay an annual rent (the *cens et rentes*) and levies when they sold immoveable property (the *lods et ventes*). The concession contract also committed the peasantry to clearing and farming the land and to taking their grain to the seigneurial mill. Failure to fulfill these obligations could result in eviction.

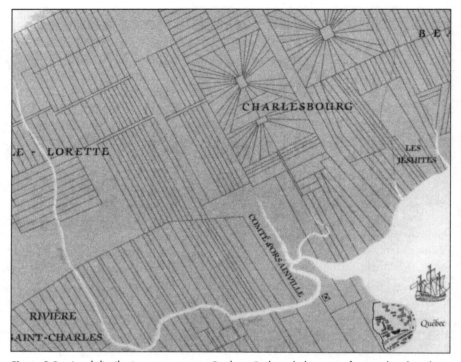

Figure 2.1 Land distribution patterns near Quebec, Cadastral plans are often used to describe the seigneurial system and to highlight the uniformity of peasant holdings. The distinctive radial villages, visible in the upper part of the figure, were created by the Jesuits in the 1660s and are often wrongly attributed to intendant Jean Talon. Farmers took little heed of the surveyor's lines but cleared patches close to one another.

In addition to the seigneurial dues the seigneur had honorific rights such as a front-row pew in church and the privilege of receiving communion first. They had other valuable privileges. Through the corvée they could exact labour from their censitaires; they could reclaim peasant holdings by the *droit de retrait* (the right to repossess a concession in the event of its sale by matching the sale price); they had monopolies over fishing and water-power sites; and, in many cases, they had the right to establish a court of law. This manor court was used by the seigneur to collect seigneurial dues as well as to settle local disputes: conflicts over property lines and complaints that trespassing livestock was trampling or eating the harvest. Most of the active seigneurial courts were located on lands owned by religious orders around Quebec City. Not only were they an important tool for seigneurial administration but the seigneurial courts also offered a useful service to local inhabitants since they charged much lower fees than the royal courts (Dickinson, 1974b). None, however, survived the Conquest.

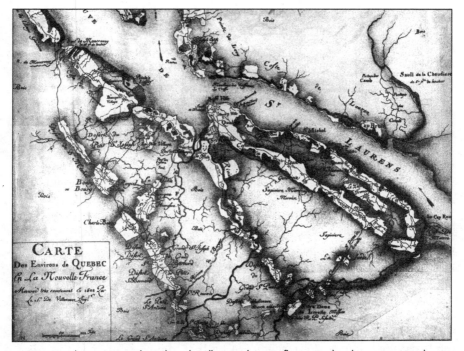

Figure 2.2 This 1688 map by Robert de Villeneuve better reflects actual settlement patterns than does figure 2.1. Clearings did not develop uniformly, but as patches in the middle of the forest, as peasants sought to clear land next to others. A sense of community was essential in opening new lands, and settlement was not a haphazard venture. The Huron village of Lorette is in the lower right part of the map (see also left centre of figure 2.1). Less than a decade after this map was made, the encroachment of white settlers on Huron land forced them to move their village farther north.

The Company of One Hundred Associates, and later the crown, had hoped that seigneurs would become colonization agents since it was in their interest to settle their lands. Few seigneurs paid immigrants' passage, however, since business or government administration interests, rather then seigneurial revenues, initially provided the bulk of their income. Religious orders were the exception and their well-populated estates produced considerable revenue from the end of the seventeenth century. Settlement spread out progressively from the lands near the towns until, by the end of the eighteenth century, the revenue of most lay seigneuries was a significant part of their owners' income (Greer, 1985).

Seigneurialism had little influence on the geographic pattern of settlement. The physical layout of seigneurial grants was established during the regime of the One Hundred Associates and was determined by geographical considerations. Estates were rectangular tracts with frontage on a major river; concessions to peasants were about 150m wide and 1600m deep (Figures 2.1 and 2.2). This system of land tracts facilitated surveying, construction and maintenance of roads, and enabled the first settlers to have access to the river. It inhibited the development of villages, however, and made homes difficult to defend. When the first *côte* (a line of farms along the river) was full, a second *côte* or, as it was later known, *rang*, was opened along a parallel interior road. Peasant social life centred on the *côte*, where relatives grouped their holdings. Seigneurs could of course determine where and how land on their estate was to be opened for settlement, and had the right to expropriate holdings in order to create a village or build a mill.

Although few Canadian seigneurs descended from the old French nobility, they nevertheless constituted a Canadian aristocracy confident in their privileges and social position. Through the many onerous and honorific dues owed to the seigneur, the peasantry could easily identify their social superiors.

Historians disagree over the significance of seigneurial tenure. Marcel Trudel (1956) described it as a social system of mutual aid established to facilitate settlement. He also saw it as a protection for the French Canadian nation from outside influences in the nineteenth century. Richard Colebrook Harris (1984, 1979), on the other hand, downplayed its importance. He argued that the pattern of settlement owed more to the physical characteristics of the land than to seigneurial activity before the Conquest, but that seigneurs became more demanding during the British regime. Research by Louise Dechêne (1971; 1974; 1981) has shown the broad implications of seigneurialism for both the peasantry and the urban population from the seventeenth century on. Recent studies focus on seigneurialism as a source of social inequality and emphasize the power of seigneurs to appropriate the peasantry's agricultural surpluses (Greer, 1985; Dépatie, Lalancette, et Dessureault, 1987; Wien, 1988; Lavallée, 1992).

⌒⌣⌒

INSTITUTIONAL AND POLITICAL DEVELOPMENT

In most societies, socio-economic conditions shape political and institutional structures. In other words, political and legal systems generally develop as a population settles. In New France, however, the basic administrative, religious, and legal infrastructure existed before the settlement of a significant European population. New France was modelled after French legal custom, which had evolved through the Middle Ages before being codified in the sixteenth century.

From its inception, New France was regulated by the Custom of Paris (although until 1664 other customs were allowed). The Custom of Paris was a coherent body of law influenced by a religious and state ideology that valued paternal authority and responsibility. The family patrimony was protected by marriage clauses that prevented important assets from being seized by creditors; by mortgage traditions that favoured family members over creditors; by the right to interfere in contracts to preserve the integrity of an estate; and by restrictions on the right to will property freely (Zoltvany, 1971). Minors (people under twenty-five) and married women were considered under the control of the male head of the family and could not manage property or act in any legal capacity without his consent. The Custom of Paris, based on a concept of property whereby all land belonged to a seigneur, encouraged an egalitarian outlook among non-aristocratic classes of society by forcing them to divide land equally among heirs.

Colonial government was based on mercantilism. Colonies were founded to serve the needs of the metropolis, and economic development was closely monitored and controlled by the imperial state. Whether it was the French Ministry of Marine or the British Colonial Office, colonial policy was always judged by its potential impact on the economy of the metropolis. Formed in Europe over the centuries, state and religious institutions were imposed on the colony and administered by Europeans who often had little sympathy for colonial realities.

FRENCH COLONIAL ADMINISTRATION

Before 1627 there was little need for complex administrative structures because there was little immigration. When the crown ceded the colony to the Company of One Hundred Associates in 1627, settlement became an important goal and administrative bodies were created. During the period 1627–1663, New France was ruled by a governor who, as the European population grew, appointed judicial officials and a council to help him administer the colony. By 1663, when the French king Louis XIV took over the colony, most of the essential institutions of France were in place: the *sénéchaussée*, a court enforcing the Custom of Paris; the seigneurial form of land tenure; and a bishop to oversee religious institutions such as schools and hospitals. Royal control merely meant that New France became a province with the same royal administrative structures as French provinces: a military governor; an intendant in charge of justice, public order, and financial administration; and a system of royal courts.

Colonial affairs, like those of French provinces, were directed from Paris. In 1663, it was decided that the Ministry of Marine, headed by Jean-Baptiste

Colbert, Louis XIV's principal minister, would have control of New France. Policy, appointments, and even pensions were decided in Versailles and the minister gave precise instructions to the governor general and the intendant. Because of the distance and the short shipping season, letters reached the colony only once a year. This infrequent communication left Versailles poorly informed about colonial problems. As a result, decisions made in France were sometimes totally inappropriate for the colony and local officials could only delay implementation while they tried to convince the ministry to change direction.

In 1696, for example, in an attempt to reduce the number of beaver on the market, the ministry ordered the abandonment of western military posts. For two decades, until the posts were reopened, the governors and intendants lobbied for reversal of this policy which curbed trade in the colony's most important product and disrupted alliances with native peoples (Zoltvany, 1974).

The governor general was responsible for military and diplomatic affairs, including relations with the native peoples. He was assisted by lieutenant governors stationed in towns such as Montreal and Trois-Rivières, and by captains of militia in each parish. Although the duties of militia were primarily military, they also had local administrative duties such as conveying orders on road work and reporting the quantity of harvests.

Given the colony's significance as a major theatre of Anglo–French imperial rivalry, the military establishment was very important to New France (Figure 2.3). From the arrival of the first royal troops—the Carignan-Salières regiment sent to quell the Iroquois in the 1660s—until the War of the Conquest a century later, the colony always had a large garrison to defend itself from the British and the Iroquois. During the eighteenth century the officer corps, recruited from local aristocrats, played an important role in the fur trade as agents for Montreal merchants as well as in the defence of the colony. The other ranks were made up of Troupes de la Marine sent from France. Many of these soldiers opted to settle in the colony after their tour of duty. Military pay and provisioning, important elements in the local economy (Eccles, 1971), accounted for a large part of the colonial government's annual budget.

The intendant and his officials administered financial affairs, economic development, and justice in the colony. As the colony developed, the intendant delegated authority to other officials: the director of the king's domain, who administered crown lands and collected customs duties; the chief road officer, who was in charge of road construction and town planning; and the port captain, who supervised maritime activity. The intendant's large staff worked in his palais in Quebec City, which doubled as the courthouse (Vachon, 1969).

Since some of the intendant's responsibilities overlapped those of the governor, conflict resulted. The governor was in charge of military matters but the intendant controlled financial affairs. The intendant controlled trade but the

Figure 2.3 Quebec from Pointe Levy, 1761. This view of Quebec illustrates the important strategic position occupied by the colonial capital. The citadel, on top of Cape Diamond to the left of the picture, had a commanding view of the river and was the heart of a fortification network encircling the city to the southwest. The large building on the cliff above the Lower Town is the Château Saint-Louis, the governor's residence. Ramparts lined the cliff, while shore batteries protected the port and the shipyard, where the hull of an unfinished warship can be seen.

governor gave out licences for travel in the West and determined official policy towards native peoples. The intendant was responsible for justice but the governor sat on the highest colonial court, the Sovereign Council, where he claimed precedence as the king's most important representative. Competition for patronage exacerbated personality conflicts, and the tensions that ensued were brought to the public's attention by the spectacle of officials jostling for precedence in public ceremonies (Eccles, 1964: 77–98).

Although public offices were not purchased in New France as they were in France, administrators considered their position as property on which there should be a personal return. This concept of political morality is reflected in the correspondence of Elisabeth Bégon (daughter of a Montreal official and widow of a lieutenant governor of Trois-Rivières) to her son-in-law, the intendant's representative at New Orleans. Using the example of intendant François Bigot, who was accumulating a fortune selling goods to the state at inflated prices, she encouraged her son-in-law to imitate the intendant's behaviour.

> M. de la Filière told me that Bigot should make two hundred thousand livres [a day labourer made about two livres a day] on his sales of flour to the state. . . . If you don't have enough wits to make some money where you are, you should be beaten since everyone knows what civil servants do and those who do not have a profitable trade are treated as idiots. You don't pay enough attention to these matters. It is all very well to do one's duty, but you should try to look after your own affairs as well.

THE JUDICIAL SYSTEM OF NEW FRANCE

As a royal province, the colony's judicial system consisted of the Sovereign Council and subordinate royal jurisdictions at Quebec, Montreal, and Trois-Rivières. The Sovereign Council, created in 1663, was made up of the governor, the bishop, the intendant, and five councillors. For a short time, the council had important responsibilities and law-making powers. By the 1670s, however, all important regulations were drafted by the intendant before they were made public at sittings of the council. The council had been reduced to an appeal court for the civil decisions and criminal sentences handed down by the royal courts. The judicial structure was completed in 1719 when an admiralty court, which heard shipping cases, was established at Quebec. Although the intendant had jurisdiction to judge any case brought before him, he almost always referred cases to the royal courts. The intendant appointed all court officials, as well as notaries attached to the royal court system, and ensured that they followed the Custom of Paris.

The royal courts were central to the legal system. They judged both civil disputes and criminal cases, as well as supervising the enforcement of regulations.

Civil jurisdiction—debt recovery and disputes over property or seigneurial dues—was by far the most frequent activity. At the Prévôté, Quebec City's royal court, this type of case made up about 98 percent of the work load. Theoretically, courts were cheap and accessible to all. However, they were located in the three major towns while the vast majority of the population lived in the countryside; the result was that courts were used mainly by the urban population: artisans, merchants, and members of the colonial elite.

In civil suits at the Prévôté, artisans made up over 35 percent of litigants, whereas merchants and the elite made up almost 20 percent each; the peasantry, which made up about 80 percent of the total population, constituted only 18 percent of litigants. Although court costs were reduced by forbidding lawyers to practise in the colony, in all cases some fees had to be paid to judicial officials—the judge, clerk, and huissiers—and litigants were often obliged to be present for several sittings. The courts thus reinforced the advantages of the elite (Dickinson, 1982b).

Criminal justice in New France differed significantly from today's. To open a case, the victim of a crime had to make an official statement before a judge. If it was not known who had committed a crime, finding suspects posed a problem since there was no official police force in the colony. However, the military was often used to track down suspects such as the following:

> height, about four and a half feet (1m 45); black hair cut at the top of the ears, blue eyes, a wrinkled forehead, a wispy blond beard, a pug-nose, a dry and narrow face, ruddy complexion; he has a crooked gait with one foot on the outside and the other turned to the inside; his voice is sharp and loud and he does not speak well; age 23 to 25 years; was wearing a blue vest with copper buttons (Lachance 1984: 135–37).

Once apprehended, a suspect was put in irons and taken to jail in Montreal, Trois-Rivières, or Quebec to await trial. The accused was not informed of charges and was not assisted by a lawyer.

When convinced that the suspect was guilty, judges could use torture to extract a confession or to learn the names of accomplices. Corporal punishment, seizure of property, exile, and capital punishment were common penalties. Although beheading, breaking on the wheel (breaking a criminal's limbs with an iron bar), and burning at the stake were used, hanging was by far the most usual form of the death penalty. Of thirty-eight people condemned to death between 1712 and 1748, eight were women (Lachance, 1984). Imprisonment in preindustrial society was never envisaged as a punishment.

Though the royal courts dealt mainly with civil disputes and crimes, they also had some administrative functions. In the absence of municipal governments during the French regime, the intendant issued by-laws concerning public order,

health and safety, trade, and roads. Publication and enforcement of these regulations were left to the Sovereign Council and the royal courts. Most of the legislation clearly underlines the major social preoccupations of administrators in
preindustrial society: hunger, fire, disease, and scandalous behaviour.

To ensure that urban populations had enough to eat, stringent regulations
required butchers and bakers to provide sufficient meat and bread at fixed prices
and forbade retailers from buying up stocks at the semi-weekly markets.
Regulations also covered town planning, the inspection of weights and measures
used by merchants, and the standards for road construction and maintenance.

Fire was a major concern to officials because it was so dangerous and there
were only limited means of controlling it. Montreal was almost destroyed in 1734
when a slave set fire to her owner's house in revenge for being punished: forty-six
houses and the Hôtel-Dieu hospital burned to the ground. Authorities regulated
house construction, chimney inspection, the distribution of water buckets and
axes, and the installation of ladders on roofs.

Public health was based on medical conceptions that emphasized pure air.
Human and animal waste had to be removed from towns and all dwellings had to
have outdoor latrines, since it was believed that odours from this waste carried
disease.

Civil and religious authorities considered inns and taverns to be the main centres for scandalous and seditious behaviour. All proprietors had to have licences,
and had to obey strict opening hours and serving rules. Native people could not
legally purchase any alcohol except beer, while servants and labourers could not
drink during the day without their employers' permission. Establishments had to
be closed during mass and had to post royal ordinances against blasphemy
(Dickinson, 1987).

⌐⌐

RELIGION

In seventeenth-century France, the king ruled by divine right and was the protec-
tor of the church; rigorous Catholic doctrine permeated legislation. The church
enjoyed high social status. It was the first estate of the realm and protected the
prevailing social structure by preaching obedience and submission. The state also
gave religious orders responsibility for education and health care. The church,
then, was a central force in the establishment of New France's institutional
framework. Even before the creation of the first parish, New France had two hospitals, two schools, and a college, all run by the church.

To maintain the social position of the clergy, the church required large revenues. Although it received some financial support from collections, donations,

royal subsidies, and fees paid by the state for the care of soldiers and the poor, the most important sources of revenue were the tithe and large land grants. (The tithe was a levy on agricultural production in the form of a percentage of the grain harvest.) To help support missions, the One Hundred Associates gave the Jesuits huge seigneuries and by the end of the French regime one-quarter of all seigneurial land was held by the church (Figure 2.4). Most of the church lands were located near Montreal, Quebec or Trois-Rivières, where population was the densest. Over one-third of the colonists lived on church seigneuries and they provided significant revenue for the clergy.

During the early years, the Jesuits were active in the government of the colony, and this tradition was maintained after the arrival in 1659 of Bishop François de Laval. Given the close ties between church and state, it was normal for Bishop Laval to sit on the Sovereign Council. Relations between civil and religious officials were not always harmonious, however, notably where the brandy trade was concerned. Laval, who considered the exploitation of native people a sin, complained that alcoholism prevented conversions, and he threatened to excommunicate anyone who traded brandy for furs.

For their part, the governor and intendant criticized Laval for overstepping his authority. They tolerated the brandy trade because they deemed it essential for the colonial economy. Laval also disagreed with civil authorities over the tithe. The governor, responding in 1663 to complaints from the local population, set it at one-twentieth of the harvest rather than at one-thirteenth as Laval had proposed. In 1707, the government finally set the rate at one twenty-sixth. Despite Laval's disagreements with colonial officials, no one really questioned state control of the church—especially not Laval's successors, who were mostly absentee bishops spending as much time in France as in the colony.

The social composition of the church reflected the existing social hierarchy. Bishops all emanated from the French aristocracy, as were many Jesuits and Sulpicians. Parish priests, recruited mainly from among the local bourgeoisie and trained at the Quebec seminary after 1663, had considerable local influence. Yet the clergy was never a dominant local force, since scarcity sometimes forced them to serve more than one parish. Apart from their religious duties, parish priests also had important civil functions; they kept the parish registers—the official record of births, deaths, and marriages—and in communities without notaries they could draw up legal documents such as marriage contracts and deeds.

Cloistered life was an important aspect of preindustrial society. The French church of the seventeenth century was strongly influenced by the Counter-Reformation. Within France, interior missions sought to strengthen the faith of the peasantry by emphasizing a rigorous morality, devotion to the Virgin Mary, and strict observance of holy days. The clergy in New France did not escape this reforming zeal. The Jesuits and Sulpicians led the drive for a better educated and

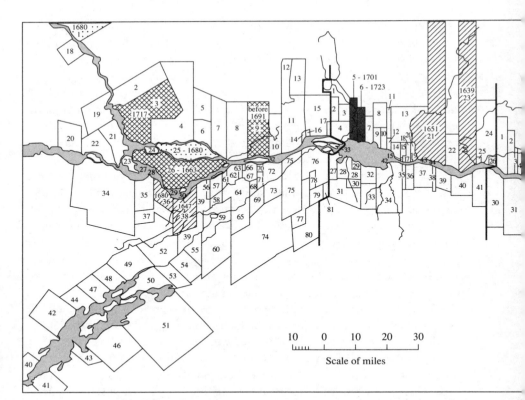

Scale of miles

10   0   10   20   30

GOVERNMENT OF MONTREAL

1	Petite Nation	27	Iles de la Paix
2	Argenteuil	28	Iles Courcelles
3	Deux Montagnes	29	Ile aux Hérons
4	Mille Iles	30	Ile St-Paul
5	Plaines	31	Ile Ste-Thérèse
6	Terrebonne	32	Iles Bouchard
7	Lachenaie (La Chesnaye)	33	Ile St-Pierre
		34	Beauharnois
8	L'Assomption, or Repentigny	35	Châteauguay
		36	Sault St-Louis
9	St-Sulpice	37	La Salle
10	Lavaltrie	38	La Prairie de la Magdeleine
11	Lanoraie		
12	Ailleboust	39	Longueuil
13	Ramezay, or Jouette	40	Rocbert
		41	Daneau de Muy
14	Dautré	42	Ramezay-la-Gesse
15	Berthier	43	La Perrière
16	Dorvilliers	44	Beaujeu
17	Ile Dupas et Chicot	45	Pancalon
18	Pointe à l'Orignal	46	La Moinaudière
19	Rigaud	47	La Gauchetière
20	Nouvelle Longueuil	48	Livaudière
21	Vaudreuil	49	Lacolle
22	Soulanges	50	Foucault
23	Ile Perrot	51	St-Armand
24	Ile Bizard	52	De Léry
25	Ile Jésus	53	Noyan
26	Ile de Montréal	54	Sabrevois

55	Bleury
56	Tremblay
57	Boucherville
58	Montarville
59	Chambly
60	Monnoir
61	Varennes
62	Cap de la Trinité
63	Guillaudière
64	Beloeil
65	Rouville
66	St-Blain
67	Verchères
68	Cournoyer
69	St-Charles-sur-Richelieu
70	Vitré
71	Cabanac
72	Contrecoeur
73	St-Denis
74	St-Hyacinthe
75	St-Ours
76	Sorel
77	Bourgchemin
78	Bonsecours
79	St-Charles
80	Ramezay
81	Bourg Marie

GOVERNMENT OF TROIS-RIVIÈRES

1	Lac Maskinongé, or Lanaudière	22	Champlain
		23	Batiscan
2	Dusablé	24	Ste-Anne-Ouest
3	Carufel	25	Ste-Marie
4	Maskinongé	26	Ste-Anne-Est, or Dorvilliers
5	St-Jean		
6	Rivière du Loup	27	Yamaska
7	Grandpré	28	St-François
8	Dumontier	29	Lussodière
9	Grosbois-Ouest	30	Pierreville
10	Grosbois-Est, or Yamachiche	31	Deguire
		32	Baie du Febvre, or St-Antoine
11	Robert		
12	Gastineau	33	Courval
13	St-Maurice	34	Nicolet
14	Tonnancour, or Pointe du Lac	35	Roquetaillade
		36	Godefroy, or Linctôt
15	Not conceded		
16	Boucher	37	Bécancour
17	Labadie	38	Dutort
18	Vieuxpont	39	Cournoyer
19	Jésuites	40	Gentilly
20	Seigneuries in or on outskirts of Trois-Rivières	41	Lévrard
		42	Ile Moras
21	Cap de la Madeleine	43	Ile Marie
		44	Iles du St-Maurice

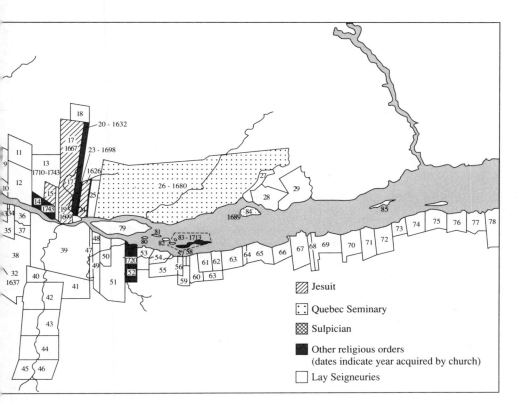

Figure 2.4 Seigneuries controlled by the church in New France. After the Conquest, Jesuit seigneuries became crown lands but the other orders retained their holdings (Source: Harris, 1984).

more devout priesthood and, although they did not train priests in New France, they became the dominant male religious orders in the colony.

The Jesuits' missionary work in New France has become famous, especially in Huronia where father Jean de Brébeuf and three of his companions suffered martyrdom at the hands of the Iroquois in 1648 and 1649. The Jesuit college at Quebec City, founded in 1635, was the first postsecondary educational institution in America north of Mexico. Jesuits also served the state as explorers (Charles Albanel, who crossed Quebec from Tadoussac to James Bay, and Jacques Marquette, who helped discover the Mississippi, are good examples), and helped maintain alliances with the native peoples by distributing gifts at their missions in the interior. With eight seigneuries around Quebec, Trois-Rivières, and on the south shore of the St. Lawrence opposite Montreal, the Jesuits were the largest landowners in the colony. After the Conquest, the order was dismantled, its college closed, and its lands taken over by the British crown.

The Sulpicians were involved in the founding of Montreal in 1642 and became the seigneurs of the Ile de Montréal in 1663. With two other seigneuries nearby, they were the dominant male religious order in the Montreal region. Important landowners, parish priests, and missionaries, the Sulpicians opened a classical college—the Collège de Montréal—at the end of the eighteenth century.

Female religious communities were active in health care and education. The first nuns, the Ursulines, arrived in the colony in 1639 to teach native girls. When they realized the futility of trying to educate native people in European-style institutions, the nuns established schools for daughters of the colonial elite at Quebec, Trois-Rivières, and New Orleans in which the catechism and reading and writing were taught alongside the domestic skills of needlework and good manners. The Ursulines were accompanied by the Hospitalières de la Miséricorde-de-Jésus, who established a hospital for native converts. As native distrust of French medicine increased, however, the hospital primarily served the European population.

The religious zeal that animated the first immigrants to Montreal led to the founding of new orders. Jeanne Mance founded Montreal's famous Hôtel-Dieu hospital in 1642 to take care of both Europeans and native peoples. Sixteen years later, the Congrégation de Notre-Dame was established by Marguerite Bourgeois. This order set up many elementary schools for girls throughout the colony from Montreal to Louisbourg. Elementary education in New France was not systematic. If schooling was available, girls and boys started at six or seven and stayed for three or four years in most cases. The first years were devoted to catechism and basic reading and counting skills. Education taught people to keep their place in society and for girls this would imply respect for patriarchy, and contentment with the role of wife and mother. Later, general hospitals were established in both Montreal and Quebec to care for the poor and the aged. These institutions, useful for social control, ensured that poverty was less visible by caring for the poor within the confines of a segregated, regimented community.

Although deep religious conviction motivated some candidates, religious life also fitted into the family strategies of the elite by reducing the number of off-spring who had to be provided for by the estate. Convent entrance fees were significant, but they were inferior to marriage dowries. The female orders rapidly became Canadianized and by the eighteenth century a majority of nuns had been born in the colony. Many daughters of the Canadian nobility joined the nursing orders and the Ursulines; indeed, about 20 percent of all adult women in this class were nuns. (Gadoury, 1988). The Congrégation de Notre-Dame admitted seventeen girls from the aristocracy but also drew from a broader social spectrum.

Sons of the colonial elite had fewer options. Apart from the Récollets, who acted mainly as military chaplains, male religious orders recruited new members almost exclusively in France. Before the 1770s only three Canadians entered the Jesuit order and none joined the Sulpicians. The reasons remain unclear. There seems to have been an anti-colonial bias on the part of the clergy but the Canadian aristocracy's preference for military careers was also partly responsible. The secular clergy—who served mainly as parish priests—was more open to Canadians but it did not draw members of the colonial elite since the most important functions such as vicar general or bishop were reserved for Frenchmen until after the Conquest. In 1776, Jean-François Hubert became the first Canadian to be consecrated bishop.

IMPERIAL RIVALRY AND THE CONQUEST

Throughout the seventeenth and eighteenth centuries, France and Britain competed for supremacy in Europe, India, the West Indies, and North America. Although France had four times Britain's population and ten times its army, its navy had shrunk to half the size of Britain's by the early 1700s. In a conflict involving colonies scattered around the world, naval supremacy proved decisive.

During the seventeenth century, neither empire was dominant and territories such as Acadia changed hands regularly. Acadia, which included present-day Nova Scotia, Prince Edward Island, New Brunswick, and Maine, was claimed by both France and England. The French, English, and Scots all unsuccessfully tried to found settlements there in the first third of the seventeenth century. In 1632, Acadia was in the hands of France and the Company of One Hundred Associates established a small base at Port-Royal on the Annapolis Basin. New Englanders conquered the territory in 1654 but were forced to give it up again in 1670. English expeditions ravaged French settlements in 1690, 1696, and 1704 before

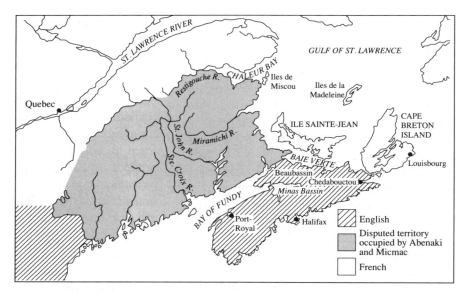

Figure 2.5 Acadia in 1754

finally conquering the colony in 1710. Thereafter, England controlled most of Nova Scotia and western Maine, while France controlled Cape Breton and Prince Edward Island (Figure 2.5). Eastern Maine and New Brunswick was a disputed territory controlled by the Abenakis and Micmacs allied with France.

The War of the Spanish Succession (1702–1713) marked an important change. France lost the war both in America and in Europe and had to cede its claims over vast territories in the Treaty of Utrecht in 1713. On the Atlantic coast, France gave up claims to peninsular Nova Scotia and Newfoundland, retaining only fishing rights to the "French shore" along the northern coast of the island. In the North, the French had to recognize British control over the Hudson Bay drainage basin, where fur traders from both countries had been competing since 1670. Finally, France had to recognize British control over the Iroquois and all their lands; this ensured that British American traders based in New York had access to the Great Lakes region.

This treaty shaped the future of imperial relations in North America. France strengthened its determination to block British expansion on the continent by building forts to link Montreal and Louisiana and by reinforcing its Indian alliances. The fortifications at Quebec, Montreal, and at stone forts along possible invasion routes from the south, such as at the Chambly rapids on the Richelieu River, were built or improved. The fortress of Louisbourg on Cape Breton Island was also erected as a naval base to protect the fishing fleet and the Gulf of St. Lawrence.

The French and British colonies in the Americas were strikingly different. New France's small population was concentrated along the St. Lawrence but its territory extended from the Gulf of St. Lawrence to the Gulf of Mexico. Its export economy was based on the fur trade, and the large garrison needed to stop English expansion reinforced the autocratic nature of its government.

In mercantilist terms, the French colony produced little benefit for its metropolis and this burden was recognized by Governor Roland-Michel Barrin de La Galissonière, who reported in 1750 that the French North American colonies "cost and will cost for a long time far more than they bring in." They were valuable, however, because they provided a market for French industry and their fisheries trained sailors for the French navy. They were also a source of labour, "a form of wealth far more precious for a great king" than any colonial produce. Their strategic position was also evident since Canada was "the strongest barrier that can be opposed to the ambitions of the English" (Groulx, 1970). La Galissonière's pleas to strengthen the colony went unheard, however, since the crown's financial difficulties and the protection of the more profitable sugar colonies were foremost in the minds of metropolitan administrators.

The thirteen colonies, on the other hand, had a much larger population, a more varied economy, and produced considerable wealth for Britain. The New England colonies specialized in fishing, the slave trade, shipbuilding, and the carrying trade (the shipment of local and imported goods between colonies); the middle colonies (New York, Pennsylvania, New Jersey, and Delaware) produced large agricultural surpluses; the southern slave colonies grew tobacco and cotton for the British market. British industries found a huge market in the colonies, and colonial trade was important for the prosperity of the British merchant navy.

Although imperial rivalry set the stage for conflict, war was precipitated by a local event. By the 1750s, British American settlers were encroaching on the rich Ohio valley, a French fur trading area. The Seven Years War began in July 1754, when British soldiers led by George Washington attacked a French reconnaissance party near the site of present-day Pittsburgh. Within months the two empires were at war in North America, on the oceans, and in Europe.

The Acadian deportation was one dramatic result of the early war years. Although conquered in 1710 by the British, Acadia attracted few English settlers and for two generations the Acadians had retained their lands and traditions. When war broke out in 1754, Nova Scotia's governor, Charles Lawrence, ordered the Acadians to swear allegiance to the British crown.

Hoping to maintain their traditional neutrality, the Acadians refused to take an oath that implied taking up arms against the French. Lawrence ordered their deportation, citing supposed Acadian support for Micmac raids against British colonists and an Acadian presence at the French forts Beauséjour and Gaspereau. Demands by New Englanders for land, however, were an equally important consideration.

Although some Acadians escaped to Quebec or France, more than 10 000 were herded onto ships and dispersed among the thirteen colonies. Family separation, loss of property, and the Acadian legend of Evangeline were the result. (The legend stressed the barbarity of a deportation that purposely separated family members.) Some Acadians made their way back up the Atlantic seaboard to what became New Brunswick, while others sought refuge in Louisiana (Griffiths, 1973). To this day, some of the population of Louisiana is French-speaking, although the "Acadian" culture has become "Cajun."

Despite initial French victories, British naval strength and Prime Minister William Pitt's determination to ensure British commercial superiority led to the conquest of France's North American colonies in 1760. Pitt, freed from European obligations by his new alliance with Frederick II of Prussia, sent 20 000 regular troops to reinforce the 22 000 colonial troops and militia already in North America. France, in contrast, was hindered by a lack of both troops and strategy. It had only 7000 regular troops in the colony, and the defensive strategy.of General Louis-Joseph Marquis de Montcalm allowed the British to close in on the St. Lawrence, especially after the fall of Louisbourg in 1758. In the summer of 1759, a British fleet, with some 20 000 soldiers and sailors aboard, sailed up the St. Lawrence and laid siege to Quebec.

Initial attacks on French positions were unsuccessful. By pillaging the countryside around Quebec City, the British commander, General James Wolfe, hoped to force Montcalm out of his defensive position and into a pitched battle. While reducing much of the city and especially the port area to rubble through a summer of bombardment (Figure 2.6), Wolfe ordered General Robert Monckton to ravage the countryside:

> I shall burn all the houses from the village of Saint-Joachim to the Montmorency River, and I would have you burn every house and hut, between the Chaudière and the River Etchemins; Churches must be spared. The houses, barns etc. from your camp down to the Church of Beaumont may be consumed at the same time.

In September, the Kamouraska region met the same fate: "Upon the whole," reported Major George Scott, "we marched fifty two Miles [83 km], and in that distance, burnt nine hundred and ninety eight good buildings, two sloops, two schooners, Ten Shallops and several Batteaus and small craft, took fifteen prisoners (six of them women and five of them children), killed five of the enemy." At Beaupré, Americans scalped the local priest and thirty militia, and burned the villages of Sainte-Anne and Château-Richer.

In a last attempt to draw out Montcalm before winter set in, Wolfe and 4500 elite troops scaled the cliffs at Anse-au-Foulon on September 9 and drew up on the Plains of Abraham. French troops were stationed primarily at Beauport to the east

Figure 2.6 The Bishop's palace after the bombardment of Quebec. During the French regime, important religious buildings—the cathedral, the Jesuit College, the Seminary, the Ursuline convent, the Hôtel-Dieu hospital—had symbolized the power of the church in a preindustrial society. During the 1759 bombardment the Lower Town near the port was almost completely demolished. The Bishop's palace, overlooking the Lower Town, suffered extensive damage, as did many of the houses on the street leading down to the port, as can be clearly seen here.

of the city while another force, led by Colonel Louis-Antoine de Bougainville, was located behind the British army at Cap Rouge. Instead of waiting for Bougainville to come up behind Wolfe, Montcalm brought his troops from Beauport, left the fortifications, and hurried out to meet the British in the open field. Tired from their long march and lacking strong leadership, the French were defeated in twenty minutes.

In the spring of 1760, the French won a battle at Sainte-Foy, but the arrival of the English fleet forced the French to retreat to Montreal. British forces moved in on Montreal by three of its river systems—upriver from Quebec City, down the Richelieu, and down the St. Lawrence from Lake Ontario. To avoid further bloodshed, the besieged French army surrendered in September. Thus, unlike Quebec, Montreal was spared the agony of a long siege.

Despite the defeat of the French colony, Canada's fate hinged on the outcome of the war in Europe, and in the meantime the colony was put under military rule. The articles of capitulation of Montreal (September 1760) guaranteed the preservation of the "entire peaceable property and possession of the goods, [lands], merchandizes, furs and even their ships." The rights of Catholics were not guaranteed, however, and the death of Bishop Henri-Marie Dubreuil de Pontbriand posed a problem by leaving Catholics without a bishop to confirm children or ordain new priests. Native peoples were also in an uncertain position since the British refused French requests to protect their native allies, native lands, and missionaries.

The articles of capitulation gave all inhabitants of the colony the right to return to France. Yet only a few hundred people chose to do, mostly important bureaucrats with careers closely linked to the French empire and some merchants who represented French companies. Members of the clergy also opted for Canada. While the Jesuits could no longer return to France because the order had been banned in 1764, the Sulpicians transferred ownership of property from the mother house in Paris to Canadian members.

The colony had been devastated by six years of war. With the area around Quebec City in ruins, the military authorities assisted in rebuilding and in getting fields back into production while trying to minimize British intrusion on daily life. At Quebec, General James Murray visited the Lorette mission, and ordered his troops to respect Catholic processions. He also let the Huron live on their lands and confirmed their right to hunt in the territory from the Saguenay to the St. Maurice rivers. Most important, he ordered inventories of the harvests, organizing the shipment of foodstuffs to stave off starvation.

THE DEBATE ABOUT THE EFFECTS OF THE CONQUEST

The Conquest has traditionally been seen as a watershed in Canadian history. For French-Canadian nationalists it is at the root of over two centuries of national oppression. For English Canadians it marks the beginning of a distinct, bi-ethnic North American society developing within the framework of British institutions. Although the Conquest's political impact must not be underestimated, its socio-economic impact was not dramatic.

The Conquest introduced greater ethnic diversity to Quebec but changed little in the colony's economy or class structure. Peasants continued to pay their tithes and seigneurial dues. Since seigneurs could no longer rely on revenue from military positions, they administered their lands with greater care to extract more from the peasantry. Fur traders continued to ship European trade goods to natives in the West and local merchants functioned as before. Most Roman Catholic institutions remained in place, although their financial and legal position was less assured. The change in metropolis did modify trading patterns and alter the business climate by increasing competition, but these changes were not sufficient to destroy the colonial mercantile community (Igartua, 1974b).

Because of the Conquest, the French, who had been the dominant power, became a conquered people. While generations of English Canadians have been taught to perceive the Conquest in the same light as American historian Francis Parkman, who declared, "A happier calamity never befell a people than the conquest of Canada by British arms," it is seen by French-Canadian nationalists as a major catastrophe. The French regime became a golden age; the period after the Conquest a long struggle for survival.

During the 1950s, the Conquest took on new significance as neo-nationalist historians such as Maurice Séguin and Guy Frégault interpreted it as the root of the social and economic inferiority of modern Quebec. In interrupting the normal process of development, the Conquest had prevented the colony from becoming an independent state.

> As long as French Canada remained alone, as long as the reasons for its birth and for its growth as a people [continued], the mother country sustained it, protecting it from a military point of view, colonizing it with her sons, her institutions, her capital resources. As long as these conditions existed it was in a position to become a normal nation (Séguin, 1968).

In this interpretation, the Conquest also meant the loss of a dynamic class, the bourgeoisie. The failure of modern French Canadians to dominate Quebec's economy was attributed to the destruction, or "decapitation," of the colonial elite in 1760. Because the embryonic bourgeoisie of New France was destroyed, French Canada was forced to turn inwards and to idealize rural life as the best means to preserve its nationality (Séguin, 1970).

> In 1760 Canada was completely crushed. The colony which passed to Britain three years later was an economic ruin. It was also a political ruin. Finally, in 1763 the country was ruined socially. During the years 1760–1763 Canada was not merely conquered and ceded to England; it was defeated. Defeat means disintegration. . . . The Canadians, eliminated from politics, from commerce and from industry, turned back to the soil. If they came to boast that they were "children of the soil," it was because defeat had affected not only their material civilization but also their ideas. They had higher pretensions when their community was more complete (Frégault, 1964).

This interpretation was widely accepted during the Quiet Revolution of Quebec in the 1960s, and helped shape the nationalist outlook towards English Canada. The Parti Québécois government used it to support its 1980 proposal for sovereignty association:

> Sooner or later [New France] would have rid itself of the colonial yoke and acquired its independence, as was the case in 1776 for the United States of America. But in 1763 the hazards of war placed it under British control.

> Deprived of their leaders, many of whom had to go back to France, subject to
> new masters who spoke another language, kept out of the civil service by the
> Royal Proclamation of 1763, our ancestors, lacking influence and capital, and
> ruled by British law, saw the entire commercial and industrial structure they
> had built pass gradually into the hands of English merchants (Quebec,
> *Québec–Canada: A New Deal*, 1980).

Although satisfying to many Québécois, this interpretation does not account for important differences in the social and economic structures of preindustrial and modern Quebec. Another current interpretation denies that New France had a viable business community and insists that the colony's ancien-régime mentality condemned it to a conservative outlook that contrasted sharply with the progressive business attitudes of the Anglo-Saxon merchants who arrived after the Conquest (Creighton, 1956; Ouellet, 1980). This interpretation is equally unsatisfactory.

Administrators and military officers were closely tied by patronage to the metropolis but at the same time they developed roots in the colony through their extensive land holdings. At the Conquest this group had to decide whether to remain in Canada and retain their seigneuries or to pursue their careers in the French empire. Most of the important administrators left but most military officers remained.

Merchants faced the same choice. The import–export trade, the most profitable sector of New France's economy, was dominated by agents to metropolitan trading companies and these merchants opted to return to France. Most merchants, however, were completely integrated into colonial society. Not only the rural merchants but also the Montreal fur traders, for example, had few direct links with France. They therefore chose to continue in familiar business surroundings. The Conquest forced them to find new suppliers and sources of credit but they did have a base of clients and superior knowledge of local business conditions (Igartua, 1974a).

The Conquest had an obvious effect on the composition of the administrative elite. Between 1763 and the Quebec Act of 1774, for example, Catholics could not hold office in the colony. This meant that francophone seigneurs had to give up their army commissions and turn to revenues from their seigneuries. After 1774, British administrators named a significant number of the seigneurial elite to official positions, but most of these were anglophones who had recently obtained seigneuries. Government positions were an important form of work for professionals in preindustrial society and, with the creation of a legislative assembly in 1791, patronage became hotly disputed as francophones sought their fair share (Paquet et Wallot, 1973).

The influx of anglophone traders after the Conquest, and especially after the American Revolution, changed business practices in Quebec. The most powerful anglophone merchants, who had strong ties to British firms and sources of credit, were able to drive many of the smaller francophone and anglophone merchants out of business. By the 1790s a new commercial elite had developed, centred around the essentially Scottish North West Company. The emergence of the timber trade after 1800 created new opportunities but entrepreneurs in this sector were usually recent immigrants with close family ties to important British or American merchants. These family links brought access to capital and technological innovation and to imperial and United States markets. British and American immigrants therefore often had an advantage in the mercantile community over native-born Canadians, regardless of ethnicity. Francophone merchants continued to be important in local trade and as large landholders in the growing urban centres, but they were no longer at the apex of the commercial hierarchy.

Integration into the British empire brought greater prosperity to the colony and more commercialization of agriculture. A growing francophone bourgeoisie made up of local merchants, notaries, and other professionals acted as a link between the local economy and the wider world of imperial trade in furs, timber, textiles, and manufactured goods. As population and trade grew, the business of notaries, particularly in land sales, and the wholesale and retail activities of merchants expanded greatly. In the village of Assomption forty miles to the northeast of Montreal, for example, the wealth and social status of the local merchants rose sharply in the decades 1760–1790. Across the period, the landed and movable wealth of the merchants of Assomption was five times greater than that of local notaries and doctors and ten times that of the general population (St. Georges, 1986).

At the same time, the wealth of the local clergy increased as the expanding population contributed more tithes, pew rentals, and fees for baptisms, marriages, and burials. By the end of the nineteenth century the local bourgeoisie and clergy were competing for dominance of the social and political life of the seigneurial countryside.

Within the popular classes there was greater diversity by the beginning of the nineteenth century than had been evident in the early years of settlement. Artisans continued to be independent producers, but they were joined in the towns by an increasing number of day labourers. Farmers with large holdings in the rich Montreal plain benefited from greater integration into the Atlantic economy, but more and more farmers with small holdings and those in outlying regions were forced to abandon agriculture for work in construction, the timber trade, or in artisanal shops in expanding cities and towns.

Constitutional Change under British Rule, 1763–1791

The Treaty of Paris in 1763 finalized the Conquest and gave Britain a new colony, the Province of Quebec, inhabited primarily by French Catholics who knew nothing of British traditions. In October 1763, the Royal Proclamation established the province's territorial and administrative structures. The priorities of the British government of the day, under prime minister Grenville, were to reorganize imperial administration and strengthen central control over taxation, commerce, and politics. Through the proclamation, it showed little understanding of the realities of Quebec. The government attempted to transform the colony into one with both British institutions and a British population; it promoted an elected assembly, British laws, and British immigration. At the same time, it separated Montreal from its natural fur trade hinterland by creating a vast Indian reserve in the interior of the continent (Tousignant, 1979).

Despite the instructions Governor James Murray had been given to establish English law and the Anglican church and to use English schools as vehicles of assimilation, he understood that—with the exception of the institution of British criminal law—such a policy was unworkable. Of the 70 000 French Canadians, 85 percent were rural inhabitants isolated from contact with the British and their institutions. Most of the few hundred British merchants who had come to the colony lived in Quebec City and Montreal and there was little immediate prospect of substantial British immigration.

Murray's dilemma was made more difficult by the Test Act, an English law in force in Great Britain since 1673, which prohibited Catholics from holding public office. By extension, French Canadians could neither hold government positions nor sit in an assembly in the colony. Governor Murray, because of his social origins in the Scottish land-owning class and his professional experience as a military commander, had more in common with the ancien-régime clerical and aristocratic elite of Quebec than with the newly arrived British merchants, whom he was determined to keep from power. He never held elections for an assembly, preferring to rule through a council sympathetic to the French Canadians. He also helped the Catholic church maintain its position in the colony by authorizing Jean-Olivier Briand to go to France to be consecrated as bishop, and by allowing female and most male religious orders to function normally.

The Jesuits were a significant exception to what would become an important alliance between the Catholic church and the state. As early as May 1760, Murray expelled the Jesuits from Quebec City. Their college was turned over to the army and their important library was broken up. In 1764, the order was suppressed in France and in 1773 hostility to the Jesuits across Europe culminated in their disbanding by the pope. In Canada, although forbidden to recruit members, the Jesuits, still wealthy with revenues from their ten seigneuries, struggled on. When the last Jesuit in Canada died in 1800, the crown took over their estates.

Murray's sensible reaction to political reality enraged British merchants in the colony, who demanded and finally obtained his recall. They were angry with his refusal to call an assembly, with his sympathy for the francophone seigneurs, with his toleration of Catholics, and with the failure of his bureaucrats to support the merchants' goals for a great commercial empire. They accused his administration of being "vexatious, oppressive and unconstitutional," and demanded "the blessings of British Liberty." For his part, Murray responded to the attacks of the British merchants who were trying to have him recalled by dismissing them as "ignorant, licentious, factious men."

Murray's successor, Sir Guy Carleton, came from the Anglo-Irish elite and, like Murray, came to view the clerical and seigneurial aristocracy as the natural leaders of French Canada. It was therefore fitting for him to follow Murray's policies.

By the 1770s, it was clear that the Royal Proclamation was not realistic since, failing strong British immigration, the colony retained its French Catholic character. The administration of justice, and of Indian lands, and the impracticality of instituting representative institutions remained pressing problems. Growing unrest in the thirteen colonies convinced the ministry in Britain that concessions were in order, to ensure the loyalty of the French Canadians. These were intended to reinforce, not to weaken, control by London and, moreover, were viewed by one of their principal architects, Lord Wedderburn, as "essentially a temporary" measure (Tousignant, 1979).

The Quebec Act of 1774 recognized the right of Catholics to exercise their religion and officially allowed the clergy to collect the tithe. Although the British crown still had the right to nominate the bishop, the Catholic clergy was in no immediate danger; the Test Act was replaced by an oath of loyalty that allowed Catholics to hold office. Seigneurial tenure was confirmed. The act provided for a council appointed by the crown that combined executive and legislative functions; no assembly was planned. A dual judicial system was adopted: English criminal law was retained but French law was normally used in civil cases. The boundaries of the colony were also changed to give the colony control over a large part of the Indian territories in the West (Figure 2.7).

With their social position recognized, the clergy and the seigneurs expressed satisfaction with the Quebec Act. Anglophone merchants were unhappy with the reinforcement of French institutions and the refusal to grant an assembly. Boundary modifications, however, did give them control over the western fur trade. The act changed little for the rest of the population.

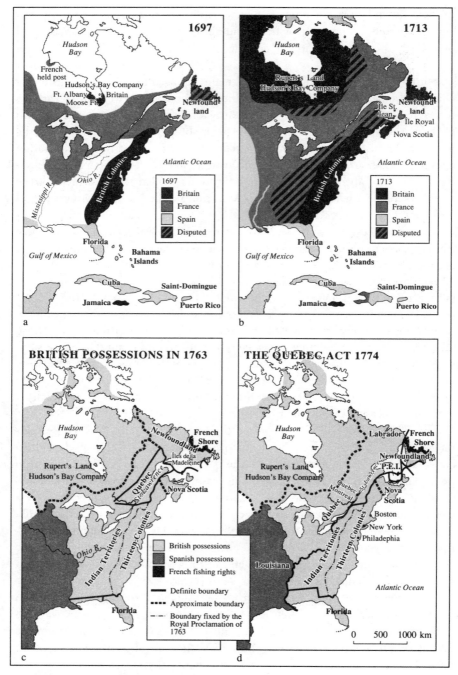

Figure 2.7 (continued on next page)

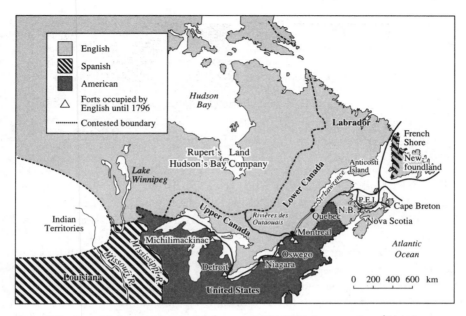

Figure 2.7 Imperial claims and territorial changes, 1697–1791. Incorporation of New France into the British empire had important effects on the colony's boundaries. In 1763, the Province of Quebec was limited to the St. Lawrence Valley from Gaspé to the Ottawa River. The Quebec Act gave it back the Magdalen Islands, Labrador, and an extensive territory around the Great Lakes. In the aftermath of the American Revolution, Quebec's boundaries were again reduced to the area east of the Ottawa River. In 1911, Quebec obtained control of the Ungava district (that part of present-day Quebec attributed to the Hudson's Bay Company in 1713) from the federal government. Labrador was lost to Newfoundland by a decision of the British Privy Council in 1927, a decision that the Quebec government has never recognized.

The Quebec Act also had an impact on the thirteen colonies, where it was considered one of the "intolerable acts" passed by the British government. To many Americans, the autocratic nature of the administration envisaged for Quebec was symptomatic of the thrust for greater centralized power inherent in much British legislation. The new boundaries of the province alienated New York merchants because Albany was cut off from the fur trade. The boundaries also offended many in Pennsylvania and Virginia by preventing settlement in the Ohio valley, while the act upset puritan New England because the Catholic church had been protected.

As unrest in the Thirteen Colonies continued to grow, Americans anticipated support from the conquered population in Canada. In its address to the people of Quebec in October 1774, the Continental Congress, meeting in Philadelphia, was particularly disdainful of the Quebec Act's violation of the principles of liberty:

> Seize the opportunity presented to you by Providence itself. . . . A moment's
> reflection should convince you which will be most for your interest and hap-
> piness, to have all the rest of North America your unalterable friends, or your
> inveterate enemies. . . . Be assured that the happiness of a people inevitably
> depends on their liberty, and their spirit to assert it.

Although the address found a sympathetic ear among the anglophone merchants
of Montreal, who distributed it throughout the colony, it was strongly opposed by
the clergy and seigneurs; the peasantry remained largely indifferent to American
appeals.

In 1775, two American armies invaded Quebec to drive the British out.
General Richard Montgomery marched down the Richelieu River route and captured Montreal without a fight while Benedict Arnold, coming down the
Chaudière Valley, laid siege to Quebec City. The two American armies joined
forces at Quebec in December but were held off by Carleton until the arrival of
British reinforcements in the spring forced the Americans to withdraw and
removed the threat of another invasion.

French-Canadian attitudes to the Americans were ambiguous. The seigneurs
and the clergy urged support for the British; Bishop Briand went so far as to order
Catholics to be loyal to the British king. The peasantry, however, remained neutral. Peasants sold supplies to the Americans for coin but refused when paper
money was offered. Over 500 militia took up arms to defend Quebec in 1775 but
none volunteered to join the British army in attacking the American colonies
later in the war.

The American colonies were granted independence by the Treaty of Versailles
in 1783. This pivotal event had important consequences for the remaining British
colonies, which we can now call British North America. With the creation of the
United States, Quebec lost its territory south of the Great Lakes, although
Canadian merchants continued to trade in the area until the end of the century.
Britain, did, however, keep the richest fur trading areas in the Northwest, and
many traders moved north from Albany to Montreal. Most important, peace saw
the arrival of Loyalists, who would challenge the predominantly French nature of
Quebec and force the British to seek a new constitutional solution.

The Quebec Act, which had reinforced French Canadian religious, seigneurial, and judicial structures, was unsatisfactory to both the anglophone merchants
of Montreal and the Loyalist immigrants. Members of the seigneurial elite told
the governor that an assembly would be "useless," but the emerging francophone
bourgeoisie—made up of merchants, notaries, and lawyers—joined their anglophone compatriots in petitioning him to have the Quebec Act repealed and to
grant an elected assembly.

The Constitutional Act of 1791 amended the Quebec Act, establishing a
political structure that maintained strong imperial control in order to fulfil the

traditional mercantile needs of the empire. British authorities were fearful of democratic excesses, which they saw as partly responsible for the American Revolution. They therefore maintained strong executive power, exercised through the governor, an executive council, and a legislative council. These councils served to cement the crown's alliance with its traditional allies among both francophones and anglophones in the ranks of the upper clergy, seigneurs, bureaucrats, and important merchants. Collectively, this group came to be known as the Château Clique.

At the same time, certain limited democratic institutions were permitted and the colonies were encouraged to assume a larger share of the costs of their own administration and defence. To this end, a legislative assembly, the first popularly elected assembly in Quebec's history, was created. Almost all rural property holders and tenants had the vote (Ouellet, 1980: 25), and although the franchise was less generous in towns, it still enfranchised many artisans. Besides a minimal property qualification, the voter also had to be twenty-one, a British subject by birth, naturalization, or conquest, and could not have been convicted of treason. Women who met the requirements had the vote but, since property was in the name of the male family head, only widows and unmarried women of majority age qualified.

Not only did the act fail to meet the political expectations of the anglophone merchants, but the division of Quebec into Upper and Lower Canada separated them from the 10 000 Loyalists who settled around Lake Ontario. The act left intact important parts of the Quebec Act that guaranteed institutions with strong French, Catholic, and ancien-régime connotations, such as the seigneurial system. At the same time, it introduced British elements to the structure of property ownership and religious institutions. State support was given to the Church of England (as an established church), for example, in the form of clergy reserves, and to educational institutions through crown reserves. These reserves made up one-seventh of the unceded public land in townships established outside the seigneurial zone. Land grants in the townships were made in freehold tenure. Property was therefore held outright by individuals in these areas, without the restrictions of the seigneurial system.

The duality created by these provisions further complicated the contradictions within the legal system, which remained a mixture of British and French traditions. Lower Canada would continue to use French civil law while English common law would be applied to Upper Canada. It was not clear, however, if anglophone settlers in areas of Lower Canada (in the Eastern Townships, for example, where freehold tenure prevailed) could use English common law in contracts and business deals among themselves. And, of course, the anglophone merchants in the colony's major towns continued to be subject to French commercial law.

THE EMERGENCE OF FRENCH
CANADIAN NATIONALISM

The legislative assembly established under the Constitutional Act became the political forum for deepening social and ethnic conflict in Lower Canada. The first session of the assembly opened in 1792 with "a determined spirit of party amongst the French members," who voted as a block to have French recognized as an official language of the House. Anglophone members quickly sided with the governor, while the francophone bourgeoisie used the legislature to challenge the leadership of the seigneurial elite and the autocratic nature of government.

In the 1790s, authorities were particularly nervous about the effects of the French Revolution on French Canadians. The Revolution broke out in 1789 and, in the early years, smashed the privileges of the crown, the church, and the aristocracy. Members of the colonial elite feared that the assembly might spread such ideas. For example, Toussaint Pothier, a powerful fur trade merchant and Montreal landowner, described the elected members of the assembly as members of the lower class who had lost "their sense of subordination," and the clerical elite strongly supported British institutions in sermons praising monarchic institutions. These fears proved largely unfounded, however, as membership in the British empire started to pay economic dividends. Demand for Canadian grain was high and, after the imposition of Napoleon's continental blockade in 1806, Canadian timber products became a major element of imperial trade. With general prosperity in the colony, neither peasants nor the francophone bourgeoisie acted to sever links with England.

Nevertheless, prosperity did not stop conflict. Attempts to bring the Catholic church under government control and to institute a public anglophone education system met with sharp francophone resistance. Ethnic conflict peaked in the period 1805–1811 with taxation bills, battles for control of the civil list (which made financial provision for members of the civil service), and projects to ban government cronies from sitting in the assembly.

Although Whig historians often interpret the conflict as one between a vibrant anglophone bourgeoisie and a retrograde francophone professional class (Creighton, 1956; Ouellet, 1981), more important issues were at stake. The Gaol Bill of 1805, by which a tax on wine and tea was levied to build new jails at Montreal and Quebec, is an excellent example. The anglophone merchants, seeking to protect the old colonial system, objected: "The taxing of trade will lessen bonds to the Mother country and the metropolitan centre's control over trade and commerce . . . as it may hereafter be applied to discourage the Importation of British Manufactures in order to encourage such as are local." They proposed a tax on land, which would have fallen heavily on the mainly francophone rural population. The francophone bourgeoisie, on the other hand, sought to establish the assembly's prerogatives in matters of local taxation.

Ethnic conflict was made more visible by the publication of party newspapers: the *Quebec Mercury* by the anglophone elite, and *Le Canadien* by the francophone reformers. The *Mercury* bitterly attacked all that was French.

> This province is already too much a french province for an english colony. To *unfrenchify* it, as much as possible . . . should be a primary object, particularly in these times. . . .
>
> A french system is an arbitrary system, because it is a military one, it becomes therefore the interest, not of englishmen only, but of the universe, to raise mounds against the progress of french power. To oppose it is a duty. To assist it . . . is criminal. To a certain extent the french language is at present unavoidable in this province; but its cultivation, beyond what may be necessary, so as to perpetuate it, in an english colony, can admit of no defence, particularly in the present times.

Le Canadien defended francophone rights:

> You say that the [French] Canadians use their privileges too freely for a conquered people, and you threaten them with the loss of those privileges. How dare you reproach them for enjoying the privileges which the British Parliament has granted them? . . . You ask absurdly whether the [French] Canadians have the right to exercise these privileges in their own language. In what other tongue could they exercise them? Did not the parliament of Great Britain know what their language was?

Beyond the ethnic confrontation lay more fundamental constitutional issues. The Reform party, or *parti canadien*, closely followed constitutional development in both Britain and other colonies such as Jamaica, and demanded that the assembly be given increased powers resembling those of the British House of Commons. Members of the *parti canadien* remained loyal to British parliamentary institutions in the pursuit of their goals; republicanism, whether of the French or the American variety, was frowned upon. Debate centred around the civil list and the control of government patronage. The patronage system had favoured members of the Château Clique, and reformers demanded that the assembly have complete control over appointments. Autocratic governors, of course, resisted this attack on their privileges and were supported by the anglophone bureaucrats who benefited from this patronage (Paquet et Wallot, 1973). As the *parti canadien's* constitutional demands became more articulate, an exasperated Governor James Craig seized the presses of *Le Canadien* in 1810 and jailed twenty of its owners and distributors for "treasonous practices."

The ethnic and constitutional clashes were more than a struggle between different concepts of government. In preindustrial society, civil expenditures focused on general administration, justice, and the army; capital expenditures on public works to modernize the economy were not yet important. The civil list was therefore a key element of power and controlling it was essential if the assembly was to have real power in the colony.

Despite these tensions, French Canada remained loyal when Britain went to war with the United States in 1812. Agents working for France tried unsuccessfully to rouse French Canadians to join the Americans. The *parti canadien* did not support the Americans, and *Le Canadien* opposed French interference in Canadian affairs, describing Napoleon as "the lawless leader of France." The assembly voted funds for the British military and raised 6000 militia to defend Canada. The first French-Canadian regiment of regular soldiers, the Voltigeurs led by Charles-Michel de Salaberry, actively defended the colony at the Battle of Châteauguay in 1813.

The church also called for loyalty to Britain, with Bishop Joseph-Octave Plessis reminding francophones of the religious freedom and "good government" that they enjoyed under British rule. The unflinching loyalty to the crown by successive bishops did much to ingratiate the church with colonial governors. In 1818, Mgr. Plessis was officially recognized by the British government as Catholic bishop of Quebec and was nominated to the legislative council. The creation of auxiliary bishoprics in the Maritimes, Montreal, Upper Canada, and the Red River colony by 1821 placed the Catholic church on an even firmer footing.

CONCLUSION

British attempts to find a constitutional solution to the problems of governing a French Catholic population led the government to guarantee the basic institutions of the French regime such as seigneurial tenure and French civil law. Despite the creation of an assembly in 1791, the ideology of colonial government had not changed. The Colonial Office continued to direct policy through a governor, much as the Ministry of Marine had done in New France. Political power and patronage in the colony were vested in the hands of a small elite which continued to favour class and family connections. Although the seigneurial elite found it more difficult to pursue careers in the army, its land revenues enabled it to maintain an aristocratic way of life.

The other main factor in the institutional framework of the French regime, the Roman Catholic church, faced many difficulties. The threat of domination by an Anglican king was ever present. Although the Jesuits and Récollets had disappeared from Canada by the beginning of the nineteenth century, most religious orders were preserved. Indeed, the French Revolution helped to reinforce communities such as the Sulpicians, who welcomed emigré priests fleeing anticlericalism in revolutionary France. Although the loss of royal subsidies had been a hard blow, the rapidly growing Catholic population and the prosperity of rural regions at the end of the eighteenth century ensured a solid financial base for the church through the tithe, fees, and donations. Thus the church was consolidating both its financial and its political position by the beginning of the 1820s.

FURTHER READING

HISTORY OF NEW FRANCE

On the general history of New France, readers should consult William John Eccles' works and notably *Canada Under Louis XIV* and *The Canadian Frontier*. Marcel Trudel's *An Initiation to New France* is succinct and useful. The best summary of the administrative structures can be found in André Vachon's introduction to the *Dictionary of Canadian Biography*, Volume II. Civil judicial administration is treated by John A. Dickinson in *Justice et justiciables: La procédure civile à la Prévôté de Québec, 1667–1759* and criminal administration by André Lachance in *La justice criminelle du roi au Canada au XVIIIe siècle: Tribunaux et officiers* and *Crimes et criminels en Nouvelle-France*.

SEIGNEURIALISM

The traditional view of the seigneurial system can be found in Marcel Trudel's *The Seigneurial Regime*. A geographer's perspective on this question is given by Richard Colebrook Harris, *The Seigneurial System in Early Canada*. The best recent studies of seigneurial tenure are Louise Dechêne's "L'évolution du régime seigneurial au Canada. Le cas de Montréal aux XVIIe et XVIIIe siècles," and Allan Greer's *Peasant, Lord and Merchant: Rural Society in Three Quebec Parishes, 1740–1840*.

THE CHURCH IN NEW FRANCE

The church in New France has been examined by Cornelius Jaenen in *The Role of the Church in New France*. On the problems faced by the clergy in its quest for official recognition, the reader should consult Lucien Lemieux, *L'établissement de la première province ecclésiastique au Canada, 1783–1884*. Conflict between the church and the *parti canadien* has been outlined by Richard Chabot in his *Le curé de campagne et la contestation locale au Québec de 1791 aux troubles de 1837–38*.

THE CONQUEST

Two collections are available that give summaries of the debate over the Conquest: Cameron Nish's *The French Canadians, 1759–1766: Conquered? Half-Conquered? Liberated?* and Dale Miquelon's *Society and Conquest: The Debate on the Bourgeoisie and Social Change in French Canada, 1700–1850.* The best single article that points out the weaknesses in the arguments put forward is Serge Gagnon's "Pour une conscience historique de la révolution québécoise."

BRITISH ADMINISTRATION

On British Administration, the two most useful surveys are Hilda Neatby's *Quebec in the Revolutionary Age, 1760–1791* and Fernand Ouellet's *Lower Canada, 1791–1840: Social Change and Nationalism.* Pierre Tousignant gives an insightful analysis of "The integration of the Province of Quebec into the British empire" in the introduction to Volume IV of the *Dictionary of Canadian Biography.* Also useful on the conditions under which the Constitutional Act was adopted is his "Problématique pour une nouvelle approche de la constitution de 1791." Gilles Paquet and Jean-Pierre Wallot, *Patronage et pourvoir dans le Bas-Canada (1794–1812)* is useful for an understanding of political conflict at the turn of the nineteenth century.

Preindustrial Society and Economy

ecause preindustrial Quebec evolved within a colonial framework, its society and economy were partially shaped by transatlantic metropolitan centres. Yet much of its development was due to local factors beyond the control of a central administration. Although the basic social, economic, and administrative structures of the colony remained constant from 1650 to 1815, it was not a static society. The population grew rapidly as the agricultural frontier expanded and merchants exploited staple products. Quebec was fashioned by the institutions and cultural traditions of two European peoples, but its agricultural economy (based on extensive mixed farming because of the scarcity of labour), its abundant land that enabled most families to establish their offspring on viable farms, and its staple-based export economy made it quite different from either of the European mother countries.

DEMOGRAPHY

The fur trade required little European labour before 1650. French settlement in Canada therefore grew slowly, reaching a population of about 1200 by mid-century. The Company of One Hundred Associates, which had been granted the colony in 1627, faced immediate problems in its settlement projects when its first two fleets were captured by English pirates in 1628 and 1629. Defaulting on its commitment to bring out 4000 settlers by 1642, the company tried to pass on the costs of settlement by granting seigneuries with the provision that seigneurs recruit colonists; few did. Instead, most settlers before 1650 were sponsored by missionaries who had a variety of motives: eagerness to expand their activities beyond a native constituency; their need for adequate supplies of local foodstuffs; or, in the case of missionaries in Montreal, the wish to create a model Christian community.

Dispersion of the Huron by 1650 had important repercussions on work and agriculture in the colony. The French now found work in the fur trade, replacing the Hurons as intermediaries. Markets for foodstuffs expanded as the local French population grew and the semi-nomadic tribes in the French alliance sought food to replace that produced by the Hurons. In the decade 1663–1672, the European population reached 7000; the French crown paid the passage of several thousand immigrants and forced the disbanded soldiers of the Carignan-Salières regiment to settle in the colony. Of these immigrants, 770 were young women (*les filles du roi*). Contrary to popular opinion, these women came from varied social and geographical backgrounds. While almost half were from the Parisian orphanage, L'Hôpital général, a third were from Western France (mainly Normandy and Poitou). Most were from the popular classes and about one-third of the poorest were provided with dowries by the crown. Given the shortage of nubile European women in these early years, all but one of the *filles du roi* married, most of them within five months of their arrival at Quebec (Landry, 1992a).

Immigration had slowed by the 1670s, however, when work opportunities declined and government sponsorship disappeared. Population growth became largely dependent on natural increase, and the government therefore attempted to encourage large families. It instituted fines for bachelors and bonuses for families with ten or more living children, providing none had entered religious life. Yet these policies were largely ineffectual. Despite the *filles du roi*, the imbalance between male and female immigrants was such that many men remained unmarried. (The sex ratio in 1681 remained about three adult men for every two women.)

Since a farm required female as well as male labour, many men were unable to farm. Some found work in the fur trade, eventually living with native women in the West. Their descendants were assimilated into their mothers' culture. Later they developed a distinct culture and became known as Métis. Because contraception was unavailable, married women had children at regular intervals (about every second year) throughout their childbearing years. The size of families was regulated by the age of women at marriage, by social attitudes that valued numerous offspring, and by infant mortality (one-fifth of the children died before their first birthday). Except during the war years (1744–1748 and 1754–1760), when it declined, the annual birth rate remained stable at about fifty-five births per 1000 population. (The Canadian birth rate in the 1980s was about eighteen per 1000.) Families averaged seven children, well below the requirement for a government bonus. Indeed, demographer Hubert Charbonneau (1975: 222–23) has estimated that less than 2 percent of families could have met the requirements. Despite the average age of marriage of twenty-two for women and twenty-seven for men, society tended to obey the religious stricture against premarital sex, and premarital conceptions and illegitimate children were very rare (Bates, 1986; Paquette et Bates, 1986).

During the French regime most immigrants came from western France, particularly Normandy and the La Rochelle area, or Paris. Although the vast majority of settlers were French, there was some diversity. Pedro Dasilva, for example, was among the Portuguese immigrants who founded families in Quebec in the seventeenth century. During the intercolonial wars of the second half of Louis XIV's reign (1689–1713), more than 1000 captured New England settlers were taken to Montreal and Quebec where many—mostly orphaned children—were adopted by Canadian families (Axtell, 1985). Other American colonists, such as Quebec merchant William Strouds, came to New France to escape legal difficulties.

By 1650, almost all of the original native inhabitants of the St. Lawrence Valley had been killed by disease or warfare; the few survivors distanced themselves from white settlements. Between 1650 and 1760 Iroquois and Abenaki from the South, Huron from the West, and Algonquin and Nipissing from the

North were settled along the St. Lawrence in villages that the missionaries established for their Christian converts. Usually isolated from French settlements, these formed the basis for present-day reserves. The first such village, established at Sillery near Quebec City in 1637 to assimilate Montagnais and Algonquins, had not been a success. Huron refugees occupied several locations near Quebec City after 1650 before moving to a permanent village at Lorette in 1697.

In the 1660s, the Jesuits established a village for Iroquois Christians at Sault-Saint-Louis, the present site of Kahnawake. In the same period, the Sulpicians started a mixed Iroquois and Algonquin village on the outskirts of Montreal. Ostensibly to isolate its inhabitants from the brandy trade, the Sulpicians moved this village twice, finally locating it in 1721 at Kanesatake near Oka on the Lake of Two Mountains. (It was over land at Oka considered sacred by the Mohawks and desired by municipal authorities for a golf course that the Oka crisis of 1990 erupted.)

The changes in village site benefited the Sulpicians because they increased the value of their seigneurial domain by using native labour to clear land. Some of this land was later sold to European settlers (Tremblay, 1981: 84–88, 111–15). Other villages were established at Bécancour and Saint-François for Abenaki refugees who had fled the English colonists in Maine. Life in these communities was patterned after that in traditional Iroquois villages, with women tilling the soil and men participating in the fur trade and in war parties against New England.

Three-quarters of the colony's European population throughout this period was rural, spreading out along the St. Lawrence before occupying lowlands along rivers such as the Richelieu and the Chaudière. Most settlers lived near Quebec and Montreal, however. Elsewhere the population was spread thinly in a ribbon along the rivers. Quebec, with a population of some 8000 in 1760, was the only city; Montreal had only half the population of Quebec and remained a frontier community; Trois-Rivières, whose population never exceeded 800 during the French period, was little more than a large market and an administrative and service town. Although the small villages of Beauport, Boucherville, Charlesbourg, La Prairie, Pointe-aux-Trembles, Terrebonne, Varennes, and Verchères acted as service centres for the surrounding rural population, one could hardly speak of an urban network.

The Conquest did not alter the basic characteristics of the Canadian population. Marriage, birth, and death rates remained relatively constant and despite immigration being cut off from France, a healthy rate of natural increase ensured the predominance of a French Catholic peasantry in the new British colony. Settlement continued to spread out in the seigneuries along the St. Lawrence and Richelieu valleys. Only at the beginning of the nineteenth century, as new generations had increasing difficulty finding new seigneurial land, did overpopulation in the St. Lawrence lowlands become a problem.

Period	Average population	Annual birth rate per 1000	Annual marriage rate per 1000	Annual death rate per 1000
1711–1715	19 800	55.9	9.5	27.8
1716–1720	22 900	57.8	10.3	21.5
1721–1725	27 200	52.6	9.4	20.3
1726–1730	31 600	54.2	10.2	26.1
1731–1735	36 200	58.1	9.9	30.4
1736–1740	42 300	54.7	8.9	21.2
1741–1745	49 100	51.2	8.7	25.1
1746–1750	55 000	50.9	10.3	33.1
1751–1755	61 200	54.5	10.1	29.5
1756–1760	67 200	51.4	10.0	37.9
1761–1765	74 400	56.8	11.6	29.3
1766–1770	86 200	56.8	8.3	27.3
1771–1775	98 100	55.7	9.2	27.2
1776–1780	110 400	52.8	8.1	30.3
1781–1785	125 700	51.6	8.1	27.7
1786–1790	141 900	50.6	8.2	25.7
1791–1795	160 300	52.5	9.2	25.9
1796–1800	183 700	51.9	8.3	24.6
1801–1805	208 900	52.6	8.8	27.8
1806–1810	238 600	50.4	8.3	25.2
1811–1815	269 300	50.1	9.1	26.9

Table 3.1   Population Change in Quebec's Catholic Population, 1711–1815
(Charbonneau, 1973: 43)

Before the American Revolution, British immigration was largely limited to a small number of merchants, artisans, bureaucrats, and soldiers, most of whom settled in the towns. More than the Conquest, it was the American Revolution that brought significant demographic change; Loyalists quickly constituted a sizable anglophone minority (Figure 3.1). The Americans portrayed the Loyalists as an elite of Anglican clergy, bureaucrats, and merchants living off government favours, but most of them were of humbler origin: recent immigrants from Britain, members of religious or ethnic minorities, Indians from the Iroquois confederacy, and farmers.

Although New France had welcomed native refugees from the south, Loyalist migration in the 1780s was much more diverse and larger in scope. Several hundred remained in the more settled areas, especially around Montreal and Sorel (then known as William Henry), but the vast majority moved west of the seigneurial

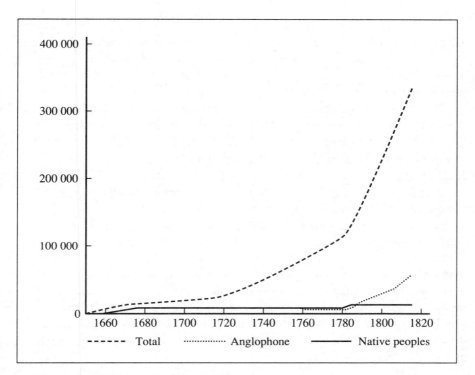

Figure 3.1 The population of Quebec, 1650–1815

lands. Some 6000 Loyalists settled along the upper St. Lawrence and Lake Ontario. Colonists were granted 100 acres in freehold tenure plus fifty acres for each member of their families, with some officers receiving special grants up to 5000 acres.

As can be seen by settler John Stuart's comments in 1783, a sense of community was already developing in towns such as Kingston:

> I have 200 acres within half a mile of the garrison, a beautiful situation and tolerable good land. The town increases fast; there are already above 50 houses built in it and some of them very elegant. It is now the port of transport from Canada to Niagara, having a good harbor. The number of souls to the westward of us is more than 5000 and we gain daily new recruits from the States—we are poor, happy people, industrious beyond example. Our gracious King gives us land gratis and furnishes provision and clothing, farming utensils etc. The greatest inconvenience I feel here is there being no school for my boys. If I succeed in erecting an Academy, I shall die here contented.

Anglophone settlements existed in Nova Scotia and Newfoundland before the Conquest. The arrival of the Loyalists signalled the expansion of a significant anglophone population across British North America. From a small merchant and military population of 500 in the 1760s, the anglophone population of Lower Canada grew to 50 000 by 1815. A majority of immigrants between 1785 and 1815 were New Englanders, many of whom settled in freehold lands in the Eastern Townships. By 1815, 15 000 anglophone settlers had moved to this region, most around Missisquoi Bay and in the Stanstead area.

The division of Quebec into Upper and Lower Canada in 1791 separated Lower Canada's anglophone population from the British and American immigrants who settled west of the Ottawa River. Although anglophones constituted a majority in the Eastern Townships and significant minorities in Montreal, Quebec City, and the Gaspé, they were insignificant elsewhere in Lower Canada. In areas where they had no contact with a sizable anglophone community many were assimilated by their francophone neighbours.

For their part, native peoples remained distinct minorities, either occupying lands set aside for them during the French regime or living in new communities established for them in regions such as the Gaspé. Many Huron, Iroquois, Algonquin, and Micmac men had work experiences similar to those of whites—as canoeists, forest workers, river drivers, timber rafters, and fishermen—while women sold artisanal products in urban markets. Only in northern Quebec, where the Hudson's Bay Company forbade settlement until the 1840s, did the Cree, Montagnais, Naskapi, and Inuit continue to follow traditional subsistence patterns, little affected by European society.

STAPLES IN THE PREINDUSTRIAL ECONOMY

The staple theory, which took form in the 1930s in the works of Harold Innis, dominated the study of Canadian political economy until recently (Innis, 1956; Easterbrook and Watkins, 1967: 49–73). Innis emphasized Canada's dependency on foreign trade and maintained that trade in staple commodities such as cod, beaver, wheat, and timber constituted the motor of Canada's economic and social development.

During the French regime fish and furs were the main staples but by 1800 they were being overtaken by exports of wheat and timber. Although exports of these staples did dominate trade with metropolitan centres throughout the preindustrial period, the staple theory has underestimated the importance of local markets and the dynamics of the peasant economy.

Despite the emphasis placed on fur in Canadian historiography, the fishery was the first North American staple and it remained the most valuable North American export to France throughout the French colonial period (Brière, 1986; Turgeon, 1981). Centred on Newfoundland and Cape Breton Island, the French fishery was dominated by ships from Saint-Malo and Granville which exploited the rich Mediterranean market through forwarders at Marseilles. Nonetheless, colonial merchants also became active in this trade. Early in the eighteenth century, Quebec City entrepreneurs such as Denis Riverin and Pierre Haimard set up fishing bases in the Gaspé, and Marie-Anne Barbel developed sealing operations along the Labrador coast. These Quebec merchants supplied the local market's strong demand for fish for the fast days of Fridays and Lent and also exported some of their catch to the French West Indies. Sealing operations provided exports of train oil and pelts for the metropolitan market.

Although France retained lucrative fishing rights along the "French shore" of Newfoundland after the Conquest, the Gulf of St. Lawrence fisheries, and especially those in the Gaspé, came under the dominance of Channel Island families such as the Robins. By 1800, the Robins were exporting some £16 000 of cod annually. The fishery also encouraged the creation of a local shipbuilding industry, not only for the schooners and shallops used for fishing but also for larger ships and brigs that were later sold in Europe. Population growth in the Gaspé started with the arrival of Acadian refugees in the 1750s and was bolstered by the arrival of some Loyalist families in the 1780s.

Despite significant local production, the 5000 settlers in this region at the turn of the century remained dependent on the great merchants of the fishery. Instead of paying cash, merchants used the truck system—paying for the catch by extending credit to buy equipment, clothes, and food at their stores. The truck system resulted in a growing indebtedness for the fishing population, and thereby reinforced their dependence while increasing merchant profits in the local retail trade (Lee, 1984).

Despite the greater economic importance of the fishery, it was the fur trade that had drawn Europeans to the St. Lawrence Valley and eventually led to settlement. As we have seen, the destruction of the Huron forced the French to seek out new suppliers. In 1653, Médard Chouart, sieur des Groseilliers, the first coureur de bois, set out to encourage western tribes to bring their furs directly to Montreal. His success showed that French agents in the interior could guarantee the supply of pelts. This led the French crown to send agents (often members of religious orders) such as Charles Albanel, Jacques Marquette, François Dollier de Casson, and René de Bréhant de Galinée to find new trade routes and to start missions in the Great Lakes and Hudson Bay drainage systems.

Although native peoples did all the work of trapping and preparing pelts, native canoeists (especially the Ottawa, who had provided much of the labour to transport fur between 1653 and 1670) were increasingly replaced by coureurs de bois, who sought complete control of trade in the interior.

The period 1670–1681 was one of anarchy in the fur trade. Metropolitan officials, who wanted Indians to do all the labour of collecting and transporting furs

Figure 3.2 The coureurs de bois have been romanticized as freedom-loving individualists who adapted quickly to life in the woods. Exploration and work in the fur trade was very demanding. Carrying heavy bales over long portages, paddling through mosquito-infested waters, coping with weather conditions and the very real threat of drowning were among the daily hardships. This illustration of exploration in the Labrador peninsula in the 1850s shows the difficulties encountered during such expeditions.

to Montreal, tried unsuccessfully to stem the proliferation of coureurs de bois by outlawing them: they were seen as a drain on the colony because they did not farm. The coureurs de bois were, however, an essential link in the staple trade. They contacted tribes, exchanged European metal wares, textiles, and brandy for furs, and transported pelts to Montreal. Local officials, particularly governor Louis de Buade de Frontenac and his associate Robert Cavelier de La Salle, continued to encourage the expansion of the fur trade in the hope of personal gain.

Apart from men like Frontenac and La Salle, only the Compagnie des Indes occidentales, which had the monopoly over fur exports, profited during this period. Although the coureurs de bois were independent traders, fierce competition cut heavily into their profit margins and hardly made worthwhile the threat of prosecution, the danger of Indian attack, and the physical hardships of paddling and portaging (Figure 3.2). (Authorities estimated that 500 men were trading in the West in 1680; in the single year 1684, 39 French traders were killed in the West (White, 1991).) Merchants who supplied trade goods to the coureurs de bois fared little better. Competition and the difficulty of recovering debts from outlawed coureurs de bois eliminated many after a couple of years. Only Jacques Leber and Charles LeMoyne managed to accumulate significant capital (Dechêne, 1974).

To put an end to this disorder, the monopoly company, the government, and the most important merchants joined forces in the 1680s and important structural changes resulted. After 1681, the company dealt only with established traders, while the government started issuing special permits, called *congés*, to trade in the West. The establishment of army posts at strategic portages enabled the government to police the trade effectively. It had also become evident that only important Montreal merchants who had enough capital to maintain large stocks of trade goods and extend credit could survive. By the 1690s the coureurs de bois, who had acted as independent traders, had been replaced by employees called voyageurs. Although some voyageurs maintained their independence and shared in the profits, the vast majority were wage labourers who contracted with a merchant to transport goods and furs to and from posts in the West.

The expansion of New France across almost half the continent in the late seventeenth century renewed conflict with the English and their Iroquois allies. When French trading in the Mississippi cut off the Iroquois's main supply of furs, they started attacking French traders in the West. The attacks began in 1681 and by 1689 the Iroquois were ravaging settlements near Montreal. Until peace was concluded in 1701, the Iroquois continued to disrupt both the fur trade and settlement in the Montreal region.

Rapid expansion of the trade also brought an oversupply of beaver. In good years before 1650, about 30 000 pelts were exported; the volume rose to about 50 000 pelts by 1670, and to over 100 000 pelts by the 1680s. As the number of poorer quality pelts from the Mississippi Valley increased, French markets became flooded. Prices fell and expansion was temporarily halted. Indian alliances, however, could be maintained only through trade. The alliances were vital to the economy of New France and to the colony's ability to limit British expansion; colonial officials therefore fought successfully with the French ministry to maintain a limited number of posts in the West.

After 1717, markets for beaver improved and the fur trade expanded again. Army officers such as Pierre Gaultier, sieur de la Vérendrye, and his sons extended the fur trade across the prairies and integrated scores of tribes into the French alliance. Yet, this period of expansion was slower than that of the seventeenth century. By granting army officers monopolies over specific territories, the metropolitan government ensured that the trade was rationally exploited to safeguard the stability of supply and profitability. These officers formed partnerships with important merchants and hired men to transport trade goods and supplies to the West (Allaire, 1987). The types of pelts became more varied as exports of deer, marten, bear, moose, seal, and lynx skins supplemented the beaver trade.

The value of exports was fairly stable after 1720 at just over 1 000 000 livres, or about twice the value of fur exports in the early 1690s.

After the Conquest the fur trade continued to dominate exports. In the 1760s and 1770s, Montreal traders pushed ever farther into the West. The expansion culminated in Alexander Mackenzie's voyages along the Mackenzie River to the Arctic Ocean in 1789 and across the Rockies to the Pacific in 1793. The basic structure of the fur trade remained unchanged until the 1780s, and francophone merchants continued to play an important role. They and the smaller anglophone merchants were gradually eliminated, however, by the large influx of Albany traders after the Quebec Act and the ensuing fierce competition. As distances between the supply of furs and the ports grew, the increased capital and credit required were available only to the most important anglophone merchants such as Robert Ellice, John Forsyth, and John Richardson, who benefited from trading partnerships with English companies. These traders formed the North West Company and dominated the trade out of Montreal by the end of the 1780s.

With the lengthening distances, work for voyageurs also changed. Some, called "winterers," stayed in the West permanently. They transported goods in the shipping season from posts such as Fort Chipewyan on Lake Athabaska to Great Lakes transfer depots like Grand Portage or Fort William. However, most of the transport workers remained seasonal and paddled the large canoes from Lachine to the Great Lakes depots (These workers were known as "pork-eaters" because of their staple food.) The Montreal region continued to be the main source of voyageurs, many of whom were urban dwellers. Others came from out-lying parishes such as La Prairie and Sorel.

Seasonal labour in the fur trade fitted into a rural family economy that relied on outside cash to provide subsistence in poorer areas and to enable sons to buy farms in richer ones. In the sandy region of Sorel, for example, inadequate farm surpluses forced families to obtain cash by having a male member in the fur trade. In the 1790s, one-third of the adult males in Sorel served as voyageurs, a fact that has led Allan Greer (1985) to describe them as a semi-proletariat.

The labour of native trappers and francophone voyageurs enabled the great Montreal merchants like Simon McTavish, William McGillivray, and Joseph Frobisher to make fortunes. In the 1780s, the North West Company shipped more than 100 000 beaver, some 50 000 muskrat, and tens of thousands of other types of pelts to England for local hat and clothing production, or for re-export to France and the Baltic. Profits can be gauged from the example of 1791, when the North West Company spent about £16 000 and sold its furs in London for £88 000.

The North West Company competed vigorously with the Hudson's Bay Company. While the Hudson's Bay Company had an enormous geographical advantage, the North West Company benefited from its experienced and tough traders, who maintained good contacts with the native trappers.

For its part, the Hudson's Bay Company followed the 1770 construction of its first inland post at Fort Cumberland on the Saskatchewan River with dozens of posts across the West. In 1812, it threatened the North West Company's trade routes and food supply by permitting Lord Selkirk to establish a Scottish settlement at the junction of the Red and Assiniboine rivers. The Nor'Westers burned settlers' buildings and tried to starve the Scots by cutting off the pemican supply. In the Seven Oaks Massacre of 1816, twenty settlers were killed. Competition between the two companies was ruinous, however, and in 1821 the Hudson's Bay Company absorbed the North West Company.

Although colonial administrations had long attempted to encourage the export of agricultural staples, they were hindered by the small population and isolation from large markets. In the eighteenth century, New France exported wheat and peas to the fortress of Louisbourg and to French sugar colonies in the West Indies, but the export of foodstuffs never became a staple during the French regime.

With the Conquest, Quebec was integrated into the larger trading network of the British empire. During the American Revolution, Quebec foodstuffs were in demand to supply British forces. In the 1780s, wheat became an important export commodity and by 1802 a record million bushels were shipped from the port of Quebec to growing markets throughout the empire (Ouellet, 1981). The situation changed in the second decade of the nineteenth century, however, as bad harvests, the beginnings of rural overpopulation, and the appearance of cheaper Upper Canadian wheat combined to turn Lower Canada into a net importer of wheat. The peasant economy adapted by producing more oats and hay for sale in the rapidly growing timber shanties. At the same time, potatoes became an important crop for domestic consumption.

At the beginning of the nineteenth century, timber became a significant part of the export economy. When the Napoleonic wars closed British access to Baltic timber, Britain turned to British North America's white pine and oak forests, particularly for naval construction. By 1810, lumber and timber products made up 75 percent of the value of exports from the port of Quebec. Timber was exported to the British markets in several forms, of which square timber was the least processed. Barrel staves, deals (7.5-centimetre planks of pine, oak, or elm), smaller planks, and potash made from ashes were also exported.

The trade in square timber and deals created new forms of work in the lumber shanties, along the rivers, and on the timber beaches and shipyards of Quebec City. Lumberjacks felled and squared the timber and teamsters hauled it to small rivers. Then drivers floated it to the Ottawa or St. Lawrence rivers, where timber

Figure 3.3 Timber rafts passing Oka on the Lake of Two Mountains. Every year hundreds of rafts floated down the Ottawa, Richelieu, and St. Lawrence rivers to Quebec City, providing employment for timber rafters and river pilots.

rafters and river pilots rafted it to Quebec City (Figure 3.3). Finally, it was measured and marked by cullers. Apart from providing seasonal employment for farmers in frontier regions, these activities brought a great increase in employment opportunities outside of agriculture and marked a significant change in the rural economy of Quebec.

THE STRUCTURE OF PREINDUSTRIAL COMMERCE

In the preindustrial period, merchants profited from both international and local trade. Their activities ranged from those of the Dugard Company's Quebec City representatives, Havy and Lefebvre, who integrated New France into trading ventures involving France, the West Indies, and Holland, to rural merchant François-Augustin Bailly de Messein's work of supplying the needs of the local community around Varennes.

Imperial policy was largely dictated by mercantilism, in which monopoly was standard and colonies were seen as suppliers of natural products and as markets for goods produced in the metropolis. In France, Louis XIV's principal minister, Jean-

Baptiste Colbert, issued numerous regulations to improve and standardize the quality of French products. He also used tariffs and privileges to protect metropolitan industry. Colonial commerce was encouraged but not the production of goods that might compete with metropolitan commodities. The main goal of mercantilism was to assert centralized state authority over the economy and it was accompanied by detailed control, meticulous inspection, and reliance on privilege (De Vries, 1976).

Merchants were an important element in the colonial system, often occupying important positions in government. During the French regime they specialized to a degree, with Quebec merchants handling the import–export business and Montreal traders focusing on the fur trade. At the top of the hierarchy were import–export merchants, usually the agents of French trading houses.

François Havy and Jean Lefebvre, for example, represented the Dugard Company of Rouen from 1732 until the 1750s. They imported French textiles, wines, brandy, and hardware, and supplied these commodities wholesale to merchants such as Montreal fur trader Pierre Guy, or retail to customers in their Quebec City store. They also exported agricultural produce to Louisbourg and the West Indies, built ships to be sold in France, and invested in sealing expeditions along the Labrador coast. At the height of their success, Havy and Lefevre controlled about one-third of Canadian trade. Like other important import–export merchants of their time, they remained tied to France and returned after the Conquest (Miquelon, 1978).

Alexis Lemoine Monière (1680–1754) is representative of a Montreal merchant-outfitter in the fur trade, and his career emphasizes the importance of matrimonial alliances in the commercial capitalist environment of the preindustrial period. The son of a small trader in Trois-Rivières, he moved to Montreal and first worked as a voyageur before financing his own trips beginning in 1712. Three years later he married Marie-Louise Zemballe, established a store in Montreal, and began financing the fur trade expeditions of his brothers-in-law and other traders.

After the death of Marie-Louise, Monière's second marriage in 1725 to Marie-Josephte Couagne, daughter of one of the wealthiest Montreal merchants, helped him to consolidate his position with the military and merchant elite. Although the fur trade dominated Monière's business, his Montreal store also served the local inhabitants, particularly retired voyageurs, and military officers. Like many successful merchants, Monière invested some of his capital in land. His son married into the same social class and carried on the family business even after the Conquest.

Although Quebec remained the most important port during the preindustrial period, developments in the fur and wheat trades increasingly enabled the Montreal directors of the North West Company to deal directly with their suppliers in England. This trend continued after the turn of the nineteenth century as Montreal became the major forwarding centre in servicing the rapidly growing population of Upper Canada.

Merchandise	Percent of sales
Textiles	35
Clothing	10
Alcohol	21
Foodstuffs (seed, spices, sugar)	8
Hardware	10
Kitchenware	5
Farm implements and tools	5
Diverse goods (leather, wood, tobacco, etc.)	6

Table 3.2   General Store Sales by Joseph Cartier, 1794–1797

(Desrosiers, 1984)

Simon McTavish (1750–1804) was a dominant fur trader in the North West Company who left an estate of £125 000. Born in Scotland, McTavish emigrated to New York and traded at Detroit and Michilimackinac before moving his opera-tions to Montreal at the end of the American Revolution. With capital accumu-lated in the fur trade, McTavish imitated other rich anglophone merchants by buying a seigneury. His seigneury of Terrebonne represented more than status and a secure investment for his merchant capital. Besides the seigneurial gristmill, McTavish opened a biscuit bakery, a sawmill, and a barrel factory to supply fur traders in the West. Known as the "Marquis" because of his elegant style, McTavish built a Montreal mansion and, when forty-three, married an eighteen-year-old French Canadian, Marie-Marguerite Chaboillez. After her husband's death, she retired to England with his fur trade capital.

Although the colony's small population confined trade to urban centres throughout much of the seventeenth century, traders did move into the country-side as the rural population grew. Rural merchants such as Joseph Cartier at Saint-Hyacinthe sold imported textiles, hardware, and alcohol (Table 3.2), buy-ing wheat and other agricultural produce in return. Over a thirty-eight-month period from 26 October 1794, to 30 December 1797, he sold over 55 000 livres of goods to 317 different clients. Since there was little currency in circulation, credit was an essential part of this trade, and rural merchants became important lenders and mortgage-holders in their communities. Cartier's experience is a useful exam-ple: at the end of the period discussed above, only six clients owed nothing. The other 311 had accumulated 38 000 livres in debts. A bad harvest in 1796 undoubtedly accounts for the magnitude of the debt, but peasant indebtedness was nonetheless a dominant feature of rural trade.

Some rural merchants, such as François-Augustin Bailly de Messein (1709–1771) and Samuel Jacobs (d. 1786), built up thriving businesses and left considerable fortunes. Bailly, the son of a Quebec City army officer, moved to Varennes in 1731. Within a decade he became the most important retailer in the region, with a clientele spread over adjoining parishes. As an older man, Bailly entered semi-retirement but continued to administer his extensive land holdings and to lend money to peasants (Michel, 1979).

Although Samuel Jacobs's career followed a similar pattern, his wealth was due as much to lucrative government contracts during the American Revolution as to local trade. Jacobs arrived in the colony with Wolfe's army in 1759 and after unsuccessful attempts to establish a distillery and potash works at Quebec, he settled at Saint-Denis in 1770. He became the dominant merchant in the Richelieu Valley with his chain of stores selling cloth, hardware, and rum and buying wheat in return.

The American Revolution provided Jacobs with a key opportunity to expand; he was named assistant commissary-general and given responsibility for laying in provisions for the large number of British troops in the region. He left an estate of almost £20 000, made up mainly of accounts receivable, merchandise, and real estate in the Saint-Denis area (Greer, 1985).

Merchants in preindustrial society had difficulty investing their money. As the extensive real estate holdings of Bailly and Jacobs illustrate, land appeared to guarantee the best and safest return on capital. Near cities, merchants like Henri Hiché and William Grant, John Mure and George Pozer opened subdivisions on which artisans and labourers could build houses in return for a perpetual rent (Dechêne, 1981). Seigneuries also offered interesting investment opportunities. Besides, wealthy merchants were attracted to the status of seigneur. By 1791, 32 percent of the seigneuries in Quebec were totally or partially owned by anglophones, and about the same percentage had been acquired by members of the francophone bourgeoisie (Harris, 1987: Plate 51).

⌒◦⌒

ARTISANS

While merchants lived by exchanging goods, artisans lived by producing them. In preindustrial society artisans used craft methods: they worked alone or with a limited number of journeymen and apprentices and controlled their own work, tools, and shop (Figure 3.4). Since there were no guilds or corporations to control standards and admission into trades, Canadian artisans had greater liberty than their European counterparts and market forces determined the evolution of trades. Butchers and bakers, whose numbers, production, and prices were regulated by the state, were notable exceptions. Although some crafts were relatively prosperous—the leather and metal trades, for example—seasonal unemployment was a

Figure 3.4 A blacksmith's shop. This painting gives a strong sense of the scale of a shop, the tools used, and the wide variety of objects that the blacksmith produced or repaired.

recurrent problem, especially because many crafts depended on commerce. Coopers and carters, for example, worked mainly during the shipping season. Seasonal unemployment was heightened by the winter shutdown of the construction and shipbuilding industries.

Artisans did not immigrate to the colony at the same rate as its population grew, and expansion of a trade therefore depended on the apprenticeship system. Boys—and, for specific trades such as dressmaking, girls—were apprenticed to masters for three to seven years. Apprentices provided cheap labour but in return they learned a trade, were incorporated into the master's household, and received a modest payment at the end of their apprenticeship. In the Canadian context, apprenticeship proved a rational means of adjusting the supply of labour to the needs of the marketplace (Hardy et Ruddel, 1977). As in other preindustrial societies, the apprenticeship system was important in the community's broader value system and in family survival across generations.

Throughout the preindustrial period, artisanal shops usually remained small family enterprises in which a master and his wife worked alone or with one apprentice. Personal relationships dominated the workplace and there was little division of labour since journeymen and more experienced apprentices could produce a finished product. A wife's work in the artisanal household might include handling sales, keeping books, maintaining the home, and monitoring the private lives of apprentices.

Figure 3.5 Les forges du Saint-Maurice. Canada's first industrial establishment, the ironworks produced bar iron and stoves for more than a century before being put out of business in 1883 by competition from Montreal. When the works first opened in 1741 there were only a dozen permanent employees but over 150 part-time workers.

Some shops in the more prosperous trades were larger, employing several journeymen and apprentices. Already in 1744, Richard Corbin's Quebec City forge had four employees. By the same date cooper Louis Paquet had three assistants. As the local market grew at the beginning of the nineteenth century so did the number of larger shops employing over five workers. This period also saw a greater division of labour. And whereas master craftsmen produced goods on order, merchant artisans began producing standardized items for sale to customers (Bluteau et al., 1980).

The relatively small population of the colony gave little opportunity for a vigorous rural artisanry to develop. Although some artisans such as carpenters, millers, and blacksmiths were established in most rural communities, they were usually dependent on farming to supplement their trade. Unlike preindustrial Europe, rural industry in New France was slow to develop, and only the Saint-Maurice ironworks offered part-time industrial labour to neighbouring peasants (Figure 3.5). Established just north of Trois-Rivières in 1739, the ironworks offered employment to peasants in extracting ore and making charcoal, or as carters, enabling them to supplement their farming income.

Some production went beyond the scale of the artisan's shop. From the 1660s on, colonial officials encouraged local mining, shipbuilding, and pitch and tar production in order to reduce France's dependence on foreign sources for these products. Apart from the Saint-Maurice ironworks, the naval shipyard at Quebec was the most important industrial site of the French regime. It built several men-of-war for the French government, and employed almost 200 workers (Mathieu, 1971). As well, private shipbuilders with yards employing between fifteen and thirty labourers built oceangoing and coasting vessels. Shipbuilding continued to grow during the British regime and became a leading sector of the economy in the early nineteenth century, along with the timber trade.

THE PEASANT ECONOMY

Across the preindustrial period, the vast majority of the population was engaged in agriculture for home or local consumption. Although Canada was barely self-sufficient in essential foodstuffs half a century after its establishment, by the eighteenth century an expanding agricultural population was producing regular surpluses for export to other colonies or to western trading posts. Agriculture was always risky and subject to climatic vagaries. A cold, damp summer did not allow time for grain to mature in the short growing season of the St. Lawrence Valley (120 frost-free days in the region around Montreal and about five days fewer near Quebec City). Late spring or early autumn frosts such as those in 1815 and 1816 were disastrous. Parasites, such as the Hessian fly that started decimating Lower Canadian wheat in 1809, were another danger. As long as land was plentiful and the initial fertility was not exhausted, there were few regional variations in Quebec agriculture. As settlement progressed in the mid-eighteenth century, however, regional variations became more pronounced. The rich Montreal plain, with its better soil and climate, was the most productive area.

Getting land into agricultural production was arduous. Settlers in the St. Lawrence lowlands were granted land in seigneurial tenure. It normally took a family two years to clear a hectare of hardwood forest and to build a log cabin, and five years to clear three hectares, the minimum for self-sufficiency. During this period, the family consumed locally produced foodstuffs which they sometimes bought at the market but more often had supplied by relatives. The strategy of most peasant families was to keep the farm intact by leaving it to a single heir. Most members of a new generation therefore had to start their own farms. In the period while they were clearing land, they became important consumers of locally produced foodstuffs. As a result, much of the colony's production was geared to meeting these and other local needs such as payment of the tithe and seigneurial dues. Only a small part of each harvest was left for sale in the towns or for export.

Rural families were never completely self-sufficient; they needed to buy cloth, clothing, alcohol, tea and coffee, salt, tools, furnishings, and kitchenware. In the older settled areas, peasants were already purchasing imported copperware, crockery, and linen by the 1740s. Christian Dessureault's study of Saint-Hyacinthe (1986) reveals that by the early nineteenth century even the poorest peasant households bought items such as copper pots and pans, iron tools, and clothing. The average peasant family owned an iron stove—a major expenditure—as well as a wide variety of consumer goods. The richest families had an abundance of copper, pewter, and iron kitchenware and some acquired china and silverware as well.

By the end of the eighteenth century, the custom of the *donation* and the *pension alimentaire*, by which elderly parents donated their farms to one of their children in return for guaranteed material support, was well established. It provides further evidence about consumption patterns. Annual supplies of tobacco, lamp oil, salt, pepper, rum, wine, and tea appeared on a list Joseph Blanchard promised to his parents in 1791:

30 minots flour	200 onions
91 kilos of pork	5 kilos of candles or 3 pots of
1 fatted sheep	lamp oil
2 minots peas	14 kilos tobacco
1 minot salt	4.5 kilos butter
450 grams pepper	25 steres of firewood
100 heads of cabbage	1.5 kilos wool
3 pots rum	a milk cow, six hens, and a rooster
3 pots wine	4 shirts of homespun and a complete
11 kilos maple sugar	suit of work clothes
450 grams tea	Sheets and shoes as needed

Blanchard also promised to purchase a set of Sunday clothes for each parent from a merchant every three years (Greer, 1985: 35).

Wheat was the main crop in Canada, accounting for about two-thirds of all grain produced. Whereas newly developed land was sown almost exclusively in wheat to capitalize on its commercial value, equal amounts of wheat, oats, and peas and/or beans would be planted on well-developed farms of about ten hectares to ensure self-sufficiency. Wheat, peas, and oats were the main cash crops and some hemp, flax, and corn were also marketed. Farm gardens and small orchards produced carrots, cabbages, onions, salad vegetables, squash, strawberries, apples, pears, and other fruits for family consumption (Figure 3.6). Surpluses were sold in areas with access to an urban market.

The emphasis on wheat rather than fodder crops and the limited market for meat combined to keep herds small. Livestock had to be sheltered and fed over

Figure 3.6 Château-Richer, c. 1785. This watercolour by Thomas Davies is one of the best illustrations of a settled rural landscape. The garden in front of the whitewashed stone house produced vegetables for home consumption as well as for the nearby urban market in Quebec. The weirs in the river were used to catch eel which were smoked and sold to urban residents.

the winter, so most farmers slaughtered all except the animals needed for traction and breeding. The strategy provided a winter meat supply, but resulted in insufficient manure to fertilize all fields and led to declining yields as the soil lost its initial fertility.

During the seventeenth and early eighteenth centuries agricultural growth was steady and closely tied to demographic expansion. Later, the opening of new export markets in the second quarter of the eighteenth century and again after the beginning of the American Revolution acted as a stimulus for agricultural production, and the amount of new land cleared vastly surpassed population growth. At the beginning of the nineteenth century, the growth of towns and the introduction of new crops such as potatoes created greater local demand. (Potatoes were consumed by anglophone immigrants and also used as animal fodder.) Expansion continued until the second decade of the nineteenth century, when climatic disasters and the Hessian fly undermined the wheat basis of Quebec's agricultural economy.

	1695	1734	1784
Population	12 786	37 716	113 012
Lands cultivated (hectares)	9 610	55 768	536 721
Land in pasture (hectares)	1 230	6 037	(not given)
Domestic animals			
Horses	580	5 056	30 146
Cattle	9 181	33 179	98 951
Sheep	918	19 815	84 696
Swine	5 333	23 646	70 465

Table 3.3   Agricultural Production

(*Census of Canada*, 1871, vol. 4)

The devolution of land was a central dynamic of peasant society, especially since the Custom of Paris stipulated equal inheritance for all children of a marriage between commoners. Peasant families had various solutions to the resulting social, economic, and legal dilemma between equal division of land and movable goods and the wish to favour a particular son or daughter. Some tried to acquire large holdings to offset the effects of inheritance. In areas where land was plentiful, farmers sought additional land concessions to ensure viable farms for their children when they married. Another common family strategy was for the heir of the family farm, quite often the youngest child, to pay an indemnity to his or her siblings (Michel, 1986; Paquet et Wallot, 1986). Thus land holdings rarely remained divided in small parcels.

As settlement became denser and families could no longer obtain new land in the same community, more prosperous farmers bought established farms from poorer neighbours, who used the capital to start new farms in other parishes. Over time, those who could not maintain viable farms increasingly turned to wage labour to supplement their incomes. Another important element in the structure of rural society was the unequal possession of draught animals. The more prosperous peasants had at least one team of oxen whereas poorer ones had to rent this important means of production from their neighbours (Dechêne, 1974; Michel, 1986; Dessureault, 1986). The peasantry had therefore become quite hierarchical by the early nineteenth century, although it had been fairly egalitarian during the seventeenth.

By the beginning of the nineteenth century, land in the seigneurial zone was at a premium. Expansion to freehold areas, on the other hand, was impeded by poor road and river communications and the existence of numerous clerical and royal reserves. Subdividing plots became a more common practice, leading to the

Figures 3.7 and 3.8 Although many English observers criticized the Canadian plough made of wood and iron (Figure 3.7), it was well suited to the heavy soils of the St. Lawrence Valley. They preferred the swing plough (Figure 3.8) which had gained acceptance both in England and the United States. It required less animal power and was easier to manoeuvre. Quebec farmers were not hostile to innovation; in St. Hyacinthe, for example, a minority of farmers owned swing ploughs by the 1830s. Some used them as second ploughs for specific tasks; small farmers adopted them because they could not afford the team of oxen needed to pull the heavier Canadian plough (Dessureault and Dickinson, 1992).

emergence of villages inhabited by a growing class of day labourers. These workers took advantage of expanding economic opportunities in rural industries and activities such as carting, ferrying, and milling (Courville, 1984; 1990).

Foreign observers were critical of peasant farming methods at the turn of the nineteenth century. These criticisms have been reiterated by Fernand Ouellet

(1981), who argues that an agricultural crisis beginning in 1802 was caused by the conservative mentality of Quebec farmers. English agronomists who visited Canada failed to understand the particularities of colonial agriculture, however, or the rationale behind peasant strategies. Because there was a limited market for meat and hides, Canadian farmers concentrated on cereal crops. This reduced manure production, and instead of spreading a limited amount across their land, farmers used this fertilizer primarily in the garden or on the more demanding crops such as potatoes (Figures 3.7 and 3.8).

The expansion of settlement onto marginal lands was an important phenomenon at the beginning of the nineteenth century. Here, work in the forest was as important as agriculture. Census statistics for the province as a whole do not take into account this mixing of an agricultural and forest economy and give a misleading image of agricultural production. The opening of new regions also increased local food demand as the new settlers looked to more established areas to feed them, thereby lessening the amount of surplus available for export (Dechêne, 1986).

The absence of reliable statistical series on agricultural production—aggregates for the colony found in the infrequent census reports are often misleading (Courville, 1984)—complicates attempts to make overall assessments of Quebec agriculture during the preindustrial period. Historians have traditionally stressed the self-sufficient nature of the peasantry and its failure to take advantage of market opportunities (Séguin, 1970; Ouellet, 1980). Recent research, however, has demonstrated that peasants in the richer agricultural regions accumulated significant capital (Dessureault, 1986; Paquet et Wallot, 1986). Rather than a generalized crisis affecting all of Quebec's agriculture, the problems of the early nineteenth century reflect growing regional diversity. Farmers on the Montreal plain and near Quebec City were prosperous, but those in remoter regions suffered, as did the growing rural proletariat.

<hr>

DAILY LIFE

Rural life was bound to the seasons: from May to October the farm population ploughed, planted, mowed, weeded, and harvested; in the winter the people threshed grain, marketed the surplus, and cleared new land. Farming necessitated a well-defined division of labour among family members. Men, with the help of their adolescent sons, performed the heaviest, outdoor physical labour: ploughing, cutting wood, removing stumps, digging ditches. Women took care of the children, cooked, cleaned, made everyday clothing, worked in the garden and orchard, and looked after livestock. Young children helped their mothers and thus provided an important source of labour in the peasant family. All family members from an early age participated in the harvesting.

Rural homes were normally built of squared logs; 93 percent of rural housing on the Ile de Montréal in 1731 was still made of wood. Houses were small (about six by eight metres), and with only one or two rooms they afforded little privacy. Towards the end of the French regime, stone houses became more widespread in the countryside, especially in the older parishes near Quebec and on the prosperous south shore of the St. Lawrence near Montreal. In more recently settled areas wooden houses were predominant throughout the preindustrial era. When seventy-year-old German settler Johannes Monk decided in 1810 that he was too old to farm, his lease with Peter Buss of Sorel described his Missisquoi property in the townships as including "dwelling log house, old but in middling good repair, [and] a framed barn (also in good repair)." Most farms would have a barn and a stable, and some had more specialized buildings such as sties, coops, sugar shacks, and icehouses.

During the seventeenth century, home interiors were austere and often smoky. The main furnishings consisted of a large curtained bed for the parents, a chest, a table with benches, cooking utensils, and straw mattresses for the children. In the summer, houses were infested by mosquitoes and flies; in the winter, family activity centred around an open fireplace. Living conditions improved in the eighteenth century as rural prosperity enabled people to buy more elaborate furniture and imported textiles. With the beginning of iron production at les forges du Saint-Maurice in the 1740s, stoves became widespread and this had a dramatic effect on heating and cooking.

Urban housing and living conditions varied sharply depending on class (Figure 3.9). Merchants, administrators, and the clergy lived in large stone houses, some of which were quite luxurious. Wall tapestries reduced the cold and damp; expensive silverware graced dining tables, and parlours were furnished with several comfortable chairs. Parents had private bedrooms, and most children had beds, even if they had to share their rooms. Artisans' homes, on the other hand, were of similar size and appearance to those of the average peasant and, in addition, often contained their shops. Quebec City fire regulations dictating that houses be built of stone added to artisans' housing costs. In Montreal, wood houses prevailed until after the Conquest; this apparently allowed artisans to spend more on furniture and clothes (Hardy, 1987).

At the turn of the nineteenth century, wooden buildings in the suburbs provided low-cost housing for the popular classes while the core areas increasingly became the preserve of the elite. Although some transient merchants, artisans, and day labourers were tenants (one-third of Montreal's households rented their accommodation in 1741) most urban families owned their own homes (Massicotte, 1987: 52). Merchants lived above their stores and warehouses.

Figure 3.9 Montreal at the corner of Notre Dame Street and the Market (today Place Jacques Cartier) at the beginning of the nineteenth century. In this period, housing for the popular classes was concentrated in the suburbs because of the higher cost of housing within the city's walls. The city centre remained the major site for the exchange of goods. Here, in the streets in front of the substantial stone houses, shops, and offices of the bourgeoisie, the popular classes worked, carted, and traded. Of particular note are the Iroquois artisans, the female public traders, and the use of dogs to pull carts.

Towns were dirty and unsanitary. Court records show that inhabitants permitted cattle and pigs to forage freely, and that passersby had to watch out for chamber pots being emptied from upper-floor windows. "Speeding" horses were also a threat.

When ships arrived from Europe, Quebec City was filled with sailors anxious to celebrate. Paradoxically, while the garrisons served to enforce the public peace, soldiers were often the cause of criminal activity. André Lachance (1984) indicates that in the eighteenth century over 20 percent of criminals were members of the military.

Bread was the staple food in both France and Canada. An adult male consumed about 500 grams of bread a day. Bakers were closely supervised and had to supply loaves at fixed weights and prices. Meat, especially pork, was important in the peasant diet; families normally slaughtered pigs in the autumn and ate the smoked and salted pork through the winter. Calves were sold to urban butchers. During Lent, cod and smoked eel became staples. When the fresh vegetables and

fruit of summer were exhausted, families began using their supply of onions, cabbages, carrots, pickles, and various beans stored in a root cellar.

Although some beer was brewed in the colony, most men drank French wine
and brandy. Women usually drank water. With the colony's integration into the
British empire, tea became a common drink and rum replaced wine and brandy
among the popular classes. English preferences gave a new importance to beer
and breweries, such as John Molson's, developed in 1786 by using local agricultural produce.

EDUCATION AND CULTURE

While most of the elite and many artisans could read and write, the majority of
the popular classes were illiterate. Allan Greer (1978) has estimated that fewer
than 10 percent of peasants could sign their marriage act during the second half
of the eighteenth century. Since there were no printing presses in New France,
there were no newspapers, and books were imported from France. In the absence
of public libraries, some religious colleges lent their books to graduates.

After the Conquest, printing presses were imported and the first newspaper, the
Quebec Gazette, started publication in 1764. Newspapers like the *Gazette* were published once or twice a week by printers who worked alone or with a journeyman or
an apprentice, on hand-operated, wooden, flat-bed presses that printed about sixty
copies an hour. Initially sales were low—the first issue of the *Quebec Gazette* sold
143 copies—and publishers relied on government advertising to survive.

By the beginning of the nineteenth century, however, newspapers such as the
Montreal Herald were selling about 1000 copies of each issue. Montreal's first
newspaper was the bilingual *Montreal Gazette*, established in 1778 by Fleury
Mesplet, a Lyonnais printer who came to Montreal to encourage Canadian support for American independence. With Mesplet's arrest, the *Gazette* was suspended in 1779. It began publishing again in 1785 and by 1822 had become an
English newspaper closely identified with anglophone merchants. The Quebec
tradition of political journalism really started after 1805, when papers with clear
political affiliations started publication. The *Quebec Mercury* represented the
anglophone merchants and *Le Canadien* represented francophone professionals.

Education in preindustrial Quebec society was dominated by the established
churches. During the French regime, the Jesuit College at Quebec provided males
in the colonial elite with a postsecondary education comparable to that in a
provincial French town. The Quebec seminary ran the most important elementary
school, the Petit Séminaire, and trained Canadian priests in its theological college.

From its base in Montreal, the Congrégation de Notre-Dame dominated female education, establishing elementary schools in the largest towns. The disappearance of the Jesuit College after the Conquest was a serious blow. Postsecondary education started to recover only at the beginning of the nineteenth century, with the creation of a province-wide system of classical colleges. The curriculum emphasized the classics and liberal arts, in particular literature, rhetoric, and philosophy. The eight-year program began for boys about the age of ten.

One of the earliest of the classical colleges was the Collège de Montréal established by the Sulpicians, using their French mother house as a model. After 1803, this elite boys' school with pleasant grounds on the western extremity of the city had 120 resident students. They lived in fine, large dormitories that featured indoor toilets. Each student paid substantial fees and provided his own bedding and silverware. Pupils rose at 5:30 a.m. and, after mass and breakfast, were in class by 8:00; the Sunday regime featured a procession by the student body to the parish church.

Despite the classical nature of these schools, scientific education was not completely absent. The Jesuits played an early and important role in teaching hydrography, and many missionaries showed considerable interest in North American flora and fauna, and in ethnology. Apart from members of religious orders, the leading scientific figures in the history of New France were governor La Galissonière—who amazed Swedish naturalist Pehr Kalm with the breadth of his scientific knowledge—and doctor Michel Sarrazin, whose botanical observations and experiments received recognition from the French Academy of Sciences.

Professionals, such as notaries and lawyers, normally attended classical colleges and then entered into apprenticeship as clerks to be trained in the profession. Family partnership or the transfer of a practice from father to son; the intimacy of pew, parish, and school; and intermarriage all cemented the bourgeoisie. The necessity of financing studies in a classical college, finding a professional willing to train a clerk, and having social contacts to establish a practice ensured that boys from the popular classes did not often enter the professions.

Since the church opposed most theatre, opera, and much of the literature written during the Enlightenment, bourgeois culture was underdeveloped in the colony. In 1694, the bishop attempted to ban Molière's controversial play *Le Tartuffe*, which poked fun at religious bigotry. (The bishop was not very successful, however. He offered Governor Frontenac 1000 livres to halt the production. Frontenac accepted the money and allowed the play to proceed. Having bribed the governor, the bishop could not very well complain that his ploy had not worked.) In 1753, Bishop Pontbriand incited Catholics to shun impious books in circulation. Occasional plays were staged by college students but lay theatre, apart from performances by military officers, did not develop until the Molson Theatre was established in 1825. By encouraging members of the francophone elite to join religious confraternities (the Congrégation de la Sainte-Famille and the Congrégation des hommes, for example) priests tried to control morality. They wanted the elite to practise model behaviour as an example for the popular classes to encourage them to shun secular entertainment in favour of piety. Musical production was centred on religious ceremonies and the surviving scores produced in this period all relate to church music.

Despite clerical censure, dancing was a favourite pastime of the colonial elite in both the French and British regimes. French fashions featuring "scandalously" low-cut dresses were imported for the winter social season of balls and dinners given by leading members of the colonial administration. When governor La Galissonière and intendant François Bigot visited Montreal during the pre-Lenten carnival in 1749, members of the local elite outdid each other. Madame Bégon describes dances lasting until 6:30 in the morning and sermons threatening to withhold Easter communion from those who dared participate.

Little is known of popular culture although there is evidence of such activities as card playing (Figure 3.10). In the countryside fiddlers and storytellers maintained the oral and folkloric traditions of their French ancestors and added original elements of their own. Feast days provided opportunities for processions and socializing. (In addition to Sundays, there were thirty-seven annual feast days before 1744 and twenty thereafter.) Few artisans or peasants owned books, and pious literature, especially the lives of saints, predominated in the private libraries of all social classes (Drolet, 1965; Dickinson, 1974a). The advent of newspapers provided some cultural content but local literary production did not become important until the mid-nineteenth century.

Religiosity is difficult to measure. Protestants were not allowed in New France, and so all inhabitants were officially Catholics. This monopoly gave the church a strong influence over colonial cultural life. In the eighteenth century some Protestant merchants, such as François Havy, came to the colony but they could not marry or hold religious services. One must be wary of generalizations based on Bishop de Saint-Vallier's criticism of the transgressions of the faithful or on the letters written by a couple of overbearing priests about the deviant practices of their parishioners (Jaenen, 1976b). The standards set by a rigorous clergy could not have been met by even the most pious population.

In all preindustrial societies, religion was a central feature of popular culture. The importance of religion was reflected in pilgrimages, religious clauses in wills, low rates of illegitimacy, the small number of children conceived out of wedlock, and participation in religious confraternities (Cliche, 1978; Bates, 1986; Paquette et Bates, 1986; Caulier, 1986). (See also Figure 3.11). Nonetheless, evidence points to a sharp decline in religious fervour late in the eighteenth century; mem-

Figure 3.10 Card playing was an important leisure activity for all social classes. George Stephen Jones's diary emphasizes the importance of cards and singing as evening entertainment for this Quebec City clerk (Ward, 1989).

bership in religious confraternities, for example, suffered a long period of decline from the 1760s until the 1820s. When the Jesuits and the Récollets were banned, the number of faithful per priest jumped. From 350 in 1759 the ratio went to 1075 per priest by 1805, at which time almost a hundred parishes lacked a resident

Figure 3.11 An *ex voto* thanking St. Anne. Most sculpture and painting produced by artisans in New France was destined for churches and chapels but there are also examples of popular art, often in the form of *ex votos*. In this example, Jean-Baptiste Auclair, Louis Bouvier, and Marthe Feuilleteau thank St. Anne for saving them in a canoe accident in which two of their friends drowned. This picture also highlights the most common form of accidental death in New France.

priest. From the Conquest until 1774, uncertainty over the right to collect tithes encouraged evasion (Wallot, 1971). Although the influx of a few émigré priests during the French Revolution helped improve theological training, many priests were of marginal quality.

Protestant religious practice centred on the established churches—the Church of England and the Kirk of Scotland—in urban centres. Much of the popular religion of the Eastern Townships, however, was brought by non-conformist American circuit riders using Vermont as a base. One such missionary made his rounds by following a line of marked trees between settlements; he supported himself by farming in the summer and shoemaking in the winter (Smith, 1975: 81). Despite the official declaration of war in 1812, a border-area Methodist minister organized what he called a "love feast," which had parishoners on both sides of the border holding hands during a service (Smith, 1975: 54). Even so, the war ultimately did lead to a break between the New England and Canadian non-conformist churches (Smith, 1975). The construction of small Protestant churches throughout the region is testimony to the importance of non-conformist religion in anglophone pioneer life.

SOCIAL RELATIONS AND POPULAR PROTEST

Analysing criminal activity provides unique insights into social relations. Court records from the French regime are fairly complete and have been used as the bases for several excellent studies. Those of the British period, in contrast, have received almost no archival treatment and are still largely unexploited.

New France is often depicted as a harmonious and peaceful society in which religion and strict morality dominated. Examples of popular protest and criminal activity abound, however, particularly in the form of physical violence. André Lachance (1984) counted eighty-two cases of serious crimes like murder, duelling, and infanticide during the period 1712–1759. (Suicide is included in Lachance's list since it was considered murder.) Brawls in taverns and barracks and among neighbours were commonplace, accounting for half the activity of criminal courts. In one case, two Quebec shoemakers, Louis Rousseau and Joseph Dugas, argued over a game of billiards. Dugas accused Rousseau of cheating, and after exchanging insults, the two men attacked each other. Rousseau bit off two of Dugas's fingers and Dugas bit off part of Rousseau's cheek.

After physical violence, theft was the most prevalent crime. Although the poor occasionally stole food the most prevalent form of property crime was night-time break-and-entry into homes or stores.

Crimes against the state took two major forms: assault on judicial officials and forgery. For example, when bailiffs François Clesse and Pierre Courtin came to seize Joseph Ménard's property in 1737 as part of a judgment for debt, the two

Type of crime	1650–1699 Total number for the period	Percentage	1712–1759 Total number for the period	Percentage
Crimes against the church	19	3.9	12	1.2
Crimes against the state	32	6.5	149	15.0
Murders	43	8.8	82	8.2
Assaults	141	28.7	357	36.0
Insults	54	11.0	83	8.4
Thefts	83	16.9	204	20.4
Sexual offences	105	21.4	55	5.5
Others	14	2.8	53	5.3

Table 3.4 Criminal Activity in New France

(Lachance, 1984)

officials were threatened with an axe. Forgers were active in the colony. Because of shortages, paper money at the time was often made of playing cards on which the intendant simply wrote the amount of money owed by the government. Many forgers were soldiers who made or altered such card money.

Crimes against the church such as blasphemy and witchcraft were the exception, but there were a significant number of sexual offences, as defined by the church's strict moral code. Seduction was the most common but other offences such as rape, adultery, and bigamy did occur. There are recorded cases of couples charged for co-habiting before marriage.

The state tried to prevent social protest by measures such as denying people the right to congregate to discuss public issues except in the presence of a judge. In British North America, protest took the form of petitions, public meetings, and demands for an elected assembly. Occasionally, popular unrest escalated into riots. In 1714, for example, the habitants of the parish of Saint-Augustin, twenty kilometres southwest of Quebec, marched on the colonial capital—some armed with muskets—to protest their poverty and the cost of imported goods. The state used troops to bar their entrance into Quebec and force their dispersal.

Popular resistance often focused on forms of taxation such as the tithe and the corvée. When grand voyer (roads commissioner) François-Marie Picotté de Bellestre ordered a bridge to be built by the inhabitants of Boucherville, Varennes, and Verchères in 1781, for example, the local residents refused to obey. Their continued resistance delayed the project until 1788, when it was finally abandoned (Robichaud, 1989: 104–14).

⌒

NATIVE PEOPLES

Popular resistance during the preindustrial period was not limited to the European population. Native peoples are sometimes seen as passive, their dependence on trade goods making it easy for missionaries and governors to manipulate them. This was not the case. In the Montreal area, violence committed by drunk natives living in mission communities was a common occurrence. Although most of the victims were other natives, over a dozen white settlers were reported killed or wounded during the French regime. Even missionaries were occasionally beaten. Since the authorities were hesitant to alienate the Iroquois—whose military support was essential for the defence of the colony—natives were never prosecuted by the regular courts. The only recourse authorities had was to fine the French suppliers of alcohol.

Natives also resisted government control by carrying on trade with the British at Albany. Although the French maintained mostly peaceful relations with natives in the St. Lawrence Valley, they could not stop the Iroquois from trading with the British and could not depend on their military support in times of war. In the West, the French had greater difficulty. The Fox tribe harassed French traders and settlers from 1712 until governor Beauharnois ordered a war of exter-mination against them in the 1730s. With the resolution of the "Fox problem," the Sioux stepped in to resist the French. In the Mississippi valley, the Natchez, Choctaws and Chickasaws constantly resisted French presence on their territory. Western natives who resisted the French paid dearly; hundreds were enslaved for service in the West and in the St. Lawrence Valley. Despite the emphasis that historians place on the harmonious relations between the French and their native allies, governors continually complained that natives were unreliable barbarians (Trudel, 1990; Dickinson, 1987; Belmessous, 1990).

The British administration also faced problems with native peoples. In 1763, western tribes under Ottawa chief Pontiac attacked British traders throughout the Great Lakes region and captured all British forts except Detroit. During the war years (1754–1760), Indians had received few trade goods and had complained of the prices British traders charged, of the poor quality of their goods, and of the lack of presents traditionally given to confirm alliances. Although the Royal Proclamation of 1760 had guaranteed native peoples possession of all lands that had not already been ceded or sold, this did not dispel their fears that the British-American colonists would take their territory. The different tribes were not suffi-ciently united, however, and with the official disappearance of the French after the Treaty of Paris in 1763, the Pontiac alliance fell apart; peace was finally signed in 1766.

During the American Revolution, native allies in Quebec and most of the New York Iroquois sided with the British but their support was never more than tepid. They viewed these events as foreign to their immediate concerns and put their collective survival first (Ostola, 1989).

WOMEN IN PREINDUSTRIAL QUEBEC

In preindustrial societies, collective rights and responsibilities, particularly those of the family, took precedence over individual rights. As we have seen, marriage was normally part of a larger family strategy that involved helping all children to obtain land. Parental permission to marry was required for minors (those under twenty-five), and even when they were of majority age marriage that did not fit family goals was frowned upon. The role of women must be considered from the vantage point of family imperatives: childbearing, childraising, domestic responsibilities, caregiv-ing, and unpaid work in family enterprises.

French law was based on a paternal and authoritarian ideology in which women were subordinate to their fathers and husbands. As minors, women were under paternal control and could neither marry nor enter into any other contract without permission. In a marriage the husband exercised legal powers over the family, and his wife and children were to respect his authority. He was to provide for his family and was permitted to punish them physically; battered wives had to prove that their lives were in danger before being granted separation.

Although men managed their wives' estates, property that women brought into marriage or that they inherited could not be mortgaged or alienated without their permission. Occasionally, a married woman would seek a court separation of estates on grounds that her husband was mismanaging her affairs or beating her. In the former case, the court could accord the wife a separation of property; in the latter, she might be granted a separation of bed and board. Divorce was of course prohibited by the church and couples were considered married even if they lived apart (Savoie, 1986).

Single women and widows did have some autonomy and could use their legal rights to manage property or to run a business. Married women, with the written permission of their husbands, could become female public traders, a status that allowed them to enter into contracts. Widows were a particularly important economic force. Marie-Charlotte Denys de la Ronde, widow of Montreal lieutenant governor Claude de Ramezay became an important businesswomen. When her husband died in 1724, Denys took over his interests, notably a Chambly sawmill that produced planks for the local market and for export. She and her unmarried daughter, Louise de Ramezay, were important landowners and also became involved in other industrial activities including a brickyard, a tile factory, and a tannery. Marie-Anne Barbel became one of the colony's most successful merchants after her husband, Louis Fornel, died in 1745. She expanded the business by establishing a pottery and in 1748 obtained a monopoly over all trade on the North Shore from Charlevoix to Labrador (Plamondon, 1986).

Businesses usually involved the labour of several family members. Freed from domestic chores by servants, wives might help their husbands keep the books or operate the store. It was not unusual for a man to give his wife full legal powers to administer his affairs during an absence, or to represent him in court. Female religious communities operated under the bishop's authority but did have a certain amount of autonomy and thus offered women an avenue to exercise limited power.

Legal dependence was accentuated by the lack of employment opportunities for women in the colony. Women could not hold any official position and were barred from the professions. Clerical work, such as that of the scribes who worked in the intendant's offices, was a male occupation. Girls and unmarried women were employed as domestic servants but married women were expected to work in the home. Widows from the popular classes often had to take in boarders, wash clothes or in some cases become domestic servants in order to survive. As the notarial contract between Catherine Thibault and Pierre Couraud illustrates, destitute widows often hired their children out as servants:

> Catherine Thibault, widow of Nicolas Benoist, habitant of Rivière-des-Prairies, now living at the sieur de l'Espérance's house in Longue-Pointe, who has the care of four young girls and is without any financial means, has decided to place them in the domestic service of honest families to ensure their survival. To achieve this end, she promises to send her twelve year old daughter, Marie-Joseph Benoist, to serve Pierre Couraud de Lacoste for six years. Mister Lacoste promises to feed and clothe her, to bring her up in the Catholic religion. Marie-Joseph Benoist promises to serve her master faithfully and loyally and to look after his interests in all things. At the expiration of the contract, Mister Lacoste will give her a new set of clothes fitting her social condition, which will consist of a new coat, a new skirt, a pair of stockings, a pair of shoes, and six new shirts, along with all the other clothes that she might have.

Other widows operated small businesses such as taverns; of twenty-three people fined for operating a tavern without a licence in Quebec in 1751, six were widows.

⌒ ᴐ ᴄ ⌒

CONCLUSION

The social system of preindustrial Quebec was based on a farming population with reasonable access to new land. The peasant household was the basic unit of production, and its surplus supported a seigneurial and clerical establishment. Through rural merchants, the peasant economy was linked to the larger market economy. While local exchange was important, much of the colony's trade was based on the export of staple commodities.

Quebec remained a rural, preindustrial society across its first two centuries. Quebec City and Montreal were the only real urban centres and both had modest populations of around 10 000 by the beginning of the nineteenth century. Montreal at the end of the Napoleonic Wars was a city without large public buildings; few were over two storeys and its most important church, the original Notre Dame, was small, unimpressive, and squarely blocked a main thoroughfare. The city's elite—from the garrison, merchant houses, seminary, and royal bureaucracy—lived cheek-by-jowl with artisans and day labourers and their taverns and boarding houses, all within the confines of the stone fortifications.

The city's grain, firewood, and vegetables came largely from the Ile de Montréal; some of the city's flour was ground at Pointe Sainte-Anne, whose seigneurial mill was in sight of the port. Except in winter, when foreign trade was stopped by ice, timber, fur, and wheat staples passed through the city. Much of the city's flavour, its smells and sounds, came from daily life: carters, hay, market odours, woodsmoke, human and animal waste, hawkers, anvils, soldiers tramping, and church bells. Wood remained the most important fuel and building material; the horse, the human, wind, and water produced the city's energy.

Away from Montreal and Quebec City, regions developed with little interference from central political or judicial authority. Peasants in the Richelieu Valley produced wheat, peas, and oats as they had for the past century—primarily for family consumption, with surpluses going to pay the seigneur, the church, and the local merchant. Remote areas like the Gaspé had no land connections to Quebec City and remained in an Atlantic orbit.

In these preindustrial, locally defined economies, women had essential roles in providing food, drink, and clothes, and in agricultural work and certain forms of urban work. Dressmaking was the important female artisan trade. The wives of shopkeepers, butchers, and artisans supervised apprentices, books, stocks, and sales. Girls and young women from the popular classes worked as domestics in bourgeois homes. Widows retained their husbands' shops and trades or found work in the victualling, hawking, millinery, tavernkeeping, ferryboat, boarding house, or innkeeping professions.

<hr />

Further Reading

PREINDUSTRIAL QUEBEC

Among the better general introductions to preindustrial Quebec are R.C. Harris and John Warkentin, *Canada before Confederation*. Along with works cited in the previous chapter, readers should consult Marcel Trudel, *The Beginnings of New France* and Dale Miquelon, *New France, 1701–1744*. André Lachance's *La vie urbaine en Nouvelle-France* gives an excellent overview of urban life. The first volume of the *Historical Atlas of Canada* is also essential.

The Programme de recherches en démographie historique of the Université de Montréal has played a leading role in demographic studies in Canada. Along with Jacques Henripin's pioneering *La population canadienne au début du XVIIIe siècle*, Hubert Charbonneau's *Vie et mort de nos ancêtres* and *Naissance d'une population* are the best introduction to this science in the context of New France.

THE STAPLE THEORY

The importance of staples has been long debated. Work on the fisheries has regained vigour with the studies of François Brière ("Pêche et politique à Terre-Neuve au XVIIIe siècle: la France véritable gagnante du traité d'Utrecht," "Le commerce triangulaire entre les ports Terre-Neuviers français, les pêcheries d'Amérique du Nord et Marseille au 18e siècle: nouvelles perspectives"), and Laurier Turgeon ("Pour une histoire de la pêche: le marché de la morue à Marseille aux XVIIIe siècle," "Pour redécouvrir notre 16e siècle: les pêches à Terre-Neuve d'après les archives notariales de Bordeaux"). The fur trade has received more attention. Harold Innis, *The Fur Trade in Canada*, is essential and is complemented by a recent debate between William John Eccles, "A Belated Review of Harold Adams Innis's *The Fur Trade in Canada*," and Hugh M. Grant, "One Step Forward, Two Steps Back: Innis, Eccles and the Canadian Fur Trade." W.T. Easterbrook and M.H. Watkins, *Approaches to Canadian Economic History*, is also useful.

COMMERCE

Preindustrial commercial enterprises have not drawn as much interest as their later counterparts, but Dale Miquelon's *Dugard of Rouen* is an excellent case study of colonial commerce in the eighteenth century. Equally important is James Pritchard's article on shipping, "The Pattern of French Colonial Shipping to Canada before 1760." Jacques Mathieu's *Le commerce entre la Nouvelle-France et les Antilles au XVIIIe siècle* analyses inter-colonial trade. The fur trade has been treated by José Igartua, *The Merchants and Négociants of Montréal, 1750–1775: A Study in Socio-Economic History*, and Gratien Allaire, *Les engagés de la fourrure, 1701–1745: une étude de leur motivation*. Lately, much attention has been paid to rural merchants, notably by Louis Michel, "Un marchand rural en Nouvelle-France: François-Augustin Bailly de Messein, 1709–1711."

INDUSTRIAL PRODUCTION

The best English-language study of preindustrial Quebec artisans is Peter Moogk's *The Craftsmen of New France*. Jean-Pierre Hardy and Thierry Ruddel's *Les apprentis artisans à Québec, 1660–1815* includes changes wrought by the introduction of British practice after the Conquest. Large enterprises have been covered by Jacques Mathieu's *La construction navale royale à Québec, 1739–1759* and by Cameron Nish's *François-Etienne Cugnet: Entrepreneur et entreprises en Nouvelle-France*.

PEASANT SOCIETY

Indispensable for the understanding of peasant society and the peasant economy is Louise Dechêne's *Habitants and Merchants in Seventeenth-Century Montreal*, and her "Observations sur l'agriculture du Bas-Canada au début du XIXe siècle" is brilliant. Fernand Ouellet has had an important impact on the study of this period through his *Economic and Social History of Quebec*. Along with Allan Greer's book cited in the previous chapter, readers should refer to Christian Dessureault's *Les fondements de la hierarchie sociale au sein de la paysannerie: les cas de Saint-Hyacinthe, 1760–1815* and Louis Lavallée's *La Prairie en Nouvelle-France*.

RELIGION

Cornelius Jaenen's overview of religion in New France cited in the previous chapter and Jean-Pierre Wallot's "Religion and French-Canadian Mores in the Early Nineteenth Century" should be tempered by Marie-Aimée Cliche, *La religion populaire dans le gouvernement de Québec sous le Régime français d'après la pratique des actes surérogatoires*, and Brigitte Caulier, *Les Confréries de dévotion à Montréal du 17e au 19e siècles*, which are less impressionistic.

WOMEN

Women's history has not yet fully embraced the preindustrial period. The attempt to reconstruct a woman's view of history in the Clio Collective's *Quebec Women: A History* is only partially successful for the preindustrial period. More provocative is Jan Noel, "New France: Les femmes favorisées." Lilianne Plamondon, "A Businesswoman in New France: Marie-Anne Barbel, the Widow Fornel," gives an example of a businesswoman's career.

Economy and Society in Transition, 1810s–1880s

At the beginning of the nineteenth century, Lower Canada was predominantly preindustrial. Its agricultural and artisanal production was based largely on the family and goods were consumed locally. Montreal, which was to become the pivot of industrial capitalist society in Quebec later in the nineteenth century, was still a preindustrial city (Figure 4.1).

During the nineteenth century, Quebec was characterized by two major phenomena: urbanization and the transition to industrial capitalism. The number of farmers increased rapidly and the land area devoted to agriculture doubled in the second half of the century. Yet the percentage of the Quebec population living in urban centres expanded even faster. In 1809 the first steamboat service was established between Montreal and Quebec; by 1891, several daily trains as well as telegraph and telephone service linked the province's two major cities.

The complex process that historians refer to as the transition to industrial capitalism was characterized by a growing importance of capital in the colony. Lower Canada had little in the way of formal financial institutions until banks were formed after the Napoleonic Wars, and the important presence of Spanish currency symbolized the colony's perennial specie problems. In 1875, sixteen banks had their headquarters in Quebec City or Montreal (Rudin, 1985: 46); in 1900, one financial institution, Sun Life, had assets of $10 486 891 and $58 000 000 of insurance in force. The transition was also characterized by the expansion—albeit uneven by region and by trade—of industrial production in larger shops at the expense of artisanal producers. Changing gender relations were another central part of the transition, particularly the role of women in capitalist work settings and the deepening patriarchy of Victorian Quebec. State bureaucracies and new institutions of education, health, and other social services flourished in the transition as did expanding professions like the law, the notariat, and medicine. Science and the idea of the Canadian nation took on new importance across the period.

In 1816, small-scale artisanal activities using muscle power prevailed. By the 1890s the share of manufactured goods in the Canadian Gross National Product was almost as high as it was in the 1980s (Pomfret, 1981: 123). In Quebec, the value of manufacturing rose from $600 000 in 1851 to $15 000 000 in 1861, and to $104 660 000 in 1881. Productivity per worker also increased dramatically. An increasing percentage of this industrial production was destined for local consumption; the growing importance of meat packing, sugar refining, and the factory production of butter, cheese, bread, cigars, and textiles emphasize that family self-sufficiency in certain types of food and clothing was declining.

It was not only the use of steam or new technology that brought fundamental change to traditional work and social relations. For those who were able to accumulate capital, the period was one of growing power and social privilege. To

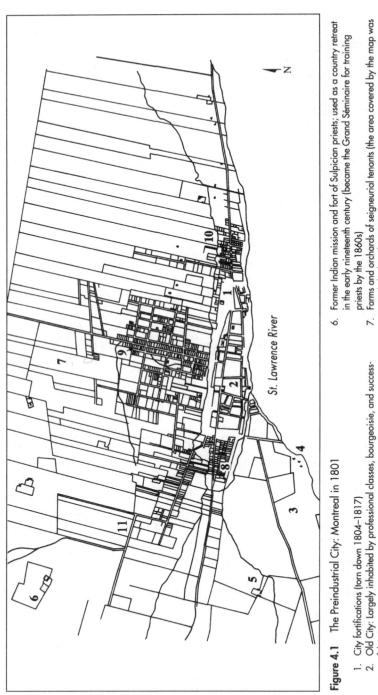

Figure 4.1 The Preindustrial City: Montreal in 1801

1. City fortifications (torn down 1804–1817)
2. Old City: Largely inhabited by professional classes, bourgeoisie, and successful artisans
3. Seigneurial commons (disappeared after the 1830s)
4. A banal windmill (converted to factory use by the 1860s)
5. Estates of religious communities (crossed by the Lachine Canal in the 1820s and Grand Trunk Railway in the 1850s)

6. Former Indian mission and fort of Sulpician priests; used as a country retreat in the early nineteenth century (became the Grand Séminaire for training priests by the 1860s)
7. Farms and orchards of seigneurial tenants (the area covered by the map was entirely built up by 1885)
8–11. Suburbs of Saint-Joseph (8), Saint-Laurent (9), and Sainte-Marie (10): occupied essentially by popular classes. By the 1850s the bourgeoisie was moving to the suburb of Saint-Antoine (11) and in 1871 this suburb had the highest number of servants per household in Canada.

defend their position, those with authority were able to exploit the widening civil functions of the state, the changing police and judicial powers, ethnic divisions, the ideological influence of the church, and its expanding network of institutions.

For pioneers, peasants, wage labourers, and widows, survival was often a daily struggle to find work and make ends meet. Amid ethnic conflicts, epidemics, and strikes, resistance to the transformation of work and social relations can be discerned. Opposition took various forms. Sometimes it was organized into riots, strikes, and political demonstrations. Sometimes resisting authority meant individual acts of arson, aggression, or refusal to attend church, to take the sacraments, or to pay tithes, taxes, or seigneurial dues. None of these forms of action were particularly new but represented, instead, a persistent process of social struggle.

In the area of work, we can see the effect of the transition on the work site, on the way work was done, on the gender and age of the labour force, on certain artisanal skills, and on the ownership of tools. In the financial sector, industrial capitalism brought new banking and insurance institutions to the fore for which accumulating and investing capital were more important than the earlier function of banks as exchange and clearing houses for merchants.

Quebec's institutional structure—its bureaucracy and social system, its land and mortgage system, its land law and civil code—took new forms during the transition. The nineteenth century saw growing public subsidies for roads, canals, and railways; the formation of a federal state in 1867; and the implementation of John A. Macdonald's National Policy encouraging immigration, tariffs, and transcontinental railways. These were clear indications that, by the end of the period, Quebec was an integral part of a larger Canadian state.

The transition was also characterized by significant changes in social relations and these brought forth numerous conflicts: the rebellions of 1837–1838; popular resistance in the 1840s to school reforms and local taxation in the "guerre des éteignoirs"; the sacking of the parliament in Montreal in 1849; and strikes and the development of unions in the 1850s and 1860s. The dismantling of seigneurialism and consequent decline of the seigneurial class, and a revitalization of the power of the Catholic clergy, hinted at a new alliance among Quebec's religious, political, professional, and entrepreneurial elite. At another level of the social scale, women in the popular classes, landless peasants, children, immigrants, and the urban unskilled formed distinct elements in a growing Quebec proletariat.

During the nineteenth century, bourgeois democracy was established in Lower Canada. Ancien régime institutions such as authoritarian government, the seigneurial landholding system, and the preindustrial legal system gave way to elected officials, parliamentary institutions, new bureaucracies, and a new civil code and judicial jurisdictions. The whole was legitimized by an ideology that emphasized the individual, and the competitive qualities of capitalism, and freedom to use one's property and to contract one's labour.

The transition was not an even process. Some rural regions remained peripheral to the market economy. Other regions developed into dynamic service centres which, with the major urban centres, were characterized by both higher production and specialization for specific markets. Industrial production—as opposed to artisans' work—was introduced at different times in various trades. At large construction sites, shipyards, foundries, breweries, and distilleries, industrial production occurred early in the century, while artisanal production methods remained strong much later in other sectors. In leather, for example, different modes of production co-existed: artisanal production, the "putting-out" system of people working at home, and factory production. And steam power, even at the end of the century, was less important than power generated by watermills.

The period of transition began in the 1810s. The end of the Napoleonic Wars marked a new demographic pattern as immigrants poured in from the British Isles. In 1816, the worst harvest in memory underlined the problems of Lower Canadian agriculture. The 1810s also saw the establishment of formal banking institutions in Quebec, and mounting pressure from industrial producers for the reform of seigneurial and legal structures.

By the other end of the period, the commercialization of agriculture had advanced significantly, aided by access first to American markets with the Reciprocity Treaty of 1854 and then to Great Britain's markets for cheese and butter. Cities, as we have seen, changed dramatically too. Montreal in particular, solidified its position as the corporate headquarters for the country's major transportation, financial, and industrial enterprises.

In preindustrial Canada, merchants, seigneurs, the upper clergy, and colonial administrators formed the elite. During the transition, they were joined and often superseded by industrial capitalists and professionals. Industrial producers objected to the seigneurial system, its dues, its domains, and its impediments to the unhindered use of property. They also pushed for a strong centralized state, abundant labour and cheap food, new canal and rail facilities, and tariff protection for their capital and manufactured goods.

DEMOGRAPHY

Despite nineteenth-century British immigration, Quebec remained overwhelmingly francophone as the province's overall population quadrupled from 340 000 in 1815 to 1 359 027 in 1881 (Figure 4.2). Urbanization was an important factor in demographic change. Dramatic increases in the size of Montreal and in the number of small urban centres reduced the relative importance of the rural population. Montreal's population rose from 9000 in 1815 to over 58 000 in 1852,

Year	Total population	Urban population	Urban percentage	Emigration (previous decade)
1815	340 000	c. 30 000	8.8 (approx.)	—
1822	427 000	—	—	—
1831	553 134	56 668	10.2	—
1844	697 000	—	—	—
1851	890 261	—	—	35 000
1861	1 111 566	—	—	70 000
1871	1 191 516	271 851	22.8	100 000
1881	1 359 027	378 512	27.9	120 000

Table 4.1 The Population of Lower Canada, 1815–1881
(Bernier et Boily, 1986; Lavoie, 1972)

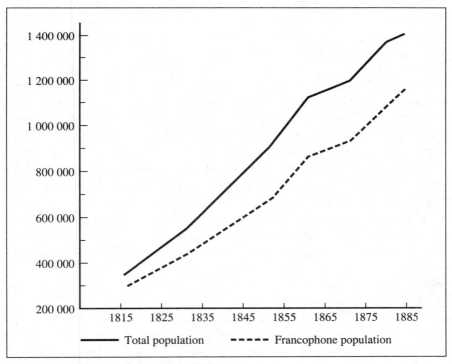

Figure 4.2 Quebec population, 1815–1885

and, including suburbs, to 327 000 at the end of the century (Linteau, 1992b).
Villages, as Serge Courville and Normand Séguin (1989) have pointed out, also
grew rapidly, accounting by the 1840s for 12 percent of the population of rural

parishes. These villages were important centres of trade, of production, of services, and of links to the larger world. The percentage of the Quebec population that was urban rose from 10.2 percent in 1831 to 27.9 percent in 1881.

The growth of Quebec's francophone population was due to natural increase. With stable birth and death rates, the French Catholic population rose from 288 000 in 1815 to 929 817 in 1871. The number of births per Catholic marriage (including anglophone Catholics) was 7.1 in 1816–1820 and 6.7 in 1876–1880. The significance of these rates must not be exaggerated, however, for they are comparable with general birth rates in the United States and other parts of Canada. In 1871, for example, the Quebec birth rate was lower than that of Ontario. It was only after the 1810–1890 period that Ontario's birth rate began dropping faster than Quebec's. Nor did the death rate change significantly over the period. The annual number of deaths per 1000 Catholic inhabitants of Quebec was 24.5 in 1816–1820 and 24.3 in 1876–1880 (Charbonneau, 1973).

The size and heterogeneity of the anglophone population increased rapidly. In chapter three it was clear that immigration from the United States was the dominant factor in the growth of the anglophone population before the Napoleonic Wars. American settlement was concentrated in Montreal and along the border from the counties of Huntingdon, Missisquoi, and Beauharnois into the Eastern Townships. After the Napoleonic Wars, agricultural depression and industrial crises in the British Isles brought new immigrants. Between 1815 and 1851, almost 800 000 British and Irish immigrants were recorded at the port of Quebec. Although most of them were en route to Upper Canada and the United States, some 50 000 did settle in Lower Canada.

Immigration raised the percentage of anglophones in the total population from 15 percent in 1815 to a high of 24.3 percent in 1861; thereafter, anglophones began a slow decline as a percentage of the Quebec population. With concentrations in the Gaspé, the Eastern Townships, the Ottawa Valley, and the urban centres, in 1871 anglophones represented about 20 percent of the Quebec population. Of the province's population, 5.9 percent was English in origin, 4.2 percent Scottish, and 10.4 percent Irish. Only a handful of the anglophone immigrants were gentry or (as was the case with Hugh Allan and William Price) the offspring of prominent British merchant families.

Most immigrants arrived in the unhealthy and overcrowded holds of timber ships deadheading back to Canadian ports. Wily shipowners and captains managed to cram as many as eighty or ninety people in spaces about eight metres square. James Hunt, an Irish immigrant on the brigantine *William*, which brought ninety-seven adults and forty-four children from Dublin to Quebec City in 1823, testified that he embarked with his pregnant wife and two relatives:

Year	England	Ireland	Scotland	Total
1829	3 500	9 600	2 600	15 700
1830	6 700	18 300	2 400	27 400
1831	10 300	34 100	5 300	49 700
1832	17 400	28 200	5 500	51 100
1833	5 100	12 000	4 100	21 200
1834	6 700	19 200	4 500	30 400
1835	3 000	7 100	2 100	12 200
1836	12 100	12 500	2 200	26 800
1837	5 500	14 500	1 500	21 500
1838	700	1 400	500	2 600
1839	1 500	5 100	400	7 000
1840	4 500	16 200	1 100	21 800
1841	5 900	18 300	3 500	27 700
1842	12 100	25 500	6 000	43 600
1843	6 400	9 700	5 000	21 100
1844	7 600	9 900	2 200	19 700
1845	8 800	14 200	2 100	25 100
1846	9 100	21 000	1 600	31 700
1847	31 000	54 310	3 700	89 010
1848	6 000	16 500	3 000	25 500
1849	8 900	23 100	4 900	36 900
1850	9 800	17 900	2 800	30 500
1851	9 600	22 381	7 000	38 981
Total	192 200	410 991	74 000	677 191

Table 4.2   Arrivals at the Port of Quebec from the British Isles, 1829–1851

(Ouellet, 1981)

that neither he or his family had a berth excepting his wife, who was nearly starved with cold [sic], and was permitted for three nights to sleep in the cabin; that during the first ten nights, they were obliged to sleep between the berths; and at other times in the long boat upon deck. For the last three weeks of the passage, he says they lay in the hold on some ropes, where the child he had with him died, and where his wife was delivered of another.

Infectious diseases like typhus, measles, and cholera were often carried on immigrant ships. Thousands died at sea or at the quarantine station at Grosse Ile near Quebec City. Epidemics then spread to the general populace. Of Lower Canadian cholera epidemics in 1832, 1834, 1845, 1851, 1854, and 1867, the worst, the Asian cholera of 1832, was introduced from the immigrant ship, the *Voyageur*. There were 2723 cholera-related deaths in Quebec City in 1832, 2547 in Montreal, and an undetermined number in the countryside (Dechêne et Robert, 1979; Bilson, 1980: 179).

While Don Akenson (1984) has focused on those Irish who became rural inhabitants, it is clear that significant numbers became the labour of industrial society. About 5 percent of Irish immigrants stayed in Quebec; 15 percent went to Upper Canada, mostly to rural areas; and the rest emigrated to the United States. The Irish who did stay in the ports of Montreal and Quebec City became an important source of wage labour. It was a significant factor in Lower Canadian ethnic politics that by 1831 over 40 percent of the day labourers in Montreal were anglophones.

Anglophones took on growing economic importance. As contractors, bankers, and industrial producers, they were often favoured in competition for British government, military, or institutional contracts. Anglophone merchants dominated the Lower Canadian banking system as well as the Canadian network of involvement in international finance. Foreign capital in Quebec was predominantly British, but American capital became increasingly important by the 1880s. In the transportation and manufacturing sectors, many of the engineers, entrepreneurs, patent holders, and importers of technology were American and British.

The growing anglophone presence in certain regions contributed to the development of francophone nationalism, particularly in the years before 1837–1838. Francophone professionals in Montreal, merchants and peasants in the Richelieu Valley, and forest and river labourers in the Ottawa Valley were rankled by the expansion of anglophone communities and their growing vociferousness. Their power in local economies added to this hostility. The case of Stephen Tucker in the Ottawa Valley seigneury of Petite-Nation is an example. Although 21 percent of the seigneury's 1842 population was anglophone (primarily from New England), the seigneury was overwhelmingly francophone and Catholic. Yet ninety-six of the 145 debt contracts signed before a local notary during 1837–1845 recognized debts owing to Tucker, an anglophone general merchant and sawmill operator. In the mid-1840s Tucker, who was rumoured to have offered $40 to any Catholic who would convert to the Baptist church, owned forty-four properties. Most of these were repossessed from debtors among the francophone peasantry (Baribeau, 1983: 30, 136).

Francophones were also frustrated with monopolistic and imperialistic land companies that speculated in development schemes and gave preference to British settlers. In 1833, for example, the British American Land Company controlled over 1 400 000 acres of crown land in the Eastern Townships. Working with landlords and emigration and parish officials in Britain as well as immigration officers in Canada, the Company attracted first paupers from southern

England and then, after 1836, starving crofters from the western Highlands and islands of Scotland (Little, 1989a: 38–50).

These aggressive settlement projects prompted what Jack Little describes as "a defensive reaction" by Catholic officials against "the encroachment of a modern, individualistic, and secularizing society." Privately accusing the British of swamping Lower Canada with its landless and cholera-ridden proletariat, the upper ranks of the Catholic clergy were prominent in the formation of colonization societies. Aided by a colonization roads program in 1848 and the Colonization Societies Act of 1869, which subsidized the cost of crown lands, colonization societies such as the Société Générale de Montréal were established to promote Catholic and francophone settlement, particularly in the Eastern Townships.

Francophone settlement in the Ottawa Valley was characterized by diversity and individual or family immigration. Of 161 francophones in Petite-Nation from 1815 to 1854 whose origins can be traced, twenty-six had already lived for a period in Upper Canada—usually in counties just across the Ottawa River— eleven were from the urban centres of Montreal, Trois-Rivières, and Quebec, and the remaining 124 were from fifty-three different Lower Canadian rural localities (Baribeau, 1983: 39).

Unlike settlers, industrial workers earned immediate cash and, thanks to railways, often had easier access to their home communities. As well, women and children were valuable wage workers in mill towns while the seasonal, waged forest labour force was essentially male. Between 1840 and 1880 some 325 000 Quebecers, overwhelmingly francophone, emigrated to the United States.

Emigration significantly changed the demography of industrializing Quebec. Railway networks facilitated travel, and much of the surplus rural population began to seek work in the industrial centres of Quebec or New England. Bruno Ramirez (1991: 27–28) has argued that emigration became a more attractive family strategy than colonization for the rural proletariat in counties like Berthier, where the landless and day labourers formed 14 to 20 percent of the population in older rural parishes and up to 26 percent of the population in the town of Berthierville. Families sent out members to specific New England towns that had parish links to their community. Emigrants from the Berthier area near Montreal favoured Rhode Island mill towns, while Rimouski emigrants preferred southern Massachusetts industrial communities like Fall River.

The overcrowding, migration, and new forms of work inherent in the transition to industrial capitalism had profound effects on family life and social relations. The number of illegitimate births in Quebec City increased sharply, especially in the 1860s (Figure 4.3). Postponement of marriage for economic reasons and expansion of the urban proletariat led to increased illegitimacy. Montreal's Grey Nuns Foundling Hospital took care of an increasing number of infants, even if it is not clear how many of these were abandoned by married

Year	Abandoned	Number placed in families	Number who died
1820	64	6	55
1825	98	3	88
1830	108	9	98
1835	131	13	108
1840	152	8	135

Table 4.3 Children Abandoned at the Grey Nuns Foundling Hospital in Montreal, 1820–1840 (Gossage, 1983)

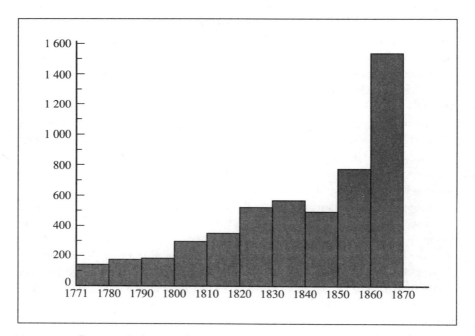

Figure 4.3 Illegitimate births in Quebec City, 1771–1870 (Canada, Census of Canada, 1871, 5: 359)

women—among them rural women who came to Montreal to have their babies. Infants were placed in the care of wet nurses and, as elsewhere, the death rate was extremely high.

Census data consistently underestimate native populations. Many natives, especially hunting families, were missed by census enumerators. Even settled groups such as the Lorette Hurons were missed in the 1881 census, which listed only 36 natives as living in the Quebec City region. In 1881, the census enumerated 7515 native peoples living within the boundaries of the province and another 5016 in the territories east of Hudson Bay. Iroquois in the Montreal region and Micmacs in the Gaspé lived alongside white communities but the majority of natives lived in hunting bands scattered throughout the Canadian Shield. Even though there might have been 15 000 or more native peoples living within the boundaries of present-day Quebec, their status and influence were increasingly marginal to white society.

URBANIZATION

From the perspective of the staples trades, Montreal's future was not bright in the first decades of the nineteenth century. The city was losing the fur trade and its political influence in the West to the Hudson's Bay Company, and the square-timber trade of the St. Lawrence was concentrated in Quebec City. Although Montreal did have an important commercial vocation forwarding goods to Upper Canada and exporting its wheat, the city's extraordinary growth across the period of the transition forces us to look beyond a staples interpretation of Canadian history.

Growth was due mainly to the city's expanding industries, which provided work for both the skilled and the unskilled. In 1881, Montreal and its suburbs produced 52 percent of the value of Quebec's manufactured goods; Quebec City accounted for only 9.3 percent (Hamelin et Roby, 1971: 298). Montreal's metropolitan dominance was enhanced by water power, canals, and railways, and by the expansion of its financial institutions, which concentrated capital in the city.

In the 1840s and 1850s, Montreal's political elite used increasingly powerful local institutions such as the municipal government, the Board of Trade, and the Harbour Commission to foster a transcontinental dimension to their bailiwick. Politicians such as George-Etienne Cartier, who had clear links to industrial capitalists, were instrumental in obtaining state support for the improvement of the ship channel downstream from Montreal to deep water and of upriver routes such as the Lachine Canal to American and Upper Canadian hinterlands. The Grand Trunk Railway was completed in the 1850s, its head office was located in Montreal, and its huge shops were developed in the Pointe St-Charles suburb of the city. All of this reinforced Montreal's position as a transportation hub. The opening of the railway's Victoria Bridge at Montreal gave the city the province's only bridge over the St. Lawrence, and by 1885 Montreal was a terminus for international and continental railway systems that included the Grand Trunk, Canadian Pacific, Vermont Central, and Delaware and Hudson. Railways stimulated industrial production. The Montreal area accounted for 40 percent of Canadian production in the food and beverage sector and the same percentage in transport equipment.

Figure 4.4   The Anse-au-Foulon timber cove and shipyard. During the first half of the nineteenth century, Quebec City lived by the timber trade and shipbuilding. Large rafts coming from the Ottawa River were beached at Sillery before the square timber was loaded on board ships or used in shipbuilding. After the 1860s, exports and wooden ship construction declined dramatically; from an average of over 18 million board feet of square timber in 1862–1866, exports declined to just over 7 million board feet in 1882–1886.

Quebec City fared badly in the transition to industrial capitalism because it was dependent on shipbuilding and the square-timber trade, both of which declined in the second half of the century (Figure 4.4). Britain abolished its duties on Baltic timber, and in the United States there was a rising demand for sawn lumber that could be shipped on north–south canals and railways from Montreal and the Ottawa Valley regions. The Reciprocity Treaty of 1854, which permitted the free entry of lumber into the United States, further damaged the trade for Quebec City. As a result, its population grew only slowly and its ocean port declined. Even before 1867 its political and administrative functions were in decline and in 1871 the British garrison was removed.

A major seaport without a bridge over the St. Lawrence, the city was isolated from canal and rail networks. Politicians and entrepreneurs in Montreal worked to ensure that Quebec City did not receive state help to build a bridge over the St. Lawrence and that its railways remained subservient to main lines operating out of Montreal. As early as 1844, a Maine newspaper, the *Eastern Argus*, predicted Quebec City's death knell as a commercial and industrial city:

> Quebec has for many years ceased to be a place of any considerable business . . . and though a place of great attractions for its military fortifications and historical incidents, its junctive position in the midst of a mountainous region, renders it comparatively forbidding as a place of residence, and with the exception of its lumber trade, its business is still on the decrease. Nine tenths at least of all the travel to, and from Quebec is by the way of Montreal.

A number of Quebec towns became regional industrial and service centres. Historically an important administrative centre, Trois-Rivières, at the junction of the St. Maurice and St. Lawrence rivers, was still Quebec's third largest city in 1871, with a population of 7570. Its size was due in large part to expanding leather, textile, and wood industries such as furniture making. Sherbrooke was the dynamic, younger service centre for the Eastern Townships and, with its water-power resources and rail links to Montreal, Lévis, and New England, became an important industrial centre. In 1866, Canada's largest woollen mill was located there and by 1871 the city had a population of 4432. Hull, with its supply of Ottawa Valley lumber and abundant water-power resources, had grown to 3800 in 1871. Saint-Hyacinthe (3746 in 1871) and Saint-Jean (3022 in 1871) were both regional service centres with water-power and transportation facilities that encouraged industrialization. In 1850, Quebec had fourteen towns with a population of 1000 to 5000, compared to thirty-three towns in Ontario. By 1870 the figure had risen to twenty-two towns in Quebec and sixty-nine in Ontario (Table 4.4).

Trois-Rivières illustrates the transformation of a preindustrial service town into an industrial city. In 1852, when it was given diocesan status, Trois-Rivières had a population under 5000. In that year George Baptist built his sawmill in the Saint-Maurice Valley and the government began constructing sluices and booms to prevent logs from being smashed by the falls and rapids of the Saint-Maurice. The development of its hinterland gave Trois-Rivières new regional importance. In1865, the 182 oceangoing ships that docked in Trois-Rivières loaded over

Town size	Quebec		Ontario	
	1850	1870	1850	1870
25 000+	2	2	1	2
5000–25 000	0	3	4	10
1000–5000	14	22	33	69

Table 4.4 Number of Towns in Quebec and Ontario, 1850–1870

(McCallum, 1980: 55)

Sector	Number of manufacturers	Number of employees
1. Food, drink and tobacco	14	25
2. Leather	24	193
3. Textiles, hats, clothing	30	206
4. Wood, furniture	25	454
5. Metal	21	91
6. Other	10	49
Total	124	1018

Table 4.5   Industrial Activities in Trois-Rivières, 1871

(Hardy et Séguin, 1984: 182)

20 000 000 board feet of lumber for export to British, American, and Latin American markets. In 1878, a railway was built along the Saint-Maurice River and by 1881 Trois-Rivières had rail connections to Montreal and Quebec City. The population of Trois-Rivières grew from 4900 to 8600 during the period from 1851 to 1881, and in 1871 the city had over 1000 people working in manufacturing. Industrialization accelerated in the 1880s with the opening of several new sawmills, a biscuit factory, woodworking shops, ironworks, and a shoe manufacture.

TRANSPORTATION

Transportation was a crucial factor in Quebec's transition to industrial capitalism. In 1809, brewer John Molson launched Canada's first steam vessel, the *Accommodation*, and it transformed shipping between Montreal and Quebec City. The paddlesteamer *Royal William* was constructed in 1831 at Quebec City; powered by a 200-horsepower engine built in Montreal, it was the first merchant vessel to cross the Atlantic largely under steam. Steamships and railways brought new dimensions of industrial production, capital, company organization, and labour concentrations. Although rail networks covered much of southern Quebec by 1885, more remote regions were still served only by rough roads and sailing ships.

As a major port for ocean vessels, Montreal tried to protect both the St. Lawrence system and its Upper Canadian and American midwest trade against American competition, particularly from New York, Boston, and Philadelphia. Completion of the 605-kilometre Erie Canal in 1825 gave New York a strong advantage but by the late 1840s Montreal's access to the interior had been improved along the Richelieu, Ottawa, and St. Lawrence river axis. The Lachine

Canal, originally completed in the 1820s, was rebuilt in the 1840s with new locks and turning basins, and the Beauharnois, Cornwall, and Welland canals were constructed. These developments permitted ships to run from Montreal to Lake Ontario and beyond.

Trading along the banks of the St. Lawrence, the Gulf, and the Gaspé was also dependent on transportation networks. Although anglophone merchants in Montreal predominated in the upriver forwarding trade to Upper Canada, trade downstream from Montreal was dominated in the early period by francophones. The Richelieu Company, for example, was established in the 1840s by local merchants such as Jacques-Félix Sincennes of Sorel. The company flourished by trading to important riverfront agricultural, service, and sawmill communities such as Saint-Césaire, Beloeil, Saint-Denis, and Saint-Jean, and by shipping lumber to American markets via the Richelieu–Lake Champlain system. After 1853, declining trade on the Richelieu, construction of the Grand Trunk Railway, and the increasing dominance of integrated steamship systems led to the transfer of company control to Montreal and its incorporation into a larger steamboat and rail network.

Even during the heyday of canal construction, attention was shifting to rail transportation. Steam engines rolling on iron rails permitted freight to move year round. Railways attracted the attention of both merchant and industrial capital, permitting access to new markets and resources and extending the political, financial, and industrial influence of rail-line owners.

The first major interprovincial and international railways were proposed in the 1840s. In 1846, railways were chartered by Lower Canadian and American entrepreneurs to join Montreal and the ice-free port of Portland, Maine. When completed in 1860, the Grand Trunk Railway—under the direct control of its major British shareholders—extended from Sarnia, Ontario, through Montreal and the Eastern Townships to Portland. The Grand Trunk continued to expand its network on the south shore of the St. Lawrence, extending its line to Rivière-du-Loup. In 1861, the Grand Trunk Railway had 2904 employees, and some 14 000 people in Montreal were directly dependent on the railway (Hamelin et Roby, 1971: 267). In 1876, the Intercolonial Railway linked Montreal to the Maritimes via the Matapedia Valley and New Brunswick's north shore. In the 1880s the Grand Trunk built its own line between Detroit and Chicago.

Construction of the Grand Trunk Railway was much more than an isolated engineering and entrepreneurial feat. Its significance for the Montreal economy can be seen from its influence on independent carters. Hauling goods and people was an essential ingredient in the urban economy and carting was an important nineteenth-century occupation. Its transformation shows changes both in how work was done and in the power structure of industrializing Montreal. Carters—who traditionally competed among themselves—faced a new scale and form of

Figure 4.5 Victoria Bridge. Plans for the Victoria Bridge were drawn up by Robert Stephenson, the bridge engineer and son of the inventor of the steam locomotive. Work began in 1854 with the crucial centre span being erected in the winter of 1858–1859. Scaffolds were built on ice, and work continued around the clock to assemble the bridge before spring breakup. The opening of the bridge in December 1859 gave Montreal access to the ice-free port of Portland, Maine.

competition from the centralized industrial capital that accompanied canal and rail transportation. In 1861, some 70 percent of Montreal's 1188 carters were still independent operators, owning their own horses and carts. A minority had become wage labourers, driving for employers with large stables and fleets.

The opening of the Lachine Canal in the 1820s had already deprived carters of the important Montreal–Lachine route. By mid-century, access to railway stations was vital to the survival of the independent Montreal carter. Before the completion of the Victoria Bridge in 1859 (Figure 4.5), the Grand Trunk Railway stimulated business for local carters. They hauled goods from the port to the railway depot in Pointe St-Charles, or across the St. Lawrence ice. With the rationalization of Grand Trunk operations, however, an exclusive contract was awarded in 1863 to John Shedden. His cartage company had already expanded rapidly in Upper Canada by winning a monopoly to serve certain Grand Trunk stations. The railway's contract with Shedden in Montreal gave him privileges in delivering and picking up goods at the Grand Trunk's Montreal depots and station. It had an immediate effect. When Shedden hired twenty-four carters and built a stable for sixty-four horses, independent carters protested that the contract jeopardized their livelihood.

In September 1864 the carters went on strike, accusing the Grand Trunk of instituting a monopoly. Although the carters were well organized and could paralyze transportation in Montreal, they did not rally significant political support from merchants or municipal authorities. When they ended their strike a few days later, their cause was effectively lost. The power of the Grand Trunk and its form of business had been reinforced (Heap, 1977).

Construction of the Grand Trunk, heavily subsidized by the Canadian government, greatly disadvantaged other communities, particularly in the Quebec City and Trois-Rivières regions along the North Shore of the St. Lawrence. Although Quebec had 1235 km of railway in 1871, almost none served the North Shore. A rail trip from Quebec City to Montreal in 1854 took twenty-one hours and entailed crossing the St. Lawrence by ferry at Lévis and (until completion of the Victoria Bridge in 1859) again at Montreal.

Lack of capital, fierce hostility from the Grand Trunk, and the weakness of the Quebec City and North Shore economy hindered construction of railways in the region. In addition, the combination of the Quebec City region's weak lobby in both the federal government and the Grand Trunk management meant that this railway project dragged on for thirty years and brought Quebec close to bankruptcy. Railways joining Quebec City to Montreal and Ottawa were only completed in the 1880s.

As was clear from the effect of the Grand Trunk on Montreal carters, railways were much more than commercial enterprises. Historians Tom Traves and Paul Craven (1983) have shown the importance of the Grand Trunk as an industrial producer, its development of modern management, accounting, and labour organization, and its crucial influence on Canada's industrial economy. They point out that even before its completion, the Grand Trunk was rebuilding its line and repairing track, communicating by telegraph, and operating grain elevators and steamships. It also had complex management, accounting, and engineering structures.

Railways represented a heavy investment of capital. The Grand Trunk's shops, where its rolling stock was constructed and maintained, were built on farm land located southwest of Montreal between the Lachine Canal and the St. Lawrence River. The 41-hectare site was bought from four religious communities. With nearby milling, shipbuilding, and iron-working industries along the Lachine Canal, the shops stimulated the growth of Pointe St-Charles and other working-class communities that spread along the canal to St-Henri (Hoskins, 1987). By 1871, the area had fifty-nine factories employing 4963 workers (Triggs et al., 1992).

The Grand Trunk's 1854 plans show 1000-metre-long foundations for its Pointe St-Charles shops. The shops included a forge, a foundry, a warehouse, and facilities for erecting locomotives. As part of the company's organization, independent contractors were systematically eliminated. In addition to manufacturing its own cars, locomotives, and rails, the Grand Trunk added ancillary shops such as a sawmill, a planing mill, and a paint-and-varnish shop to its Pointe St-Charles facility. In the 1860s the shops had hydraulic presses and screwing and drilling machines, and were illuminated by 700 gas lights and steam-heated by burning sawdust from the sawmill. By 1871, the Pointe St-Charles shops had 790 workers. Although many of its employees were skilled, the Grand Trunk was characterized by factory production and rigorously organized management: steam hammers, huge drilling machines, and daily work reports.

INDUSTRIAL PRODUCERS

Well before the transportation revolution, the brewing, shipbuilding, and milling trades in Montreal had developed industrial production methods. As early as 1831, the Ogilvies had a steam mill in Montreal. The businesses started by brewer John Molson and mason John Redpath illustrate the transition from artisanal to industrial production.

As families became less self-sufficient and, particularly in the cities, began buying more of their provisions, urban producers found themselves with expanding markets. By the 1850s, Montreal breweries had annual sales of £750 000 (Pomfret, 1981: 122). As early as 1785, John Molson, Sr. owned a Montreal brewery and early in the nineteenth century, he and his three sons began using their capital to branch into steamshipping and steamship construction, foundries, whisky distilling, sawmilling, land speculation, warehousing, banking, and railways. The Molsons are an indication of the important relationship between industry, the accumulation of capital, and its investment in landed property. By mid-century the Molsons were by far the largest lay land proprietors in Montreal; the property of just two Molsons was evaluated at £43 296.

Redpath's career also illustrates the path to industrial capitalism. Scottish-born, he became an important Montreal stonemason in the 1820s and 1830s and accumulated capital through large building projects. He constructed canals, churches, and other public institutions. The scale of contracts for large projects such as Notre Dame Church and the Rideau Canal facilitated new business and work practices. In an eighteen-month period (1826–1827), Redpath submitted fourteen tenders for contracts that included the Montreal Water Company, the British and Canadian School, a house for the Molsons, a store for merchants Forsyth and Richardson, and the lock-keeper's house on the Lachine Canal. With his profits, Redpath built Canada's first sugar refinery (Figure 4.6).

Anglophones in Quebec owned much of the capital and the means of production. A cultural interpretation of this phenomenon (such as Everett Hughes's emphasis on the family structure of French Canada and its "closed rural system" (1943)) poses difficulties. There is ample evidence of francophone participation in railway and industrial development. The anglophone elite did, however, have

Figure 4.6 The Redpath sugar refinery. The seven-storey Redpath sugar refinery was built in 1854 and represented an investment of £40 000. Within a year it had 100 employees and was refining 3000 barrels a month of sugar from West Indian cane. The illustration emphasizes the importance of the Lachine Canal and gives a sense of the distance between this emerging canal-side suburb and Montreal. Also of note is the presence of carters and both sail- and steamshipping.

advantages: the concentration in their hands of merchant capital from furs, wood, and forwarding; the transatlantic network of family and friends that gave access to British political and economic power; and the importance of Britain and the United States as sources of immigration, industrial technology, and engineers and other professionals.

Yet urban francophone professionals such as George-Etienne Cartier adapted effectively to the changing conditions of nineteenth-century capitalism. He thrived in the masculine, extrafamilial, and bicultural world of Montreal business and politics. He was a lawyer, and his corporate clients included the government of France, the Seminary of Montreal, the Grand Trunk Railway, and various mining, railway, and insurance companies. He supplemented his law and political income with property investments that returned substantial rents. By the 1860s, he was investing his surplus capital in bank and, to a lesser extent, industrial stocks.

The traditional francophone elite—the clergy and seigneurs—cannot be labelled as opposing industrial capitalism either. To take one example, the Seminary of Montreal was one of the two largest Canadian investors in the Grand Trunk Railway, while in Quebec City the local clergy invested in regional railways. Calling the railway to Quebec City "a work of patriotism," the archbishop of Quebec bought shares, as did the Seminary of Quebec and the Ursulines.

Figure 4.7 A student's view of the opening of the railway in Joliette

There is ample evidence of the sustained involvement of seigneurs in industrial activity. The seigneur of Lotbinière spoke out strongly in favour of railways by comparing them to the sustaining blood of the human body and predicting that "wherever those iron arteries do not carry life there will be decay." Seigneurs saw the industrial potential of their water-power sites, forests, and mines. While some opted to lease or sell mill sites or timber reserves, other seigneurs participated directly in industrial development.

As early as the 1820s, seigneurs like Barthélemy Joliette saw the potential of their seigneuries to produce lumber. Using capital from seigneurial dues, Joliette built a sawmill, alongside which he constructed a church and classical college. In 1837, he built a second mill and a distillery. By 1850 he had constructed one of the first railways in Quebec (Figure 4.7), which was used to transport timber from his mills to the St. Lawrence (Robert, 1972).

Even more important to industrialization was the attitude of Quebec's political leadership after 1840. From the first years of collaboration between Louis-Hippolyte La Fontaine and Francis Hincks in the 1840s, through the careers of George-Etienne Cartier, Hector Langevin, Joseph-Adolphe Chapleau, and Honoré Mercier, it is clear that the alliance between some of the most important Quebec politicians and industrialists was a fundamental reality of Quebec politics. This translated into strong Quebec support for a variety of railway enterprises.

The Guarantee Act (1849) and Municipal Loan Act (1852) facilitated public subsidies, particularly for the Grand Trunk.

By the 1870s, Quebec, much more than Ontario, was borrowing heavily in British, French, and American money markets to build railways deemed politically important to the province. In the budget year ending June 1877, the province spent $3 481 670 on railways and $407 176 as charges on the public debt, much of which had been caused by earlier investments in railroads. All other government expenditures for the year totalled under $2 000 000.

Despite the importance of certain rural and village industries, much of Quebec's early industrial production was concentrated in Montreal, and more particularly, along the Lachine Canal. By the late 1840s, manufacturers benefited from improved shipping facilities and used the water power of the recently expanded locks to run their flour mills, sawmills, cooperages, shipyards, sugar refineries, and manufactures for nails, beds and chairs, doors and sashes, saws, axes, and hammers. In 1856, 1203 workers were employed in water-powered industries along the canal. By 1871, forty-four industrial establishments along the canal employed 2613 workers, and another 938 were employed in the Grand Trunk shops (McNally, 1982: 117; Willis, 1987: 220).

The shops, mooring basins, sawmill, and engine foundry of Augustin Cantin, Montreal's most important steamboat builder, covered eleven acres around the first lock. Cantin, a native of a small village near Quebec City, mastered the construction of steamships in New York. In 1850 he invested £10 000 to build a dry dock; in 1855 his shops turned out seven steamships for domestic and export markets. Employing 200 to 250 workers, Cantin's manufacture was one of the first to put a marine engine in an iron-hulled ship (Tulchinsky, 1977: 210).

⌒

THE ORGANIZATION OF WORK

Industrial production necessitated changing the organization of work. In some instances this brought new forms of discipline and management; in others it implied work rhythms, work relations, and standards of accuracy and regularity that differed sharply from the work traditions of home, farm, or artisanal shop. In the process, artisans experienced a loss of status and labour became proletarianized.

The apprenticeship system seems to have undergone transformation after 1810. Masters took less parental responsibility for their apprentices and replaced board, lodging, and instruction with increased payment. An increase in the number of apprentices per master implied larger shops, a division of labour in some trades, and the transformation of apprenticeship from a process of acquiring skills into a simple labour contract. In 1815, Montreal area sculptor Louis Quévillon, for example, had fifteen apprentices and journeymen who had well-defined tasks assembling church furniture and ornaments. Employing cheap labour and standardized patterns, he used mass production to furnish and decorate dozens of churches across Lower Canada.

With increasing urbanization these changes in the labour process became evident in other trades. After 1820, a third of all artisans in Montreal worked in construction. They found their traditional work challenged on two fronts: the growing power of the general contractor often reduced the independence allowed to or skills required of the carpenter, plasterer, glazier, and mason; and, by the 1840s, competition from ever larger Lachine Canal manufacturers posed a serious threat. The canal manufacturers sold standardized building products such as doors and sashes.

This process was not uniform, and artisans did not receive it docilely. Joanne Burgess (1988) shows that in the first third of the nineteenth century Montreal's francophone population of leatherworkers was "a vital and dynamic community with longstanding craft traditions, able to reproduce itself and to attract large numbers of new recruits." Although there was a large influx of British leatherworkers into the Montreal tanning, shoemaking, and saddling trades, French Canadians remained a strong force. As the leather trades expanded, French Canadians from both Montreal and the surrounding region provided much of the labour force. For their part, many of the British craftsmen were transient but 17 percent integrated into the French Canadian community.

Peter Bischoff (1992) makes the same argument for the dynamism of francophone iron moulders after 1850, demonstrating that the trade was transmitted from father to son, that workers from the St. Maurice area migrated to foundries near the Lachine Canal in Montreal, and that artisanal families maintained solidarity in both their neighbourhoods and their workplaces. Both Burgess and Bischoff insist on the strong relation between rural industries, the strength of Montreal industries, and the mobility of labour.

Leather processing—tanning, shoemaking, and the production of gloves, belts, saddles, and harnesses—permits different stages of industrial production to be observed across an entire sector and in a region outside Montreal. Historically, tanneries were artisanal family operations. Many tanneries were concentrated along rue Saint-Vallier in Quebec City and in the Rolland Tanneries area west of Montreal. Most tanners were proprietors of their own shops, which usually adjoined their houses. Normally they employed little labour (in 1842 an average of 3.5 people per tannery in Quebec City). The average investment per Quebec City tannery was $7500 (Ferland, 1985: 52). In the early nineteenth century small tanneries were established in other areas and by 1851 there were over 100 across Quebec.

The leather industry was changing, however, and migrating west. An 1865 Montreal Board of Trade report emphasized changes in production and markets for sole leather:

> The manufacture of sole leather is becoming concentrated in the hands of men possessing capital and experience. The production last year was largely in excess of the demand and a considerable quantity of stock was shipped to Great Britain. . . . The black or curried leather which seeks a market in Montreal is made chiefly at small tanneries scattered through [Upper] Canada.

Some of this change came from the increasing influence of Americans in the Quebec leather industry: their capital, their technology (splitting machines, hide mills, new presses, vats, and ovens), and their skill in organizing all levels of production. The Shaw Brothers of Massachusetts, for example, improved the use of hemlock bark in the tanning process and then exploited the Eastern Townships' huge hemlock reserves. By 1871, the Shaws had invested $255 000 in their factories, particularly in their hydraulic and steam facilities. They had 126 employees in their Waterloo, Roxton Falls, and Montreal factories. Once local hemlock was exhausted by the end of the century, large rural tanneries such as the Shaws moved to Ontario.

In shoemaking, changes in artisanal production were a half-century process that began decades before the introduction of machines and steam into the leather trades. In the 1820s, Montreal merchants and bootmakers challenged the traditional practice of producing custom-made shoes by advertising ready-made shoes and boots. At the same time wholesalers were encouraging large-scale production of cheaper shoes for distribution across Upper and Lower Canada. In the late 1840s, new technologies brought further change: the Brown and Childs shoe manufacture in Montreal offered a 10 percent reduction in shoe prices thanks to "labour-saving machinery." The next three decades saw increased investment in new technology, particularly the sewing machine in the 1850s and steam facilities in the 1860s. Large shoe factories developed as a consequence, the traditional craft and outwork system broke down, and artisans lost control of the trade (Burgess, 1977).

By 1871, the largest shoe manufacturers in Montreal and Quebec City were producing nearly 500 000 pairs of shoes annually. Production per employee was high. Joseph Poirier's Quebec City manufacture turned out 19 000 pairs of shoes a year with twenty-three employees. Within the shoe factories there was an increasing mixture of skilled and unskilled labour. Skilled workers—the lasters and leather cutters—worked in the same building as unskilled hand labour and machine operators.

Industrial work was often repetitive and organized so that cheaper, unskilled labour could be used. From the point of view of employers, women and children were an excellent source of cheap labour. In 1871, 25 percent of boys in Montreal between the ages of eleven and fourteen were working, and women represented 33 percent of the Montreal labour force, with particular strength in the textile, clothing, and rubber sectors.

Changes in the form and place of work and in ownership of the means of production were often resisted. Despite the difficulties of organizing strikes and other forms of resistance, labour militancy was particularly strong in the leather, construction, and transportation sectors. Riots and strikes by Irish navvies at Lachine and other St. Lawrence construction sites occurred periodically through the half century after 1820. In 1844, stone carters threatened to kill their contractor if wages and working conditions were not improved; the employer's carts were destroyed at night and threatening notices posted (Willis, 1987: 97). The bloodiest confrontations in the construction sector occurred at Beauharnois in 1843, where twenty strikers were killed by British troops. The number of strikes increased later in the century with sixty-one strikes across Quebec from 1843 to 1879 and 102 from 1880 to 1895.

An important strike occurred in 1866 among Quebec City ship labourers. Their struggle was for more than wages; it represented an attempt to regain control of the work site. Among their demands were the refusal to use steam-driven machinery for certain kinds of tasks and insistence on the right to regulate the number of workers employed for specific jobs.

Violence occurred regularly within and between ethnic groups. Along the Lachine Canal, immigrants from Cork and Connacht fought openly, while throughout the 1830s and 1840s confrontations known as the Shiners War occurred between Irish and francophone workers in Ottawa Valley lumber camps. With completion of the Rideau Canal, Irish labourers (known as Shiners perhaps because of the shiny silk hats of immigrants or as a corruption of the French *cheneur*, or oak cutter) moved into forest work. This had been a traditional preserve of francophone farmers, for whom winter wage labour was essential, and conflict ensued (Cross, 1973). Along the Quebec City port and shipyards, ethnic relations between francophone and Irish workers had traditionally been good. The francophones predominated in shipbuilding and the Irish in longshoring. With the decline of shipbuilding, however, francophones moved into longshoring. After ethnic riots in 1878 and 1879, the Ship Labourers' Benevolent Society adopted a by-law providing for the employment of equal numbers of francophones and Irish on a job.

The effects of paternalism, new forms of work, and changing relations between capital and labour were evident in a broad cross section of crafts and trades in the 1830s and 1840s. In these two decades tailors, shoemakers, bakers, carpenters, printers, mechanics, firemen, painters, stonecutters, and milkmen all formed unions (Palmer, 1992).

By the 1880s labour militancy had focused on the Knights of Labor, an organization formed to unite all working women and men. Established in Philadelphia in 1869, the Knights spread rapidly in Canada in the 1870s and 1880s. By the early 1880s, they were an important force in Quebec. Despite direct interdiction from Archbishop Taschereau, who described membership in the Knights as a mortal sin (1886), the Knights program had a strong appeal to Quebec workers. It emphasized class solidarity, collective principles, and the nine-hour day. The Knights' symbolism and secret rituals; the solidarity of class and community suggested by their picnics, galas, and parades; and their program of self-help and temperance all reflected the interests of many anglophone and francophone workers. Stressing labour's solidarity, the Knights organized female workers.

Although Montreal and Quebec City were the strongholds of the Knights in Quebec—the Montreal order had 2500 members in 1887—communities such as Hull, Sillery, Buckingham, Valleyfield, Sherbrooke, and Bedford also had members. The Knights participated in 1886 in important Quebec strikes by coopers, shoemakers, and metalworkers. While the organization quickly faded in most parts of North America, the Knights held out much longer in Quebec and New England and remained a major force into the 1890s.

BANKING AND FINANCIAL INSTITUTIONS

Access to capital was crucial for industrial producers (Figure 4.8). In addition to the clearinghouse facilities offered by older merchant banks such as the Bank of Montreal (1817) and the Quebec Bank (1818), industrial producers needed substantial capital to build and expand their physical plants. This encouraged banks and other financial institutions to develop lending and saving facilities that permitted the capitalists who controlled the banks to collect capital in new forms.

Later in the century, building societies, the stock exchange, insurance companies, and municipal bonds began competing with local self-help and benevolent societies for the savings of rural parishes, white-collar workers, and the working class. The Montreal Stock Exchange was chartered in 1874 and this facilitated, legitimized, and institutionalized the raising of capital in Quebec. Many of the stocks were in banking or commerce, but ten of the sixty-three companies listed on the exchange in 1874 were industrial (Sweeny, 1978: 184).

Life insurance, another means of accumulating capital, became important in the 1870s. The largest Canadian insurance company, Sun Life, was founded in 1871 by a group of Montreal capitalists. The company quickly amassed huge sums from its insurance premiums. These were invested first in mortgages but increasingly in public utilities. In 1877, the company began writing insurance in the

Figure 4.8 Economic and institutional power on Place d'Armes. Attached to Notre Dame parish church, which was rebuilt in the 1820s, can be seen the business office of the Seminary of Montreal. Here the Sulpicians collected seigneurial rents and dues from across the Ile de Montréal. Construction of the Bank of Montreal's head office across the square from the parish church and seminary symbolized the conjuncture of merchant, clerical, and seigneurial economic power in mid-nineteenth century Montreal.

West Indies and by 1900 it was a force in the Orient, Great Britain, the United States, and Africa. This spread gave the company a huge pool of capital that it could invest in industrial activities in Quebec and elsewhere.

The relationship between investment capital and industrial production, the function of family networks, the importance of access to financial institutions, and the nature of power in industrial capitalist society can all be seen from the career of Hugh Allan. By his death in 1882, Allan had become Quebec's foremost capitalist. Although his empire lacked the rationalization of later industrial organization, Allan was able to use his resources of private and public capital to develop an integrated financial, transportation, and manufacturing complex.

Born into an important Scottish shipping family, Allan emigrated to Canada in 1826. With his father's help, he became a partner in a company that built one of the largest merchant fleets on the North Atlantic. Steamshipping led to producing goods for his ships and ensuring that rail routes led to his major ports, particularly Montreal. Allan became the chief backer of the original Canadian Pacific Railway syndicate. He was also president of the Montreal Telegraph Company (1852) and the Montreal Warehousing Company (1865). In addition, he became a director of other companies: the Montreal Railway Terminus Company (1861); the Canadian Railway Station Company (1871); the St. Lawrence International Bridge Company (1875); and the Detroit River Tunnel Company. He took an active role in financing dozens of companies in cotton and wool textiles, tobacco, shoemaking, iron and steel, rolling stock, and paper.

President of the Cornwall Woolen Manufacturing Company and the Canada Cotton Manufacturing Company, Allan was also a founder of the Montreal Cotton Company which, thanks in large measure to the tariff protection offered by the National Policy, declared dividends of 11 percent in 1880, 20 percent in 1881, and 14 percent in 1882. Allan also served as president of the Adams Tobacco Company (1882). He was a director of the Canada Paper Company, one of the first industrial stocks listed on the Montreal Stock Exchange. Pulp-and-paper was another growth industry and it doubled its production twice between 1861 and 1881.

Allan was also active in developing natural resources such as land, cattle, fish, and minerals. President of the Montreal and Western Land Company, the North-West Cattle Company, and the Canada and Newfoundland Sealing and Fishing Company, he was also a director of three Ontario mining companies and a Vermont marble company. Coal was the most important mineral resource to industrial capitalists like Allan. It was the energy source for his railways, steamships, and many of his factories. Director of several maritime coal mining companies, he was also president of the Vale Coal, Iron and Manufacturing Company (1873), supplier of coal to many of Montreal's largest industrial consumers.

Financing for these industrial activities came in part from the credit and banking facilities of Allan's bank and six fire, marine, and life insurance companies.

Bank	Established	Fate
Banque du Peuple, Montreal	1835	Closed 1895
Banque Nationale, Quebec City	1860	Merged 1924
Banque Jacques Cartier, Montreal	1862	Reorganized 1900
Banque Ville-Marie, Montreal	1872	Closed 1899
Banque de St-Jean, Saint-Jean	1873	Closed 1908
Banque d'Hochelaga, Montreal	1874	Reorganized as the Banque Canadienne Nationale 1925
Banque de St-Hyacinthe, Saint-Hyacinthe	1874	Closed 1908

Table 4.6   Francophone Banks Established before 1874

(Rudin, 1985b: 5)

His bank—the Merchants Bank—was chartered in 1861 and quickly established a reputation as Canada's most aggressive bank; by the late 1870s it was second in size only to the Bank of Montreal. Many of its loans were directed to Allan's companies.

Allan was part of a family dynasty in which succeeding generations inherited economic power. His younger brother, Andrew, helped found the Montreal Ocean Steamship Company and became rich in his own right. One of Hugh's sons, Hugh Montague Allan, became president of the Merchants Bank two decades after his father's death.

Francophone entrepreneurs were well aware of the significance of banks and investment capital, but they found it difficult to compete with their anglophone counterparts, many of whom had family ties to merchant capital or links to international financial or political interests. In 1835, the Banque du Peuple was established and in 1846, francophone and anglophone business leaders established the Montreal City and District Savings Bank. Although primarily founded to collect savings from the popular classes for investment by its directors, this bank was promoted by the Montreal Catholic hierarchy as a philanthropic organization.

In the period before 1874, seven small banks were established by francophones in an attempt to overcome the older banks' neglect of secondary regions in favour of the major commercial and industrial centres. In their efforts to promote local savings deposits, note circulation, and investment, the banks were characterized by insufficient capital and were tied to their respective regions. In this they had much in common with smaller anglophone banks such as the Eastern Townships Bank.

COMMERCIAL CAPITALISM

Merchants had, of course, been an important force in preindustrial Quebec and trade had co-existed comfortably with other preindustrial activities. While nineteenth-century merchants were supported by an increasingly complex commercial network of banking, insurance, brokerage, warehousing, shipping, and legal services, the nature of their local and international trade activities did not change significantly in the transition. What did change were the opportunities to invest capital accumulated through trade.

Local and regional trade remained the bread and butter of many Quebec coastal traders, urban retailers, and general merchants in the villages. Behind the very visible square-timber and wheat trades were feed suppliers who shipped oats for Quebec City's horses; local producers and merchants who supplied butter, apples, eggs, potatoes, and flour for the timber shanties of the Ottawa, Saint-Maurice and Saguenay; firewood suppliers in Châteauguay and Saint-Jérôme who kept the stoves of Montreal burning; and Eastern Townships pork dealers who fed British troops stationed in the province. There was also a small army of tavernkeepers, boarding-house and ferry boat operators, market-stall holders, victuallers and peddlers who ensured consumer supplies of food, alcohol, medicine, and dry goods. The diversity and scale of trading activities can be seen in the number of peddlers reported by provincial census takers: it quintupled from sixty-seven in 1851 to 344 in 1891.

The square-timber trade remained important until the mid-nineteenth century, although it was ultimately surpassed by potash, construction lumber, barrel staves, deals (spruce planks), and paper. Some of the great family fortunes in Quebec—the McLarens of the Ottawa Valley and the Sharples and Prices of Quebec City—originated in the timber trade and sawmilling. The Prices are perhaps the best example of the accumulation of capital in the forest industry.

William Price (1789–1867) arrived in Canada in 1810 as the representative of a British timber firm but by 1820 he was exporting square timber on his own account to the British navy. By 1833, Price and his partners had individual contracts worth up to £200 000 and were dispatching 100 shiploads of timber a year to Britain. In the 1840s he controlled some 19 940 square kilometres of forest reserve in the Saguenay–Lac Saint-Jean area, as well as 384 square kilometres on the south shore of the St. Lawrence. As sawn lumber became more important, Price ploughed his square-timber profits back into sawmill sites and construction of a network of sawmills. His forest concessions supplied his thirty-three sawmills along the Saguenay and both sides of the St. Lawrence.

These mills produced 500 000 planks a year for the British market and huge quantities of sawn lumber for American markets. By 1861, 12 000 settlers in the

Lac Saint-Jean area assured Price of a dependable source of labour for summer work in his sawmills and for cutting timber in the winter.

Price took steps to control the food supply for his workers. His 325-hectare farm near Chicoutimi employed up to 100 workers. The farm supplied his lumber camps with butter, pork, wheat, beef, and sugar beets. In 1860, the local priest reported that Price's farm harvested as much grain as all the rest of the parish (Ryan, 1966: 142). His biographer, Louise Dechêne (1976), is unequivocal in describing his monopoly and his character: "Price ruled the region; charitable when his men were docile, he was ruthless towards those who disputed his dominion."

Trade with Upper Canada assumed new dimensions as the population grew, the Rideau Canal system was completed (1832), the Lachine Canal underwent improvements (1840s), and the first railways to Upper Canada were built (1850s). Forwarding became an increasingly important activity for Montreal merchants, who shipped hardware, tea, coffee, cotton, woollens, silks, and sugar to Upper Canada. Upper Canadian products such as wheat, flour, oatmeal, butter, pork, square timber, staves, deals, and potash came down to Montreal for local consumption or export. Wheat was of particular importance because by 1851 Lower Canada was importing half of its total consumption, most of it from Upper Canada. In that year, almost 4.3 million bushels of Ontario wheat were imported to Quebec. Of the total tonnage passing down the St. Lawrence canals, 78 percent consisted of wheat and flour (McCallum, 1980: 35, 71).

AGRICULTURE, SETTLEMENT, AND THE RURAL ECONOMY

Agriculture, as we have seen, had already been integrated into markets in preindustrial society, and the Quebec peasantry were not unaccustomed to being in debt to either merchants or seigneurs. Perhaps the major transformation in agriculture during the transition period was the greater rural migration to both new agricultural regions and industrial centres within the province, and to New England as seigneurial lands were filled after 1830. At the same time, farmers increasingly depended on industry for goods that had previously been produced locally, such as leather products. To afford the new commodities, farmers were forced to produce specialized agricultural products for sale. Agriculture was also affected by changes in the legal structure of land ownership as seigneurialism was phased out after the 1850s. Finally, the poorer areas outside the St. Lawrence lowlands experienced increasing regionalism, and underwent a shift to agro-forestry, an economic system in which farmers were dependent on revenues from the forest industry.

Wheat exports from Lower Canada declined from 1815 to 1840 because of climatic conditions, including attacks from parasites like the Hessian wheat fly. There were several other factors in decreased wheat production. Without large herds, farms did not have enough manure to fertilize the fields. Settlement began to expand onto lands that were marginal for grain production. Finally, growing local markets provoked a shift to other crops. The importance of these factors varied across Lower Canada. As regional disparities became more evident young people began leaving rural areas, to become a major source of industrial labour for Lower Canada and New England.

As described earlier, the Montreal plain seems to have fared best. It was highly fertile and new land remained available until the 1830s. Saint-Hyacinthe, another lowland area, was still under development in the first half of the century, offering farm conditions comparable to those of the New France period. In the Quebec City region, Montmagny continued to produce surplus grain.

Conditions in Charlevoix, however, deteriorated as its limited arable land became densely occupied by an expanding population. Seigneurial concessions at Malbaie became larger in the 1820s but since they were concentrated in the unproductive, hilly back-country, farm families had to spread themselves across fishing, forest, and farm occupations. In parts of the Ottawa Valley, population pressure forced farmers to settle on the unproductive flanks of the Canadian Shield.

According to René Hardy and Normand Séguin (1984), the marginal farming population's dependence on cash income from forest work characterized the agroforest economy of the Ottawa, Saint-Maurice, and Saguenay valleys. Saint-Maurice provides a good example. Here families farmed in the short growing season to produce both their own food and cash crops such as firewood for Montreal and Trois-Rivières (Figure 4.9), and hay, oats, potatoes, and peas for the local lumber shanties. For family survival, men supplemented farm production with winter work in the forest.

Not all regions had an agro-forest economy. In the Eastern Townships, for example, farmers had few links to forest industries and produced essentially for home consumption. Winter labour in company forests was drawn from the mill labour force (Little, 1989a).

Forest labour paid $7 to $10 a month in the 1850s and $12 to $22 in the 1880s (Hardy et Séguin, 1984: 131). Much of this wage labour came from adolescent or unmarried males; boys under sixteen and men over forty-five rarely went. Married men aged twenty-two to forty-five generally took forest work only if their sons were too young to work.

Figures 4.9 and 4.10 Wood in the local economy. The trade in wood is often seen as synonymous with the export trade in square timber. In contrast, these two photos illustrate the importance of local markets for wood products and emphasize the inadequacy of the staple theory in explaining the dynamics of economic activity in Quebec. In the 1820s, for example, 23 000 cords of hardwood were sold as firewood in Montreal. This suggests that about as much wood was consumed in the local market as was exported. Figure 4.9 illustrates the firewood market in Trois-Rivières.

The Lambkin Furniture Manufacture represents another industry that developed to serve local markets. It used both water power and steam power for its woodworking machinery. The three-storey building served as a warehouse and showroom; the kiln was located across the street. Using local maple, ash, and pine, a dozen employees produced furniture, caskets, and woodwork for local churches and houses. Although the industry used modern woodworking machinery and steam power it retained some artisanal characteristics. A well-known artist decorated the fancy furniture; barter, particularly in lumber, was used instead of cash to settle many accounts; and the owners doubled as Missisquoi County's first architects.

Cutting began with the first snows and moved into high gear with the freeze-up, which permitted transportation by sleigh of food and timber. Until the 1920s, when piecework replaced wage labour, cutting teams consisted of five men: two cullers, a team driver, a clearer, and a piler. Early in the nineteenth century the lumberjack's traditional axe was being replaced by the two-person crosscut saw. Spruce was the primary product of the Saint-Maurice. Dragged to the banks or piled directly on the frozen rivers, it was driven downstream to the mill or port after spring breakup in mid-April.

These regional forest economies were dominated by lumber producers such as William Price who controlled the forests, the transportation systems, the marketing of lumber products, and the labour market. The lumber producers also controlled local consumption by instituting truck payments at their company stores. The trade-off for the peasantry was that, while their labour contributed to the fortunes of Quebec's great timber capitalists, they were able to ensure the survival of their families and transmission of their property.

The growing body of rural, landless day labourers contributed to the development of rural industries and to the expansion of villages in the Montreal region, particularly in the period 1815–1831 (Courville, 1984). There had always been artisans such as tanners and blacksmiths in the villages and towns, but now commodities were produced in smaller centres (Figure 4.11). In the Richelieu Valley village of Saint-Charles, for example, hat-making and pottery became important occupations. Further up the Richelieu, Saint-Jean became a centre for earthenware production. The appearance of coopers, tailors, and carriage makers in other small centres emphasizes the growing differentiation of the rural economy.

New crops and more specialization indicated that fundamental changes were occurring in the structure of Quebec farming. By the second decade of the nineteenth century, potatoes had become a staple in the peasant diet. The dairy industry had expanded in response to growing demand from both local urban populations and, later, export markets. Quebec livestock improved as a result, and greater quantities of fodder crops such as clover and hay were grown. By the end of the century, Quebec had 1992 cheese factories, many specializing in the production of cheddar for export to the British market.

The decline of Quebec wheat production and its disappearance from export markets is part, then, of a larger adjustment to changing economies and markets. Far from being backward, however, as Fernand Ouellet has suggested (1980: 120), these shifts in production were rational responses to market realities, enabling farmers to exploit expanding local markets and, later in the century, new British markets for dairy products.

The transition in dairying had important implications for the sexual division of labour in farm families. Farm women in preindustrial Quebec had traditionally been in charge of both animal husbandry and the production of butter for the family or for barter in the local community. Once export markets grew larger, so did

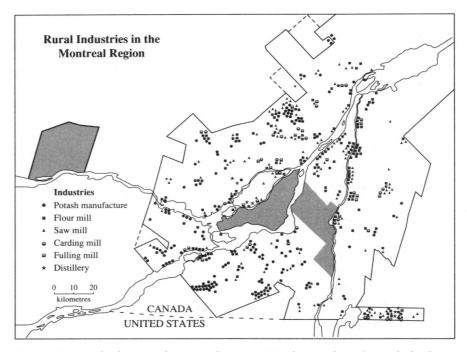

Figure 4.11 Rural industries in the Montreal area in 1831. The map shows their wide distribution and diversity. Relying on local agricultural surpluses, these industries produced for both local and export markets (Serge Courville, 1988).

investment in herds, buildings, and in new technology such as cream separators. The production of cheese and butter shifted from the home to local manufacturers, and women became distanced from economic power in dairying (Cohen, 1984).

During the period of the Reciprocity Treaty (1854–1866), exports of Quebec butter and cheese to American markets grew rapidly, especially from Huntingdon, Châteauguay, and Missisquoi counties. An infrastructure of dairy-production laws, inspectors, and producers' organizations, and improved refrigeration and ventilation on trains and ships led to greater Canadian access to British markets, accelerating the shift from production for home consumption to market production. The first Quebec creamery was opened in 1873 and by 1891 there were 112 in the province.

There is clear evidence of a growing landless peasantry during the nineteenth century who had no choice but to emigrate from some of the oldest rural regions. On the Ile d'Orléans near Quebec City, 41 percent of the heads of families in 1831 did not own property (Ouellet, 1980: 143). And although Quebec farmers had traditionally kept their farms a viable size rather than subdividing them infinitely among heirs, some farm division did occur in these conditions. Heavy colonization out of the St. Lawrence lowlands was underway by mid-century. Despite strong support from family networks, Catholic clergy, government, and colonization societies, colonists faced serious difficulties. Arable parts of the Shield and the Appalachians were isolated, and colonization roads proceeded only slowly, making it difficult to obtain supplies and to market potash, pork, and butter.

Francophone settlement of available parts of the Eastern Townships was often blocked by the presence of large land companies. With charters giving them ownership over huge tracts, these private companies responded to shareholders' considerations. Whatever their attitude to francophones, company officials had little enthusiasm for settlers without capital to buy land. Land settlement companies such as the British American Land Company simply abandoned their settlement mandates in favour of exploiting the pine and spruce resources of their lands through logging and sawmilling.

Francophones did migrate to forested regions of the townships, often as young married couples. Here they competed with the large timber companies as independent producers. In the 1850s the demand for unskilled labour in expanding industrial centres like Sherbrooke increased the presence of francophone wage labourers (Little, 1989a). By 1871, francophones were a majority in the Townships, although the anglophone minority remained dominant in economic power, in the wealth of their educational institutions, and in the visibility of the English language.

To the north of the St. Lawrence, settlers colonized Shield areas along the Ottawa, Saint-Maurice, and Saguenay systems. The Saguenay population grew from 3000 in 1844 to 19 800 in 1871; this represented about 1 percent of the Quebec population. North of Trois-Rivières, 1 200 000 hectares of grassland along the rivers of the Saint-Maurice system were suitable for agricultural settlement. A 160-kilometre colonization road was built in the Saint-Maurice Valley to help open up the region. Railway development also played an important role on the North Shore. Construction of the Grand Trunk Railway on the other side of the St. Lawrence in the 1850s led to the construction of four small steel mills in the Saint-Maurice Valley, while completion of the North Shore Railway in the 1870s stimulated local agricultural and industrial production. Between 1850 and 1875, fourteen new parishes were established in the region. The local population (including Trois-Rivières) grew from 30 000 in 1851 to 50 000 in 1881 (Hardy et Séguin, 1984:138).

∽◦∽

SOCIAL LIFE

Several benchmarks of social change can be examined for the transition period: the growth in power of the Roman Catholic Church (discussed in ch. 5); manifestations of popular resistance; religious and ethnic clashes; and the development of neighbourhoods segregated by class and ethnicity. Popular-class housing in

Figure 4.12 Saint-Roch, 1866. The Saint-Roch suburb of Quebec City was a popular-class community without public lighting, water, or sewers until the second half of the nineteenth century. Although labourers worked in the nearby shipyards, many artisans worked in shops near their homes. Households raised animals and produced food to meet part of their requirements. The housing and outbuildings in poorer urban areas were constructed of wood, whereas stone and, later, brick were favoured for bourgeois housing. Fires occurred regularly and their catastrophic dimensions are evident from this photo. The Saint-Roch fire of 1845 destroyed 1630 houses and 3000 workshops, boutiques, and outbuildings (Dechêne, 1981). This suburb was again ravaged in 1866. The Saint-Laurent and Sainte-Marie suburbs of Montreal were devastated by a major fire in 1852.

Quebec City suburbs developed near the shipyards and tanneries along the Saint-Charles River (Figure 4.12). By the late 1850s, working-class suburbs were developing in Montreal along the Lachine Canal and to the northeast of the old city. In Pointe St-Charles, the railway shops and canal-side factories had a range of industrial employees: labourers, foremen, ironworkers, rope makers, carpenters, mill workers, guards, paint-shop workers, bolt makers, and coppersmiths. Until tramways were extended into this area in the 1870s and 1880s, workers had to live near their work site. Some of these suburbs were ethnically mixed (Sainte-Anne and Pointe St-Charles for example), while farther along the canal Sainte-Cunégonde and Saint-Henri were predominantly francophone.

Until the 1840s, Saint-Henri was a tanning and shoemaking village separated from Montreal by the open countryside of the Sulpicians' seigneurial domain. In 1825, its population was 466, of whom 63 percent were involved in the leather trades: tanning, cobbling, saddlemaking. Lachine Canal expansion, road and rail construction, and subdivision of the seigneurial domain and local country estates into industrial estates and popular housing, placed Saint-Henri in the path of industrial development.

By the 1850s, leather production in the artisanal shops of Saint-Henri was giving way to "putting out," the system by which shoes were stitched by men and women working at home. By the 1870s, both putting out and artisanal shoemaking were declining fast in the face of a shoe factory with fifty employees, a steam-operated tannery with eighty employees, and two brick manufactures. In 1871, Saint-Henri's population was nearly 2500. Between 1879 and 1881, Saint-Henri reached another industrial plateau with the construction of huge industrial abattoirs, the Williams sewing machine factory, and the Merchants' Cotton Mill. The two latter factories employed large numbers of women (Lauzon and Ruelland, 1985).

Seventy-four percent of Saint-Henri residents were tenants. Onézime Bourelle and Philomène Mire were what might be considered a typical working-class couple in their community. Married in their home village of Saint-Isidore in 1857, they had worked in New England before settling in Saint-Henri where Bourelle found work as a policeman and later in the Redpath sugar refinery. With a household of nine, the Bourelles rented a four-room, second-floor flat in a wooden building of four apartments. One of the tenants, a milkman, paid extra rent for the backyard stable in which he kept seven cows. Each apartment had access to the courtyard where tenants had separate outside toilets and storage sheds. The Bourelles had neither a garden nor animals but their landlord, who occupied one of the apartments, kept a pig in the courtyard.

Bourgeois housing in Montreal was built in response to that class's demands for communities that would be isolated from popular-class housing and industrial activities. The housing in bourgeois neighbourhoods was characterized by single-family dwellings, and used different building materials and larger lots than did working-class housing. The francophone bourgeoisie built fashionable greystone houses up Saint-Denis and Saint-Hubert streets, while farther west their anglophone counterparts moved into the villa, terrace, and rowhouse subdivisions near the Mount Royal estates of the great Montreal capitalists. In one streetcar suburb, near what today is the Montreal Forum, ninety-three of ninety-four purchasers over a twenty-five-year period after 1860 had anglophone names. Property owners in this subdivision had six months to erect fences and to plant trees along their property fronts. Their deeds restricted land use to private residences, dictated fireproof roofs and stone and brick building materials, and prohibited construction within twelve feet of the street.

Like housing, cultural life was a function of class. In Saint-Hyacinthe, girls of the local elite spent their school holidays riding, walking in the woods, visiting friends, going to parties, flirting, making lace, and playing the piano. In the summer of 1876 the Dessaulles family took the train for a holiday on the Maine coast at Old Orchard Beach.

Despite her apparently frivolous lifestyle, fourteen-year-old Henriette Dessaulles had a sharp, critical mind, which she revealed in her observations of convent life, priests, and retreats.

> March is a time of tedious and ridiculous goings-on at the convent. If you are good, you earn a tissue-paper rose which you go and deposit solemnly in front of a tall ugly statute of St. Joseph. Every week you exchange your roses for a lily branch—made from the same dirty paper—that has a certain number of flowers on it according to how many roses you have earned. At the end of the month we all carry in procession our supply of lilies to poor old St. Joseph who looks as foolish as ever. I'm not blaming him because I realize he was *made* to look like this (1 March 1875).

> The retreat continues. All of it bores me except silence which I relish. . . . No, really, this [priest] is laughable with his way of seeing baseness everywhere, of talking only about the ugly side of human nature and of death and eternity, and with his senseless descriptions of the punishments that await us! (4 October 1875).

> He [Curé Prince] is much better at blowing his nose noisily in his red handkerchief than at hearing girls' confessions. I even think he has no idea creatures like us exist. For him there are priests, nuns, old parents, and perhaps boys (31 January 1876) (Dessaulles, 1971: 32, 68–69, 91).

In Montreal, the bourgeoisie established curling, cricket, tandem, and hunt clubs, and also enjoyed bowling (Figure 4.13). Men from the urban popular classes played lacrosse, hockey, and baseball. Horseracing, wrestling, boxing, and cockfighting drew large crowds. Swimming, previously confined to the dangerous and frigid St. Lawrence, became immensely popular with the opening of public

Figure 4.13   After lunch in the bowling alley, Cacouna. A village on the Lower St. Lawrence, Cacouna was a favourite holiday site for the Montreal bourgeoisie. As late Victorian women's dress became more formal, bowling must have been difficult.

baths in the 1880s. When a bath on a waste weir of the Lachine Canal was opened, 3296 men and boys came to swim in the first four days. Aside from overcrowding, which led to twenty-minute restrictions for swimmers, municipal authorities made a gesture for public morality by insisting that "frequenters of public baths wear bath trunks." Skating was another popular sport and by the 1870s private pay-rinks had been opened on vacant lots across the city. Other popular recreational activities included parades, sledding, picnics, circuses, band concerts, fireworks, and music halls. After 1853, Viger Gardens with its three acres of trees, its greenhouse, fountains, walks, and free public concerts became the most popular park in Montreal.

Taverns were an important part of the popular culture of Quebec males, and Montreal was reputed to have a tavern for every 150 inhabitants (DeLottinville, 1981–1982:12) In addition to being places to drink, taverns served as centres for other forms of popular recreation: gambling, billiards, music, and political debate (Figure 4.14).

Figure 4.14 Victorian authorities' concept of prevalent vices. There was a sharp gender division in morality: men succumbed to drink, snuff, card-playing, and gluttony while women were prone to vanity, tea, and gossip.

WOMEN

The transition period posed particular problems for women, especially those who could not fall back on family networks. Their responsibilities in the preindustrial family—preparing food, caring for domestic animals, and providing clothing—had different dimensions in an urban, industrial society that emphasized wage labour, tenancy, the exchange economy, and consumerism. Until pressure from city fathers made it increasingly difficult, urban families persisted in keeping animals: horses, cows, poultry, and pigs. The latter two were of particular importance in the diet of the popular classes; the decline of pigs after 1861 (Table 4.7) emphasizes the effect of municipal regulations on the popular classes' family survival strategies. Urban families were forced to buy rather than to produce meat.

Widows and unmarried or deserted women without capital faced desperate conditions. The number of female family heads was large: in 1881, 30 percent of women in Montreal over the age of forty were widows. Generally without capital or wage-labour experience, they took work in which they used their domestic skills—cleaning, washing, cooking—or ran boarding houses or taverns:

> When Widow McGrath lost her husband, she was left with three children aged 4 to 9. She took in two other widows, one with an 11-year old child. Two of them worked as a washerwoman, one sold goods at market. Between them they kept five pigs, probably eating some, and raising cash by selling others (Bradbury, 1984).

Women had traditionally worked alongside their husbands in shops and market stalls representing what has been called "the hidden investment" of women in family enterprises. Deserted wives or single women found a means of livelihood in the markets, grocery shops, and taverns. Four of thirty-one stalls at the Saint-Anne market in Montreal (1834) were leased to women. In 1850, Montreal's sixteen female tavernkeepers represented 9.2 percent of the city's licensed taverns.

Year	Horses	Milk cows	Pigs	Poultry
1851	2077	1528	1877	—
1861	2892	2160	2644	—
1871	3530	1837	831	—
1881	4479	1658	180	—
1891	6751	1290	92	9589

Table 4.7   Animals in Montreal, 1861–1891

(Adapted from Bradbury, 1984: 15)

POPULAR RESISTANCE

Popular resistance was often manifested in the transition period. In the early part of the century, traditional signs of community control such as charivaris were evident in Montreal. In 1821, for example, popular mores were offended by the marriage of an older widow to a younger man. A crowd of 500 gathered outside the newlyweds' house in Montreal and, after a battle with the constables, extorted some money for the Female Benevolent Society from the couple.

Mobs, riots, and strikes were regular features of urban life; indeed, arson and riots became regular parts of the popular celebration of holidays. By Confederation, Queen Victoria's birthday had become an important occasion for gang wars in Irish neighbourhoods of Montreal:

> armed with bludgons and stones, they escaped the vigilance of police who were too busily engaged at the Champs de Mars. They arrived at the Bonsecours market and commenced an onslaught on the French Canadian street arabs who reside in that locality. Stones and sticks flew about in all directions until the arrival of a few policemen dispersed the juvenile delinquents (*Montreal Gazette*, 25 May 1867).

Judicial records show a broad variety of social deviance within the popular classes. Crimes associated with drunkenness (drunk, disorderly, disturbing the peace) accounted for 5358 (4313 men, 1045 women) of the 11 135 Montreal arrests in 1870. The largest occupational groups among the arrested were labourers (2121), vagrants (895), prostitutes (843), carters (727), shoemakers (302), clerks (235), and tavernkeepers (170). Some measure of work-site resistance early in the transition period can be gleaned from "crime" statistics for servants. The four most important crimes, representing eighty-two of 144 arrests of servants in Quebec City, 1816–1820, were for desertion (38), absence without leave (18), poor conduct (14), and disturbance, nuisance, and damage (12) (Lacelle, 1987: 52).

Election disturbances were endemic and the Riot Act, stones, clubs, and firearms were never far from the poll box. In the particularly bitter 1844 election, a brewery worker was knocked unconscious, stripped, and wakened to "find himself naked except his legs." In Quebec City and Montreal, anti-Catholic speeches by the ex-monk Alexandre Gavazzi brought Irish Catholics into the streets and left ten dead. During the 1885 smallpox epidemic, whole neighbourhoods in Montreal resisted violently as public health officials tried to vaccinate the population. The Archbishop of Montreal ordered his priests not to interfere with doctors and to reassure their parishoners.

Some of the strongest popular resistance occurred in the countryside. The creation of municipal governments and school commissions in the 1840s and particularly the local bureaucracies and taxation that accompanied them, led to widespread revolt. In the second half of the decade, the "guerre des éteignoirs"—social protest against school taxes—raged in the Trois-Rivières region. Clergy and professionals generally supported the education reforms, but the landed elite and the peasantry openly revolted:

> "The Municipal council [of St. Grégoire]," the MLA for Nicolet wrote [to] L.-H. LaFontaine in March 1850, "could not meet last Monday because Mr. L.M. Cressé brought down 150 Irishmen armed with bludgeons. There is an organized conspiracy in the parishes to destroy schoolhouses and burn the property of school commissioners who do their duty. The county will soon be in a state of anarchy" (Nelson, 1989).

NATIVE PEOPLES

Native peoples' work experience in industrializing society was often parallel to that of white workers. Like other forest workers in the Ottawa Valley, the Mohawks, established at Kahnawake since the 1670s, combined garden-farming with work in the fur and timber trade. Esteemed across Canada as canoeists, transport workers, and packers in the fur trade, Kahnawake men were later highly skilled river drivers and timber rafters. At Kanesatake on the Lake of Two Mountains seigneury, the Seminary of Montreal had 200 homes occupied by Mohawks and Algonquins who lived as tenant farmers or forest workers (Dessureault, 1986: 219).

In the North, the Cree and the Inuit had important resources with which to maintain their cultural independence from the influence of both white traders and missionaries. Along James Bay, the Cree worked with the Hudson's Bay Company as labourers, guides, provisioners, voyageurs, and manufacturers of essential means of transportation such as canoes and snowshoes. Inland Cree had only limited contact with the company. By the mid-nineteenth century, the company negotiated peace between the Cree and Inuit and started benefiting from Inuit whale-hunting, sealing, and trapping (Francis and Morantz, 1983).

With the intrusion of William Price's logging activities along the North Shore, the Montagnais increasingly saw their traditional subsistence patterns threatened. In 1849, the Montagnais living at Betsiamites demanded compensation and a large territory for a reserve. The government refused compensation, finally establishing a smaller reserve in 1861. The decline in hunting and trapping led many Montagnais to seek employment in the timber shanties and as canoeists and guides for prospectors and recreational hunters (Bédard, 1988).

CONCLUSION

The impact of the transition on Quebec as a whole can be symbolized visually by using Saint-Hyacinthe as an example. Great changes occurred here from the mid-1830s to 1881 (Figures 4.15 and 4.16). On the other hand, the process was complex

Figure 4.15 Saint-Hyacinthe circa 1836. In the 1830s, Saint-Hyacinthe was a village of 1000 inhabitants. Its size, the physical dominance of its parish church, and its intimate relationship to the countryside emphasize its preindustrial vocation. The seigneur, Jean Dessaulles (1766–1835), was the dominant local figure. As well as sitting in the Assembly, he decided the sites for the bridge, market, courthouse, and classical college.

Figure 4.16 A bird's-eye view of Saint-Hyacinthe in 1881. By 1881, the village had become an industrial city of 5321. Indicative of its transition to industrialization are the urban growth, the railways, the new bridges, dams, and water technology, as well as the expansion of educational facilities evident from the seminary at the top right of the picture. In the foreground, water power is being used in the knitting mill and tannery, while closer to the railway a foundry smokestack is evident. The city also included a corset factory, a shoe manufacture, its own bank, and a cathedral.

within regions, and within sectors such as leather processing, agriculture, and even manufacturing, the transition to industrial capitalism was uneven. The overlapping of preindustrial and industrial life, the new power of capital, and changing forms of labour had profound influence on social relations, political life, and institutional structures in Quebec.

⌒

FURTHER READING

GENERAL WORKS

Both strongly contested, Fernand Ouellet's *Lower Canada 1791–1840: Social Change and Nationalism* and Stanley Ryerson's *Unequal Union: Confederation and the Roots of Conflict in the Canadas, 1815–1873* are useful starting points for the economic history of the period. Two important works show differing elements of the rural economy: Serge Courville, *Entre ville et campagne*, and Jack Little, *Crofters and Habitants: Settler Society, Economy, and Culture in a Quebec Township, 1848–1881*. For a challenge to the staple thesis see the provocative case study of firewood in Robert Sweeny, Grace Laing Hogg, and Richard Rice, *Les relations ville/campagne: le cas de bois de chauffage*.

RURAL LIFE

For the rural crisis debate see Joseph Goy and Jean-Pierre Wallot, *Evolution et éclatement du monde rural, France–Quebec, XVIIe–XXe siècles*, especially the articles by Louise Dechêne and Louis Michel. Rural life is described succinctly in Serge Courville and Normand Séguin's booklet, *Rural Life in Nineteenth-Century Quebec*. Agriculture and settlement in the townships has been described in several places by Jack Little; a good starting place for Little's work is *Nationalism, Capitalism, and Colonization in Nineteenth-Century Quebec: The Upper Saint-Francis District*. This should be compared to Normand Séguin, *La conquête du sol au 19e siècle*, and René Hardy and Normand Séguin, *Forêt et société en Mauricie*. Emigration is soundly treated through a case study of Berthier county in Bruno Ramirez's *On the Move: French-Canadian and Italian Migrants in the North Atlantic Economy, 1860–1914*. The careers of seigneurs Papineau and Joliette are described in R. Cole Harris, "Of Poverty and Helplessness in Petite Nation," and Jean-Claude Robert, "Un seigneur entrepreneur, Barthélemy Joliette, et la fondation du village d'Industrie (Joliette)." For discussion of the seigneur as industrial producer see David Schulze, "Rural Manufacture in Lower Canada: Understanding Seigneurial Privilege and the Transition in the Countryside."

URBANIZATION AND CLASS RELATIONS

For cholera, see Geoffrey Bilson, *A Darkened House: Cholera in Nineteenth-Century Canada*. On Irish immigration H.C. Pentland's *Labour and Capital in Canada* should be compared to Donald Akenson, *The Irish in Ontario: A Study in Rural History*. The development of an urban parish is described effectively in Lucia Ferretti's *Entre Voisins. La Société paroissiale en milieu urbain: Saint-Pierre-Apôtre de Montréal, 1848–1930*. Bettina Bradbury's several works are the best source for family relations in Montreal. A useful starting point for her work is "Gender at Work at Home," in her collection *Canadian Family History: Selected Readings*.

BUSINESS

The Montreal business community is discussed in Gerald Tulchinsky's *The River Barons: Montreal Businessmen and the Growth of Industry and Transportation, 1837–53*. Still useful is Tom Naylor's *The History of Canadian Business, 1867–1914*. For francophone banking see Ronald Rudin, *Banking en français: the French Banks of Quebec 1835–1925*. Paul Craven and Tom Traves's emphasis on railways as industrial producers is found in their "Canadian Railways as Manufacturers, 1850–1880." For the significance of the Victoria Bridge see Stanley Triggs, Brian Young, Conrad Graham, and Gilles Lauzon, *Victoria Bridge: The Vital Link*. For development of the Lachine Canal see Larry McNally, *Water Power on the Lachine Canal, 1846–1900*, and John Willis, *The Process of Hydraulic Industrialization on the Lachine Canal 1840–80: Origins, Rise and Fall*. For a case study of industrialization in a regional centre see Kathleen Lord, *Municipal and Industrial Development: Saint-Jean, Quebec, 1848–1914*.

LABOUR

Fernand Harvey's *Le mouvement ouvrier au Québec* describes the Knights of Labor in Quebec. A repertory of strikes can be found in Jean Hamelin, Paul Larocque, and Jacques Rouillard, *Répertoire des grèves dans la province de Québec au XIXe siècle*, while Bryan Palmer's *Working-Class Experience: Rethinking the History of Canadian Labour, 1800–1991* gives a useful overview of the Canadian situation. For examples of carters and shoemakers see Margaret Heap, "La grève des charretiers à Montréal, 1865," and Joanne Burgess, "L'industrie de la chaussure à Montréal: 1840–1870—le passage de l'artisanat à la fabrique." Much of the material on tanning is taken from Jacques Ferland's *Evolution des rapports sociaux dans l'industrie canadienne du cuir au tournant du 20e siècle*. Although the focus of her book is Ontario, Marjorie Griffin Cohen describes women's work effectively in *Women's Work, Markets, and Economic Development in Nineteenth-Century Ontario*.

Politics and Institutions
in Transition, 1810s–1880s

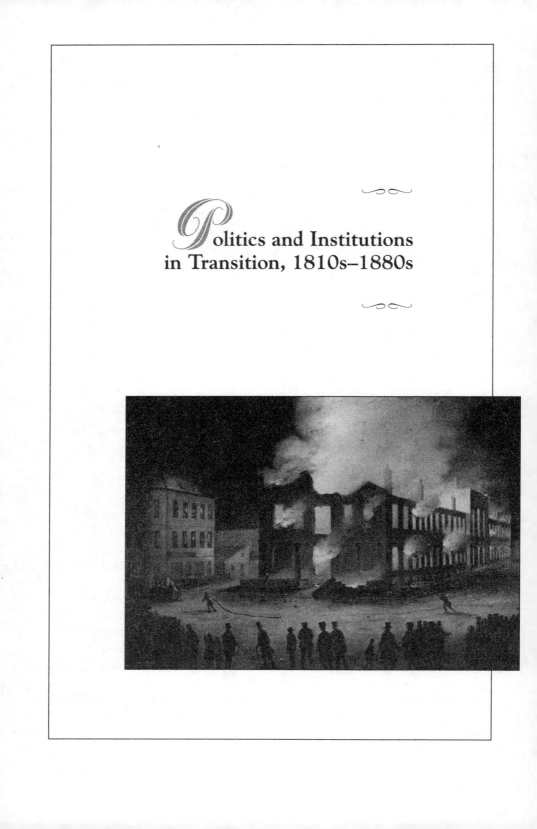

*I*mportant social, political, religious, institutional, and cultural change accompanied the transition to industrial capitalism in Quebec. Despite the presence of an elected assembly, real political power in 1816 was still in the hands of the governor and executive. Lower Canadian institutional structures were rudimentary, although important for enforcing authority.

The rebellions of 1837–1838 and consequent restructuring of Canadian public life in the 1840s were a watershed in Canadian political development, ending the struggle between legislative and executive power in Quebec constitutional history. Responsible government, a party system, and an alliance of centrist political elements in Upper and Lower Canada were evidence that the legislature now asserted power over the executive and that the main elements of the British cabinet system had been installed.

Bourgeois democracy on the British model was accompanied by other important political changes. In the 1840s, the first significant elements of federalism appeared in the political and administrative structure of the united Canadas. Education, justice, and local government assumed their Ontario and Quebec particularities. Federalism came to fruition in Confederation. By the 1880s, the Riel crisis and other John A. Macdonald government policies confirmed that Quebec had only the status of a minority in the Canadian state and that its provincial government was simply a local administration.

The final important political element of the period was the formation in Quebec of a centralized and bureaucratized state. Justice, education, and the administration of crown lands, local railways, municipalities, and colonization gave Quebec greatly expanded powers over isolated regions.

Bourgeois democracy, federalism, and the formation of the bureaucratic state corresponded to changing social relations. By the 1880s, the preindustrial autocracy—the colonial bureaucracy, seigneurs, clerical elite, and great merchants—had ceded much of its power to industrial capitalists and their allies in the francophone professional and political elite. Far from being reactionary, this elite used its new political power to reshape preindustrial structures into forms that responded to its economic and social interests.

As part of the realignment of classes after the 1838 rebellions, an important element in the Quebec bourgeoisie allied itself with the Roman Catholic church, which had emerged in a stronger position. The bourgeoisie and the clergy had a common interest in French-Canadian nationalism and the power that would result from increased Lower Canadian autonomy in social, educational, and moral matters. The realignment of elite groups in Lower Canada produced vigorous state sponsorship of transportation and industrial development, and also extended the church's authority to shape social and educational institutions for the popular classes.

The function and power of the Catholic church changed dramatically during the transition. At the end of the preindustrial period, the Lower Canadian church was weak. The number of clergy had been declining and the religious, property, and civil powers of the church were in question under British administration. In the countryside, the church faced an increasing challenge from the petty bourgeoisie over ideological, social, and taxing power.

The church had been a consistent supporter of established authority, in both the French and British regimes. This support was particularly precious in 1837–1838 and was symbolized by bishops Lartigue and Signay describing insurrection and violence as "criminal in the eyes of God and of our Holy Religion." The church had a particularly important role in defusing popular unrest. In the countryside, parish priests received clear instructions from the bishops to support established British authority and the divine right of the monarchy. As parish priests of Montreal, the Sulpicians had a strong influence on Irish Catholics and were a key force in channelling Irish popular discontent away from the Patriotes, a political group they perceived as radical, anti-establishment, and potentially anticlerical. Governor general Lord Durham recognized the importance of this intervention: "The priests have an almost unlimited influence over the lower classes of Irish; and this influence is said to have been very vigorously exerted last winter, when it was much needed, to secure the loyalty of a part of the Irish during the troubles."

Other fundamental elements of social organization, particularly the law, landholding structures, and political, educational, and social institutions, took new form in the 1840s and 1850s. Quebec seigneurialism and civil law were reformed in favour of freehold property and individual rights such as freedom to contract and to sell one's labour. New institutions were directed at controlling the rural and urban popular classes. A universal education system, a province-wide judicial fabric of courthouses, rural police, and jails, new municipalities, and new forms of taxation subjugated Quebecers' minds and wallets to a bureaucratized and centralized state.

Culture was an important force in this changing structure. It may at first seem paradoxical that French-Canadian nationalism was encouraged, on the one hand, by elements in the church that rejected the values of the French Revolution and, on the other hand, by francophone leaders who supported Quebec's integration into the larger Canadian state. The explanation lies in the changing Quebec elite and its need to manage popular ideology. The popular classes resisted being told what to think and so adhered to their network of family, tavern, friendly society, labour union, and neighbourhood. To combat such independence, lay and clerical intellectuals formulated a unifying, conservative national ideology rooted in

Catholicism, the French language, the preindustrial family, and an idealization of rural life. Women became important deputies in propagating this ideology in the enclaves of both convent and domestic life.

THE STATE AND ECONOMIC DEVELOPMENT

In preindustrial society, the state had provided little infrastructure for transportation or communication. Fortifications, troop expenditures, and administrative costs for the colony far outdistanced moneys spent on public works to facilitate trade or industry. The mercantilist state favoured its friends with monopolies, army contracts, and protection on the high seas.

State attitudes to economic development changed in the early nineteenth century as military and economic conditions evolved. Symbolically, the fortifications of Montreal were torn down by 1818 and the state began to invest its military budget in canals and roads (Legault, 1986). The Lachine, Chambly, St. Lawrence, and Rideau canals represented massive injections of state capital and most served double duty: acting as military routes and enabling St. Lawrence trade routes to compete with American systems.

By mid-century Lower Canadian/Quebec governments entered enthusiastically into the railway lottery as communities and regions competed for rail service and access to trunk lines. In the budget year 1876–1877, the Quebec government spent $3 481 670 on railways and $407 176 to service public debts for railway construction, compared to $66 000 on provincial police (1875), $233 410 on education (1875), and $11 000 on colonization roads (1875).

A fundamental change in ideology accompanied this process. Taxation in preindustrial society often took the form of labour or customs duties. Road construction had traditionally been accomplished by statute labour (the corvée). In the 1760s, every habitant—under penalty of a 20-shilling fine—was to provide eight days of road labour as well as maintaining the roads on his land. After 1815, the crown began to subsidize royal roads while municipalities assumed responsibility for local roads; later in the century, colonization roads giving access to timber regions were subsidized by the state. Statute labour was replaced by tenders, toll roads, and taxes (Robichaud, 1989: 23, 33).

Under the Guarantee Act of 1849 and the Municipal Act of 1852 both the central government and the municipalities helped to finance railways. In 1870, the Quebec government put aside 3 208 500 acres of crown land to sponsor railway construction on the north shore of the St. Lawrence; in 1872, Montreal taxpayers approved a subsidy of $1 million for the Montreal Colonization Railway. The result was a new partnership of capital and state in Quebec's transportation system. Politicians and entrepreneurs, enthusiastically supported by the church, moved freely from board room to cabinet.

POLITICAL STRUGGLE

The early decades of the century were characterized by political and social struggle between the preindustrial elite that controlled the executive and the francophone professionals who dominated the assembly. The governor and executive council came under increasing attack in the press and in the assembly from lawyers, notaries, doctors, innkeepers, and small merchants. Of the members of the assembly in the pre-rebellion period of 1792–1836, 77.4 percent were merchants or professionals (Ouellet, 1980: 188).

The assembly challenged the executive for control of patronage in the bureaucracy, militia, and judiciary. An 1829 report noted that twenty-two of thirty-nine magistrates in Montreal were natives of Great Britain and only seven were French Canadians. The same report accused government official Robert Christie of abusing judicial autonomy by dismissing hostile magistrates at will, "of acting as a spy upon the conduct and votes of the Members of this House," and of bringing "contempt upon this office of the Magistracy."

Military and canal construction represented the largest building projects of the period, and government contracts were therefore important factors in the local economy. At the same time, provisioning the British army produced some of the largest supply contracts for local merchants. British patronage in these sectors usually favoured well-placed anglophones in what was known as the Chateau Clique.

As well, francophone professionals, politicians, and speculators resented the large, anglophone land companies that by the 1830s controlled development in the Eastern Townships. Attacks on the monopoly and settlement practices of these companies raised issues about colonization and French-Canadian nationalism and thus appealed to both the landless peasantry and the church.

The bad blood of contracts, patronage, and power was worsened by conflict over status. Ethnic slurs became common coin as prominent francophone notaries, lawyers, surveyors, and doctors found themselves far down the local colonial pecking order. Social precedence and the order used at official gatherings was that of England: royalty, clergy, nobility, royal household officials, military, professional classes, artisans, labourers (Senior, 1981: 39). But more was at stake than the defensive action of what Fernand Ouellet calls a class looking "for someone to blame" (cited in Cook, 1969: 54). The basic issue was power in a flotsam that included centralization and bureaucratization of the state, urbanization and industrialization.

Despite ethnic tension, there is strong evidence of political consensus on financial, regulatory, and developmental policy for projects such as roads, bridges, canals, and railways. Alan Dever (1976) has shown, for example, that 82 percent of the motions for economic development in the assembly passed unanimously and he concludes that "conflict was the exception rather than the rule." Many members supported the efforts of millers, urban landowners, and manufacturers to lift preindustrial restrictions on the free movement of property and labour. Nor were all anglophones associated with reaction and toryism. Some in the assembly were members of the *parti canadien* and later the Patriotes: Marcus Child of Stanstead, Ephraim Knight of Missisquoi, and James Stuart and Robert Nelson of Montreal. Some of them, John Neilson, W.H. Scott, and E.B. O'Callaghan, represented francophone ridings.

After 1840, consensus in favour of economic development was clear in the all-party support given to canal, railway, and industrial development. Etienne Parent, editor of *Le Canadien*, emphasized that the future of the francophone bourgeoisie was tied to industrial capitalism:

> the industrialists are the lords of America; and their claim to nobility is better justified and more enduring than that of your noblemen in the old world. Neither misfortune nor revolution can destroy them. It is through industry's struggle against hostile elements that countless cities and empires have been conquered, not with sword and bloodshed, but with spade and sweat. For this, gentlemen, industry must be honoured, not just through words and gestures but through action (1846).

Until the 1830s, reformers generally favoured British parliamentary democracy, despite talk of republicanism and French-Canadian nationalism. There was less consensus among them on the separation of church and state, reform of the Custom of Paris, and the abolition of seigneurialism. The issue of control, particularly financial, in proposed systems of universal primary education acted as a perennial lightning rod in relations between the church and liberal elements in the francophone bourgeoisie. Attempts in the first decades of the century to establish education on the British model of the Royal Institutes of Learning remained largely a dead letter in francophone communities. The 1824 church-wardens' law represented a compromise by the assembly. While respecting clerical sensitivities, it would have established some secular control over parish finances and therefore some control over school construction. It gave the churchwardens—lay officials who were on a middle ground between the parish priest and the community—the right to use one-quarter of their funds for school construction. An 1829 law went further and separated education from local clerical influence by entrusting school authority to civil officers: members of the assembly and an elected syndic (Chabot, 1975).

As local doctors and notaries became more radical and contested clerical power, parish priests began worrying about their ability to control the peasantry. In 1831 a prominent priest warned, "It is time to organize ourselves before the nationalist and liberal effervescence turns everyone's head. Already they are speaking out against the priests and episcopal authority in the legislative assembly." The ideology of local professionals and merchants was rendered more dangerous by their growing numbers in relation to the clergy.

In its struggle in the political arena, the bourgeoisie who controlled the assembly concentrated on three main demands: responsible government, control of the civil list (most taxes needed to pay local officials required assembly approval), and an elected legislative council. Until the 1830s these fundamental political reforms were demanded within the cadre of British constitutional tactics: attempts to impeach the chief justice, petitions to Westminster, and blockage of government bills. For their part, British authorities, frustrated by the actions of the popularly elected assembly, drew on their autocratic political powers. Sessions were suspended, elections were rigged, the assembly's nomination of Patriote leader Louis-Joseph Papineau as speaker was refused, and opposition newspaper editors were jailed. In the escalating political crisis, the Riot Act, the army, and ultimately martial law were used to impose authority.

As the issues of educational policy, taxation, control of the bureaucracy, and reform of the landholding and judicial systems became more crucial in industrializing society, the stakes became higher. In Westminster, the Union Bill (1822) was introduced into the British Parliament. Proposing to unite Upper and Lower Canada and to abolish French as an official language, the terminology of the bill—"all written proceedings of the [assembly and legislative council] shall be in the *English* language and none other"—left no doubt as to the future of French Canadians and their bourgeoisie in a united Canada.

Although never passed, the bill was a milestone in the evolution of what became the Patriote movement. John Neilson, a Scot and editor of the *Quebec Gazette*, was among those who joined the reform movement. He wrote to Papineau: "What fate have the inhabitants of this country to hope for from people who proceed in such fashion?" Protest delegations were sent to England and some 50 000 Lower Canadians signed petitions opposing the bill.

THE REBELLIONS OF 1837-1838

By the late 1820s, Louis-Joseph Papineau was becoming more nationalist, more republican, and more critical of British constitutional practice. In the early 1830s, rallies, marches, secret societies, riots, and radical newspapers like *La Minerve* and the *Vindicator* made it clear that the struggle of the bourgeoisie in the assembly had larger revolutionary potential. Following the July 1830 revolution in France, law and medical students scaled the wall of Montreal's most prestigious classical college, le Collège de Montréal, hanged a teacher in effigy, and left the tricolour of the French Revolution on the school flagpole.

The term *parti patriote*, first used in 1827 to designate the *parti canadien*, became common after 1832—a year that saw the arrest of leading reformers, riots, and a cholera epidemic. The Patriotes approved a tricolour flag of green, white, and red (not the red, white, and blue of the French Revolution) and, under Papineau's leadership, attracted broad support that included Louis-Hippolyte La Fontaine, Etienne Parent, and Ludger Duvernay.

In 1835, protestors broke windows at the Seminary of Montreal and threw into the courtyard an effigy of the superior wearing the ears of an ass. In the 1830s, Saint-Jean Baptiste day was a rowdy, nationalist festival that celebrated French Canada's patron saint with revolutionary songs and toasts to the United States.

Social unrest was not limited to the bourgeoisie. Francophone artisans and labourers in Montreal, Quebec City, and the Ottawa Valley had to compete with cheap Irish labour and with new forms of labour organization that included large work sites, company stores, and contract day labour.

The Quebec peasantry faced failing local economies, emigration, and, in certain regions, increasing dependence on wage labour in the agro-forest economy. In 1825, censitaires petitioned that seigneurs were violating seigneurial law by refusing to make concessions, by stripping land of timber before conceding it, and by increasing the rates of seigneurial dues. On Papineau's own seigneury, only ten of his censitaires were not in debt to him by 1832 and during the 1830s he used the courts to obtain judgments and enforce payment (Baribeau, 1983: 138). In 1838, the Sulpicians reported that the annual arrears of their rural censitaires on the Ile de Montréal averaged a total of £433 over the past thirty years. On another seigneury in the Montreal area, two-thirds of the censitaires were in arrears by the late 1830s.

The peasantry had a long tradition of poaching, evading tithes, and cheating on seigneurial dues. Debts, lack of land for their children, and the possibility of famine in the 1830s made their mood potentially dangerous.

The bourgeoisie tried to instill more submissive attitudes in the peasantry. Joseph-François Perrault, chief clerk of Quebec City, drew up rules for justices of the peace (1789) and a student manual for criminal law (1814). His *Rural Code* (*Code rural à l'usage des habitants tant anciens que nouveaux du Bas-Canada*) (1832) outlines the civic and religious duties of peasants and shows the merging of church and state in principles such as the civic duty to serve as churchwarden, to pay tithes, to educate children, to serve in the militia, to repair roads, and to have all contracts drawn up by a notary. His support for the church was clear: "One can judge the zeal of the habitants for their religion by the beauty of their church, by their consideration for their priest, by the size of the presbytery, and of their respect for the dead by the state of the cemetery." Far from being stuffy, remote legal processes, these codes directly affected everyday life and were part of a larger attempt to regiment the population.

Throughout the 1810s–1880s period, imperial, provincial, and municipal authorities took measures to control the popular classes of countryside and city. The British Combination Acts (1800), Master and Servant Laws, and provincial legislation concerning the desertion of apprentices (1802) and worker sabotage (1841) impeded union formation and strikes. In 1821, special police regulations in Montreal required workers to give fifteen days notice before quitting their employment (Tremblay, 1983).

In the same period, tavern and market regulations were tightened. Leisure time was perceived as a particular threat. Between 1817 and 1826, Montreal magistrates forbade not only charivaris, gaming at city markets, and firing guns to celebrate birthdays, but even skating and sledding within the city.

At the same time, the struggle between the Patriotes (whose power base was in the assembly) and the executive intensified. Particularly in Montreal, magistrates were increasingly forced to call out the troops. An especially bloody riot broke out in 1832 in Montreal's West Ward, where the Patriotes nominated Daniel Tracey for election. Tracey was editor of the *Vindicator*—which supported Irish and Patriote measures—and had been recently released from jail for libel. There was no secret ballot in this period and voting occurred over several days. After recurrent clashes, the Riot Act was read, the troops opened fire, and three French Canadians were left dead on St. James Street (Figure 5.1). While Governor Aylmer described it as an "accidental circumstance," Patriotes renamed St. James Street the "Street of Blood" (Senior, 1981: 20). Two days after his bloody election victory, Tracey died of cholera.

The Patriotes' fate was increasingly linked to Louis-Joseph Papineau's leadership and ideology. Papineau's grandfather had been an artisan; his father's professional success as a notary and surveyor improved the family fortunes and enabled him to purchase a seigneury. Papineau studied law but spent most of his life in politics. Personal idiosyncrasies, incapacity to provide forceful leadership in an armed rebellion, and ideological confusion over the relative importance of Catholicism, the bourgeoisie, and seigneurialism marked his career. Many of his

Figure 5.1 Riots in Montreal. As the political system imposed in 1791 became increasingly paralysed by constitutional deadlock between the assembly and executive, British authorities turned more frequently to garrison troops. According to military historian Elinor Senior (1981: 72), the use of troops became "almost a normal military operation during Montreal elections." The Riot Act and troops were used in elections in 1832, 1844, 1846, and 1847, during strikes in 1843, for the civil disturbances of 1849, and in the religious riots of 1853. The imposition of martial law, with its suspension of ordinary government and justice, was more serious. Virtually unused in England, martial law was applied in Lower Canada for several months during the rebellions of 1837 and again in 1838. Legal historians like Jean-Marie Fecteau (1987: 495) see a parallel between the application of martial law and the War Measures Act, which was applied in Quebec in 1970.

colleagues shared his ambiguity over social, religious, and nationalist goals, shaping the first rebellion in 1837 into an essentially socially conservative and nationalist effort.

Papineau concentrated his increasingly ethnic attacks on the great commercial capitalists, deflecting Patriotes who wanted to stir latent popular hostility into a common front against the church, seigneurs, great merchants, and British authoritarianism. Ultimately, he defended the church, Quebec civil law, and the seigneurial system as bastions of his definition of the "national" cause:

> in Papineau's scheme of thought the social equilibrium would rest upon two fundamental institutions, so far as these could be restored to their original meaning: seigneurial tenure and French common law. The first seemed essentially favourable to an equal distribution of landed property, when the seigneur was conceived of as the guardian of social equality and as an insurmountable

> obstacle to capitalist speculation. It possessed, moreover, what seemed to
> Papineau a further great advantage, that of maintaining the individuality of
> Lower Canada in the face of the surrounding Anglo-Saxon bloc. Thanks to
> the French common law, the indispensable support of the seigneurial regime,
> Lower Canada would be ready to develop in the true sense of its traditions
> (Ouellet, 1964: 12–13).

In February 1834, the assembly, complaining that it had been "insulted" and "trampled under foot" by the governor, passed the Ninety-two Resolutions. Expressing support for American republicanism, the resolutions threatened to impeach the governor. Although passage of the document cost the support of many moderates, 80 000 Lower Canadians signed petitions supporting the resolutions and in elections held later in 1834, Patriote candidates won seventy-seven of the assembly's eighty-eight seats.

By 1835, frustrated anglophone militants were holding mass meetings and forming vigilante groups: the British Rifle Corps, the Montreal British Legion, and the Doric Club. William Lyon Mackenzie, leader of the radical faction in Upper Canada, and Papineau in Lower Canada both leaned towards militancy. The Patriotes formed a liaison with British reform groups like the Chartists. A paramilitary group, the Fils de la Liberté, was established as an offshoot of the Patriotes and acted as a security force for them. The group was modelled after the American Sons of Liberty.

Colonial Secretary Lord Russell's rejection of the principles of the Ninety-two Resolutions brought the political crisis to a climax. With warrants out for their arrest in the fall of 1837, Patriote leaders fled to the countryside where revolutionary activity centred in the Richelieu Valley and Two Mountains areas. On 23 October, a six-county Patriote rally in Saint-Charles denounced executive oligarchy and called for the popular election of magistrates and militia officers. Bishop Lartigue's pastoral letter was read in Montreal on 24 October, in which he urged people "not to be seduced by those who want to entice you into rebellion against established government." In response, 1200 Patriotes massed in front of his cathedral singing the Marseillaise and chanting "Long live Papineau."

The first important confrontation with British troops took place on 23 November 1837 in the Richelieu Valley community of Saint-Denis. In an all-day battle 800 Patriotes under Dr. Wolfred Nelson beat back British troops. Nonetheless, the church's condemnation of revolution, Papineau's weak military leadership, the failure to marshal peasant support, and ineffective military organization hindered sustained Patriote resistance. After a British victory in Saint-Charles on 25 November the rebellions subsided in counties on the south shore of the St. Lawrence. Papineau and other Patriote leaders escaped into exile in the United States.

In Montreal, the church hierarchy feared all-out attack. Montreal remained quiet, however, and it was to the north in the Two Mountains area where resistance was sustained. On 14 December, some 2000 troops attacked Patriotes barricaded inside the church at Saint-Eustache; fifty-eight Patriote defenders were killed. In the sack that followed, sixty houses and barns were burned and two days later the Patriote village of Saint-Benoît was torched and looted.

The rebellions of 1838 were more revolutionary in their goals. With Papineau in exile, leadership was taken by the more radical Robert Nelson: "Papineau has abandoned us for selfish and family motives regarding the seigneuries and his inveterate love of the old French laws. We can do better without him. . . . " (Ouellet, 1980: 312). There was also a deep reservoir of hostility against authorities, particularly magistrates.

On 28 February, Nelson entered Canada near Alburg, Vermont with 160 men. Before being forced back into the United States by local militia, Nelson declared Lower Canada a republic and issued a Proclamation of Independence calling for separation of church and state, and state expropriation of the clergy reserves and the lands of the British American Land Company. Confessional schools would be abolished; French and English were both declared official languages; the Chartist goals of universal suffrage, a secret ballot, and freedom of the press were affirmed; the death sentence was abrogated; and native peoples were to enjoy the rights of all other citizens. The most important differences between the goals of 1837 and 1838 were over land tenure and the social relations of seigneurialism. The Proclamation stated that "seigneurial tenure is hereby abolished as if it had never existed in this country. Every person who bears arms or furnishes help to the Canadian people in its struggle for emancipation is discharged from all debts [. . .] due to seigneurs for seigneurial arrears."

After border incursions such as Nelson's failed, secret military lodges—the Frères Chasseurs—were established in the United States and across western Lower Canada in July 1838. In the Richelieu area around Saint-Denis 1500 men took the oath of Chasseurs, and uprisings across Lower Canada were planned to coincide with renewed rebellion in Upper Canada (Senior, 1985: 165). The actual outbreaks were minor; in early November, insurrection in the Beauharnois, Napierville, and Châteauguay areas focused attacks on seigneurs.

The insurrection was limited in both region and duration. It may have been dampened by the strong opposition of the church, by Lord Durham's grant of an amnesty to all but eight of the 1837 leaders, and by strong military force. The estimated 2500 Chasseurs faced regular troops backed by local militia units, including the 2000-strong Montreal Volunteers, the St. Regis Indians, and troops from Upper Canada (Figures 5.2 and 5.3). After several skirmishes through the southwestern counties, the rebellions were over.

Figure 5.2   Rebels as painted in November 1838 by Jane Ellice. Without arms, military training, or support from native peoples, organizing a military uprising against British forces was problematic. Of the 150 to 300 men who occupied the seigneur's manor in Beauharnois, only half had muskets; the rest carried pikes and clubs.

Figure 5.3 Grenadier Guards. By July 1838, British authorities had 4704 rank-and-file troops and 527 officers in Lower Canada. As well, 3000 infantry, a troop of cavalry, and three artillery companies were stationed in Upper Canada.

After the first rebellion in 1837, martial law was proclaimed, the Canadian constitution was suspended, and Lord Durham was named governor of all British North America. Unlike the leniency that followed the first rebellions, punishments imposed after November 1838 were severe. Some 850 Patriotes were arrested, 108 were courtmartialed and ninety-nine of those condemned to death. Ultimately, twelve were hanged and fifty-eight deported to Australian penal colonies. The legislature of Lower Canada was suspended and replaced by an appointed Special Council that ruled from 1838 until the Union Act of 1840 came into effect.

∽∽∽

THE EFFECTS OF THE REBELLIONS

Despite the emphasis of historians such as Stanley Ryerson (1968), Jean-Paul Bernard (1983), and Allan Greer (1981, 1984), many anglophone historians have marginalized the rebellions from the course of Lower Canadian political development. Unsuccessful, un-British, and nationalistic, the rebellions are interpreted as having diverted Canadians from constitutional solutions and subjected Lower

Canadians to an authoritarian and anti-francophone regime. French Canadians, this Whig interpretation continues, took years to overcome the legacy of rebellion. They did so only by making compromises: by forging a new ethnic alliance (symbolized by Baldwin and La Fontaine) and working in a bicultural partnership in the emerging Canadian party and federal system; and by working within the British constitutional framework, "the organic vitality of the British constitution in which freedom wears a Crown" (Monet, 1969: *vii*). For their part, francophone historians like Maurice Séguin saw the result of the rebellions as simply a deepening of French-Canadian "serfdom" under "British occupation" (1970: 250).

The rebellions must be seen, however, as an integral part of a political chain of resistance, authoritarianism, and bourgeois democracy. The Quebec Act (1774) and the Constitutional Act (1791) had left Lower Canada with a preindustrial institutional structure. The rebellions served to clean house, purging some members of the francophone bourgeoisie, giving short-term power to the authoritarian Special Council, and preparing the terrain for a profound adjustment of judicial, landholding, social, educational, and religious institutions.

The rebellions were an important step in the long-term accession to political power of certain elements in the Lower Canadian bourgeoisie. This group would subordinate seigneurialism and preindustrial French law to economic development, local autonomy, and the formation of a centralized bureaucratic state. It saw that many of its social and economic goals were synonymous with those implemented by the Special Council. Charles Poulett Thompson, Lord Sydenham, who was sent out in 1839 as governor, was not from the preindustrial elite. He was an aggressive administrator whose family had important merchant, industrial, and mining interests in the Baltic and in South and Central America. Sydenham's goals were to restore stable British government, to modernize administrative structures, and to make Canada attractive for British investors.

⌒⌒

THE ROLE OF THE SPECIAL COUNCIL

The Special Council governed the province from 1838 to 1841 and set in motion a process of fundamental changes that would affect institutional structure, social relations, and forms of land ownership. The state took a new, active role in organizing and financing social and educational institutions. Although its legislation was only temporary, was often hastily conceived, and was unlikely to receive popular support, the Special Council's crucial contribution was to build an institutional framework that would be legitimized later by Lower Canada's own politicians under the rubrique of responsible government.

The Special Council established new institutions for the urban proletariat, such as the Montreal Lunatic Asylum (1839). Across Lower Canada, dozens of schools, Catholic colleges, literary societies, and institutions for indigents, orphans, widows, foundlings, and the elderly or sick were funded. The Special Council responded to local demands for improved transportation by subsidizing bridges, roads, and the Chambly Canal. Longstanding complaints about seigneurial land in Montreal were addressed, giving landholders the option of commutating their seigneurial lands into freehold tenure.

Local capitalists had also complained that their capital lacked security because there was no public registry system to publicly record land sales, mortgages, and encumbrances. This was remedied with the Registry Act of 1841, which required that all conveyances be registered in county registry offices. Important municipal and judiciary ordinances also increased central control over the countryside. Circuit courts for small-debt claims were established in the Montreal, Trois-Rivières and Quebec districts, for example, and rural police were established in the Montreal area.

The Special Council moved quickly to reassure the Catholic clergy, which feared the worst from Durham and the authoritarian regime. Religious communities were forced to give a full accounting of their property and social services, but they were treated respectfully. While the ordinance concerning its property in Montreal was being drawn up, the Superior of the Seminary of Montreal and his lawyer met for eight consecutive days with Charles Buller, Durham's first secretary. The superior described the resulting ordinance as "the most Catholic and Papist law that it [Britain] had sanctioned in over three hundred years."

The Special Council recognized the important social role of the Catholic church and accorded it new corporate powers and reinforced property rights. At the base of these privileges was the reality that the church's capital and ideological influence were to serve the state. New Catholic orders were permitted into Lower Canada; the right of religious institutions to hold property without taxes (in mortmain) were clarified; seigneurial lands held by religious orders were to be fully compensated in their transformation to freehold tenure; and male religious communities like the Sulpicians were permitted to expand their numbers.

Preindustrial institutions that had served the elite well were to prove inadequate for an industrializing society. The Collège de Montréal, for example, a classical college for bourgeois youth, could no longer respond to the educational needs of an industrial city like Montreal, which had a growing wage labour force. Nor was the peasantry amenable to new forms of taxation and state control. As a result, the institutions of law, land holding, education, welfare, and health were restructured. State and business changed as new bureaucracies, forms of management, and ways of organizing the work site evolved.

Seigneurialism and Law

The industrial activities of seigneurs like Barthélemy Joliette had shown that seigneurialism was compatible with industrial activities such as sawmilling, railways, and town development. Yet, industrial producers objected to seigneurial monopolies over water-power sites and mills and to restrictions on the free transfer of property. Looking to new urban and export markets, they wanted to build flour mills, woollen mills, and sawmills without seigneurial interference and dues. As early as 1816, industrial miller William Fleming challenged the milling monopoly of the seigneurs of the Ile de Montréal by building a mill at Lachine. And urban speculators, particularly in Montreal, objected to paying *lods et ventes* as a surcharge on improvements they made to their properties.

Seigneurial land blocked industrial expansion in other ways. The Sulpician seigneurial domain of St. Gabriel, for example, along the Lachine Canal on the outskirts of Montreal, was used for storing grain and pasturing the seigneur's animals. This frustrated speculators and industrial producers who wanted to develop manufactures along the canal. Until seigneurial law was changed, seigneurs could not be forced to release their land for industrial use. Immediately following the rebellions, the Special Council introduced free tenure principles into property relations in Montreal. Censitaires who wanted to commute their land to freehold tenure were allowed to form a capital from the seigneurial rents previously paid. Hundreds of propertyholders, usually large urban capitalists, availed themselves of the option. Legislation in 1854, the Special Court of 1855 (Figure 5.4) and a new law in 1859 extended these principles across the province, making them universal and, more and more frequently, mandatory.

Industrial producers' demand for an end to seigneurial rights and for a "free" market for land and labour led inevitably to attacks on the legal system. Legal reform became a central element in the formation of a modern, centralized Quebec state. Reflecting its preindustrial origins, the Custom of Paris had integrated property rights into a seigneurial, familial, and religious framework; since individual property rights were not always absolute, the transfer or sale of land was often complicated. From the standpoint of universality, it was important to have an English translation of the Custom since some anglophones, particularly in the Eastern Townships, continued to use American practices (in sales contracts, for example), arguing that French customary law was foreign to their common-law traditions.

In their demand for a new legal culture, large capitalists called for a system in which all individual creditors would receive equal treatment. To protect their capital in landed property, they demanded changes in mortgage and registry regulations and restrictions that would end both secret liens on property and the special privileges accorded under the old law to wives, children, and artisans with

Figure 5.4 The Special Court, formed from the legal elite and with La Fontaine presiding, was established in 1855 to examine the problem of seigneurialism. Dismantling seigneurialism raised the dilemma of what form property relations should take in a society in which a capitalist ideology was becoming dominant. On one hand, the seigneurial system clearly interfered with individual rights and the principle of freedom of contract; on the other, it was rooted in the fundamental rights of property. The solution was to force censitaires to reimburse seigneurs for lost revenues and for the state to provide additional subsidies for seigneurs to replace *lods et ventes.* "Because the vast major-ity [of censitaires] could not afford such a price, they paid in its stead an annual constituted rent [. . .] thereby remaining in basically the same subservient position as before. The true beneficiaries were the commercial and industrial entrepreneurs. [. . .] As former seigneurs, their annual rents would not diminish; [. . .] as capitalists, it was now easier for them to speculate in land, to control timber reserves, and to build mills at water sites within the old seigneuries" (Little, 1982).

respect to real property. The pressure to revise preindustrial legal codes was clear in a Quebec journal, the *Revue de législation et de jurisprudence* (1846):

> The conquests which modern society has made in politics, science, the arts, agriculture, industry, and commerce necessitate the reform of the old codes which directed ancient societies. Everywhere, one feels the inadequacy of laws made for an order of ideas and things which no longer exists, and the need to remodel ancient systems and of promulgating new ones, in order to put ourselves at the level of society's progress.

Figure 5.5 The Saint-Jean courthouse and jail. Similar courthouses can be seen in Rimouski, the Beauce, Bedford, and Huntington. A centralized judicial apparatus was an important part of the extension of the institutional state into all regions of Lower Canada. With the formation of nineteen judicial districts, at least fourteen new courthouses and jails were built between 1859 and 1863. With the exception of a rare asylum, penitentiary, or military installation, the courthouses were the largest public buildings in their districts. A standard set of courthouse and jail plans was drawn up by the architect for the public works department. The central government controlled the exact position of the building, and imposed details such as the height of the judge's bench, the structure and drainage of the building's six toilets, and the quality and number of coats of paint. Regional judicial expansion stimulated the formation of local legal elites.

It was Attorney General George-Etienne Cartier who masterminded codification. A careful and pragmatic politician who came to believe in federalism, his career was based on balancing the political and economic unity of the St. Lawrence—symbolized by his long alliance in the Conservative Party with John A. Macdonald—with meticulous attention to fundamental Quebec institutions like the church and civil law. Established under Cartier's codification bill of 1857, the codification commission was made up of his old political and legal colleagues, René-Edouard Caron, Charles Dewey Day, and Augustin-Norbert Morin. It submitted eight reports in the early 1860s, which were referred to a special legislative committee chaired by Cartier. One year before the 1867 Confederation, the new code went into effect. Among other reforms, it clarified contract law and gave new definitions to master–servant relations (Cairns, 1987). Cartier also presented two bills (1857) that helped to develop a uniform, centralized legal system. The bills reorganized the Lower Canadian court system, established nineteen judicial districts, provided for courthouses and jails (Figure 5.5), and clarified the way in which the legal system was to be applied in the Eastern Townships.

EDUCATIONAL INSTITUTIONS

Most Lower Canadians did not know how to read or write in the early industrial period. School acts in the 1840s shaped a school system based on religion, which resulted in a church–state partnership in education. In the Catholic sector, newly arrived religious communities such as the Christian Brothers provided teachers, while long-established orders such as the Congrégation Notre-Dame greatly expanded their teaching activities. In 1853, 11 percent of the teachers in Catholic schools were clerics; by 1887 this had risen to 48 percent. The number of elementary school students had risen to 178 961 in 1866.

As the working class was being introduced to elementary education, the expansion of higher education in Quebec was solidifying and perpetuating the position of the bourgeoisie. Agronomy, engineering, law, and medicine were professionalized, separating the working classes and women from scientific knowledge, access to capital, and real power in the burgeoning institutions and factories. Université Laval was established in Quebec City in 1852 and opened a Montreal campus in 1876; the Ecole Polytechnique, a school of applied sciences, was formed in 1873 and affiliated with Laval in 1887. Anglophone universities benefited from the industrial capital of the Molsons (beer), Redpaths (sugar), and Macdonalds (tobacco). The arts faculty of McGill University was established in 1843 and by the end of the century McGill had five faculties. Anglophones in the Eastern Townships were served by Bishop's University.

Medicine provides a good example of professionalization in Lower Canada. Before the mid-nineteenth century, most doctors, as was the case with lawyers and notaries, learned their trade by apprenticeship. By mid-century doctors were establishing their professional credentials. They began publishing medical journals and expanded their power over hospitals and competitors such as midwives. In 1847, the provincial College of Physicians and Surgeons was established and a law forced all future practitioners to attend recognized medical schools and pass standardized examinations. Universities played a central role in legitimizing the profession. Anglophone doctors began receiving medical degrees from McGill University in 1833, while francophone doctors trained at l'Ecole de médecine et de chirurgie and at Laval University's Faculty of Medicine. A second anglophone medical school, Bishop's, was established in 1871 (Bernier, 1989).

Medical students were largely from bourgeois backgrounds. Unlike McGill, whose students came from across North America, Laval and the Ecole de médecine et de chirurgie de Montréal tended to train local graduates of the classical college system. In 1870, for example, 72 percent of Laval's students came from Quebec City and eastern Quebec; 82 percent of Bishop's medical students came from Quebec's anglophone community in 1872–1905; and only 30 percent of McGill medical students came from the province during 1849–1939 (Weisz, 1987).

⌐○○⌐

Public Health and Environment

As typical small, preindustrial cities in the post-Napoleonic period—without municipal governments, sewer systems, garbage collection, or sterile water supplies—Quebec City and Montreal were vulnerable to epidemics. In the spring of 1832, faced with the spread of Asiatic cholera from Europe, authorities hastily passed quarantine laws, established public health offices, and constructed a quarantine station at Grosse Ile, an island some fifty kilometres downstream from Quebec City. These measures proved ineffective in stopping the spread of cholera, which accounted for 82 percent of deaths in Quebec City in 1832 and 74 percent in Montreal (Dechêne et Robert, 1979). In 1847, about a third of the 60 000 Irish immigrants quarantined at Grosse Ile died of cholera; gravediggers on the island were paid $4 a day and used hooks to drag the dead to open graves.

Riots occurred regularly during epidemics, as the popular classes struck back at both authorities and immigrants. In 1847, some 2000 rioters in Quebec City's Lower Town attacked the immigrant hospital which they identified as the source of cholera. The same phenomenon occurred during the smallpox epidemic of 1885 when public health and police officials were attacked in their attempts to systematically innoculate the popular classes.

Whereas the threat to public health from epidemics such as cholera has disappeared since that period, environmental hazards have of course increased. Rivers in the St. Lawrence lowland have become major environmental hazards through sewage and industrial and agricultural pollution. In the mid-nineteenth century, however, these rivers—as well as being major transportation routes and water-power sites—were important sources of food, water, ice, and leisure (Figures 5.6 and 5.7). Many islands were commons where animals grazed; commercial fishing was practised throughout the region. Once the forests had been cleared, fishing became particularly important to native peoples in Kahnawake, Akwesasne, and Kanesatake. Soldiers swam in the river off Ile Sainte-Hélène while Scottish men curled on the ice in front of Montreal.

Figures 5.6 and 5.7 These two photographs illustrate two uses of rivers near Montreal: fishing for shad on the Rivière des Prairies in 1866 and commercial ice cutting on the St. Lawrence in 1884.

RELIGIOUS INSTITUTIONS

The church played an ever more important role in controlling the popular classes after the 1840s. In preindustrial Quebec, churches had not been immune to civil disobedience. Drinking, heckling, and obstructing services were apparently sufficiently common that a law "for the maintenance of good order in churches, chapels and other places used for public worship" was passed in 1821. Churchwardens were empowered to arrest loiterers, tipplers, or disturbers of the peace and to bring them before magistrates. If necessary, magistrates could appoint constables to assist the churchwardens.

The physical presence of the church was in decline before the rebellions of 1837–1838: from 750 Catholics per priest in 1780, there were, by 1830, 1834 Lower Canadian Catholics per priest (Gagnon et Lebel-Gagnon, 1983: 377). At Petite-Nation, where the first settler arrived in 1805, the seigneury was without a resident priest until 1828. In the early years, the seigneur fed, lodged, and provided a chapel in his manor house for the visiting missionary priest. Once the parish was established, the priest complained that parishioners refused to pay the tithe and that he was reduced to "scratching among the stumps" (Baribeau, 1983: 125; Harris, 1979: 347).

Urban conditions were not any better. In the 1830s, one-third of adult burials in Montreal were conducted without a religious ceremony. Only 36 percent of the parishioners at Montreal's parish church bothered to take Easter communion, the most important religious service of the year, while at the Récollets' church in the Montreal suburbs, pew holders petitioned against the behaviour of their rougher compatriots and "the ridicule of the irreligious" who obstructed the services.

After 1840, however, the apparatus of the Catholic church expanded rapidly. The number of priests in Quebec escalated, and the number of faithful per priest dropped from 1834 in 1830 to 1080 in 1850 and 510 in 1890 (Gagnon et Lebel-Gagnon, 1983; Linteau, Durocher, Robert, et Ricard, 1989: 261). Membership in male religious communities increased from 243 to 1984 between 1850 and 1901. The Congrégation Notre-Dame, which had never had more than eighty members in the seventeenth and eighteenth centuries, saw its membership grow fivefold between 1830 and 1870 (Danylewycz, 1987). By 1891, the Congrégation was running ten schools in Montreal alone. New dioceses were established across the province: Trois-Rivières (1852), Saint-Hyacinthe (1852), Rimouski (1867), Sherbrooke (1874), Chicoutimi (1878), and Nicolet (1885).

The membership of female religious communities, which had remained steady in the decades before 1840, doubled in the 1840s and by 1881 had reached 3783. In the second half of the nineteenth century, twenty-five female religious communities and twelve male orders were established in Quebec (Figure 5.8). Nine of the female communities and all of the male ones were founded in France.

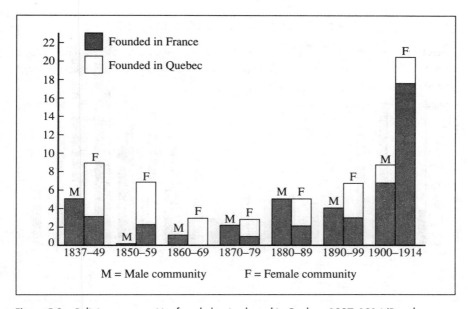

Figure 5.8 Religious communities founded or implanted in Quebec, 1837–1914 (Danylewycz, 1987: 47).

In imposing social and educational institutions on industrializing Quebec, male and female religious communities could draw on their preindustrial experiences with communal living, authority, and discipline, and on their understanding of the relationship of isolation, work, and prayer. The clergy encouraged parishioners to establish lay, burial, and philanthropic societies like the Dames de la Charité and Saint-Vincent-de-Paul. Brigitte Caulier's work shows the sharp growth of Montreal burial societies after 1820 (Figure 5.9).

The extent of urban poverty and suffering in Montreal was, however, overwhelming. In 1847, a nun who visited the waterfront sheds where immigrants were marshalled and lodged was shocked to find 1500 cholera victims, two to a bed, "suffering and abandoned." In 1848, 332 of the 650 immigrants lodged in the sheds died before being moved to alternative shelter. In the great Montreal fire of 1852, 1100 houses were destroyed. To serve these expanding social needs, the church found itself responsible for hospitals, orphanages, maternity hospitals, day-care centres, houses of industry, food depots, and hospices and asylums for the indigent, elderly and insane (Lapointe-Roy, 1987).

The Seminary of Montreal (Figure 5.10) is an example of the enormous problem of staffing. This seminary was responsible for the administration of three seigneuries, as well as overseeing the parish of Montreal, an Indian mission, a college, and several convents. The seminary also had the responsibility to direct the

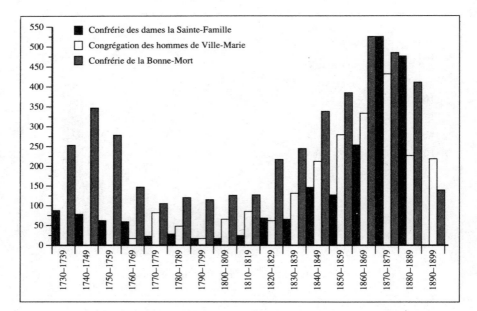

Figure 5.9 Membership in three Roman Catholic burial societies in the parish of Montreal. Burial societies provided their members with coffins, transportation, and a funeral mass. In one such society, contributions in the 1860s ranged from thirty to sixty cents a year. These societies accumulated important capital, which authorities might invest in a refuge, asylum, or in other social work (Caulier, 1986: 82).

expanding Catholic social services in Montreal. But for all this the seminary had only twenty priests (1840), two of whom were over seventy years old. Despite a seemingly impossible situation, the seminary was instrumental in rebuilding the parish church of Notre Dame, as well as establishing St. Patrick's church for the Irish and new suburban churches in working-class neighbourhoods. The seminary had a strong interest in elementary education, and subsidized teaching orders such as the Christian Brothers and Congrégation Notre-Dame. It also provided land as part of its sponsorship of a house of industry; sponsored the upkeep of thirty to forty Irish orphans in the Grey Nuns orphanage; and established a "poor depot," where nuns distributed flour, potatoes, peas, and firewood.

The subordination of the Sulpicians to the bishop of Montreal is an important part of the institutional history of Montreal. The epitome of a preindustrial institution, the Sulpicians were seigneurs and titular parish priests of Montreal. In the 1820s, they singlehandedly supervised construction of their new 4968-seat parish church, Notre Dame, and in the 1830s and 1840s they operated their social services and supervised female religious communities in a quasi-independent fashion.

Figure 5.10 Grand Séminaire and Collège de Montréal (1876). The importance of the Roman Catholic church's educational and institutional role in industrializing Quebec is clear from this picture of the Sulpicians' new seminary and classical college. Modelled on the architecture of seminaries in France, it was built on the Sulpicians' mountain domain in the 1860s with capital derived from the commutation of seigneurial land into freehold land. Of the 7529 seminarians who studied at the Grand Séminaire (the left half of the institution) in the period from 1840 to 1940, some 4000 became priests. Before 1967, the Seminary's courses were in Latin and students—including anglophones—came from 34 dioceses across Canada and the northeastern United States. Since 1967, anglophone seminarians have gone elsewhere and classes have been taught in French. In the period from 1940 to 1965, the Grand Séminaire trained 1747 priests; this fell to 413 between 1965 and 1991.

Although they retained power in the parish of Montreal, and were still responsible for training priests, they became increasingly subject to control by the state. In the 1860s, they lost important powers to Ignace Bourget, the bishop of Montreal, symbolized by the division of their Montreal parish. In 1886, Pope Leon XIII named Montreal an archdiocese and archbishops such as Edouard-Charles Fabre and Paul Bruchési came to dominate religious life in the city.

These deeply conservative bishops tried to repress sexuality and popular culture, and relegated women to a separate and subordinate sphere. The bishops opposed theatres, lotteries, mixed pilgrimages, amusement parks, carnivals, baby contests, and dancing by young people. Girls were not to attend public gatherings, and women were not to wear jewellery or watches.

Paul Deschamps, farm tenant on a religious domain on the outskirts of Montreal, had the following clause in his lease: "the lessee promises not to tolerate dancing or any other disorder in his house. In addition he will not permit the farm or woodlot to become a *rendezvous de plaisir* nor allow any picnic—even for a charitable cause" (1886).

Religiosity did seem to increase. Louis Rousseau (1986) has discerned a new popular attitude to religion as early as 1839; the first pastoral retreats were held in that year, and in 1841 30 000 faithful in the Montreal area went to Mont Saint-Hilaire for the dedication of a cross. Whereas only 36 percent of the parishioners at Montreal's Notre Dame Church took Easter communion in 1839, 97 percent of the Catholic population of the diocese of Montreal did so in the 1860s.

⌒

THE ACHIEVEMENT OF
BOURGEOIS DEMOCRACY

In the aftermath of the first rebellions, Lord Durham had been ordered to examine the causes of unrest and to propose political solutions. In his 1839 report, Durham differentiated between the rebellions in Upper and Lower Canada. He found the irresponsible rule of the Family Compact, the clergy reserves, and tough economic conditions to be important factors in the rebellions in Upper Canada but interpreted the Lower Canadian struggle as an ethnic struggle of "two nations warring in the bosom of a single state." Although he was known as "Radical Jack," Durham's roots were deep in the British élite; in 1833 he employed 2400 miners. During his Canadian visit he was primarily influenced by Tories and great merchants who detested French Canadians. He was therefore harsh with their culture, describing it as "stagnant," and he had a particular dislike for French law and Roman Catholicism: "There can hardly be conceived a nationality more destitute [. . .] than that which is exhibited by the descendants of the French in Lower Canada, owing to their peculiar language and manners. They are a people with no history and no literature."

But behind Durham's strong ethnic bias he paid careful attention to questions of capital, labour, and property and insisted on the need for what he called "industrial progress." Here, the Lower Canadian bourgeoisie, artisans, and industrial producers found their assembly speeches echoed by Durham:

> A very considerable portion of the Province has neither roads, post offices, mills, schools, nor churches. The people may raise enough for their own subsistence, and may have a rude and comfortless plenty, but they can seldom acquire wealth. . . . Their means of communication with each other, or the chief towns of the Province, are limited and uncertain.

Durham's ideology was, of course, anathema to the Papineau wing, which linked French-Canadian nationalism to civil law, seigneurialism, and Roman

Catholicism. But the La Fontaine–Cartier element of the francophone bourgeoisie sensed the possibilities of an ethnic collaboration that would stimulate urban and capitalist expansion. Within months of the Durham Report, La Fontaine was corresponding with Francis Hincks of Toronto and agreeing that he did "like the principles of government laid down in the report." Hincks was the editor of the Toronto *Examiner* and a leading Reformer. He had strong links to Upper Canadian promoters such as Welland Canal developer William Merritt, grain dealer William Pearce Howland, and merchant Isaac Buchanan.

Durham's two most important proposals were to unite Upper and Lower Canada and to let the colony conduct its own internal affairs through the British parliamentary practice of "responsible government," by which the executive would have to have the support of a majority in the assembly. Authorities in London rejected his proposal for responsible government but acted quickly to unite Upper and Lower Canada. By the Union Act of 1840, the reunited Canadas were granted a legislative assembly in which Canada East (Lower Canada) and Canada West (Upper Canada) each had forty-two seats; the government, however, did not have to maintain a majority in the assembly. The appearance of equality was in fact a denial of representation by population. Lower Canada had a significantly larger population, 650 000 compared to Upper Canada's 450 000. The policy thus ensured the political superiority of the minority anglophone population.

The obvious potential of a pragmatic, bicultural political alliance under the Union Act soon overwhelmed the more isolationist position of Patriotes and social conservatives like Denis-Benjamin Viger and John Neilson, who opposed collaboration with Upper Canadian liberals. La Fontaine called for the resources of the interior to be opened, seigneurial tenure to be abolished, and the canal system to be developed further. Although he was defeated in the elections of 1841, his program brought him into alliance with the Upper Canadian reform group led by Robert Baldwin. Baldwin had impeccable political credentials as a prominent Toronto lawyer, Anglican, and member of an elite family. He found La Fontaine a seat in a Toronto riding and over the next years the two men established the bi-ethnic Reform Party. Although the Reform Party lost the election in 1844, it had become a central political fact in Canadian politics, a legacy inherited by George-Etienne Cartier and John A. Macdonald in the 1850s.

The Reform Party's first goal was to win responsible government. A government with control over local resources, markets, and state bureaucracy would be able to create a suitable environment for capitalists: canals, railways, expanding financial institutions, a stable labour force and a supportive state. Their struggle coincided with a growing demand in Britain for free trade; the decline of mercantilism led to repeal of the protectionist Corn Laws and Navigation Acts in the 1840s and a re-evaluation of the cost, function, and political organization of the empire.

In 1847, Lord Elgin was named governor general. Although he was critical of French-Canadian use of British constitutional practice, Elgin was prepared to accept the principle of responsible government that had already been applied in colonies like Nova Scotia. When the Reformers won two-thirds of the seats in the 1847 elections, Elgin called on Baldwin and La Fontaine to form a government.

Despite legislation that permitted exiled rebels of 1837–1838 to return home and named French as an official language, the full implications of responsible government only hit home with Lord Elgin's signing into law of the Rebellion Losses Bill granting indemnity to Patriotes who had lost property during the rebellions. The act enraged the anglophone commercial elite of Montreal, who felt threatened as a minority in Lower Canada and abandoned when Britain acceded to both responsible government and free trade. On 25 April 1849 a Tory mob marched on parliament, the symbol of responsible government (Figure 5.11):

> The Assembly was still sitting at nine o'clock when a volley of stones came crashing into the chamber through the vaulted windows and a dozen ruffians erupted into the hall, swinging sticks at the gaslights. In a moment, the chamber floor was crowded with rioters. One threw rocks at the clock; another, mounting the steps of the Speaker's chair right under [Augustin-Norbert] Morin's nose, pronounced, "I dissolve this French House;" another began to hack the throne to pieces. Perry pulled down a portrait of Papineau and trampled it under foot; someone else seized the splendid mace and hurled it out a window to the excited crowd. Some members, who had hurried out to the library, now ran back to announce that fire had broken out. . . . By then the flames were licking the walls about the roof while the rioters were running around the building, singing, and yelling, celebrating the ruin of French domination. They had turned away the firemen and cut their hose. At midnight the huge fire still raged high into the black sky (Monet, 1969: 337–38).

Another crisis arose in 1849 with the annexation movement. Calling for "a friendly and peaceful separation from British connection and a union upon equitable terms with the [United States]," the annexation manifesto won support from some industrial producers and leading Montreal merchants. At the same time, the Rouges, a party whose essential program was separation of church and state and the secularization of Quebec society, used its newspaper L'Avenir to promote annexation. Popular support for annexation was weak, however, and only a determined few believed that French-Canadian nationalism had a future either with Montreal's anglophone Tories or in a larger American union.

By the end of the 1840s, the Reformers had seized centre stage. While a rump of Patriotes moved to the Rouge party, the Reformers gained power by a pragmatic approach to ideology that espoused the values of liberal capitalism while accommodating itself to the social values of the Catholic church.

Whereas Louis-Hippolyte La Fontaine and George-Etienne Cartier were active in politics and the law, the evolution of ideology can be clearly perceived in the

Figure 5.11 The burning of the parliament buildings in Montreal, 1849

career of historian François-Xavier Garneau (1809–1866). As a clerk for notary Archibald Campbell in Quebec City, he read widely on European liberalism and, after a trip to the United States, became aware of his North American identity. He was closely tied to the Patriotes, working as Denis-Benjamin Viger's secretary in London from 1831 to 1833. After the failure of the rebellions, he became a civil servant. Incensed by Durham's contemptuous remarks about French-Canadian culture, he responded with the four-volume *History of Canada (1845–48)* which emphasized French Canada's distinct identity and equated its history with a struggle for survival. Although the first edition was liberal in its interpretation, clerical concern encouraged Garneau to take a more conservative stance over religious questions in subsequent editions. Garneau's work, hailed as the most important Quebec book of the nineteenth century, was enormously successful in shaping francophone historiography for a century.

Garneau had little interest in religion for itself but rather in the relation between church and state. As ultramontanism—the belief in the supremacy of papal over civil authority—grew, the religious dimension of Quebec history was amplified by authors such as Sulpician Etienne-Michel Faillon (1799–1870). Faillon's works on New France emphasized the pre-eminent place of the church and the saintliness of the founders of French Canada.

The political reality was that the Reform Party held a strong central position. Anglophone Tories on the right were isolated, and the Rouges on the left faced perennial trouble gaining strong popular support. In 1844, they had founded a liberal reading club and meeting place, the Institut Canadien, and from then until 1877, when Wilfrid Laurier made peace with the Catholic authorities on behalf of Quebec Liberals (the party that succeeded the Rouges), they faced unceasing opposition from the church. The church had powerful means beyond the pulpit and confessional to suppress opponents. Rouge supporters like book merchant Edouard-Raymond Fabre found ecclesiastical sales dropping. Groups such as the Institut Canadien found it difficult to obtain meeting halls, most of which were controlled by the church. Radicals like labour organizer Médéric Lanctot found the bishop and clerics ranged against them, and Rouge lawyers and notaries discovered that lucrative ecclesiastical business went to their political opponents.

When Joseph Guibord, a member of the Institut Canadien, died in 1869, his wife was unable to obtain a Catholic burial for him. She buried his remains temporarily in the Protestant cemetery and took the case to court. For five years the church resisted. It was not until after her death that the highest court, the Privy Council in England, resolved the case. In November 1875, 1235 soldiers accompanied Guibord's remains to the Catholic Côte-des-Neiges cemetery, where, under court order, he was buried. Guards were posted and the coffin was protected by cement while Bishop Bourget declared that the grave was separate from consecrated ground.

The Rouges were divided over industrial development. In the ruralist tradition of Papineau, some attacked the idea of railways and insisted on the alliance of seigneurialism, civil law, and French-Canadian nationalism. A majority seems to have accepted Etienne Parent's argument, however, that industry was the means of conserving French-Canadian nationality (Bernard, 1971: 31). The ideological stresses of the Rouges and the weakness of their political base made them easy prey for the Reform pragmatists. Reformers had a comfortable relationship with the Upper Canadians, an alliance with the clergy, and were able to make use of state patronage effectively. The Rouges grappled with integrating Papineau's ruralism, idealism, and dreams of independence with the reality of industrialization and federalism. The Reformers, on the other hand, offered workable compromises: to maintain a francophone bloc within a larger bi-ethnic party; and to remain politically and institutionally separate within a nebulous, but developing, federal system. In their first cabinet, Baldwin and La Fontaine established a co-premiership; Baldwin also became attorney general for Canada West and La Fontaine took the post of attorney general east. As well, there were eastern and western ministers in portfolios such as public works and solicitor general.

The Reform Party was increasingly professional in its attention to the regional and political realities of Lower Canada. It encouraged party newspapers such as

La Minerve in Montreal and *Le Journal de Québec* in Quebec City, and subsidized local colonization, railway, and canal projects. In Quebec City, Hector Langevin was emerging as a careful, conservative politician with the necessary links to the journalistic, clerical, and local capitalist circles. Elections and government contracts were carefully supervised; all appointments of judges, militia officers, customs officials, school inspectors, prison chaplains, and postal workers crossed the desk of the local party chief.

The Reform Party paid close attention to the anglophone majority in Montreal and the Eastern Townships. Leaders like Alexander Galt, John Rose, and Thomas D'Arcy McGee were given important positions in both party and government. Strident French-Canadian nationalism was quietly abandoned in favour of bicultural rhetoric. Anglophones were assured that French Canadians had British hearts and that Canada was blessed to have two great civilizations. Nowhere was this rhetoric more evident than in the negotiations leading to Confederation, when the anglophone minority of Lower Canada was given strong assurances concerning Protestant schools, the division of school taxes, and a fixed number of ridings in the Eastern Townships. In both Montreal and Quebec City, political leaders such as La Fontaine, Cartier, and Langevin cemented the Reform Party to the major industrial interests by accepting directorships, contracts, and party contributions.

By the late 1850s, the Reform Party had evolved into the more centrist Conservative Party. One of the party's strengths was its alliance with the Catholic clergy. The issue was not religiosity but the social and political significance of official religion. In the 1840s, the Reformers had supported colonization, temperance, and increased clerical control over the national fraternal society of French Canada, the Saint-Jean Baptiste Society. They only put forward educational and social legislation after consultation with the clerical hierarchy. Also, in particularly sensitive areas such as the law, seigneurialism, and Confederation, the Reformers took great care to obtain clerical support.

Leaders were particularly careful when they saw evidence of popular unrest. The capital of the united Canadas was moved from Montreal to escape political turbulence such as the riots of 1849, when the parliament buildings had been burned. After intense sectional debate that lasted years, the capital was located in Bytown (Ottawa). The creation of new courts in regional centres and of an effective police force supplemented traditional clerical supervision to better control the countryside. In the period 1846–1850 widespread rural rioting—the *guerre des éteignoirs*—broke out against compulsory schooling and school taxes. The elite divided over the issue. In Nicolet county, for example, the local seigneur, Luc-Michel Cressé, was hostile to school taxes that would fall on landowners and helped to incite riots. On the other hand, doctors, lawyers, notaries, and other village notables in the county favoured the school laws since they believed that their influence would increase through holding the office of school commissioner (Nelson, 1989). Ultimately, charges of arson and criminal conspiracy were laid and justices of the peace dispatched to trouble spots. La Fontaine demanded stronger support from church officials to get rural obedience. When the curé of Ile Bizard called for submission to the school law, his parishioners threatened to burn down his house. Schools were burned, and priests, tax collectors, and schoolmasters threatened. Bishop Bourget responded by visiting the troubled parish and ordering the parish church to be locked until the law was obeyed.

Médéric Lanctot and his Grand Association de Protection des Ouvriers du Canada, formed in 1867 and linking twenty-six artisanal groups, posed the particularly dangerous threat of working-class political action. The Grand Association was composed of delegates from various artisanal groups. Inevitably, it linked questions of class and ethnicity. With its class interpretation of Quebec society, the Association attempted to unite French-Canadian workers in a single organization and to stop emigration to the United States.

A union of ironworkers was organized in Montreal in 1859—largely by workers of British origin—and affiliated with the Iron Molders Union of America. Francophone and anglophone members of the union were sharply divided, although seven out of ten francophone ironworkers who moved from the St. Maurice region to Montreal immediately joined. Peter Bischoff (1992) suggests that, because of ethnic strife within their union, francophone ironworkers eventually gravitated to the Grand Association.

The Association brought strong reaction from industrial capitalists, clergy, and Conservative politicians. With a strong base among workers in Montreal, Lanctot established a newspaper, *L'Union Nationale*, was elected alderman, and prepared to take on George-Etienne Cartier in the 1867 elections. Lanctot's labour sympathies were a particular threat to the industrial capitalists, who backed Cartier. The Association incorporated European socialist principles and demanded councils to ensure improved working conditions and equality before the law. It participated in two strikes, opened bakery co-operatives, and drew 15 000 people to its rallies. When Lanctot lost the election and switched his enthusiasm towards annexation to the United States, the Association disappeared from view.

WOMEN AND THE STATE

Although Lower Canadian society already emphasized marital and patriarchal rights, the period witnessed significant legal restrictions on the property and voting rights of women and the reinforcement of a husband's power in marriage. The Registry Ordinance of 1841, for example, restricted the protection of married women's property by placing their dower rights to their husband's property on the same footing as normal mortgages, which were based on priority of registration. This meant that if a wife's claims were not properly registered by her husband, her property rights could be jeopardized. The Bankruptcy Act of 1843 dealt with the same issue for merchants and their families.

The attainment of responsible government also led to the disenfranchisement of women. Although few women had the right to vote, those who could played a decisive role in some hotly contested urban ridings. Thirteen percent of Montreal West's electors in 1832 were women; 199 of the 225 women on the voters' list exercised their franchise, and most voted against the Patriote candidate. Papineau based his campaign to disenfranchise women on the need to protect them from electoral violence. Disenfranchisement was first proposed in 1834 and remained on the political agenda until it became law in 1849 (Bradbury, 1990). Women in Quebec were not re-enfranchised until 1917 for federal elections and 1940 at the provincial level.

CONFEDERATION

The federalism and party system that had emerged from the Union Act of 1840 broke down by the late 1850s under the pressure of regionalism, increasing ethnic tensions, and demands from Britain that Canada assume a larger financial share of its own defence and administration. At the same time, expanding government economic programs in canal, railway, and industrial development made it essential to maintain a strong central government.

Lower Canadian Conservatives were early and enthusiastic supporters of federation. At the 1864 Confederation negotiations in Charlottetown and Quebec City, and in the public debates that followed, Lower Canadian Conservative delegates accepted a highly centralized state despite fierce opposition from the Rouges. Protection of Lower Canadian interests was largely delegated to an upper house that did not exercise financial control and whose members were appointed for life by the central government. Nor did the Conservatives reject the federal right to disallow provincial legislation and to name the provincial lieutenant governor.

George-Etienne Cartier, who was the most important Lower Canadian at the negotiations, had become an inveterate anglophile and supporter of British institutions. He described the new federation as a new "political nationality" in which "British and French Canadian alike could appreciate and understand their position relative to each other. They were placed like great families beside each other, and their contact produced a healthy spirit of emulation." Rouge leader Antoine-Aimé Dorion was enraged at Conservative acquiescence in Confederation but because he was excluded from the negotiations his power was limited. Accusing French Canadians of being "fast asleep," Dorion charged that instead of initiating a federation in which provinces would retain important powers, Confederation would simply be "Legislative Union in disguise." Since the Conservative majority in the assembly was more than adequate to approve the federation resolutions, Rouge attacks could be largely ignored.

Unlike Ontario, Quebec made little attempt to protect its autonomy in provincial and economic matters in the first decades after Confederation. Leaders like Cartier and Langevin had built their careers on an ad hoc federal system that was now formalized in Confederation. Younger Conservatives such as Joseph-Adolphe Chapleau subscribed to the rhetoric of their elders. Although he speculated privately that Quebec's role in Confederation was to "carry water to the mills of others," his public pose was as a defender of the federal system which, he insisted, protected "the autonomy of our Province."

Although they spoke in favour of provincial autonomy, Quebec's Conservative leaders in this period were centralists. Most of them supported double representation, by which politicians could sit simultaneously in the provincial and federal legislatures. Prime Minister Macdonald's correspondence to his Quebec lieutenant Langevin leaves no doubt as to subordination of Quebec's legislation to that of Ottawa: "I have read [Premier] Chauveau's bill with not a little astonishment. . . . The Bill will not do at all but you need not say anything to him about it. I will draft a Bill which I think will hold water and do all that is necessary and will give it to you when you come up."

The financial terms of Confederation reinforced Quebec's subservience to Ottawa since over half of the province's income was in the form of a federal subsidy. As Quebec finances drained away in railway subsidies, Ottawa began warning Quebec of the implications. In 1879, Alexander Galt wrote to Premier Joly of Quebec, "You have a most difficult task before you, if the Province is to be saved from bankruptcy. If you fail, then Confederation must give way to a legislative union."

The most important attack on the increasing centralization of the Canadian state came from Judge Thomas J.J. Loranger, formerly a Conservative colleague of Cartier but by the 1870s a cogent defender of provincial autonomy. Confederation, he wrote, seemed to be working to the detriment of French Canada: "Political union, which, for other nations means increased force, natural development and concentration of authority, means for us, feebleness, isolation and menace, and Legislative Union, political absorption!" In opposition to the increasing power of Ottawa, Loranger argued in favour of what became known as the compact theory:

> In constituting themselves into a confederation, the provinces did not intend to renounce, and in fact never did renounce their autonomy. This autonomy with their rights, powers and prerogatives they expressly preserved for all that concerns their internal government; by forming themselves into a federal association, under political and legislative aspects, they formed a central government only for interprovincial objects.

Aspirations for provincial autonomy had little political influence before 1887. Confederation had locked Quebec into a federal state in which, for the moment at least, the most important powers lay with the central government. In accepting the subordination of Quebec to Ottawa, the Conservatives were only following the centralizing economic logic of Canadian industrial capitalism. Caught up with the National Policy and the rush for capital and development of the Canadian West, the province's bankers, shippers, and industrial producers had little time for constitutional niceties, Riel, or federal–provincial relations.

By Confederation, the Rouges had been rendered impotent by relentless pressure from the church, particularly the ultramontanes. In the 1870s, remnants of the old Rouge Party reorganized, realigned themselves with nationalists, and sought peace with the church. Wilfrid Laurier's speech in 1877 defending liberalism was a major factor in bringing legitimacy to the party as well as launching Laurier's career:

> It is true that there is in Europe, in France, in Italy and in Germany, a class of men, who give themselves the title of Liberals, but who have nothing of the Liberal about them but the name and who are the most dangerous of men. These are not Liberals; they are revolutionaries. . . . But, while reproaching [Quebec Liberals] with being friends of liberals our adversaries further reproach us, with . . . denying to the Church the freedom to which it is entitled. . . . No, let the priest speak and preach, as he thinks best; such is his right and no Canadian Liberal will dispute that right.

With the accession of Liberal Honoré Mercier to the premiership in 1887, Quebec politicians began for the first time to exploit the issue of provincial rights effectively.

⌒⌒⌒

CONCLUSION

Quebec in 1885 was a very different world than that of 1815. The purge of 1837–1838, parliamentary democracy, a new federal system, and the alliance of the clerical hierarchy and francophone bourgeoisie with the industrial producers left the province in the hands of conservative elements, forces that would effectively control Quebec well into the twentieth century.

FURTHER READING

NATIONALISM

Aside from the works of Fernand Ouellet noted in chapter four and his *Louis-Joseph Papineau: A Divided Soul*, political events before the rebellions can be examined in Alan Dever, "Economic Development and the Lower Canadian Assembly, 1828–40," and in Stanley Ryerson, *Unequal Union: Confederation and the Roots of Conflict in the Canadas, 1815–1873*. For the origins of Quebec nationalism see Ramsay Cook, *French-Canadian Nationalism: An anthology*.

THE REBELLIONS

For interpretations of the rebellions, consult Jean-Paul Bernand, *Les rébellions de 1837–1838*. Details of the rebellions themselves can be found in Elinor Senior's two books, *British Regulars in Montreal: An Imperial Garrison, 1832–1854*, and *Redcoats and Patriotes: The Rebellions in Lower Canada, 1837–38*. The legal elements of the rebellions are treated by Jean-Marie Fecteau in "Mesures d'exception et règle de droit: Les conditions d'application de la loi martiale au Québec lors des rébellions de 1837–1838," and Murray Greenwood, "The Chartrand Murder Trial: Rebellion and Repression in Lower Canada, 1837–1839." For treatment of the rebels see George Rudé, *Protest and Punishment: The Story of the Social and Political Protesters Transported to Australia, 1788–1868*.

UNION AND CONFEDERATION PERIOD

Politics of the Union and post-Confederation periods are described in Jacques Monet, *The Last Cannon Shot: A Study of French-Canadian Nationalism 1837–1840*; Jean-Paul Bernard, *Les Rouges: libéralisme, nationalisme et anticléricalisme au milieu de XIXe siècle*; and Brian Young, *George-Etienne Cartier: Montreal Bourgeois*. Of particular use for institutional development is J.M.S. Careless, *The Union of the Canadas: The Growth of Canadian Institutions 1841–1857*. For women and the vote see Nathalie Picard, "Les femmes et le vote au Bas-Canada de 1792 à 1849." Of particular use for state formation is Allan Greer and Ian Radforth, *Colonial Leviathan: State Formation in Mid-Nineteenth Century Canada*.

RELIGION AND EDUCATION

For the clergy see Serge Gagnon et Louise Lebel-Gagnon, "Le milieu d'origine du clergé québécois 1775–1840: mythes et réalités." For the history of the church, see Roland Litalien, ed., *L'église de Montréal. Aperçus d'hier et d'aujourd'hui*, particularly the article by Louis Rousseau. Essential for education questions and the clergy is Richard Chabot, *Le curé de campagne et la contestation locale au Québec de 1791 aux troubles de 1837–38*. Literacy is treated in Allan Greer, "The Pattern of Literacy in Quebec, 1745–1899," while the education of women is the subject of two volumes by Nadia Fahmy-Eid and Micheline Dumont, *Maîtresses de maison, maîtresses d'école: Femmes, famille et éducation dans l'histoire du Québec* and *Les couventines: L'éducation des filles au Québec dans les congrégations religieuses enseignantes 1840–1960*.

LAW

For judicial institutions and codification see Jean-Marie Fecteau, "Régulation sociale et répression de la deviance au Bas-Canada au tournant du 19e siècle"; Evelyn Kolish, "Le Conseil législatif et les bureaux d'enregistrement (1836)"; and John Brierley, "Quebec's Civil Law Codification Viewed and Reviewed." For bankruptcy see Dominique Launay, "La banqueroute au Bas-Canada: une étude des années 1840–1849." Of special interest is the July 1987 issue of the *McGill Law Journal* (33, 3) devoted to Quebec legal history.

SOCIAL ISSUES

Urban social structure and economic strategies of the elite are discussed in Jean-Paul Bernard, Paul-André Linteau, and Jean-Claude Robert, "La structure professionelle de Montréal en 1825"; Paul-André Linteau and Jean-Claude Robert, "Land Ownership and Society in Montreal: an Hypothesis"; and Louise Dechêne, "La rente du faubourg Saint-Roch à Québec, 1750–1850." For a case study of industrialization, see Kathleen Lord, "Municipal Aid and Industrial Development, Saint-Jean, Quebec 1848–1914," and Peter Gossage's excellent demographical and social-history study, "Family and Population in a Manufacturing Town: Saint-Hyacinthe, 1854–1914."

The social history of nineteenth-century Montreal's popular classes is treated in several articles by Bettina Bradbury: "The Family Economy and Work in an Industrializing City: Montreal in the 1870s"; "The Fragmented Family: Family Strategies in the Face of Death, Illness and Poverty, Montreal, 1860–1885"; "Pigs, Cows and Boarders: Non-wage Forms of Survival among Montreal Families, 1861–91"; and "Women and Wage Labour in a Period of Transition: Montreal, 1861–81." For extensive coverage of women at work see Marie Lavigne and Yolande Pinard, *Travailleuses et féministes: les femmes dans la société québécoise*. For violence in marriage, see Kathyrn Harvey's thesis " 'To Love, Honour and Obey,' Wife-battering in Working-class Montreal." Of particular interest for its analysis of both Montreal housing and the building trades is David Hanna, *Montreal: A City Built by Small Builders, 1867–1880*.

Popular culture is treated in Peter DeLottinville, "Joe Beef of Montreal: Working Class Culture and the Tavern, 1869–89." For labour see Robert Tremblay's two articles: "La grève des ouvriers de la construction navale à Québec (1840)," and "Un aspect de la consolidation du pouvoir d'Etat de la bourgeoisie coloniale: La législation anti-ouvrière dans le Bas-Canada, 1800–1850." For servants, see Claudette Lacelle, *Urban Domestic Servants in 19th-Century Canada*. For a working-class parish, see Lucia Ferretti, *Entre Voisins*. *La société paroissiale en milieu urbain: Saint-Piérre-Apôtre de Montréal, 1848–1930*. For the economic and social life of a colonization community, see Normand Séguin, *La conquête du sol au 19e siècle*; this can be compared to Claude Baribeau's *La seigneurie de la Petite-Nation 1801–1854*.

For bourgeois social activity see Alan Metcalfe, "The Evolution of Organized Physical Recreation in Montreal, 1840–1895." *Hopes and Dreams: The Diary of Henriette Dessaulles 1874–1881* is an important source for the life of the female elite.

Industrial Capitalism, 1890s–1930s

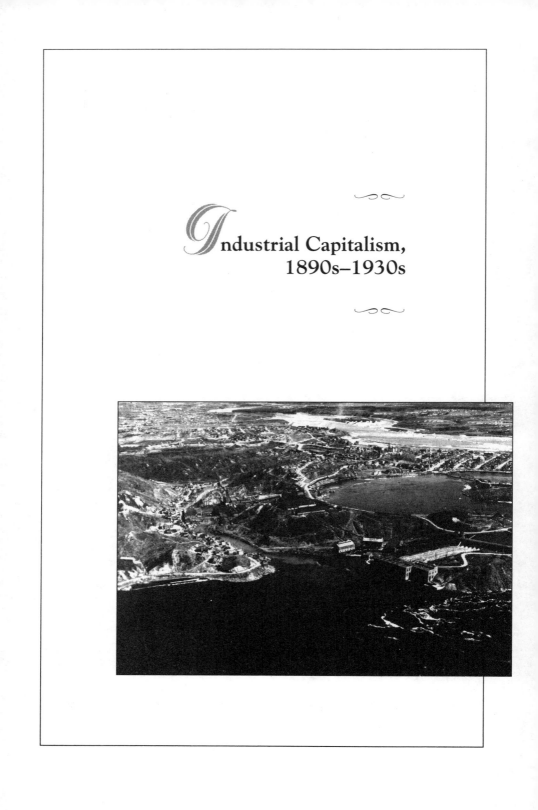

*I*ndustrial capitalism in Quebec matured from the 1890s to the 1930s as new forms of energy, particularly electricity, came into use, technology advanced, and manufacturing expanded rapidly. Most important, ownership of the means of production became increasingly concentrated; monopolies came to dominate transportation, finance, and leading manufacturing sectors such as textiles. Concentration of capital and ownership in the Quebec economy was part of the development of a centralized pan-Canadian bourgeoisie based in Montreal and Toronto.

American capital became important in the Quebec economy, particularly after the First World War, and at the same time the developing resource industries came to depend more and more on American markets. It was in this period that branch plants and resource towns became important features of the Quebec landscape.

Industrial capitalism brought new ways of organizing production, labour, management, and cost accounting. Large corporations emerged with interlocking directorships and centralized management systems. During the transition period of the nineteenth century from the 1810s to the 1880s, small workshops and skilled artisans had remained important. By the turn of the century, however, industry was increasingly large, mechanized, and specialized. The world's largest railway shops, for example—with a labour force of between 4000 and 8000—were the Canadian Pacific's Angus Works in Montreal (Ramirez, 1986: 13). At the same time, productive trades such as blacksmithing were being replaced by service trades such as the automechanic's shop.

By the beginning of the twentieth century, farming had lost its position as the largest employment sector. Although farming itself did not change much, increasing numbers of young people left farming and fishing for work in mines, forests, or factories. By the 1930s, electrification, the radio, the automobile and expanding rail networks had made the consumer products of industrial society accessible to almost all regions of the province.

Before the National Policy (1879), in which protective tariffs were the cornerstone, industrial activity had been widely dispersed across the Maritimes and Central Canada. The concentration of manufacturing in Central Canada after the 1880s was of great benefit to southern Ontario and the Montreal region. By 1919, four-fifths of Canada's manufacturing production occurred in Ontario and Quebec.

While Montreal's rapid population growth and the expansion of its financial and manufacturing power testified to its strength in the province's economic life, other industrial activities developed across the province in regions with mining, forest, and water-power resources (Figure 6.1). Some of these activities were outside the direct influence of Montreal, depending instead on Toronto or New York. Industrial development was uneven, and left important pockets of Quebec

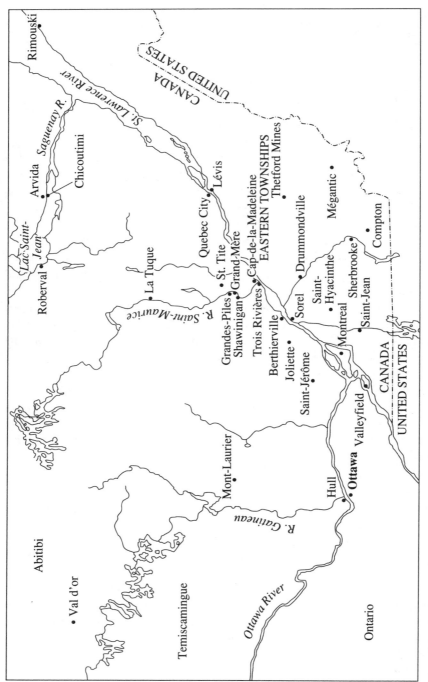

Figure 6.1 Southern Quebec in 1930

characterized by small service towns, traditional farming, and marginal contact with consumer society. Depression and world war underscored the marked differences between regions of Quebec.

The rapid growth of literacy, new forms of rail, road, telegraph, telephone, and postal communication between town and country, the changing form and ownership of the means of production, and the growing influence of capital and the state led to changing social relations. The anglophone bourgeoisie expanded particular institutions that separated it from daily contact with Quebec society; in Montreal, for example, new anglophone municipalities like Westmount and the Town of Mount Royal provided their own municipal services, such as parks and libraries, which allowed women and children to live in enclaves apart from the larger city (Figure 6.2). At the same time, in company towns across Quebec separate neighbourhoods, Tudor-style houses, and curling clubs testified to the insular existence of local anglophone managers and engineers.

Murray Ballantyne, son of a Montreal senator, expressed attitudes characteristic of Montreal's anglophone elite in the post–World War I period:

> I am a Canadian of British stock who was born and brought up in Montreal's once-powerful square mile. I lived surrounded by French Canadians and understood nothing of them. I went to McGill and did graduate and postgraduate work in History. I took every course the History Department at McGill had to offer, and I still understood nothing about the French Canadians. They didn't seem to matter very much (Association Générale des Etudiants de L'Université Laval, 1962: 25).

For labour, gains in wages and buying power, and improved working conditions, especially during the two world wars, were counterbalanced by continuing problems of public health, particularly high infant mortality rates among urban francophones. Desperate unemployment and a struggle for mere survival during the Depression were also a reality as the class inequalities of industrial society deepened.

In the twentieth century, conservative international and Catholic unionism superseded the nineteenth-century tradition of community and shop-floor solidarity, which had been symbolized institutionally by important Quebec support for the Knights of Labor. Immigration, insecurity, and the power of conservative Catholic ideology led to increased ethnic and shop-floor division among workers and, until the 1930s, little public support for progressive movements.

For the working class, adolescence usually meant entry into the paid labour force. Restricted to low-paying jobs on the shop floor, young women were increasingly directed to the gender ghettoes of teaching, nursing, and clerical work. Teaching and nursing were both subject to proletarianization under the guise of professionalization; at the same time, the professionalization of medicine reduced

Figure 6.2 Mount Stephen Avenue in lower Westmount in the early 1900s. A traditional bastion of the anglophone bourgeoisie, Westmount dates from the last two decades of the nineteenth century, and from building booms in the decades before and after the First World War. Westmount attracted the great anglophone capitalists to estates near the top of the mountain while professionals, managers, and merchants built their houses down the slope in lower Westmount. Of particular note in the photo is the use of brick and wood lathing as building materials in these semi-detached houses and the City Beautiful influence evident in the presence of trees, sidewalks, and houses set back on their lots.

The absence of a Roman Catholic church in Westmount contrasted sharply with the plethora of Protestant churches. Lawn-bowling and tennis clubs, the architecture of public buildings, and the infrastructure of parks and libraries reveal Westmount's British traditions. Its separate class and ethnicity were further emphasized by its resistance to annexation to Montreal. Twenty-three suburban municipalities were annexed to Montreal from 1883–1918; Westmount, like its francophone counterpart Outremont, remained separate.

the power of midwives, who practised a traditionally female occupation. Parked at the bottom of rapidly expanding white-collar corporate hierarchies, women's clerical work was segregated, menial, and low paid. The feminization of clerical work accelerated during the labour shortage of the First World War.

DEMOGRAPHY

The population of Quebec increased from 1 359 027 in 1881 to 2 874 662 in 1931 but it did not keep pace with the rest of Canada, particularly the Prairies. As a percentage of the Canadian population, Quebec's population fell from 31.4 percent in 1881 to 27.7 percent in 1931. By the 1920s, almost one-third of the Canadian population lived west of Ontario. The West had only a small francophone population and little contact with Quebec. In the four western provinces in 1941, there were only 138 000 residents whose mother tongue was French. Only 5 percent of these had been born in the East (Joy, 1972: 45). These facts gave poignancy to the language and school crises affecting francophone Catholic minorities in the West.

Despite important European immigration into the Montreal region in the early twentieth century, francophones continued to represent 80 percent of the province's population across the period. There was a dramatic fall in the birth rate from 50 per 1000 in preindustrial Quebec, to 41.1 in 1884–1885, and to 29.2 in the 1931–1935 period. Although Quebec still had Canada's highest birth rate, much of the province's natural increase was restricted to certain rural families. Of Quebec's married women born in 1887, 20.5 percent had more than ten children. These women produced more than 50 percent of the children of their generation (Collectif Clio, 1982: 249).

A fall in the Quebec death rate from 21.9 per 1000 in 1891–1895, to 11.4 per 1000 in 1931–1935 greatly affected population growth. Canada's overall death rate in the latter period was marginally lower (Charbonneau, 1975: 44; Bernier et Boily, 1986: 28). Diarrhea was the leading cause of death among children at the

Year	Francophone Catholics	Other Catholics	Protestants
1885	408.9	189.5	198.3
1890	249.4	204.6	146.2
1895	259.0	199.6	172.3
1900	282.5	235.4	102.8
1905	255.4	198.7	174.4
1911	225.6	179.3	140.6
1914	182.3	195.0	115.8

Table 6.1 Infant Mortality in Montreal, 1885–1914 (per 1000)

(Tétreault, 1983: 512)

turn of the century, and tuberculosis was the leading cause of death among adults. Martin Tétreault (1983) has shown that infant mortality (the death of children in their first year) was linked to class and ethnicity. In 1900, for example, the death rate among francophone Catholic infants in Montreal was almost three times that of the city's Protestant infants (Table 6.1). This can be attributed to differences in the quality of milk, water, lodging, and sewer facilities between rich and poor neighbourhoods. The construction of a water filtration plant in Montreal, pasteurization of milk, and public health programs brought the death rate down significantly in the 1920s. Even in 1961, however, more than thirty of every 1000 children in Quebec died before their first birthday (Langlois, 1990: 32).

The proportion of unmarried women in the population was also significant. The marriage rate stabilized at about seven marriages per year per 1000 women in the period 1884–1930. Across the province about 20 percent of women aged forty were not married, with the highest proportion in the Montreal area. Marta Danylewycz (1987: 52) notes that in many counties of the St. Lawrence plain around Montreal, "where land shortage was endemic and the rate of outmigration high, 25 to 35 percent of the women never married"; in Montreal itself, "at least one women in three was still a spinster at age forty." From the 1880s until at least the 1920s, an increasing percentage of these unmarried women entered religious orders.

The period was marked by sharp increases in urbanization. The urban percentage of the Quebec population increased from 36.1 percent in 1901 to 63.1 percent in 1931. The growth of Montreal was a major factor; the city's population doubled between 1896 and 1911. It reached 818 577 in 1931, which represented 28.4 percent of the province's population. This compared to Quebec City's slower growth from 63 090 in 1896 to 78 710 in 1911 and 130 594 in 1931.

Montreal's dominant urban position must not overshadow the considerable expansion of other urban centres in Quebec. The province counted twenty-four towns and cities with populations over 2500 in 1901 and forty-four in 1931. Much of this development occurred in resource areas along the St. Lawrence, Saint-Maurice, and Saguenay rivers as well as around Montreal. In Chicoutimi county, for example, pulp-and-paper mills opened at the turn of the century. As the region's port, rail, water-power, and mill facilities expanded, the population of Chicoutimi went from 17 percent urban in 1881, to 62 percent by 1921 (Figure 6.3).

As the province was urbanized, its declining anglophone population congregated in the Montreal region, and by 1941 some 70 percent of Quebec anglophones lived on the Ile de Montréal (Rudin, 1985a: 37). By 1911, all traditionally anglophone counties in the Eastern Townships except Brome reported francophone majorities (Joy, 1972: 28). The anglophone population of Quebec City continued to decline, representing only 7 percent of the city's population in 1901. Although a majority of Quebec anglophones were still British or Irish in origin,

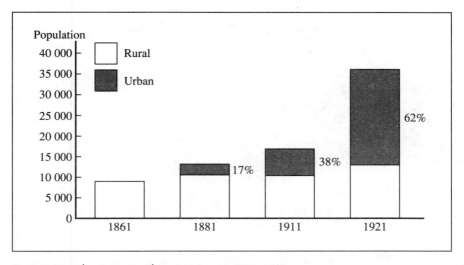

Figure 6.3 Urbanization in Chicoutimi County, 1861–1921

European immigration began to change the ethnic balance, particularly in Montreal. By 1931, 14.3 percent of the population of Montreal was neither French nor British/Irish. People of French origin made up 63.9 percent, and 21.8 were British/Irish. The relatively fast decrease in the British/Irish population of Montreal was due in part to its new concentration in developing suburbs which were not part of the census of the city. For the province as a whole, only 15.1 percent of the population was British or Irish in origin and 5.9 percent neither French nor British/Irish (Figure 6.4).

Quebec, and particularly Montreal, was a favourite destination for immigrants in the first three decades of the century. Between 1901 and 1930, 632 671 immigrants gave Quebec as their destination. The heaviest immigration occurred in the period 1911–1915, when an annual average of 46 491 people arrived in the province.

Although there had been a Jewish community in Montreal since the 1760s, it grew rapidly only after 1890. From 2473 in 1891, the Jewish population of Montreal reached 28 807 in 1911. Although some Jews were professionals, manufacturers, or merchants, many first-generation Montreal Jews worked in the garment industry. In 1931, 1608 Jewish men were working as tailors in Montreal while 1232 women were employed as sewing-machine operators. The 1931 census showed that 39 percent of the employed Jewish population worked in manufacturing, 35.1 percent in commerce, and 5.1 percent in liberal professions such as law or medicine. Most of the remainder worked in offices or construction (Bernier et Boily, 1986: 208).

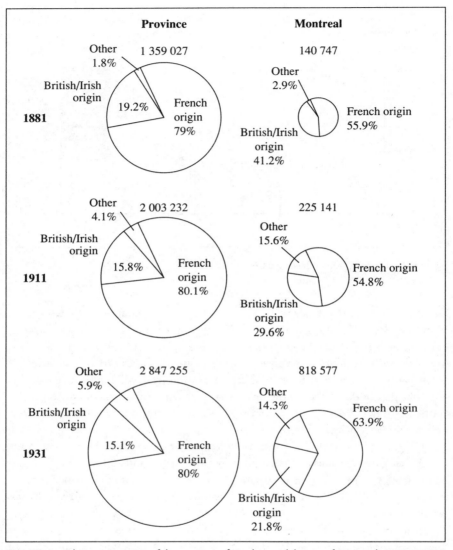

Figure 6.4 Ethnic composition of the province of Quebec and the city of Montreal, 1881–1931 (based on Bernier et Boily, 1986: 43)

Nobel prize winner Saul Bellow recounts his Montreal childhood in the 1920s:

> In our family, my parents spoke Russian between themselves. The children spoke Yiddish with their parents, English among themselves, and French in the streets. . . . I never even was aware of what language I was speaking. I made no distinction whatsoever and simply used the appropriate language for the person with whom I was speaking. I was confident in what I was. That's how I lived.

Italians became important in Montreal urban life in this period. Early in the century, many were recruited in Italy as seasonal labourers for railway or tramway construction sites. In 1903, for example, the Canadian Pacific Railway (CPR) hired over 3500 Italians, mostly through Italian hiring bosses like Antonio Cordasco (Harney, 1979: 74). Two out of three Italian workers were unskilled. Many of the CPR's employees were young and much of the work was seasonal. Some of these sojourners settled in Montreal and established families, usually with Italian wives. Montreal's first Italian parish was established in 1905 to serve an Italian community that increased from 1398 in 1901 to 13 922 in 1921 (Ramirez and Del Balso, 1980: 43).

The ethnic groups of Montreal were visible and important, but they must not be overemphasized in the city's demographic profile, which was dominated by francophones. Lucia Ferretti's study (1992) of the east-end working-class parish of Saint-Pierre-Apôtre de Montréal, 1848–1930, reiterates the nineteenth-century characteristics of Saint-Henri shown by Gilles Lauzon (1987). Family and household patterns in Saint-Pierre-Apôtre reveal the class and ethnic homogeneity of francophones, and also how a Montreal francophone working class was formed and perpetuated. Francophone workers tended to marry the offspring of their francophone peers. Sixty-one percent of the working-class marriages in the parish church were between people born in Montreal. Most of the remaining 39 percent came from rural areas in the Montreal region—particularly from the Ile de Montréal itself or from the lower Laurentians—while others migrated from urban working-class communities like Saint-Roch in Quebec City. New arrivals in the parish frequently found work and lodging through family or village networks.

⌒

Native Peoples

From the 1890s to the 1930s settlements and resource industries encroached further upon areas occupied by native peoples. Throughout areas like the Laurentians, the government set aside or sold large tracts for private hunting and fishing camps. In 1895, for example, the French chocolate manufacturer Henri Menier bought Anticosti Island (from the Indian word Natiscosti, "where bears are hunted") as a private sports reserve. In 1926, it was acquired by Consolidated Bathurst for their pulp-and-paper empire.

In 1857, the province's 3910 Montagnais-Naskapi had been separated into twenty-three different bands. Depletion of fish and game led to famines such as the one in 1892, which reduced the population of Fort Chimo from 350 to 200. In 1900 the Montagnais population was, at best, stable at about 3500. In the early 1900s, the Montagnais relied on purchased foodstuffs to support their winter trapping expeditions. Increasingly dependent on a money economy, many acted as hunting and fishing guides for wealthy whites.

The traditional disregard by the state for native land claims became more significant as resource extraction and tourism gave new importance to the North. The fate of Huron territories illustrates this well. By the 1880s, hunting from the Saguenay to the St. Maurice was the mainstay of the Lorette Huron economy. Their livelihood was totally disrupted once the Lake St. John Railway was completed in 1893 and the Parc des Laurentides was created in 1895. Promoters successfully petitioned to have huge tracts of land along their railway granted to them for private hunting clubs. Both the private clubs and the provincial government then employed game wardens to force Hurons out of their traditional territory. Only in 1990 did the Supreme Court of Canada finally recognize Huron territorial rights.

The economic and cultural consequences of engrained ignorance of native needs and rights were dramatic. Hurons at Lorette had an infant mortality rate of 331 per 1000 and the reserve suffered from outmigration in the period 1900 to 1930. Hunting became less important and agriculture had disappeared from the reserve by the end of the nineteenth century in favour of handicrafts and factory work. The last Huron speaker died in 1912 (Helm, 1981: 173).

AN INDUSTRIAL CAPITALIST ECONOMY

The importance of both industrial activity and capital make the term "industrial capitalism" apt to describe Quebec's early twentieth-century economy. Financial institutions and many traditional manufacturing sectors remained Canadian during the period but considerable American capital was invested in Canadian mining and smelting and pulp-and-paper industries. It is difficult to assess the role of foreign capital. Theoretically, American investment in pulp-and-paper grew from $20 000 000 in 1897 to $74 000 000 in 1914 (Bernier et Boily, 1986: 142), but it is not clear how much of this was new American capital and how much was simply reinvested profit from Canadian operations.

The exploitation of hydro-electric resources in the southern part of the province helped Quebec's industrial capitalist economy to mature. Four rivers provided the potential for massive power: the St. Lawrence west of Montreal; the Ottawa and its tributary the Gatineau; the Saint-Maurice; and the Saguenay. By 1933, almost half of Canada's total electric capacity of 8 000 000 horsepower was located in Quebec (Armstrong and Nelles, 1986: Table 36).

Two important political decisions influenced the development of hydro-electric power in Quebec. Unlike Ontario, Quebec did not nationalize hydro-electric

Figure 6.5 Shawinigan, 1914. The importance of electricity in Quebec's early twentieth-century economy is evident in this photo. The picture shows not only a dam and a generating station but also an aluminum smelter (established 1901), on the top of the hill to the left of the dam. With war demands, its annual production rose to 8332 tonnes in 1915. In the bay below the smelter is the Belgo-Canadian Pulp and Paper Mill, which produced eighty-two tonnes of pulp a day in 1902; in 1904 the mill began producing paper and by 1926 it produced 635 tonnes of newsprint a day. Near the generating station were also located a brickyard and cable factory (1902). Shawinigan's chemical factories are in the background (1911) (Groupe de Recherche sur la Mauricie, 1985).

power before the 1960s. Equally important, private companies were permitted to concentrate on commercial clients, giving them preferential treatment over residential service. Many companies had arrangements with important industrial consumers. Three-quarters of Quebec's hydro-electric power in the 1930s was sold to the wood, paper, and aluminum industries or was exported; and pricing structures discouraged consumption by small industries, farms, and residences. In 1931, domestic service in Quebec represented only 3.5 percent of provincial hydro-electric consumption, compared to 17.4 percent in Ontario (Armstrong, 1984: 224; Armstrong and Nelles, 1986: 299).

Canadian technology for generating and transmitting electricity was first developed in the 1890s at Niagara Falls, Ontario. In 1898, the Shawinigan Water and Power Company was formed to exploit the forty-one metre drop of the Saint-Maurice River at Shawinigan (Figure 6.5). Using American capital, the

Shawinigan generating station and dam became the world's second largest hydro-electric centre, Niagara being the largest. By 1903, hydro lines capable of carrying 50 000 volts had been built across the 134 kilometres that separated the site from Montreal. In 1905, the company's total capital was $10 600 000 (Armstrong and Nelles, 1986: Table 10). Shawinigan experienced a further boom during the First World War when electrical consumption and local chemical production, particularly of carbides, expanded enormously.

Industries in centres like Shawinigan benefited not only from inexpensive power and the availability of forest resources, but also from cheap labour. The Saint-Maurice population was already dependent on seasonal forest work; employers now depicted it to industrial investors as a pool of passive, happy wage labourers who were obedient to their priests:

> Nowhere in the world can more favorable labour conditions be found than in the province of Quebec and in the region of the Shawinigan Water and Power Company in particular. A happier and more satisfied people can probably not be found on the face of the earth. The satisfaction of the French Canadian people is a factor of great importance for employers in this region; this value of human happiness is directly attributable to the wise and good direction of their "father confessors," the Catholic priests. For centuries in this region, the first principle of the habitants' religion has been to be satisfied with their lot. Local unions are moderate and reasonable in their demands. . . . Another important factor for labour availability is the proverbial size of the French Canadian family. Since they all must eat, they must all work, and so the factory has abundant female and male labour on its doorstep; since they all must work, the wages asked for are extremely low (Shawinigan Water and Power Company brochure, 1930).

Local francophones served as unskilled labour, whereas skilled workers, company managers, and professionals were recruited in Britain and in the anglophone community. In 1911, 6.5 percent of Shawinigan's population was anglophone, a much higher percentage than in other Saint-Maurice communities. Quebec communities based on mining, pulp-and-paper, or water-power resources developed predictable class and ethnic divisions. Managers, engineers, and chemists were usually anglophones who benefited from company-subsidized housing and sporting clubs.

⌒

The Expansion of Industry

The province's largest mills were established in the Canadian Shield and Appalachians, where direct access to spruce forests and hydro-electric power was possible. Here, American capital was central to the development of pulp-and-paper towns along the Ottawa, Saint-Maurice, and Saguenay rivers. Like other pulpwood-producing provinces, Quebec was concerned that pulpwood was being exported instead of manufactured into newsprint within Quebec. In 1910 it followed Ontario's lead in forbidding the export of pulpwood. By the First World War, Canada was the world's largest producer of newsprint, with 86.4 percent destined for American markets. Despite a drop during the Depression, pulp-and-paper held its position as the largest Canadian export, representing 24 percent of the country's exports in 1954.

Mining became increasingly important in the first half of the twentieth century. Quebec's gold and copper became of world importance by the end of the 1920s as mines were opened in the Abitibi region around Rouyn-Noranda. (Compare in Table 6.2, for example, gold and copper production in 1920 with that of 1930.) By 1930, Noranda Mines had built a copper smelter and concentrator in Noranda and a refinery in Montreal. The rise of gold prices during the Depression stimulated gold production. Asbestos mining was controlled by American companies like the Johns Manville Corporation. Production of asbestos fibre in Eastern Townships communities like Thetford Mines expanded rapidly in the twentieth century; 70 percent of it was exported unprocessed to the United States. Before the First World War, asbestos was exported especially for use as roofing material. In the 1920s it found new markets in the expanding automobile industry, particularly for brake linings.

Like copper and asbestos, aluminum was an increasingly important material in the electrical, war, and automobile industries. Alcan, the major producer of Canadian aluminum, was founded as a Canadian branch plant of the Aluminum Company of America in 1902. The company helped develop the massive hydroelectric resources of the Saguenay River in the 1920s and built a smelter. Its company town, Arvida, was named after company president Arthur Vining Davis. By 1936 Alcan, owned for the most part by the Davis family, was the world's second largest aluminum producer.

The value of Quebec manufacturing doubled between 1900 and 1919 and the number of workers increased from 101 600 in 1901 to 125 400 in 1921 (Roby, 1976: 19). In Valleyfield, for example, the Montreal Cotton Company mill developed the largest concentration of textile machinery in Canada: by 1907 Valleyfield had over 5000 textile workers (Ferland, 1987: 61).

	1910	1920	1930
Gold	3 000	19 000	2 930 000
Copper	112 000	154 000	10 426 000
Asbestos	2 556 000	14 735 000	8 390 000

Table 6.2   Value of Quebec Gold, Copper, and Asbestos Production, 1910–1930 (in dollars) (Armstrong, 1984: 221)

The First World War stimulated Quebec industry. Two large munition factories were built in the Montreal area during the war, and shipbuilding expanded in Montreal, Quebec City, and Sorel. Nor was it just the transportation and iron-and-steel sectors that benefited from war. The Wood Manufacturing Company, a Montreal producer of twine, tents, and flags, saw the value of its common stock triple during the First World War.

Transportation had always been central to the Quebec economy. During the 1890s–1930s period it underwent three important changes: the advent of the automobile, expansion into resource regions, and consolidation. Quebec vehicle ownership mushroomed in the 1920s, but most Canadian automobiles were produced in Ontario. National annual production of cars tripled between 1919 and 1929. In 1929, 188 721 cars were built in Canada and the industry employed 13 000 workers in Ontario.

Two new transcontinental railways—the National Transcontinental and the Canadian Northern—had important regional ramifications for Quebec. Begun in 1903, the National Transcontinental, part of the larger Grand Trunk Pacific system, ran from Moncton to Winnipeg and crossed the St. Lawrence at Quebec City. The opening of the Quebec Bridge at the end of the First World War gave Quebec City a direct rail link to the south shore of the St. Lawrence and from there to ports open year round. West of Quebec City, the National Transcontinental reached La Tuque, followed the Upper Saint-Maurice Valley for 192 kilometres, and continued into the Abitibi region and into Northern Ontario.

The Canadian Northern Railway project, organized by William Mackenzie and Donald Mann, eventually included several Quebec regional railways in its transcontinental system: the Lower Laurentian Railway, the Quebec and Lake St. John Railway, and the Quebec, New Brunswick, and Nova Scotia Railway. Despite some success, such as their five-kilometre tunnel through Mont Royal in Montreal, the Mackenzie–Mann syndicate was bankrupt by the First World War. The National Transcontinental, as part of the Grand Trunk system, also failed as its sources of British capital dried up during the war. In 1917, the bankrupt companies were nationalized into the Canadian National Railways system. By 1923, the Canadian National, which was composed of the residual assets of 221 different railway companies, had 35 000 kilometres of rail and 99 169 employees (Stevens, 1973: 311).

Both the Canadian National Railways and the privately owned Canadian Pacific Railway had their head offices and major shops in Montreal. This had important repercussions for the concentration of iron-and-steel and rail transportation equipment manufacturers in Quebec. In the 1920s, for example, the Canadian Car and Foundry of Amherst, Nova Scotia, and the Maritime Nail Company of Saint John moved their plants to Montreal (Thompson and Seager: 1985, 106).

Food and beverage processing, much of which had undergone an early transition to industrial production, remained Quebec's most important manufacturing sector across this period. It represented 23.6 percent of the value of manufacturing production in 1880, 17 percent in 1910, and 19.3 percent in 1939. The expanding transcontinental rail system and the Canadian freight rate structure ensured that the products of the mills, breweries, canneries, and sugar refineries could be distributed nationally.

In 1911, the St. Lawrence Sugar Company's Montreal plant produced between 20 and 25 percent of Canada's sugar. Ogilvie Mills of Montreal, a flour milling company started in 1801, was reputedly the world's largest private flour company in 1900; in 1920 it controlled over 100 western grain elevators and seven mills with a daily capacity of 19 000 barrels (Sweeny, 1978: 199). Not all Quebec food and beverage production was destined for national markets. In Montreal, the Viau Biscuit Company's annual sales of $1 000 000 (1913) came largely from local consumption, and regional distillers like Melcher's of Berthierville supplied Quebecers with gin. The sector also spawned important ancillary Quebec industries such as bag, barrel, bottle, and can manufacturers.

Quebec brewers were particularly vigilant in protecting their market. Molson, Dow, Dawes, and Ekers united to defeat the Anti-Alcohol League in the 1919 provincial plebiscite over the sale of wine and beer. Monster torchlight parades in favour of wine and beer sales were held in Montreal while the Quebec Brewers' Association pointed out their centuries-old contribution to Canadian social life:

> For more than a century they have promoted temperance in its truest form. They have given the public a pure, wholesome, delicious beverage, healthful and nutritious in winter, refreshing and thirst-quenching in summer . . . YOU—who enjoy a glass of beer; you—who appreciate the goodness of beer; you—who have beer in the house—remember that if this law goes into effect on May 1st, you will get no more. WHAT ARE YOU GOING TO DO ABOUT IT? (Denison, 1955: 320).

With the defeat of the plebiscite, Molson in 1920 had its first five-million gallon year, rising to seven and a half million gallons in 1929.

Agriculture became less central in the Quebec economy. The percentage of the Quebec labour force engaged in agriculture declined from 45.5 percent in 1891 to 19.3 percent in 1941. The dairy industry remained important, with cheese exports to Britain peaking in 1904 and then falling off in the face of New Zealand competition. Cheese production, which was concentrated in the Eastern Townships, dropped significantly in the early twentieth century. On the other hand, butter production increased threefold in response to new manufacturing technology, refrigerated rail transportation, and growing domestic demand.

Year	Butter	Cheese
1901	11 193	36 650
1911	18 922	26 441
1921	22 104	24 655
1931	31 660	11 776
1941	34 666	17 737

Table 6.3   Factory Butter and Cheese Production in Quebec, 1901–1941 (in tonnes) (Séguin, 1980: 123)

Despite improvements in the dairy industry, Quebec agriculture did not modernize during this period. Colonization into the Shield was still encouraged by clerical nationalists—who feared that large segments of the population would emigrate to the United States—although the total number of farms levelled off. The growing pulp-and-paper industry maintained the traditional agro-forestry sector. More important, however, the average size of Quebec farms remained stable instead of merging into larger, more profitable units, and farm mechanization lagged far behind other Canadian provinces.

The tobacco industry became more important during this period but another consumer industry, the leather sector, declined. Tanning and saddlery industries migrated to Ontario as Quebec hemlock (used in the tanning process) was exhausted and as hide production became tied to the Ontario meat packers. The number of tanneries in Quebec City fell from twenty-seven in 1901 to twenty-one in 1911 and the number of shoe manufacturers fell from thirty-five to twenty-six in the same period. The decline was accompanied by a drop in shoeworkers in Quebec City, from 3838 to 2987. In 1871, Montreal had dominated Canadian saddlery production with twenty-three saddle manufacturers, mostly small. What was left of this dying industry by the turn of the century was largely in Ontario (Ferland, 1985: 147–48).

Shoemaking remained fragmented in both organization and capital structure, which is a reminder that not all sectors of the Quebec economy underwent centralization or concentration. Nevertheless, an American company did manage by means of patents to hold a virtual monopoly on the machines used in shoe assembly. The United Shoe Machinery Company of Massachusetts built a branch plant in Montreal in 1912 to produce shoe-assembly machines for the Canadian market, of which it controlled 95 percent (Ferland, 1985: 187). The company leased its machines and aggressively defended its proprietary rights.

Concentration in the shoe-assembly machines tended to protect small Quebec manufacturers since shoe producers had no choice but to rent rather than to invest in the equipment (Bluteau et al., 1980: 111). While a few giant shoe man-ufacturers, such as Ames-Holden of Montreal, produced over 2 000 000 pairs of shoes annually (1921), they represented only 9 percent of Canadian shoe produc-tion. Twenty-nine percent of production came from manufacturers who produced fewer than 100 000 pairs annually.

The Quebec garment industry throughout the 1890s–1930s period was char-acterized by low capital investment, limited technology, and dependence on cheap, female, piecework labour. In the late nineteenth century, social change, urbanization, new work and consumer patterns, and new marketing phenomena (department stores and catalogue-sales outlets) stimulated Quebec's "ready-to-wear" clothing industry. Canadian clothing production increased 400 percent in the last three decades of the century. Although Quebec City had 1300 workers in the garment trades in 1891, the industry was traditionally concentrated in Montreal.

Based on standard sizes, clothing production branched out from an early con-centration on men's work shirts, overalls, and coats into blouses, underclothes, and coats for the women's market. Unlike the generators of the hydro-electric station or the boilers of a foundry, the technology of the garment industry—the sewing machine, button-holer, and steam iron—was inexpensive and did not have to be concentrated on a single work site.

At the H. Shorey Company in Montreal, only 130 of the 1530 employees on the 1892 payroll worked on the company premises (Steedman, 1986: 153). Male tailors and workers in the Montreal factory did the cutting, pressing, and finish-ing, and the piecework was distributed to women in the city or surrounding coun-tryside. In 1935, a pair of pants sewed in out-work brought $0.25 to its female producer; the same pair of pants produced in a union factory had a labour cost of $1.50 (Lavigne et Pinard, 1983: 129). Low fixed capital costs meant that the industry remained open to entrepreneurs and less subject to concentration than the highly capitalized sectors.

Iron- and steelworks remained an important sector. In Trois-Rivières, the Canada Iron Furnace Company built what was reputed to be Canada's largest fur-nace. In 1908 its 800 workers produced 400 000 train wheels, 200 000 tonnes of pipe, and machinery for the pulp-and-paper industry. Production of transporta-tion equipment increased, especially in Montreal, where Canadian Pacific's Angus railway shops were opened and the British-owned Vickers Company opened its Maisonneuve shipyards in 1912. War contracts were of great impor-tance in this sector, prompting expansion of Quebec foundries and engineering companies. Over 15 000 people worked at the Vickers shipyards during the First World War, while Davie Shipbuilding of Lauzon built submarines, submarine chasers, and steel barges.

FINANCIAL INSTITUTIONS

Early twentieth-century finance capitalism in Quebec was characterized by monopoly. The links between finance and industry deepened as banks and trust and insurance companies developed interlocking directorships with the major manufacturing enterprises. The operation of what was then Canada's largest bank, the Bank of Montreal, shows how industrial and financial capital mixed. The bank was active in financing the Canadian Pacific Railway (CPR), Bell Telephone, the Laurentide Paper Company, and Dominion Textile. George Stephen, president of the bank, headed the CPR syndicate, and in the 1880s the bank's principal stockholder was Montreal's leading tobacco manufacturer, William Macdonald. In 1930, the Bank of Montreal shared three or more directors with each of ten companies, including industrial concerns such as Canada Steamship Lines, Consolidated Mining and Smelting Company, Dominion Rubber, Bell Telephone, and Dominion Textiles. Among financial institutions it shared directors with were Sun Life and Royal Trust (with which it shared eleven directors in 1930) (Piédalue, 1976: 378). Consolidation within Canada was accompanied by rapid overseas expansion as the Bank of Montreal moved into Newfoundland, the Caribbean, and Central and South America; by 1926 it was the largest financial institution in Mexico (Sweeny, 1978: 19).

Bank mergers were an important element of concentration. The number of Canadian banks dropped from fifty-one in 1875 to twenty-one in 1918, and eleven in 1925. Sherbrooke's Eastern Townships Bank, with seventy-seven branches, was acquired by the Canadian Bank of Commerce in 1912. Among the regional banks, only the two francophone-controlled ones remained: the Banque Canadienne Nationale (the result of a government-managed merger of the Banque d'Hochelaga and the Canadienne Nationale in 1923) and the Banque Provinciale. For its part, the Bank of Montreal acquired three old Montreal banks (the Bank of British North America, the Merchants Bank, and Molson's Bank) and at the outset of the Depression had assets totalling $965 000 000 (Rudin, 1985b: 120; Sweeny, 1978: 20).

The example of the Sun Life Assurance Company demonstrates how a Montreal financial institution expanded from a local capital base into an international operation. This company also illustrates the fusion of industrial and financial capital in Quebec. Life insurance began in Canada only in the 1870s, with the growth of an urban, white-collar labour force. Set up in 1871 by Montreal merchant and industrialist capitalists, Sun Life soon had agents across Canada and throughout the world, particularly within the British empire. As chapter 4 discussed, the company began writing insurance in the West Indies in 1877 and by 1900 it had made an impact in the Orient, Great Britain, the United States, and Africa. Sun Life accumulated vast amounts of capital from insurance premiums, which it invested first in mortgages and then increasingly in electric-power utilities and street railways in the United States and Canada.

As early as 1900, company secretary T. B. Macaulay emphasized to the board of directors the importance of utilities and other industries based on hydro-electric power: "We should do well to ask ourselves whether the securities of some of the corporations which depend on this new and rising power [electricity] may not be just as desirable as those which depend upon [steampower] which has already reached its zenith" (Sweeny, 1978: 241).

Having made millions from public-utility monopolies in Ontario and the American Midwest, Sun Life invested $50 million in First World War Dominion and Imperial bonds, and during the Second World War it was the largest subscriber to Canadian war bonds. In the 1920s, Sun Life took over dozens of Canadian and foreign insurance companies. By the end of that decade its assets totalled over $400 million and its office staff numbered 1500. The company's Montreal head office was the largest office building in the British empire.

Francophones were to a large degree absent from these concentrated financial groups. (Stockbroker Louis-Joseph Forget was an exception. He was president of the Montreal Stock Exchange in 1895 and 1896 and, with Herbert Holt, a dominant figure in the merger of several utility companies into the Montreal Light Heat and Power Company.) Looking at this phenomenon, Robert Sweeny (1978) rejects the explanation of the "hardy Scot" and "enterprising American" ethnic determinism. Fernande Roy (1988: 275–76) examines the ideology of francophone entrepreneurs in Montreal and insists on their liberal views on property, the role of the state, labour, progress, and success. She sees no contradiction between liberalism and a sense of French-Canadian nationalism that led them to seek an increased hold on Quebec society. Sweeny goes further in emphasizing the link between ownership of francophone financial institutions and nationalism, showing how the regional bourgeoisie developed a *maître chez-nous* strategy of controlling local capital:

> Over 90% of the shareholders in the Strathcona Fire Company were members of the Chamber of Notaries. Active in the field of real estate, these men were building on their own experience in contributing to the creation of an institutional framework which permitted the savings of French Canadians to remain within the Québec economy.

In the small cities, towns, and villages of the St. Lawrence lowlands, the established francophone elite provided capital for the small, regional industries and local agriculture. This milieu would produce conservative nationalists such as Maurice Duplessis and, a generation later, Union Nationale leader and Parti Québécois cabinet minister Rodrigue Biron.

Besides running the regional banks, francophones also started the Caisse Populaire movement, an important savings and loan co-operative. Using European co-operatives and savings and loan bank models, Alphonse Desjardins opened the first Caisse in his Lévis home in 1901. The Caisses were run as co-operatives and every member had a vote. They had the double social and nationalist aim of encouraging farmers and workers to save and of collecting capital to make available to francophones. The Caisses both collected savings deposits and made loans; in the period 1915–1920, the average loan was $182. The Catholic clergy were enthusiastic supporters of the movement and many Caisses were formally associated with parish churches, which helped their expansion. By 1920, 206 had been established across Quebec and in francophone communities in Ontario and New England; these were grouped into ten regional federations.

The Depression of the 1930s eroded Montreal's primacy as Canada's financial and manufacturing centre; its important textile and clothing manufacturing sector was particularly vulnerable to falling consumer demand. In the 1920s, 70 percent of stocks sold in Canada were handled on the Montreal Stock Exchange but by 1933 the Toronto exchange had 55 percent of the market volume (McCann, 1982: 96). The decline of the Montreal exchange was accelerated by the increasing financial and industrial strength of Toronto as the metropolis of industrial southern Ontario, and by the preference of American investors for the Toronto exchange. Most of the head offices and almost all the financing of the expanding mining sector on the Canadian Shield (especially gold) were located in Toronto.

LABOUR

In industrial capitalist Quebec the nature of work was transformed not only by changes in ownership and forms of production but by the declining importance of agriculture, by fluctuations in the demand for goods resulting from world war and depression, and by the state, church, and employers combining to suppress labour resistance. At the same time, there is strong evidence of vigorous labour resistance in certain sectors (Ferland, 1985; Rouillard, 1981).

Despite industrialization, work in Quebec remained seasonal for many workers, and not just in the forest sector. Longshoremen, construction workers, and sailors could not expect to work more than seven or eight months a year. Machinists, ironworkers, and mechanics in Quebec City came back to the docks in late February and March to prepare ships for the season. In October it was customary for many workers from the Quebec suburb of Sillery to take the train to Lac Saint-Jean, where they worked in the forest. Shoe manufacturers shut down for four to six weeks in the slow season. Of the CPR's Italian employees in Montreal in 1900–1930, 50 percent worked less than six months for the company and 19 percent worked a month or less. The instability and de-skilling of labour is clear from Bruno Ramirez's analysis of CPR employment records:

> [Italian machinist T.D.] was first hired in July 1917 as a machinist [. . .] one week later he was switched to a bolt threader job and then laid off during a staff reduction. In February of the following year, he landed another skilled job, this time as a boiler maker, but in less than two months he was laid off again in another staff reduction. Three days later, he got himself hired as a bolt threader and one month later he climbed to a machinist job. But the path to downward mobility could be a precipitous one, and one year later T. D. found himself once more at the bottom working as a labourer. . . . [I]n November 1920, he started moving up the occupational ladder again, first as a "foundry helper," then as a "skilled helper." His path was halted by another reduction in staff. It took another two years before T. D. was back in the employ of CP [as a machinist]. A few months later he had slipped down again, and was working as a rivetter (Ramirez, 1986: 24).

Across the first half of the century, improvements in working conditions came only slowly. Per capita income in 1926 was $363 in Quebec, compared to $278 in New Brunswick and $491 in Ontario (Armstrong and Nelles, 1986: 286). Many skilled workers in Quebec City had won the fifty-four-hour work week by 1909, but women and children still worked sixty hours a week. Although a provincial law in 1912 reduced the work week in the textile industry to fifty-five hours, the law was not applied.

Through the first quarter of the century, child labour continued to be important in the manufacturing sector. Fines and corporal punishment were used to control this juvenile labour force. Although Quebec was a leader in Canada with its 1909 industrial accident legislation, the government consistently failed to provide sufficient budgets to monitor infractions to its factory act. Factory inspection remained haphazard, and overworked inspectors had little power to improve plant ventilation, sanitation, or safety. There were 131 industrial deaths reported in Quebec City during the period 1904–1914. Construction was particularly dangerous (Figure 6.6). On the other hand, both the federal and provincial governments were active in passing legislation to impose arbitration of labour conflicts (Dickinson, 1986b).

As elsewhere in Canada, the Depression had an effect in Quebec that went far beyond unemployment; farm bankruptcy, acute social distress, and hunger were common (Figure 6.7). The collapse of markets for export resources such as pulp-and-paper and asbestos led to intense hardship across entire regions of the province. Despite popular myths about their self-sufficiency, farmers were not spared and, in 1931, 35 000 Quebec farmers were reported bankrupt (Lévesque,

Figure 6.6 Collapse of the Quebec City Bridge, 1916. Modelled on the Firth of Forth Bridge near Edinburgh, Scotland, the Quebec Bridge collapsed twice during construction. Thirty-five of the seventy-four workers killed on 29 August 1907 were Mohawk steelworkers from Kahnawake. On 11 September 1916, the central span collapsed while being hoisted into place. Ten men perished in the river: "the mass twisted on its side as though in pain," an observer recalled, "and plunged to the bottom in a great cloud of spray. . . . Bodies were shaken down like apples from a tree, to fall splashing into the river. One man fell from a great height like a mannequin or wooden doll."

Figure 6.7 Eviction in Montreal during the Depression. A city of tenants, Montreal was also characterized by a labour force of which one-sixth were unskilled labourers. This double vulnerability was made even harsher by the low per capita expenditure on social services: $39.60 in 1926 compared to $54.50 in Toronto (Copp, 1974: 146). The conjuncture of tenancy, limited social services, and unemployment assumed massive social dimensions during the Depression and by 1933, 38 percent of the city's francophones were on relief. Many were simply forced into the streets.

1984b: 21). In Montreal alone, 48 percent of family heads in 1931 had annual incomes of less than $1000, the minimal survival income for a family. A 1933 study of the city's unemployed showed that only 55 percent of unemployed adults had an adequate diet.

WOMEN AT WORK

While women continued to be responsible for domestic work and mothering, they also formed a growing part of Quebec's paid labour force. The number of working women rose from 98 429 in 1911 to just over 200 850 in 1931 despite the advent of the Depression (see Table 6.4).

In the labour shortage of the First World War, Quebec women moved into labour sectors traditionally reserved for men: munitions, steel, cement production, and transportation (see Figure 6.8). Female labour was synonymous with cheap labour, since women's wages were about half those of men's: 53.6 percent of male wages in 1921 and 51 percent in 1941. Gail Cuthbert Brandt (1985) has shown the salary inequities in the Quebec cotton industry: "the evidence is incontrovertible that female operatives earned less than their male counterparts. [. . .] In 1926 male frame spinners in Quebec earned the equivalent of 30.7 cents an hour while female spinners made only 24.3 cents." Competition from clerics helped keep teachers' salaries low (Table 6.5). A female Catholic teacher's starting salary of $625 in 1920 compared to her unmarried male counterpart's salary of $900; a married male started at $1200. Male Protestant schoolteachers averaged nearly $2000. Female teachers in urban schools, it is estimated, earned a little more than half the salary of the male caretakers of their schools (Lavigne et Pinard, 1983: 126; Thivierge, 1983: 176; Danylewycz and Prentice, 1986: 75).

Sector	1911	1921	1931
Manufacturing	40.1	33.5	23.4
Domestic	32.6	20.2	29.3
Office workers	—	18.5	18.9
Professional services	9.6	14.2	11.6
Commerce	13.9	8.8	8.4
Transportation	2.7	3.6	4.4
Percent of total labour force	21.6	25.2	25.4

Table 6.4   Percentage of Female Labour in the Principal Occupational Sectors, Montreal 1911–1931
(Lavigne et Pinard, 1983: 127)

Figure 6.8 Women's lunchroom in a Montreal munitions factory

As elsewhere in Canada, female work became wage work, and was ghettoized as greater numbers of women became elementary school teachers, nurses, telephone operators, office clerks, and store clerks. The Banque d'Hochelaga had only one female employee in 1901 and six in 1911. By 1921 in the Bank's head office, "where the deskilling of jobs was most advanced," women represented one-third of the work force of 179 (Rudin, 1986: 65). Comparing the sexual division of labour at the Banque d'Hochelaga in the first third of the century, Michèle Dagenais (1989) found that male work was characterized by the ability to transfer from branch to branch and to reach management positions; women were almost inevitably given dead-end work in the bank's lower echelons, particularly as clerks and stenographers. By the 1930s, Sun Life had 87 females in its stenography pool—yet another sign of the specialization and degradation of female work at the company. Across Dominion Square from Sun Life, the Canadian Pacific Railway grouped its twenty female stenographers and typists into one office in 1935 (Lowe, 1987: 124). Private secretarial schools developed as part of the feminization of clerical labour, and to serve the growing labour demand. The schools attracted female students for the most part, who were taught the inferior office tasks—typing and stenography—while accounting and bookkeeping were taught largely to the male students. In the retail sector, part-time labour and employer paternalism were effective means of keeping women's salaries low.

Year	Lay females	Lay males	Nuns	Brothers
1900	55.0	2.3	32.5	10.2
1910	51.4	2.5	33.7	12.4
1920	48.1	3.3	35.4	13.2
1930	45.6	6.1	35.1	13.2
1940	44.2	6.6	35.7	13.5
1950	47.4	8.0	32.7	11.0

Table 6.5   Percentage of Lay Females and Male Teachers, Nuns, and Brothers in Catholic Schools, 1900–1950

(Thivierge, 1983: 172)

Far from being intellectual work that offered women good working conditions and opportunities for social advancement, elementary school teaching in Quebec was a distinct element in the proletarianization of female labour because teachers were underpaid wage workers, blocked from professional advancement (Danylewycz and Prentice, 1986: 61). Female teachers were subject to increasing bureaucratization and inspection, and worked in poorly ventilated, ill-equipped, and overcrowded classrooms. Rural teachers were expected to clean the classroom, shovel snow, and light fires. Isolation, fatigue, physical breakdown, and poverty in old age were conditions that had less in common with the professions than with the working class.

While professions such as elementary-school teaching became feminized, the more prestigious professions of medicine and law in Quebec resisted even a token presence of women (Figure 6.9). Annie Macdonald Langstaff grew up in Ontario and in 1906 came to Montreal, where she worked in a legal office until she was admitted as the first woman in the McGill Law School. Graduating fourth in her class (1914), she unsuccessfully petitioned the courts against the refusal of the Quebec Bar to let her practise law. Asked in court if she had consulted her husband before entering law, she replied, "No, I did not, I did not know his address." That Macdonald Langstaff was a woman, married, and separated had a cumulative effect in Justice St. Pierre's decision that her admission to the bar "would be nothing short of a direct infringement of public order and a manifest violation of the law of good morals and public decency." For her part, Macdonald Langstaff refused to attribute this discrimination entirely to men:

> It is not merely men who oppose the entrance of women into the learned professions. There are many women who are so cowardly and so lacking in true womenhood as to take the same attitude. . . . It is all very well to say that women's sole sphere should be the home, but this shows most lamentable blindness to economic conditions which one would think were potent. The plain fact . . . is that many women have to earn their living outside the home, if they are to have homes at all (Gillett, 1981: 306).

Figure 6.9 Irma LeVasseur (1877–1964), Quebec's first woman doctor. Irma LeVasseur went to Quebec City's Ecole normale Laval after classical-college studies at the Collège Jésus-Marie. Since women were denied access to medical school in Quebec, LeVasseur went to Minnesota, obtaining her M.D. in 1900. She then had to await passage of a private member's bill in the Quebec National Assembly in 1903 before being allowed to practise in the province. During the First World War she was one of five Canadian doctors who served in Serbia during the typhus epidemic of 1915–1917. She returned in 1920 to Quebec City, where she played an important role establishing clinics for children and disabled people. "The end of her life was less fortunate. Homeless, she died in January 1964, forgotten and penniless . . . " (Michaud, 1985).

As medicine became professionalized, clinical training for doctors was entrenched and male doctors came to dominate hospital administration. As a consequence, nursing became proletarianized, and the importance of midwifery declined. Birthing, traditionally a preserve of the midwife, became a male domain as midwives were formally excluded from using new obstetrical techniques such as induced labour, surgical deliveries, anesthesia, and using forceps. At the Montreal Maternity Hospital, an important obstetrical teaching hospital attached to McGill

University, the midwife was replaced in 1886 by a resident physician. The same hospital successfully objected in 1916 to the admission of black medical students, although male (Gillett, 1981: 292). In 1917, midwives were reminded by the Quebec College of Physicians and Surgeons that they were forbidden to use forceps.

Professionalization of nursing occurred in the 1890s with probationary training, supervision by doctors, diplomas, and residences for trainees. The first nursing school in Quebec was opened by the Montreal General Hospital in 1890. The first nursing courses in French were offered at Notre Dame Hospital in 1897. By 1909, there were seventy nursing schools in Canada. The number of graduate nurses in Canada rose from 280 in 1901 to 5600 in 1911 and 20 462 in 1931 (Urquhart and Buckley, 1965: 44).

LABOUR ORGANIZATIONS

Until late in the Depression, Catholic ideology defined workers' rights within the framework of the social doctrine of Pope Leo XIII's *Rerum Novarum* (1891), which stressed the social value of manual labour within a hierarchical order. Opposing class struggle and international unions, which affirmed a principle of religious neutrality, Catholic social activists argued that French Canada's language, culture, and religion needed defending against the forces of materialism and foreign communist and labour-union threats. They focused their reform efforts on labour peace, temperance, improved education for the working class, and restricting Sunday work in the mills and factories (Ryan, 1966).

In the first half of the twentieth century, Roman Catholic authorities participated directly in the Quebec labour movement. In 1907, the first Catholic union was formed in Chicoutimi under the sponsorship of the bishop. With parish priests acting as chaplains, these early confessional unions united Catholic authorities and francophone trade union activists in defending the rights of property, in espousing a corporatist view of the workplace over that of class struggle, and of opting for arbitration over strikes. The issue of Protestants and Jews in the labour force was addressed by the provincial council of bishops in 1909 when it warned of the "false and dangerous principle of religious neutrality in trade unions." Priests intervened personally in important industrial disputes, arbitrating in the tramway strike in Montreal (1903) and the shoe industry strike in Quebec City (1911). Labour organizers, particularly Communist or American union organizers, had no doubt about the role of the church. It provided ideological support to the forces of capital, rather than mediating between capital and labour. Joshua Gershman, who organized a general strike of 10 000 francophone garment workers, understood the power of the church at the local shop level:

Very fine workers; the girls were really good operators and finishers. We got them in those days an increase of $3.50 a week which was a big thing. The shop was very happy and satisfied. Monday, a week after we settled the strike, five girls with the shop chairlady, a French Canadian girl, beautiful person, came down together with the shop committee. The girls, brought *me* back, not the boss, the increases they got in the new pay envelope and they said we have been to Church yesterday [. . .] and we were told by the priest that this is dishonest money, and they begged that I should return the money back to the boss. We had to go visit the parents of these girls and convince them that it's OK., that it's all right to belong to the union. . . . Many parents agreed with us but the Church really worked against us (Abella, 1977: 200).

In 1911, the Ecole sociale populaire was established to expound and propagate the church's social doctrine through brochures, study groups, and retreats. Under the leadership of a Jesuit, Joseph Papin-Archambault, the church trained priests to lead social action in their parishes and in unions. The Catholic union movement expanded rapidly after 1915 and in 1921 a confederation of Catholic unions was formed: la Confédération des Travailleurs Catholiques du Canada (CTCC). By 1931 the CTCC had 121 locals and 25 000 members.

One of the major goals of the CTCC was to unite workers by religion rather than by class and to protect francophones from international influence. In 1925, the treasurer of the CTCC and Catholic activist, Alfred Charpentier, established the Groupe Jeanne d'Arc des retraitants pompiers. The goal of this benevolent association of firemen was, in Charpentier's words, to "raise the moral fibre of firemen [. . .] to study and spread the social teachings of the church with a view to disaffiliate them from the International union. This is why I put our group under the patronage of Joan of Arc who drove the English out of France" (Charpentier, 1971: 71).

Catholic unionism was only one element of the Quebec labour movement. Craft unions, for example, which united skilled workers in a craft, had a long history of resisting new shop disciplines and reductions in wages. In the early twentieth century, especially with the decline of the Knights of Labor, many skilled workers joined unions associated with the American Federation of Labor (AFL). A grouping of craft unions, the AFL promoted the limited goals of collective bargaining agreements, written contracts, and union labels rather than larger issues of class or nationalism. With their strict craft orientation, they rejected unions that would unite both skilled and unskilled workers at a single workplace.

International unions grew rapidly in Quebec in the pre-war period and by 1914 they reported 30 000 members in Montreal and 3000 in Quebec City (Harvey, 1980: 146). The Depression was less propitious for the international unions and by 1933 once powerful unions like the United Mine Workers and the Amalgamated Clothing Workers were in ruins.

The craft and Catholic unions generally supported candidates from traditional parties who endorsed workers' demands but periodically labour gave strong support to independent political activity. Three labour candidates ran in working-class districts of Montreal in the provincial election of 1886; in 1888 a Knights of Labor organizer, A.T. Lépine, won a seat in Montreal; and other victories were achieved in municipal elections (Palmer, 1992: 140). In the pre–World War I period working-class candidates ran under the banner of the Parti Ouvrier, part of the Canadian Independent Labour Party movement. Its social democratic program included compulsory free education, expansion of public libraries, old-age pensions, health insurance, workers' compensation, and a ban on child labour. In the federal election of 1906 the party did succeed in electing Alphonse Verville, head of the plumbers union and president of the Trades and Labour Congress, in the Montreal working-class riding of Saint-Marie. Unlike the American Federation of Labor, which supported the war effort wholeheartedly, Verville was prominent in the anti-conscription movement. He associated World War I with class interest: "There were two major views on the War, that of the exploiter and that of the exploited" (Palmer, 1992: 199). Despite his rhetoric of class, Verville campaigned under a Labour–Liberal banner for his successful 1917 election, and in the 1920s the Liberal Party successfully co-opted Parti Ouvrier support. Nor was the Communist Party an important force among Quebec labour. In 1930, after a decade of activity in Quebec, it had 300 members (Education Committee of the CSN and CEQ, 1987: 105).

The passivity of Quebec workers has been exaggerated. Bitter strikes broke out, particularly in the transport, textile, and clothing sectors. There were at least forty strikes and lockouts in the Quebec cotton textile industry between 1900 and 1908 (Roback, 1985: 169). Jacques Ferland (1987) has shown the division between skilled and unskilled labour in an examination of 110 labour conflicts in the textile and leather industries between 1880 and 1910. While skilled workers went on strike in unilateral fashion, unskilled workers engaged in broader, multilateral strikes.

Women were prominent in labour resistance. The garment and textile sectors, both of which depended heavily on female labour, had frequent strikes. Despite clerical opposition, francophone women crossed ethnic lines to join their Jewish counterparts in garment industry strikes. In 1924, female workers went on strike for two months at the Eddy Match factory in Hull over management's attempt to reduce salaries and to replace female supervisors with men. Female teachers faced tight control from their school boards, but Catholic and Protestant teachers were able to work collectively and formed women's teachers associations for improved pensions and working conditions (Danylewycz and Prentice: 1986, 76).

Resistance took different forms. Within Catholic unions, shop leaders and labour militants struggled with priests for control of their unions and ideology.

There is also evidence that women who were isolated and not unionized protected themselves with collective action. In 1929, four female teachers in Cap-Chat closed their school when the school board did not pay their salaries on time, and in Alma four years later ten of twelve female teachers left their classrooms under the same conditions. Marîse Thivierge (1983: 181) concludes that these examples of collective action "demonstrate the awakening of combativeness of female teachers who were conscious of being exploited. However, these actions were of short duration and of uncertain influence."

Strikes often failed in the face of federal and provincial labour legislation, police action, and management's powers in the work place. The federal and provincial governments suspended strikes by forcing workers into arbitration. Regular troops and the militia were used to suppress strikers, and scabs and private security forces could be brought in rapidly by railway. In 1903, a strike by 2000 Montreal longshoremen was described as a "civil war." Troops from Toronto were used to supplement the Montreal militia and 1000 workers were imported from Britain by the shipping companies as scab labour (Roback, 1985: 169).

These obstacles continued across the period. An organizer in the garment industry described his difficulties during the early 1930s: "It was the time of the Bennett regime, our union was raided by the police many times. Workers were terrorized on the picket line by police and by gangsters hired by the police. Jewish manufacturers behaved very badly" (Abella, 1977: 200). Of 287 strikes in Montreal during 1901–1921, 115 resulted in total rejection of employee demands. Only forty-nine of these strikes were successful, mostly for skilled workers (Copp, 1974). Although labour department statistics are unreliable in counting short strikes and those in Roman Catholic unions, Table 6.6 indicates the major Quebec strikes.

Years	Number of strikes	Number of workers involved	Person days
1901–1905	131	30 516	382 275
1906–1910	106	32 311	459 080
1911–1915	75	30 120	492 586
1916–1920	186	63 728	1 475 220
1921–1925	115	30 374	739 499
1926–1930	74	21 446	313 901
1931–1935	105	39 282	289 762

Table 6.6 Labour Conflicts in Quebec: 1901–1935

(Bernier et Boily, 1986: 325)

When 3000 Quebec City shoemakers struck against the imposition of a 30 percent pay reduction in 1925, they rejected the arbitration efforts of their chaplain and his suggestion that they return to work with a 10 percent wage cut. Workers demanded justice and paraded before the factories with photographs of the archbishop, Saint Joseph, and the Virgin. Using Americans as trainers, the owners hired 1500 new workers and at the same time introduced new machines that required less skilled labour. The failure of the strike after four months crippled progressives in the Catholic union movement and it was only in the 1930s that militant Catholic unionism resurfaced.

⌒⌒

CULTURE

Despite the telephone, radio, film, and other new manifestations of consumer culture, traditional forms of cultural activity persisted among the popular classes. Family and church remained dominant influences. During *veillées*—evening family gatherings—storytelling, pipe smoking (among men), chatting, cards, singing, and dancing remained the most popular pastimes. Outside the home, most activities centred on the parish: mass, bazaars, dinners, choir singing, retreats, and service clubs. Most rural people only travelled for important family occasions such as weddings and funerals, for the annual regional agricultural fair, or for a pilgrimage to one of the several popular shrines in the province.

The village of Valcourt provides a good example of characteristic social activity. It had a population of 300 in the 1920s and, like many villages, had a racetrack, baseball diamond, and amateur theatre productions. After work, men gathered in the billiard room at the rear of the village restaurant. For Joseph-Armand Bombardier, an ambitious young garage mechanic in the village, the major opportunity to meet women was at his aunt's Saturday night socials; it was there that he met his fiancée (Lacasse, 1988). Community work activities like haying, blueberry picking, corn husking, and maple-syrup production remained important social occasions for courtship, music, and dance. A Sainte-Hyacinthe girl confided to her diary that she had "spent an afternoon under the pine trees."

In urban centres, taverns continued to provide a place for male socialization. Restricted by law to incorporated cities and towns, taverns originated as part of inns, providing the food and drink. With the formation of the Quebec Liquor Board in 1921, independent taverns could be licensed. Taverns became establishments for the sale of beer by the glass; they had a monopoly on the sale of draft beer and, until 1979, were restricted to men. The 1922 map in Figure 6.10 reveals the concentration of taverns in working-class neighbourhoods.

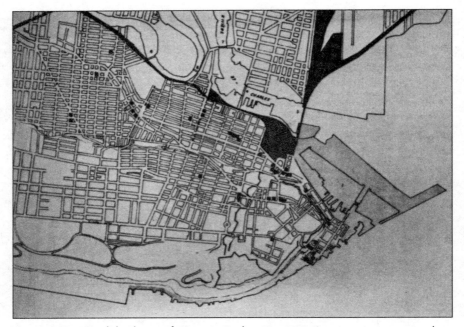

Figure 6.10 Spatial distribution of taverns in Quebec City, 1922. Taverns were concentrated near the port and in the working-class neighbourhoods of St-Roch and St-Sauveur.

Although traditional activities persisted, industrial capitalist society also saw the development of new forms of leisure for both the elite and the popular classes. With the growth of literacy, a market for local literature appeared. Newspapers could be produced more quickly and cheaply using technological innovations such as the linotype machine, manufactured by the Linotype Company in Montreal after 1891. Large circulation dailies such as *La Presse* (founded in 1884) capitalized on illustrations and clear layout for popular appeal, and on increasing consumerism for advertising revenue. During the 1880s, 305 new newspapers and periodicals were established in Quebec. Alongside dailies and professional newsletters were small weeklies that published popular literature. From 1886 to 1893, *La bibliothèque à cinq cents* regularly provided readers with twenty-four pages of excerpts from French and Canadian novels and poems for a nickel. Popular literature was a feature of most newspapers and continued in dailies such as Quebec City's *Le Soleil* until after the Second World War.

Written history continued to affirm the distinct character of Quebec culture. Alongside professional historians such as abbé Lionel Groulx, who inaugurated his chair in Canadian history at the Université de Montréal in 1915, rural notables and the urban petite bourgeoisie also wrote history. The latter contributed to the

Bulletin des recherches historiques (founded in 1895). With the establishment of the Ecole littéraire de Montréal in the 1890s, Quebec literature broke new ground. The best known representative of the Ecole was the brilliant poet, Emile Nelligan (1879–1941). Criticizing the epic poetry of Octave Crémazie (1827–1879) and Louis Fréchette (1839–1908), who had emphasized family and nation, members of the Ecole expressed a more open, exotic, and philosophical national literature.

In the 1920s, two new forms of cultural activity had a profound influence on leisure. Moving pictures rapidly gained popularity and there were 134 cinemas in Quebec by 1933. Radio started in 1922 with the first broadcasts of two Montreal stations: CKAC in French and CFCF in English. By 1931, 37 percent of urban homes in Quebec had radios whereas only 8 percent of rural homes had them. In the countryside, as Elzéar Lavoie remarks, "listening to radio was a collective act which, instead of linking individuals to a wider world, cemented local identity and underlined dependence on the rural elite, whose power was curiously strengthened by the new technology" (Translated from Lavoie, 1971).

The growth of public transportation gave the urban working classes access to new kinds of leisure. Urban amusement parks commercialized the industrial city's need for entertainment, music, food, and drink. Mount Royal Park—designed by Frederic Law Olmsted and opened in 1876—emphasized a natural, green environment. Sohmer Park (Figure 6.11) could receive up to 10 000 visitors a day seeking

Figure 6.11 Sohmer Park, 1916. This advertisement for Sohmer Park emphasizes the importance of public transportation, beer, music, and vaudeville for the success of the amusement park.

entertainment, food, and beer. Established by Ernest Lavigne, the park opened in 1889 on an east-end site surrounded by docks, railways, smokestacks, and Molson's Brewery. Its popular attractions included magicians, giants and dwarfs, fireworks, circuses, puppets, wheelbarrow contests, and vaudeville shows; while Mme Juez Palmer was renowned for picking up 200 pounds with her teeth, the park's greatest folk hero was strongman Louis Cyr. All was not simple entertainment however, and the park played an important role in educating and controlling the working classes with industrial exhibitions, concerts, and Saint-Jean Baptiste celebrations (Lamonde et Montpetit, 1986).

CONCLUSION

In the early twentieth century, Quebec's industrial economy was increasingly based on electrical power, the development of natural resources, and factory production. The period saw the rise of great corporations, interlocking directorships, and company towns. Through branch plants and American capital, important sectors of Quebec's industrial production were integrated into the American economy.

Despite this, much of the economic power in Quebec was controlled by anglophone capitalists in Montreal and Toronto. With pan-Canadian and international perspectives, they ignored much of Quebec outside Montreal. The francophone bourgeoisie did not control significant amounts of capital. They did dominate the state apparatus and, at the regional level, continued to control financial, commercial, and industrial power.

From the shop floor to the pew, the classroom, and the teller's wicket, most Quebecers found themselves subject to strict controls. To reinforce its paternalism, capital used immigrant, short-term or seasonal labour and isolated company towns. The church remained a strong ideological ally of capitalism. Although gender, union, and regional groups did demonstrate some resistance, the popular classes were handicapped by the effects of world war, urbanization, public health problems, industrial work, consumerism, and ethnic division.

FURTHER READING

INDUSTRIAL CAPITALISM

For financial institutions see Gilles Piédalue's thesis: *La bourgeoisie canadienne et le problème de la réalisation du profit au Canada, 1900–1930*. Also important is Robert Sweeny, *A Guide to the History and Records of Selected Montreal Businesses before*

1947. For banking see Ronald Rudin, *Banking en français: The French Banks of Quebec, 1835–1925.* For hydro-electric development see John H. Dales, *Hydroelectricity and Industrial Development. Quebec 1898–1940.* For the forest industry see René Hardy and Normand Séguin, *Forêt et société en Mauricie.* The ideology of francophone businesspeople is described in Fernande Roy, *Progrès, harmonie, liberté: libéralisme des milieux d'affaires francophones à Montréal au tournant du siècle.* The history of the caisses populaires is presented in Yves Roby, *Alphonse Desjardins et les caisses populaires, 1854–1920* and in Ronald Rudin's *In Whose Interest? Quebec's Caisses Populaires, 1900–1945.*

LABOUR

For Quebec labour see Fernand Harvey, *Le mouvement ouvrier au Québec,* and two books by Jacques Rouillard, *Les syndicats nationaux au Québec de 1900 à 1930* and *Histoire de la CSN (1921–1981).* Andrée Lévesque, *Virage à gauche interdit: Les communistes, les socialistes et leurs ennemis au Québec, 1929–39,* treats the left effectively. Aluminum workers are examined in José Igartua and Marine de Fréminville, "Les origines des travailleurs de l'Alcan au Saguenay, 1925–1939." For female office work see Ronald Rudin, "Bankers' Hours: Life behind the Wicket at the Banque d'Hochelaga, 1901–21," and Michèle Dagenais, "Itineraires professionnels masculins et féminins en milieu bancaire: le cas de la Banque de Hochelaga, 1900–1929." For the proletarianization of female teachers see Marta Danylewycz and Alison Prentice, "Teacher's Work: Changing Patterns and Perceptions in the Emerging School Systems of Nineteenth and Early Twentieth Century Central Canada." The relationship of Quebec workers to the larger Canadian labour movement is treated in Bryan Palmer, *Working-class Experience: Rethinking the History of Canadian Labour 1800–1991* and Craig Heron, *The Canadian Labour Movement: A Short History.*

Strikes are discussed in Jacques Ferland's "Syndicalisme 'parcellaire' et syndicalisme 'collectif': Une interprétation socio-technique des conflits ouvriers dans deux industries québécoises (1880–1914)." Of use for the leather industry workers is M.-A. Bluteau et al., *Les cordonniers, artisans du cuir.* Of interest for the unionization of female teachers is Marîse Thivierge, "La syndicalisation des institutrices catholiques, 1900–1959." For labour in the garment industry see Irving Abella, "Portrait of a Jewish Professional Revolutionary: The Recollections of Joshua Gershman."

SOCIAL GROUPS

The attitude of the clergy to industrialization is examined in William Ryan, *The Clergy and Economic Growth in Quebec (1896–1914).* Perhaps the best source for the history of the urban working class is Terry Copp, *The Anatomy of Poverty: The Condition of the Working Class in Montreal 1897–1929.* Paul-André Linteau's

Maisonneuve: Comment des promoteurs fabriquent une ville provides a good case study of the development of an industrial community. Much more than a study of women in religious orders, Marta Danylewycz, *Taking the Veil: An Alternative to Marriage, Motherhood, and Spinsterhood in Quebec, 1840–1920*, treats work and the family. For a history of the Jews in Quebec see Pierre Anctil and Gary Caldwell, *Juifs et réalités juives au Québec* and Gerald Tuechinsky, *Taking Root: The Origins of the Canadian Jewish Community*. Italians are treated in Bruno Ramirez and Michael Del Balso, *The Italians of Montreal: From Sojourning to Settlement*; padronism is treated in Robert F. Harney, "Montreal's Kind of Italian Labor: A Case Study of Padronism." For Italian labour see Bruno Ramirez, "Brief Encounters: Italian Immigrant Workers and the CPR, 1900–30." Public health is examined in Martin Tétreault, "Les maladies de la misère: aspects de la santé publique à Montréal 1880–1914."

Church, State, and Women in Industrial Capitalist Society, 1890s–1930s

From the 1890s to the 1930s, conservative forces had a strong hold on society. For much of the period, provincial politics were dominated by the Liberal Party. Under both Lomer Gouin and Louis-Alexandre Taschereau, the party established comfortable relationships with the Montreal capitalists, the Catholic clergy, and the federal Liberal Party. While region, class and gender divided its opponents, the conservative leadership of the Liberal Party was able to use the church and nationalism to its own advantage. Reform elements were greatly handicapped by the concentration of ideological power in the hands of clerics and nationalists such as Bishop Edouard-Charles Fabre, Archbishop Paul Bruchési, Canon Lionel Groulx, and journalists Jules-Paul Tardivel and Henri Bourassa. The institutional power of the church over education and social life was at its greatest in this period. Urban progressives, feminists, and political radicals were often co-opted into essentially conservative activities or were hived into marginal political groups and ethnic ghettoes.

The maturation of industrial capitalism divided Quebec into several different economic and social worlds (Figures 7.1, 7.2, 7.3). Capitalists with interests across Canada and around the world, immigrant communities in Montreal, mining regions like Abitibi, fishing villages in the Gaspé, and traditional farmers shared the province and yet they were worlds apart. Ethnicity, class, and regionalism were accentuated by different union, educational, and social institutions and, as we will see, by the efforts of the province's political leadership. These conditions fostered the contradictory social and political forces of populism, corporatism, profound conservatism, social democracy, and urban reform.

The social and economic position of women in Quebec was subject to continuing paternalism in the family, workplace, church, and state. The Catholic church retained its strong influence over women's reproductive, domestic, and paid-work activities, and intervened directly in the attempts of women to form autonomous organizations. The political and legal rights of women were sharply limited in comparison to those of men. Women only obtained the right to vote in federal elections in 1917 and in provincial elections in 1940. They had virtually no power in government, the state bureaucracy, corporations, universities, and traditional male professions. They were denied access to almost all higher education facilities and, when admitted, were directed to special segregated programs in household economics, nursing, or teacher training.

In order to get the kind of skilled jobs increasingly reserved for them—as nurses, teachers, secretaries, and telephone operators—young women underwent job training that had larger ideological implications, also preparing them for their social role as wives and mothers. Once married, women were expected to exemplify wifely, motherly, and homemaking virtues, and were permitted little access to institutional or political leadership except in philanthropic and religious societies.

Figure 7.1   A farmer in Charlevoix

Figure 7.2   St. Lawrence Boulevard around 1914

Figure 7.3 Sainte-Catherine Street at Phillips Square, 1930

These pictures illustrate the existence of several Quebecs in the early twentieth century. With its ox, thatched roof, hay crop, traditional equipment, and wooden barn, this Charlevoix farm (7.1) retained many elements of preindustrial society into the twentieth century. In 1926, there were 1585 mechanized tractors on Quebec farms, compared to 12 286 in Ontario and 50 136 in the prairie provinces (Urquhart and Buckley, 1965: 391).

St. Lawrence Boulevard (7.2), or the "Main" as it is known, has been a kaleidoscope of Montreal's ethnic diversity since the late nineteenth century. A 1913 street directory shows the presence of the garment district, a tobacco factory and a brewery, and a variety of ethnic shops, one of which was the first Steinberg grocery store (the first of a chain that finally disappeared in 1992). Horse-drawn tramways were introduced in 1864, opening new working-class suburbs like Saint-Jean Baptiste. In 1892, the tramway system was electrified, as is evident in the photo.

Farther west at Phillips Square was the centre of anglophone Montreal (7.3). The cars and tramways illustrate the changing form of transportation. Chauffeurs waiting by their limousines hint at the wealth of some shoppers. To the right is Morgan's Department Store (now The Bay), constructed of red sandstone brought from Scotland as ballast. In the background, an addition is being made to the Toronto-owned Eaton's, which had bought out the local Goodwin's Department Store. The two department stores are separated by the Anglican Christ Church Cathedral, while across from the church and just out of the photo was the prominent jeweller, Henry Birks.

The particular role of female religious communities in Quebec's hospitals and schools provided, for many Catholic women, an important alternative to marriage. To Marta Danylewycz (1987), the 133 female religious communities established between 1850 and 1960 in Quebec represent particular forms of

Year	Number of nuns	Percentage of women over 20	Percentage of single women over 20
1851	650	0.3	1.4
1871	2 320	0.9	4.1
1881	3 783	1.1	4.4
1901	6 629	1.5	6.1
1911	9 964	1.9	8.0
1921	13 579	2.2	9.1

Table 7.1   Women in Religious Communities in Quebec, 1851–1921

(Danylewycz, 1987: 17)

autonomous female activity and cannot be dismissed simply as evidence of male clerical domination of women. "Women did not stumble blindly into convents" (Danylewycz, 1987: 159). Rather, religious communities were an important institutional means for women to advance socially, personally, and intellectually, and offered a celibate existence as an alternative to motherhood.

The convent was also an important source of material security for unmarried women; the largest number of women entered female religious communities in 1930, one of the most critical years of the Depression (Lavigne et Pinard, 1983: 279, 283). The importance of female religious communities in Quebec society is evident from Table 7.1, which shows that the 13 579 nuns in 1921 represented 9.1 percent of the population of single women over age twenty.

⟋⟋⟋

THE CHURCH

With a population that remained 86 percent Catholic in 1941, Quebec was subject to profound clerical influence in all aspects of early twentieth-century life. The financial relationship of the church, the state, and industrial capital is apparent from Table 7.2.

The power of the church hierarchy over social and intellectual life remained strong, governing Sunday activities and laws concerning theatres and cinemas. Secular officials were careful with clerical opinion. In 1893, for example, when the Italian battleship *Etna* visited Montreal, Mayor Desjardins refused to meet the ship's officers. He argued that he did not want to meet representatives of a state that oppressed the pope. In addition to its direct influence on labour through Catholic unions (see Chapter 6), the church expanded its influence over women, youth, the Caisse Populaire movement, universities, and other educational institutions and social services.

Investment	Type of enterprise	Amount ($)
Richelieu and Ontario Navigation	Shipping	169 000
Sorel, Quebec	Municipality	142 000
Champlain and St. Lawrence	Railway	94 000
Port Arthur, Ontario	Municipality	90 000
Sault Ste. Marie, Ontario	Municipality	89 000
Dominion Cotton Mills	Textile	85 000
Hamilton Power Co.	Utility	73 000
Iberville, Quebec	Municipality	49 000
Lake of the Woods Milling	Milling	43 000
Montreal Light, Heat & Power	Utility	42 000

Table 7.2   Sulpician Investments in Bonds, Debentures and Shares Worth over $40 000, 1882–1909

(Young, 1986: 212–13)

The church was particularly able to use its control over education to recruit the best students to the clergy. In the March 1986 edition of *L'incunable*, Jean-Ethier Blais effectively described the entry of François Hertel into the Jesuits:

> The important event [of his years at the Séminaire de Trois-Rivières] was his decision to become a Jesuit and therefore priest and teacher. Hertel drifted into this decision without really understanding what he was doing, caught up by this immense machine which we call destiny. The basic principle of the period was that, whoever did not rise up forcefully against a religious vocation, was made for it. Hertel entered the Jesuits then, negatively one could say, *volens nolens* by the moral authority of his confessor [. . . . This] all occurred in an atmosphere of moral rectitude, and, strange as it may seem, of liberty.

The parish, the central framework of social life of Quebec communities, kept pace with demographic growth, particularly in expanding urban areas. The number of parishes in the diocese of Montreal increased from 152 in 1881 to 215 in 1941 (Litalien, 1986: 182).

The parish of Saint-Alphonse at the Baie des Ha! Ha! on the Saguenay illustrates the steady development of the institutional infrastructure of a rural parish. Early in the twentieth century, the village became an important port for shipping aluminum, pulp, and cheese. In 1901, churchwardens bought a new cemetery site for $800. In 1902, a public hall with a sacristy and a special study room for young girls preparing for confirmation was built. In 1908, churchwardens donated land worth $3600 for construction of an orphanage. In 1923, repairs to the church cost $40 000; a new presbytery was added in 1926 at a cost of $25 000. A year later a boys' academy costing $77 220 was built (Potvin, 1957).

Figure 7.4 Brochure published by the Franciscans. Asking to be protected from the "plagues of modern life," publications such as this singled out alcoholism, liberal education, theatre, cinema, divorce, and secular clubs. Also of note is the picture's idealization of small-town life, apparent in the small town seen in the background with its prominent church steeple.

Catholicism in Quebec in the early twentieth century was more than symbolic. Its omniscient institutional presence was accompanied by ideological rigour. Church fathers continued to insist upon churchgoing, particularly confession. Patients at the Miséricorde Hospital were obliged to attend chapel three times a day. Parishoners in urban parishes of Montreal took communion an average of twenty-two times a year in 1912; rural parishoners in the Montreal area averaged twenty-eight times (Hamelin et Gagnon, 1986: 355). Through fraternal self-help societies and publications, the church exerted a strong influence on morality (Figure 7.4). The pulpit was used to speak against the dangers of urban consumer society and for traditional values such as the centrality of the family. In his pastoral letter of 1923, Cardinal Bégin warned against lascivious dances like the tango, foxtrot, and polka.

The same clerical strength was apparent in daily life in the countryside. In the village of Saint-Justin, subject of an 1898 study by Léon Gérin, families had religious images in their bedrooms. Daily prayers were customary and family pews were full for Sunday mass. Feasts and holy days were strictly observed and at Easter, attendance at mass was virtually universal (Gérin, 1968: 114). When radio came to Belle-Anse in the Gaspé, whole families tuned in to the daily rosary recitation. Sociologist Marcel Rioux (1961: 44) concluded that Catholicism "was such an integral part of the personality of the Belle-Anse villagers—of their system of values—that the principles on which it was based were never enunciated; it was something which was understood and no one considered that it could be otherwise."

Farm organizations and Caisses Populaires provided other vehicles for clerical influence over social and economic life in the countryside. When the Union catholique des cultivateurs was established in 1924, the power of chaplains in the movement ensured that it would direct its attention to social and moral reform rather than to secular politics.

Pilgrimages channelled the religious practices and recreation of the popular classes into sanctioned and supervised forms. In 1903, a Quebec City typographer reported that he and his wife took three excursions a year out of the city, two to visit kin and the third as a pilgrimage. In Saint-Justin, women undertook an annual pilgrimage as their primary sortie from the village. These pilgrimages were carefully supervised. The Archbishop of Montreal forbade women to participate in mixed, overnight trips.

The three most important pilgrimage sites in Quebec—Sainte-Anne-de-Beaupré, thirty-five kilometres east of Quebec City; Cap-de-la-Madeleine near Trois-Rivières; and St. Joseph's Oratory in Montreal—all had origins as popular shrines in the early years of French colonization. Run by the Redemptorists, the basilica at Sainte-Anne-de-Beaupré had an increase in visitors from 113 560 in 1895 to 256 610 in 1923 (Hamelin et Gagnon, 1984: 349). St. Joseph's Oratory was erected on the site of a seventeenth-century shrine. It became North America's most important urban shrine with the faith healing of Brother André, an illiterate caretaker at the shrine. Despite opposition from Catholics hostile to faith healing, a small shrine was built on the site in 1904; in 1924–1925 the church hierarchy sponsored a basilica and in 1982 Brother André was beatified. Between 1898 and 1930, twenty-three new pilgrimage sites were established in Quebec (Hamelin et Gagnon, 1984: 352).

Philanthropy continued to play an important role in providing social services in industrial society before the welfare state emerged. Catholics were cared for in institutions run by female religious orders. The Protestant bourgeoisie subsidized—

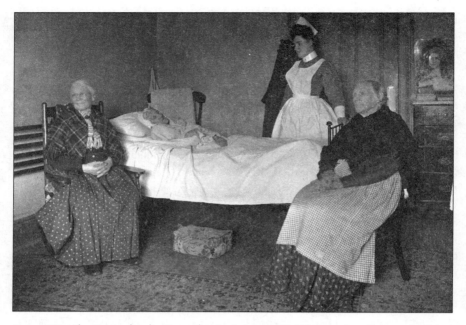

Figure 7.5 The Montreal Ladies Benevolent Institution, 1909. Whatever the religion, care of the elderly remained a female responsibility. The new profession of nursing is evident here.

and their wives administered—institutions such as the Montreal Ladies Benevolent Society, which provided care for indigent women (Figure 7.5). During the second half of the nineteenth century, sectarian lines hardened between the institutions and ideologies of Protestants and Catholics. For their part, the expanding population of non-Christian communities, particularly Jews, were welcome in neither Protestant nor Catholic educational institutions, both of which were confessional systems that gave religious instruction. After the intervention of Premier L.-O. Taillon in 1892, Montreal Jews opted to pay their school taxes to the Protestant system, where they were grudgingly accepted. But for four decades their place in the Protestant School Board of Montreal was essentially that of "second-class citizens" (Tulchinsky, 1984: 103).

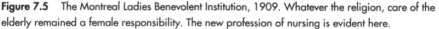

CLERICAL IDEOLOGY

Higher education was traditionally an area of particular clerical interest. In response to pressure from the chamber of commerce, Quebec's first business school, the Ecole des Hautes Etudes Commerciales, was established in 1907. Premier Gouin met the archbishop of Montreal and promised that, although the school would at first be independent, it would be affiliated with Laval University and subordinated to its religious authorities at the first opportunity. The arch-bishop was given a voice in naming the business school's first professors, two of whom were priests.

The Montreal campus of Laval became the autonomous Université de Montréal in 1920. Mgr. Georges Gauthier, auxiliary bishop of Montreal, was rec-tor. A Sulpician was named the first dean of philosophy, and the department itself became what Hamelin and Gagnon (1984) describe as "a fief" of the Dominicans for forty years.

The classical college system remained at the core of Catholic secondary school education. The clerical hierarchy tightly controlled the establishment of these colleges, their curriculum, and their faculties. Like the parish, the colleges reflected the province's changing demography. Originally located primarily in small communities, eighteen of the twenty-nine colleges founded between 1920 and 1939 were in Montreal and Quebec City. Fifteen of these were for girls (Galarneau, 1978: 59).

The most important Quebec intellectual of his generation was abbé Lionel Groulx, profoundly conservative and dedicated to soil, family, and the church. He touched Quebec's political and ideological nerve by questioning the values of industrial capitalist society and by pointing out the dangers of the decline of rural Quebec. His emphasis on an idyllic, preindustrial, and self-sufficient past had broad appeal to francophones in an industrializing and urbanizing society in which anglophone capital played an increasing role:

> One of the characteristics of the Canadian family is to be a work co-operative and a small society almost independent in the economic domain. The family budget aims at family self-sufficiency for all needs. Everyone works and makes his contribution so that from the work of all we have the wherewithal to feed and clothe ourselves.

Groulx questioned Confederation at the very time of the First World War conscription crisis, when thousands of French-Canadian males were resisting a call-up that they saw as imposed by English Canada. He wrote of a nostalgic past characterized by martyrdom and Catholic virtues that had been lost through the Conquest, compromise with the British, and the Quebec bourgeoisie's betrayal of traditional values. His emphasis on racial homogeneity and moral purity co-incided with other right-wing intellectuals' attacks on Jews and Jehovah's Witnesses in the 1930s and with the attraction that Italian, Portuguese, and Spanish fascism held for some Quebecers. Groulx gave currency to his solution of a strong French and Catholic Quebec through his chair in Canadian History at the University of Montreal and through the influential monthly, *L'Action française.*

Despite the institutional and ideological strength of Catholicism, traditional clerical prerogatives were threatened by bureaucratization and the growth of state power in the twentieth century. Clerical power was threatened also by the Depression, with its new scale of public assistance, and by new Canada-wide social programs. Bernard Vigod (1978: 180) summarizes the Church's attitude to social issues and state interference in the 1920s as one of "insecurity."

QUEBEC'S MINORITY STATUS IN CANADA

In the transition period from the 1810s to the 1880s, leaders of the francophone political bourgeoisie such as La Fontaine and Cartier had assiduously developed their credentials as political brokers between emerging industrial capitalist interests and traditional Quebec. Their power had built many of the province's fundamental social and political institutions within the framework of an industrializing but conservative and Catholic society. The perpetuation of this political stance and therefore of the tensions it generated formed the core of the Quebec political system until the end of the Second World War.

The political elite of the nineteenth century successfully reproduced itself, in terms of both families and values. Lomer Gouin, provincial premier from 1905–1920, was the son-in-law of former premier Honoré Mercier. Gouin's successor as premier for 1920–1936, Louis-Alexandre Taschereau, was the son of a Supreme Court judge and nephew of Canada's first cardinal. Their nationalist opponent, Henri Bourassa, was a grandson of Louis-Joseph Papineau. This elite governed with a sense of noblesse oblige. For them, democracy was still "in the experimental stage" and needed a guiding hand: "the task," Premier Taschereau told a student audience in 1930, "rests with a certain class of aristocracy. Not the aristocracy of blood, lineage, or money, but the aristocracy of learning, science and knowledge" (Vigod, 1986: 163).

Confederation had integrated Quebec into an increasingly larger political state. A series of linguistic and ethnic crises—from the execution of Métis leader Louis Riel in 1885 (Figure 7.6) to the conscription crisis of the First World War—made clear Quebec's vulnerability in the federation. Between 1885 and 1914, the vision of a viable French-Canadian presence in the West collapsed; Quebec members of the federal government failed to block the execution of Riel; Manitoba schools went through crisis in the 1890s; and anti-Catholic, francophobe elements in Ontario and New Brunswick grew stronger. Each incident emphasized Quebec's minority position in the federal system and the fragile status of francophones outside the province.

Figure 7.6 Louis Riel on trial, Regina, 1885. Whereas most English Canadians viewed Riel as a dangerous traitor, French Canadians almost unanimously saw him as a deranged person who was nonetheless defending the just grievances of the francophone Catholic Métis. His execution was central to Quebec's increasing ambivalence towards Canada. On one hand, Arthur Silver argues (1982: 178–79), it "served to reinforce the traditional Quebec patriotism [. . .] for the integrity of their Quebec homeland." On the other, concern for francophones living outside Quebec led some Quebecers to redefine Canada "as a bilingual, dual nationality."

Until the 1880s, Conservative politicians such as P.J.O. Chauveau, C.B. de Boucherville, and J.A. Chapleau dominated Quebec politics at both the federal and provincial levels. Ethnic tensions, scandals within the Conservative Party, and the Catholic church's newfound acceptance of moderate liberalism delivered power to a generation of Liberals. In 1896, Wilfrid Laurier was elected prime minister on a platform of "sunny ways," meaning faith in British institutions and the goodwill of anglophone allies. This stance placed him on a political tightrope, in which the defence of French-Canadian interests depended on a strong French-Canadian presence in Ottawa and a vigorous Liberal Party. Laurier's successor as Liberal leader, William Lyon Mackenzie King, also emphasized the importance of his Quebec lieutenant, Ernest Lapointe. Part of the Liberal strategy was to foster the image of the Conservative Party as hostile to francophones.

"Sunny ways," however, could not ultimately soften the reality that the majority in Canada—and an overwhelming majority outside Quebec—was English-speaking. Quebec views were inevitably subordinated to the majority. To

French-Canadian sensitivities it became clear that in the view of the anglophone majority in Canada, Confederation had not established "two nations" but rather a federation in which Quebec was only one voice among many provinces.

Canada's role in the British empire was an ongoing source of difficulty for politicians from Quebec, particularly after the 1890s as Britain sought Canadian support in imperial matters. At Queen Victoria's Diamond Jubilee in 1897, British officials began to pressure Laurier to contribute to the upkeep of the British navy. During the Boer War (1899–1902), French-Canadian nationalists were offended by a definition of the British empire that permitted Canadian troops to be sent to subdue the Boers, a minority of European origin with whom the French in Canada could identify. Many Canadians of British origin insisted that Canada support the British, and 7000 Canadian troops served in the war despite French-Canadian resistance.

The failure to achieve separate schools in the new western provinces of Saskatchewan and Alberta (1905) was followed in 1911 by Ontario's Regulation XVII. Restricting French as a language of instruction to the first two years of elementary school and the study of French in other years to one hour a day, the regulation seemed to signal the end of francophone education in Ontario.

The place of francophones outside Quebec was made perfectly clear in Eastern Ontario, where francophones formed a majority in certain border counties. In Prescott county, for example, francophones represented 71 percent of the population in 1901 but officials had no intention of granting permanent status to French schools. According to Chad Gaffield (1987: 29, 34), Ontario school officials saw French-language schools in the county as "ephemeral, a necessary but temporary phenomenon to be tolerated on the way to the goal of uniform, unilingual schooling."

It would be overly simplistic to see Quebec's minority status only in terms of linguistic questions. Establishment of the Supreme Court of Canada in 1875, for example, subjected Quebec's civil law to judges trained in the common-law tradition. While admitting the Supreme Court's jurisdiction on matters under control of the federal parliament, nationalist jurists in Quebec like T.J.J. Loranger and Charles-Chamilly de Lorimier questioned "as contrary to the principles of good justice" its power over cases emanating from issues under Quebec's control when two-thirds of the Supreme Court judges were ignorant of civil law.

The First World War, and particularly the issue of compulsory military service, further divided Canada, and much more deeply than the schools crises had done. As the number of volunteer recruits declined and casualties rose, pressures for conscription mounted. Recent British immigrants had been the most enthusiastic volunteers while French Canadians, their ties to France sundered a century and a half earlier, were among those least enthusiastic about a European war. (Farmers and organized labour outside Quebec shared their sentiments.) Furthermore, the

Canadian military service was resolutely British in its language and traditions. In June 1917, when the Military Service Act was introduced by the Conservative government of Robert Borden to raise 100 000 recruits, the Liberal Party—and Canada—divided. Although Quebec Liberals remained loyal to Laurier, most Liberals joined the Conservatives in a Union Government established to implement conscription. In Quebec anti-conscription riots, the failure of 40 percent of conscripted men to report for duty, and the election in 1917 of only three Union Government supporters (all from predominantly anglophone ridings) pointed to strong French-Canadian resistance to the views of the English Canadian majority.

In 1921, Quebec assured political power to Mackenzie King by delivering all 65 seats to the federal Liberals; over 70 percent of the Quebec population voted Liberal, compared to 30 percent in Ontario and 11 percent in Manitoba. The elections of 1917 and 1921 established a Liberal stranglehold on Quebec that only John Diefenbaker (1958) and Brian Mulroney (1984 and 1988) were able to break. Block voting in Quebec has ensured that the province, despite its minority position in Canada, has had a powerful position in cabinet.

PROVINCIAL AUTONOMY

The sense that the province was isolated within Confederation, with its institutions and language under attack from the majority, led to a growing Quebec separateness from the rest of Canada on social and moral issues. Quebec politics from the late 1880s to the Depression were characterized by greater attention to the minority status of French Canadians in Canada, to provincial rights, and to the role of the Quebec government as the defender of French Canada's religious, linguistic, and cultural traditions. "Sunny ways" were increasingly contested by hardening theories of provincial rights.

In the post-Confederation period, Cartier's and La Fontaine's provincial heirs were caught between two forces: the conflicting interests of a conservative Catholicism with roots deep in the small-town bourgeoisie and the peasantry, and the exigencies of maturing industrial capitalism. Provincial politics in the decades after Confederation were marked by instability, bitter political division between centrists and the Catholic right, and deepening provincial debt to subsidize railways and other industrial activities. Industrial capitalists insisted on various forms of state aid, a cheap labour force, and a stable economy. State aid in Quebec changed from direct subsidies to favourable investment, tax, and labour laws.

Fernand Dumont and Jean Hamelin (1981) have shown how Quebec's baggage of provincial minority status, isolation, poverty in the face of international capital, and political and economic subjugation provided nationalists with strong ammunition. On their right, politicians faced conservative Catholic and nationalist spokesmen such as Jules-Paul Tardivel, Henri Bourassa, and Lionel Groulx. The nationalists attacked the provincial government for the hemorrhage of emigration, the failure of colonization, the position of Quebec in the federal state, and the moral disintegration that they perceived in an industrializing and urbanizing society. As early as the 1880s, provincial politicians had to tie together the reality of Canadian federalism and the vigorous arguments of nationalists like Tardivel.

> It should be obvious to anyone who thinks about it, that the French race in America will never have any real influence for good unless it is solidly based in the province of Quebec, as in a fortress. We must occupy the territory of this province, which belongs to us by every sort of title. We must develop and strengthen ourselves here, under the protection of the Church which watched over our beginnings and whose magnificent institutions are still our greatest strength (Tardivel, 1975: xxx).

The contradictions between provincial rights and "sunny ways," between federal and provincial forums, and between political action in the two-party system of Liberals and Conservatives and in third parties, can be perceived in the changing alliances of Henri Bourassa's career. His ideology was rooted in conservatism, Catholicism, and French-Canadian nationalism. His attempt to integrate these principles into a larger Canadian ideal of mutual respect, biculturalism, pan-Canadian nationalism, and Canadian autonomy flew apart during the schools and conscription crises. Entering politics after the execution of Riel, Bourassa sat in both the federal (1890–1907, 1925–1935) and provincial (1908–1912) legislatures. He first sat as a Liberal but split with Laurier over the Boer War. He then sat as an Independent, founded the important Montreal newspaper *Le Devoir* in 1910, and backed the election of nationalist candidates in 1911. Later he ran as a Conservative.

Nationalists were also uncomfortable about the provincial government's close relationship with the great trusts and industrial corporations. Once he left the premier's office in 1920, for example, Lomer Gouin had moved to the board rooms of English Canadian companies such as Sun Life and the Bank of Montreal and into the cabinet of Mackenzie King. Concentrating particularly on electric power and transport monopolies, nationalists called for nationalization of water power, municipalization of Montreal transport and electric companies or, at the very least, an end to state subsidies to private companies. During the Depression, powerful nationalists like Groulx called for state action in the economy to protect Quebec culture. His speech still reflects the accepted ideology of Quebec governments:

> To be French is to remain French. More than our right, it is our duty and our mission. The state has an obligation to remember that the national good, our cultural heritage, is an integral part of the common good for which it is particularly responsible. And since the economic and the national are not with-

out relationship, the state again has the obligation to remember that the national good imposes upon it certain duties, even of economic character (Cited in Jones, 1972: 50).

These attacks on the direction of Canadian federalism had important repercussions in the law, politics, and social legislation of the province. In 1918, Pierre-Basile Mignault was appointed to the Supreme Court of Canada. One of the province's foremost civil jurists, he rejected the federalism and pro-common-law bias of early Quebec judges on the federal bench. He not only vigorously attacked the prevalence of common-law principles in areas concerning the Quebec civil code, but also placed his interpretation of the law within the framework of a compact theory of Confederation (1891):

> The provinces were not created by this charter [the British North America Act]. Confederation is only the legalization of a pact concluded between the four provinces. It seems then that one can conclude *a priori* that the provinces acted like merchants who form a corporation. They put together a part of their property, but kept the rest (Cited in Howes, 1987: 547).

Liberal provincial politicians, well-known for their sympathies with the federal government, found it in their interest to adopt the rhetoric of provincial rights. In 1927, when his government was protesting Ottawa's plan for old-age pensions, Premier Taschereau outlined to a student audience his support of the compact theory of Confederation:

> Every Canadian must understand that sixty years ago we formed not a homogeneous country but a Confederation of different provinces for certain purposes, with the distinct understanding that each of these provinces should retain things which a people, like an individual, has no right to abdicate (Cited in Vigod, 1986: 148).

Provincial separateness, language, culture, and the power of conservative institutions in Quebec frustrated the attempts of reformers to achieve solidarity across Canada. Although Quebec farmers faced similar problems of farm prices, credit, and effective political action as farmers elsewhere in Canada, they did not join in the pan-Canadian agrarian protest that resulted in farm governments in Ontario (1919) and Alberta (1921) and in a sixty-four member Progressive Party contingent to Ottawa in the elections of 1921. Still stung by the conscription crisis, Quebecers voted solidly Liberal in provincial and federal elections in the 1920s.

Nor did socialist and radical industrial unionist groups like the Industrial Workers of the World—which rose up in the mines and shops of western Canada in the early years of the century—have much success in Quebec. The One Big Union, for example, which strangled Winnipeg with a general strike in the spring of 1919, found Quebec a largely foreign terrain. Although 13 000 workers in Montreal struck in solidarity with the labour militants of Winnipeg, the rest of

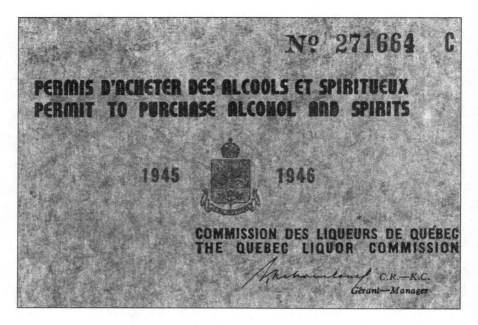

Figure 7.7 (continued on next page)

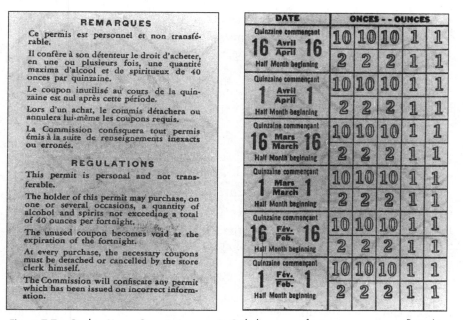

REMARQUES	DATE	ONCES - - OUNCES				
REMARQUES Ce permis est personnel et non transfé- rable. Il confère à son détenteur le droit d'acheter, en une ou plusieurs fois, une quantité maxima d'alcool et de spiritueux de 40 onces par quinzaine. Le coupon inutilisé au cours de la quin- zaine est nul après cette période. Lors d'un achat, le commis détachera ou annulera lui-même les coupons requis. La Commission confisquera tout permis émis à la suite de renseignements inexacts ou erronés.	Quinzaine commençant **16** Avril **16** Half Month beginning	10	10	10	1	1
		2	2	2	1	1
	Quinzaine commençant **1** Avril **1** Half Month beginning	10	10	10	1	1
		2	2	2	1	1
REGULATIONS This permit is personal and not trans- ferable. The holder of this permit may purchase, on one or several occasions, a quantity of alcohol and spirits not exceeding a total of 40 ounces per fortnight. The unused coupon becomes void at the expiration of the fortnight. At every purchase, the necessary coupons must be detached or cancelled by the store clerk himself. The Commission will confiscate any permit which has been issued on incorrect inform- ation.	Quinzaine commençant **16** Mars **16** Half Month beginning	10	10	10	1	1
		2	2	2	1	1
	Quinzaine commençant **1** Mars **1** Half Month beginning	10	10	10	1	1
		2	2	2	1	1
	Quinzaine commençant **16** Fév. **16** Half Month beginning	10	10	10	1	1
		2	2	2	1	1
	Quinzaine commençant **1** Fév. **1** Half Month beginning	10	10	10	1	1
		2	2	2	1	1

Figure 7.7 Quebec Liquor Commission permit. Catholic support for temperance was reflected in government liquor regulations. Liquor stores were characterized by shaded windows and bottles stored behind counters. During the war, permits were needed to buy liquor and coupons controlled consumption.

Quebec remained an infertile territory for radical unionism. In the 1920s, despite some remaining strength among Montreal packing-house workers and railway workers, the One Big Union was a waning force. Conservative unionism, symbolized by the formation in 1921 of the Confédération des Travailleurs Catholiques du Canada (CTCC), moved to centre stage of the labour movement in Quebec.

Women's rights also suffered from a lack of solidarity. While women in every other province had the provincial vote by 1922, suffragists like Marie Gérin-Lajoie were not successful in allying themselves with their anglophone counterparts even though it would have strengthened their cause. Similarly, Quebec's refusal to accept the social values of Protestants was clear over the issue of prohibition. In 1898, Quebec had been the only province to vote "no" in a prohibition referendum. In the next decades, Quebec, except for a short and theoretically dry period at the end of the First World War, continued to resist the prohibition movement. In 1919, alcohol was again being sold publicly in Quebec.

Traditionally, alcohol had been sold in Quebec by general merchants and grocers. With the establishment of the Quebec Liquor Commission in 1921, the state established a monopoly over the importation, transportation, and sale of alcoholic products (Figure 7.7). The disparity between the public sale of alcohol in Quebec and prohibition in other nearby Canadian and American jurisdictions led to widespread smuggling. The revenues of the Quebec Liquor Commission in 1929–1930 were $20 million; with depression conditions and the lifting of American prohibition in 1933, Commission revenues dropped to $5 million (*La Presse*, 29 November 1986).

∽∾∽

THE ERA OF GOUIN AND TASCHEREAU

The Liberal administrations of Lomer Gouin (1905–1920) and Louis-Alexandre Taschereau (1920–1936) tried to conciliate both conservative nationalists and the industrial capitalists. Strong support for industrial "progress" was what the Liberals described as the bedrock of their three decades of provincial power. Specifically, progress meant rapid exploitation of natural resources, low taxes, minimal state interference with business, and a paternalistic attitude to labour. They were particularly anxious to attract American capital which, as Taschereau explained, they saw as essential to the province's development: "We still don't have enough American capital interested in our enterprises. It would be difficult to get $75 for an undertaking like that at Caron Falls if we relied solely on Canadians. We need to develop ourselves with the gold of our neighbours" (Jones, 1972: 28–29).

The alliance between successive Liberal provincial governments and the major financial and industrial corporations was cemented with cronyism, directorships, legal business, sinecures, and political contributions. Even native peoples, increasingly marginal to the power structure, felt the impact. The Huron Indians of the Lorette reserve, for example, saw part of their reserve expropriated and their way of life threatened when the Quebec and Lake St. John Railway was built.

Gouin and Taschereau also tried to maintain the tradition of good political relations with the church hierarchy. In their commitment to industrial expansion, regional economic growth, and social peace, officials of both church and state usually shared a common ideology. Ideology was reinforced by social contact and systematic consultation between the hierarchies of church and state: "You know on what terms of friendship I was with your predecessor," Archbishop Bruchési wrote to Premier Taschereau in 1920. "We always got along well in all matters. I have no doubt it will be the same with you as a friend and I urge you to be the same with me."

For his part, Premier Taschereau assured the audience at a 1933 banquet for the province's leading cleric, Cardinal Jean-Marie-Rodrigue Villeneuve, that the church was an ally in maintaining social order by its teaching of "obedience to authority, respect for law and property, the sanctity of the home, the sovereignty of the father of the family in his little kingdom [and] the assurance that death is not an end but a beginning" (Vigod, 1986: 201).

The church proved a reliable force in suppressing unrest; indeed it was Premier Taschereau's uncle, Cardinal Elzéar-Alexandre Taschereau, who had condemned the Knights of Labor in 1885 (Ryan, 1966: 201). In 1907, Cardinal Louis-Nazaire Bégin founded the newspaper *L'Action sociale*, which persistently supported industrial development. In Montreal, Archbishop Paul Bruchési responded to a rash of strikes in 1903 with a pastoral letter rejecting a labour theory of value and calling on workers to be moderate in their wage demands. Strikes, he contended, forced capital to flee and resulted in cheap immigrant labour replacing striking francophone workers.

Nor was it just the upper echelons of the church hierarchy that favoured industrial development. In 1913, when government officials inquired about the needs of 270 parishes, 116 local priests replied by inviting industries into their parishes (Ryan, 1966: 198). Despite orders that they not serve on the boards of industrial companies, many priests continued the entrepreneurial tradition of curé François-Xavier-Antoine Labelle of Saint-Jérôme. In the 1870s, Labelle had been the very symbol of clerical sponsorship of regional industry and railways. To block French-Canadian emigration to the United States, he promoted mining, paper mills, and railway construction into the Laurentians. In the process, he allied himself with important anglophone capitalists like Hugh Allan, who was always pleased to pay his expenses and to invite him to mundane events such as a ball he was giving for the governor general: "although I do not expect you would dance, and more especially the fast dances, you might like to see it. I expect to have about 500 people at it. Will you come?" (Young, 1978: 35). Throughout his career, Labelle continued to blur the lines between religious and secular functions. In 1888, although a lifelong Conservative, he accepted an appointment as Assistant Commissioner in the Mercier government's Department of Agriculture and Colonization. Labelle was a model for many priests. In Lake Mégantic, for example, the local curé built the town's first electrical generating station and served as its electrician until his death.

Church–state collaboration was clear in education. The Education Act of 1875 gave every bishop in the province an automatic seat on the Catholic committee of the Council of Public Instruction. Louis-Philippe Audet (1969: 37) summed up the significance of clerical power in the provincial education bureaucracy:

> [The Education Act] resulted in a considerable growth of clerical influence to the point, that, after this date, most Catholic leaders in the francophone sector bowed gracefully before the combined power of the Catholic hierarchy, clergy, and religious communities. Conscious of the power which it held, the Church in Quebec considered its role—which historic circumstances had temporarily confided it with—as a "mission de droit."

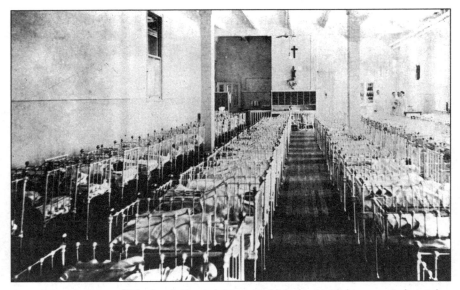

Figure 7.8 The Sisters of Miséricorde Hospital, 1900. Established in 1840, this maternity hospital was part of a wider social control network. Young domestic servants between the ages of eighteen and twenty-two formed the majority of expectant mothers. Mothers forced to abandon their babies often sent money, asked for photographs, and wrote with instructions and wishes for their infants' care: "Let her take fresh air outside. I would so like her to enjoy good health." Most babies were sent for adoption or to the Grey Nuns' orphanage. In 1933, the overcrowded institution began turning pregnant women away, accepting only local women in the last stages of pregnancy (Lévesque, 1984a: 179).

Despite some state centralization of education to oversee financing and inspection, the church successfully opposed demands for formation of a ministry of education. It continued to control curriculum and textbooks and resisted an extension of compulsory education that would reduce the responsibilities of the family and increase the power of the state. In 1908, the provincial education budget was less than $0.50 for each child enrolled in elementary school (Ryan, 1966: 216). Costs were kept low in large part by the cheap labour of the nuns and brothers, who made up 48.3 percent of elementary teachers and 85 percent of secondary and classical college teachers. The labour of clerics ensured that the salaries of lay teachers, most of them female, would remain low. Although Quebec spent very little, its literacy and school attendance rates were comparable to those of other provinces.

State participation was evident in the social sector. Although it did not challenge clerical control, the Public Assistance Law of 1921 recognized charitable institutions of public utility such as hospitals and asylums and established a statutory system of subsidies.

Church–state collaboration did not eliminate friction. State authorities had to contend with pressures for increased educational subsidies and for curriculum change from their Protestant and Jewish constituencies. As early as 1830, classical colleges received subsidies and a 1922 provincial law permitted each college to receive up to $10 000 from the state. The state assumed financing of male elementary education in 1897; female elementary education remained a preserve of the church. In 1900, the province's fifty female boarding schools received the equivalent state aid of one classical college. Permission was granted to the Congrégation de Notre-Dame to open the province's first female school of higher learning in 1908, although it was not given the status of a classical college until 1926, when it became the Collége Marguerite-Bourgeoys (Dumont et Fahmy-Eid, 1986: 21; Heap, 1987).

There were different tensions in the social sector, where clerical control and Catholic ideology were often at odds with the reality of an urban society. Quebec's reported illegitimacy rate varied between 2.9 and 3.4 percent of live births and was slightly lower than the Canadian average. Twenty percent of Quebec's reported illegitimate births took place in Montreal's Miséricorde Hospital (Figure 7.8).

As work and family patterns evolved in industrial capitalist society, the vocation of many Catholic institutions changed. From the mid-nineteenth century, day-care centres became increasingly necessary to working-class families (Table 7.3). The number of children in the Grey Nuns' day-care centres peaked at the turn of the century and then declined, leading Micheline Dumont (1980) to speculate that centres were converted into hospices for the children of the poor. Sylvie Côté argues that although the curriculum and organization of Sacré-Coeur hospice were intended to impose social control, the Sherbrooke proletariat made use of the hospice service for its own purposes. Faced with unemployment, war-time separation, or the imprisonment, illness, or alcoholism of the family head, parents interned their children at the hospice. Both parents of 63 percent of children at the school were alive.

Institution	Period	Number of children	Daily average
Saint-Joseph	1858–1899	9 793	242
Nazareth	1861–1914	14 925	—
Bethléem	1868–1903	12 853	350
Saint-Henri	1885–1920	16 700	450
Sainte-Cunégonde	1889–1922	6 000	—

Table 7.3   Number of Children in the Grey Nuns' Day-Care Centres, 1858–1922 (Dumont, 1980: 40)

State financial participation in social affairs touched nationalist and religious sensitivities. In 1924, the Taschereau government passed a Child Adoption Act designed to relieve crowding in orphanages, to find homes for illegitimate children, and to give legal safeguards to adoptive parents. Clerics, supported by Henri Bourassa and other conservatives, protested vigorously against the act, particularly the provision that Roman Catholic children could be placed in non-Catholic families. With the bogey of the French Revolution and the secularism of France always handy, clerical speakers described the bill as part of an anticlerical campaign aimed at "the successful elimination and systematic displacement of the church's maternal influences" (Vigod, 1986: 118).

─◦◦─

POPULISM IN MONTREAL

The proletarianization of Montreal that we observed in Chapter 6 resulted in urban populism. In the 1880s, working-class communities to the east of Montreal like Hochelaga (1893) and Saint-Jean Baptiste (1885) were annexed to the city. This added francophone weight to Montreal's proletariat. Working-class francophones became an increasingly important consideration in the politics of a city faced with rapid industrialization, private monopolies in municipal utilities such as electric power and tramways, persistent strikes in the transport sector, and dire public health conditions.

The smallpox epidemic of 1885 had 2500 victims and led to riots. In 1913, a sixty-foot-long crack in the city's water conduit cut off the water supply for four days. Quebec was the worst-hit province in the 1918 influenza epidemic, with 530 000 cases and 14 000 deaths (McGinnis, 1977: 128). Tuberculosis and diarrhea resulting from impure milk gave the city the highest infant mortality rate in North America. Perhaps the disaster that most shocked the public was the Laurier Palace Theatre fire of 9 January 1927.

The 1000-seat Laurier Palace Theatre was located in east-end Montreal in a working-class neighbourhood. During a Sunday showing of a children's film, fire broke out. Seventy-eight children died. Almost all of them died of asphyxiation on the stairs of the four exits. An inquiry showed that the theatre was operating without a permit, that inspection was lax, that exit doors were blocked by ropes and snow, and that safety laws had been disobeyed. By law, parents were to accompany children under seventeen, but not one of the victims was over sixteen.

Until 1914, mayors of Montreal represented the elite and the mayoralty alternated between anglophones and francophones. This changed with the victory of francophones such as Médéric Martin (mayor 1914–1924, 1926–1928) and Camilien Houde (mayor 1928–1932, 1934–1936, 1938–1940, 1944–1954), who were able to capture strong working-class support by using patronage effectively, and by attacking the big corporations and traditional patrician leadership.

In 1914, Médéric Martin ran against establishment candidate George Washington Stephens. Martin was a cigar maker from the working-class neighbourhood of Saint-Marie. Stephens was a McGill University graduate and the dominant shareholder of the Canadian Rubber Company; he lived permanently in the Ritz-Carlton Hotel. Although supported by almost all the Montreal newspapers and the Trades and Labour Council, Stephens's campaign for the City Beautiful, for a just and efficient city, for female suffrage, and for library and sewage facilities, was defeated by Martin, whose campaign contrasted his worker background against "the millionaires and rich men pretending to be working in the public interest."

Martin never forgot his origins. Instead of appealing to progressive sentiments, he promised pavement, patronage, and public works projects in working-class neighbourhoods. This formula, along with his skills as an orator and his image as an "east-end boy" who rubbed shoulders with princes and kings kept Martin in office for a decade. In 1927, the Laurier Palace fire, a typhoid epidemic caused by lax pasteurization procedures of local milk producers, and his promotion of a local beer called "la bière Martin" led to his defeat by Camilien Houde. Like Martin, Houde was a product of the working class, a store clerk who had advanced to bank clerk and ultimately bank inspector.

Houde was able to exploit the fears and conservative impulses of the Montreal proletariat with a millennial message linking the monopoly interests of the great banks and tramway and electrical companies to paganism: "I believe that the limited liability company, both from the moral and material standpoints, is the most serious error of our country. It is driving us straight to paganism which will, if it continues, lead to the disappearance of our western civilization" (1934). Houde also focused on what he saw as the profound social and sexual implications of women's participation in the paid labour force: "The man at home in a bathrobe while the women is in a factory in pyjamas, the husband taking care of the children while the wife is out fighting for their daily bread and perhaps her honor, that is the world upside down."

⌒

WOMEN'S RIGHTS IN
INDUSTRIAL CAPITALIST QUEBEC

Chapter 6 examined the ways in which working women took part in labour organization and in resistance to industrial capitalism. Yet women's participation in wage labour had not alleviated their mothering and domestic duties. The particular social dimensions of industrial society for women are revealed in early day-care centres, maternity hospitals, and hospices for the offspring of the poor, and in the economic implications of widowhood. In the church, convents at one level symbolized female subordination to male supervision and male concepts of Marianism. On another level, however, they protected female autonomy and provided legitimate and economically viable alternatives to domestic life and mothering.

Bourgeois women, disenfranchised and blocked from power in the state, the professions, and corporations, were handicapped in their efforts to take social and political action. In 1911, there were no female architects or engineers in Quebec and fewer than 1 percent of the 17 787 civil servants in Quebec were women. Of Quebec's 2000 doctors, twenty-one were women, none of whom had studied medicine in Quebec (Danylewycz, 1987: 57). Women were admitted to the practice of law in 1941 and to the notariat in 1956.

Restricted access to higher education and the professions was accompanied by ideological pressure on the symbolism of the "woman" and her function within Quebec society (Figure 7.9). Marianism emphasized female purity, humility, virtue, and subordination to men in both public and private life. It represented a strong countervailing weight to demands for female equality in politics, the law, the workplace, and family. Henri Bourassa was a leading opponent of suffragist demands for the vote and for legal equality, leading Susan Mann Trofimenkoff (1983: 305) to dismiss him as "bitter, rigid, humourless, and pharisaic." The vice-rector of Laval, an institution that finally permitted women to audit literature courses in 1904, explained his university's discrimination in the context of a social view in which women were to be trained as "devoted companions" rather than as "rivals" of men (Danylewycz, 1987: 146).

Catholic intellectuals were not the only ones to see female education as training for motherly and domestic duties. At the Montreal General Hospital, for example, entering student nurses in 1896 were reminded by a supervising doctor of their total subordination to male physicians:

> Your duty as a nurse in relation to the medical attendant of the patient is to quietly and thoroughly carry out the directions you may receive from [the doctor], to be an efficient and trustworthy aid to him in care of the sick, and not to constitute yourself in any way his censor or critic (Kenneally, 1983: 93).

At the end of the nineteenth century, Quebec women were active in a variety of women's organizations: the Montreal Local Council of Women, the Young Women's Christian Association, the Montreal Suffrage Association, and the Woman's Christian Temperance Union. With strong influence from anglophone women, these organizations were vigorous in their demands for social and legal reform and equality in the workplace. They were soon surpassed by the Fédération nationale Saint-Jean-Baptiste. The federation was established in 1907 with the approval of the archbishop by Marie Gérin-Lajoie and Caroline Béique

Figure 7.9 The courtyard of the Ursuline Convent in Quebec. Girls of the elite were brought up with stern discipline and trained to do needlework and manage servants.

as a women's section of the Saint-Jean-Baptiste Society. Its Catholicism and French-Canadian nationalism predominated over progressive feminism. Within these conservative restrictions, the federation and journals such as *La bonne parole* called for extended civil rights for women, access to higher education for women, female suffrage, and protection for female workers. One of their most important campaigns was for reform of the Civil Code of 1866, which discriminated blatantly against women. While a husband could obtain separation from his wife on evidence of adultery, a wife could obtain separation only if her husband brought his concubine to live in the family home. In 1902, Marie Gérin-Lajoie published the *Traité de droit usuel*, a manual geared particularly to women, and which explained the law in lay terminology.

Despite the reforming thrust of its demands, the federation was pressured by patriarchal institutions to concentrate on sectors traditionally considered to be of female concern: children's hospitals, workers' housing, family courts, and alcohol abuse. At times, conservative rhetoric resurfaced, as in this Fédération nationale Saint-Jean-Baptiste pamphlet for nurses. It declared that hospital training

> prepared women admirably for their duties in family and in society. . . . After three years of work and struggle, when the student has completed her professional training, especially when, under the great law of duty, the woman can subjugate all the repugnances of her nature, all the whims of will, and all the feelings in her heart, when she is mature for the world that suffers, we call her a graduate (translated from Collectif Clio, 1982: 287).

Most nuns and rural women worked within a conservative framework of traditional Catholic attitudes. In rural newspapers, and then on radio, Françoise

Gaudet-Smet encouraged women to retain their traditional domestic skills in the face of consumerism and wage labour outside the home. In any case, church authorities had already perceived the significance of the developing field of household science. It trained women for their household tasks while separating them from "male" sciences such as agriculture. As early as the 1880s, nuns in rural regions were teaching domestic skills to girls destined to become farm wives. In 1905, the Ecole ménagère agricole de Saint-Pascal de Kamouraska was established by the Congrégation Notre-Dame and a year later another home economics school opened in Montreal.

During the First World War urban society also began to focus on teaching women domestic skills. By 1917, under the patronage of parish priests and the Fédération nationale Saint-Jean-Baptiste, 10 000 Montreal women a year followed courses in sewing, cooking, and domestic skills. Night and summer courses were established for women working outside the home; between 1909 and 1922, 40 000 female workers took housekeeping courses in provincial schools.

Many women were not fooled by their circumstances. Telephone operator Juliette Richard, for example, had a lucid understanding of the nature of her employment and its implicit sexism. In 1921, she described her work in the "central" of the Kamouraska Telephone Company. Working from an office in the home of her employer for $15 a month, she had no choice but to live with her parents:

> While it was men who invented the telephone, they called on women to operate them. This was done, since with the salaries offered, men were not interested; they served as a supplement to family revenues which the women could contribute while still taking care of the family. Another determining factor in the employment of women as telephone operators, was that they were more patient, more intuitive, and their voices are softer than men's (Collectif Clio, 1982: 310).

Female campaigns for civil reforms were opposed by the state and the clerical hierarchy, and largely dismissed by the Dorion Commission (1929). This provincial commission of inquiry rejected demands that married women have jurisdiction over their own salary, that there be equality between husband and wife in the control of community property, and that female members of a family be granted expanded rights to act as legal guardians of children. The commission's findings were based on the principle that the individual rights of a married woman were subordinate to a "superior law" of the family:

> The state of marriage created for the woman—and for the man as well—obligations. . . . One is free to establish a family or to retain one's full independence; when one has made one's choice, one is no longer free to reclaim individual rights that the superior law of the family has converted into duty (Cited in Casgrain, 1971: 89).

Although female suffrage had been granted in federal elections in 1917, women did not receive the vote in Quebec provincial elections until 1940, under the Godbout government. In 1921, the Quebec suffrage movement was revived with the formation of the Provincial Franchise Committee. The committee found it politically advantageous to argue that the goal of women's suffrage was not to change the station of women in life but rather to raise and inspire social life in general.

After a schism in the suffrage movement in 1928, Thérèse Casgrain became president of the Ligue des droits de la femme and, for fourteen years, she led the fight for equality of political and civil rights. Quebec lagged far behind other North American constituencies in this regard, maintaining "the almost complete exclusion of women from the exercise of public rights and the severe curtailment of civil capacity for married women" (Stoddart, 1981: 325).

The suffrage campaign faced hostility from both clerical and political leaders. Episcopal authorities asked the premier in 1922 to oppose female suffrage because it would represent "an attack against the fundamental traditions of our race and of our faith" (Hamelin et Gagnon, 1984: 327). Eighteen years later, the most important cleric in the province, Cardinal Villeneuve, reiterated his opposition, insisting that suffrage would violate family unity and hierarchy, that it would tempt women with the passions and adventures of electoral politics, that most women did not really want the vote, and that most of the social demands called for by women could be achieved by women's groups operating outside the elected parliamentary system.

For his part, Premier Taschereau called on Quebec women to "remain faithful to their ancestral conditions, with their status as queen of the household, to their works of charity and philanthropy, to their labours of love and denial" (Hamelin et Gagnon, 1984: 327).

∽

CONCLUSION

The dominant social characteristic of the industrial capitalist period was its conservatism. Both church and state were dominated by forces committed to the status quo and to the reinforcement of traditional values. The voices of labour progressives, political reformers, and moderate Catholics were muffled by the power of conservatives controlling the state and church apparatus. For their part, female reformers across the period faced an uphill struggle for educational opportunity, legal equality, and the provincial vote.

FURTHER READING

POLITICS AND LAW

For the career of Wilfrid Laurier see Réal Bélanger, *Wilfrid Laurier. Quand la politique devient passion*; H. Blair Neatby, *Laurier and a Liberal Quebec: A Study in Political Management*; and Richard Clippingdale, *Laurier: His Life and World*. For Conservative politics one can turn to Réal Bélanger, *Alfred Sévigny et les conservateurs fédéraux (1902–1918)*. Liberal politics are treated in Bernard Vigod, *Quebec before Duplessis: The Political Career of Louis-Alexandre Taschereau*. Bourassa and the nationalists are treated in Trofimenkoff, *The Dream of Nation: A Social and Intellectual History of Quebec*, and in Joseph Levitt, *Henri Bourassa and the Golden Calf: The Social Program of the Nationalists of Québec (1900–1914)*, and his Canadian Historical Association pamphlet, *Henri Bourassa, Catholic critic*. The most accessible statement of conservative nationalism in English is in Jules-Paul Tardivel, *For My Country: "Pour la Patrie."* Urban reform is treated in Annick Germain, *Les mouvements de réforme urbaine à Montréal au tournant du siècle*. For the relationship of Quebec law to the Supreme Court of Canada, see James Snell and Frederick Vaughan, *The Supreme Court of Canada: History of the Institution*, and David Howes, "From Polyjurality to Monojurality: The Transformation of Quebec Law, 1875–1929."

THE CHURCH

The best treatment of twentieth-century Catholicism is in Jean Hamelin and Nicole Gagnon, *Histoire de catholicisme québécois*, and Nive Voisine, *Histoire de l'église catholique au Québec (1608–1970)*. There are several sociological studies of the early twentieth century. In addition to Everett C. Hughes, *French Canada in Transition*, and Horace Miner, *St. Denis: A French-Canadian Parish*, see Marcel Rioux, *Belle-Anse*, and Léon Gérin, *L'Habitant de Saint-Justin*. For the church and education see Ruby Heap's important thesis, "L'église, l'Etat et l'enseignement primaire public catholique au Québec, 1897–1920." An excellent case study of education is found in Chad Gaffield's *Language, Schooling and Cultural Conflict: The Origins of the French-language Controversy in Ontario*.

WOMEN

For women, the best sources are Collectif Clio, *Histoire des femmes* (also available in English as Clio Collective, *Québec Women: A History*) and Marta Danylewycz's *Taking the Veil: An Alternative to Marriage, Motherhood and Spinsterhood in Quebec, 1840–1920*. For male attitudes, see Trofimenkoff's "Henri Bourassa and 'The Woman Question,'" and "Les femmes dans l'oeuvre de Groulx." For the education of women see Micheline Dumont and Nadia Fahmy-Eid, *Les couventines: L'éducation des filles au Québec dans les congrégations religieuses enseignantes*

1840–1960. Women in rural milieux are treated in Yolande Cohen's *Femmes de paroles. L'histoire des cercles de fermières au Québec*. For feminism see Jennifer Stoddart, "Quebec's Legal Elite Looks at Women's Rights: The Dorion Commission 1929–31"; and Marie Lavigne, Yolande Pinard and Jennifer Stoddart, "The Fédération Nationale Saint-Jean Baptiste and the Women's Movement in Quebec." For single working-class women see Andrée Lévesque, "Deviant Anonymous: Single Mothers at the Hôpital de la Miséricorde in Montreal, 1929–39."

From Depression to Quiet Revolution

*T*he period from the Depression to the Quiet Revolution in 1960 is often called the *Grande noirceur*—a period marked by the strengthening of conservative ideology and clerical power. To outsiders, politicians such as Maurice Duplessis projected the image of a docile Catholic population that was reliable as an unaggressive labour force and respectful of hierarchy. Behind this political rhetoric reality was rather different. Demographically, economically, and socially, Quebec continued the process of modernization. Jewish, Slav, and Southern European immigration in the postwar years heightened ethnic and linguistic tensions in Montreal and was an important ingredient in a resurgence of Quebec nationalism. Labour became better organized, more secular, and more vocal. Women pressed for political rights and increased social services. Continuing expansion of manufacturing stimulated industrial growth in mining, transportation, and chemicals. Industry developed further, especially in the resource extraction sector with the exploitation of the North Shore and Abitibi regions. American corporations and capital were increasingly important in the Quebec economy, which became more closely integrated into North American markets during the period. At the same time, Montreal faced stiffer competition from Toronto for the title of Canadian metropolis.

DEMOGRAPHY

After declining significantly during the Depression, Quebec's birth rate rose during the Second World War and was maintained in the postwar "baby boom" at a level above thirty per thousand. It remained at this level until the beginning of the 1960s when birth-control devices became more widely available. By the 1950s, the *revanche des berceaux* (revenge of the cradle) was definitely over as the Quebec birth rate came into line with the Canadian average. The combined effect of natural increase and immigration maintained Quebec's position within Canada at about 29 percent of the total population.

The increase in the birth rate after the Second World War was partially due to earlier marriages. With buoyant economic conditions, young men married at an average age of twenty-five and young women at twenty-three. At the same time, death rates continued the steady downward trend begun in the past century. Infant mortality, still among the highest in Canada, fell from over 130 per 1000 at the beginning of the period to under 50 per 1000 by the 1950s. Pasteurization was primarily responsible for the drop.

Some demographers interpret the post–World War II period as the "golden age" of the nuclear family in Quebec: most couples married fairly young and had numerous children; parents lived together and survived to see their children marry and leave home; wives did not normally work outside the home; separa-tions and divorce were exceptional; few marriages were interrupted prematurely by death (Perron, Lapierre-Adamcyk, and Morissette, 1987a).

Migration patterns were altered by the Depression. Emigration of francophones to industrial centres in the United States slowed when American immigration laws were tightened and the closing of this traditional safety valve led to renewed colonization of the Abitibi clay belt. The region had initially been opened to set-tlement by the construction of the Canadian Northern Railway in 1910 but had attracted few settlers. Encouraged by conservative Catholic ideology and govern-ment initiatives to subsidize colonization, such as the 1935 Vautrin plan, new communities were established. Abitibi's population grew from 23 692 in 1931 to 64 000 in 1941. The clay belt population had two main occupations: farming mar-ginal agricultural land and mining copper and gold (Gourd, 1975).

Prosperity after the Depression did not signal a return to previous migration patterns. A new exodus of rural families benefited Quebec centres such as Quebec City, Sherbrooke, the new towns along the North Shore, and industrial centres on the Montreal plain. For emigrants who left Quebec, Ontario, rather than New England, became the major destination. In the period 1956–1961, about three-quarters of the some 74 000 people who left the province selected Ontario.

Foreign immigration declined during the Depression and war but increased sharply after 1945. Over 420 000 immigrants arrived in Quebec from 1945 to 1961, significantly altering the composition of the province's non-francophone population (Table 8.1). Those of British origin declined as a percentage of the non-francophone population, but Italian, Polish, Greek, and German communi-ties increased dramatically. Italians increased from 4.6 percent of the non-francophone population in 1931 to 12.4 percent in 1961. With the freedom to choose the language of education, two out of three immigrants sent their children

	1931	1941	1951	1961
French	2 270 059	2 695 032	3 327 128	4 241 354
British Isles	432 696	452 887	491 818	567 057
German	10 616	8 880	12 249	39 457
Greek	(not given)	2 728	3 388	19 390
Italian	24 845	28 051	34 165	108 552
Jewish	60 087	66 277	73 019	74 677
Polish	(not given)	10 036	16 998	30 790
Asian	2 793	7 119	7 714	14 801
Indian and Inuit	13 471	13 641	16 620	21 343

Table 8.1 The Ethnic Origin of the Population of Quebec, 1931–1961

to English schools. English was identified with status, the best work, and in a more global sense immigrants perceived Quebec as just one bailiwick in a larger English-speaking North American society.

Quebec anglophones became more concentrated in the Montreal region, with the proportion of Quebec anglophones living on the Ile de Montréal rising from just under two-thirds in 1941 to over 70 percent by 1961. The concentration of non-francophones in Quebec's metropolis contributed to linguistic tensions and would eventually make Montreal the focus of the movement for French-language rights.

During the 1940s, the native population of Quebec regained its precontact level. The development of universal programs such as welfare, family allowances, and health care was of particular importance to this vulnerable and materially poor population. Subsistence patterns were disrupted as resource extraction spread to remote regions such as the North Shore. Montagnais living on reserves became more dependent on government payments as railways and lumber and mining industries encroached upon their hunting territories. As a result, they spent more time in villages and population increased more than 50 percent from 1941 to 1961, as natives received better health care.

∽◦∽

AGRICULTURE

Agriculture was seen as one panacea to the Depression, but it underwent a profound transformation after the Second World War. The farming population declined dramatically after 1951, as did agriculture's importance in the Quebec economy (Figure 8.1). Mechanization in the forest industries reduced the seasonal employment that farmers in the traditional agro-forestry economy had depended upon. As a result, many farms in peripheral areas such as the clay belt of Abitibi, the Laurentians, and the Eastern Townships were abandoned. In the Montreal plain and close to Quebec City, urban sprawl encroached on rich farmlands.

Quebec agriculture rapidly modernized in the 1940s and 1950s as tractors replaced draft animals. Fewer than 2 percent of farms had tractors in 1931 but over 63 percent had at least one by 1961. Regional disparities were still evident. In the Montreal plain over 85 percent of farms had tractors whereas half the farmers in Charlevoix still relied on animal traction. Rural electrification under the Duplessis government brought refrigeration and labour-saving technology such as mechanical milking machines between 1945 and 1960 (Table 8.2).

In the 1930s, specialization was mainly restricted to the Montreal plain, the Eastern Townships (dairying), a small area on the southern shore of Lac Saint-Jean, and truck-farming areas. Mixed agriculture and subsistence farming were

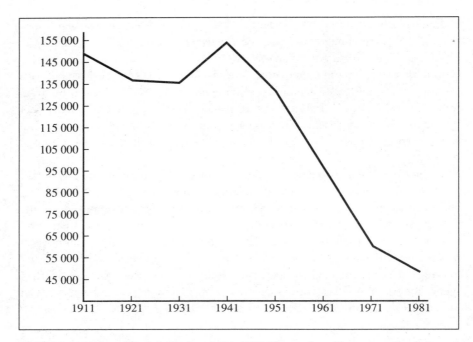

Figure 8.1 Number of farms in Quebec, 1911–1981. The number of farms started to decline slowly after 1911, but colonization movements during the Depression account for the rise in 1941. A sharp decline occurred in the postwar period.

still dominant in outlying regions such as the Gaspé, the Laurentians, the Ottawa Valley, and Abitibi. Forty percent of farms were categorized as subsistence farms in the 1941 census. By 1961, however, almost 90 percent of farmers reported a specialization; dairy farming predominated, and poultry and hog production were increasing (Figure 8.2). Turkey ranching, for example, was a minor activity in 1931 with only 150 000 birds produced annually, but by 1961 Quebec farmers were raising over 730 000 turkeys.

	1931	1941	1951	1961
Tractors	2 417	5 869	31 971	70 697
Combines	0	55	420	3 046
Milking machines	827	n.a.	17 632	34 724
Electrification (%)	14.0	—	67.1	97.3

Table 8.2 Mechanization of Quebec farms, 1931–1961

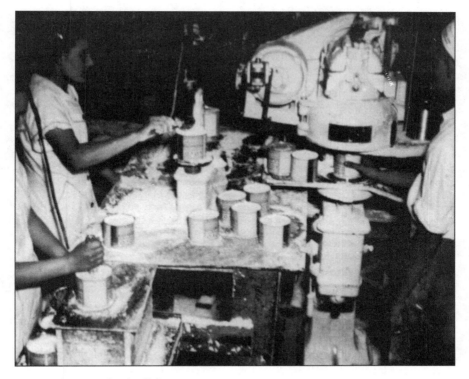

Figure 8.2   A powdered-milk factory

At the end of the war, farms were still small and relatively independent. By 1960 they were small capitalist enterprises dependent on tractors, electricity, fertilizers, outside supplies of feed, and large corporations to market their production. Government-sponsored marketing boards and educational programs for farmers flourished in the 1950s. Agricultural co-operatives prospered but as they became large businesses they faced internal conflict between their original sociodemocratic principles and the demands of modern management and big capital.

THE QUEBEC ECONOMY: FROM DEPRESSION TO EXPANSION

The decades 1930–1960 were characterized by sharp fluctuations in the labour market, as the Great Depression was succeeded by a strong labour demand during the Second World War, and then by the postwar consumer society. Between 1941 and 1951, manufacturing replaced agriculture as the most important male

	1931	1941	1951
Men			
Agriculture	223 164	251 539	187 846
Mining	6 127	9 977	12 273
Labourers	133 282	81 038	100 242
Construction	62 822	69 961	98 389
Manufacturing	111 325	173 288	235 580
Service	73 674	89 967	133 516
Women			
Manufacturing	45 367	68 227	88 032
Service	104 475	126 846	124 474
Clerical	27 887	37 373	75 638

Table 8.3   Labour Force by Occupation, 1931-1951

(Statistical Year Book, 1960: 77)

occupation; the proportion of men in farming dropped from 44.7 percent in 1901 to 27 percent in 1941 and 17 percent in 1951 (Table 8.3). Women represented 21.3 percent of the paid labour force in Quebec in 1931 (the highest percentage in Canada) and 24.5 percent in 1951. Service remained the largest paid female occupation, and office work the fastest growing female profession. Manufacturing accounted for 25.8 percent of female jobs in 1951.

The Depression left indelible scars on working people. While 40 percent of the working population of some Montreal neighbourhoods was out of work (Figure 8.3), unemployment in regions such as Chicoutimi hit 60 percent when pulp-and-paper factories closed. In some industries, the Depression was also characterized by tighter management control over the organization of work. At the Alcan aluminum plant in Arvida, for example, the company named a technical manager in 1934 and a personnel manager in 1937, and doubled the number of plant engineers from 1935 to 1940.

Armand Rodrigue remembers his experience of the Depression:

> I came from a really poor family. My father was a labourer. There were seven kids in the house; my mother gave birth to eleven. There was no question of unemployment in those days. My father worked here and there as a coal carter. . . . I didn't last long at school. At age ten or eleven you worked: one, two, or three dollars a week—that helped the family eat.
>
> In the first years of the depression I had a good job but I lost it. In those days at Stelco, I earned $17 a week. I dropped to $2.80 on "Secours direct." One survived but not much more! My rent was $8 a month—not much but if I earned $3 a week and if I subtracted $2 for the rent, that left me $1 . . .

(Translated from citation in Rouillard, 1981: 106)

Figure 8.3 Surviving in the Depression. Although thousands of Montrealers formed breadlines, many survived with poorly paid jobs.

Government incentives drew some 12 000 people from across Quebec to land-clearing and colonization projects in Abitibi and the Gaspé during the Depression. These regions were highly receptive to the Caisse Populaire movement which spread out from its core on the south shore of the St. Lawrence, the St. Maurice, and the Eastern Townships. In these colonization areas there were few chartered banks and the local petite bourgeoisie—the backbone of the Caisses—had great economic and social power. Between 1934 and 1945, some 800 Caisses were established, many in peripheral regions, and by 1945 Caisse assets were $90 million. In the Duplessis period, Caisse and government leaders collaborated to alleviate the rural crisis by using the Caisses' capital in financing the Office du crédit agricole, a provincial agency established in 1936 to provide long-term credit to farmers (Rudin, 1990: 30, 136).

The war stimulated production and employment across the province. With military demand for aluminum, Arvida more than doubled in population in the decade after 1941; the labour force in the chemical industry jumped from 5823 in 1939 to 46 553 in 1943 (Dumas, 1975: 20). Nickel mining at Noranda and ship-yards at Sorel and Lauzon boomed. Troop demand for beef, powdered milk, and other food products gave work to farms and dairy factories. The Montreal region profited from war production, especially aircraft and armament factories. The Cherrier munition works at Saint-Paul-l'Ermite, for example, had 450 buildings (Education Committees of CSN and CEQ, 1987: 110). Although Ontario received a greater value of war contracts, Montreal had the greatest number of employees in war industries and Quebec City was in third place behind Toronto (Historical Atlas of Canada, vol. 3, plate 48).

Historically, Montreal had been the metropolis of Canada; it had had the most active stock exchange, the largest number of important corporate head offices, and had been the hub of communications and transport. Its pre-eminence was challenged by Toronto during the 1920s, especially in the retailing, whole-saling, and banking sectors. Toronto's department store chains—Eaton's and Simpsons—had the strongest catalogue sales. By the 1930s, Montreal was losing its financial dominance. The Toronto Stock Exchange became the most active in 1933 and by 1960 Montreal had fallen well behind. In the period 1941–1961, six small and fifteen medium-sized insurance companies moved their head offices from Montreal to Toronto, as did the larger American Prudential and New York Life insurance companies. American capital was concentrated in the Toronto region. In 1961, 666 American-controlled companies were located in Toronto compared to 99 in Montreal. Montreal continued to be home to the head offices of many industrial concerns, but the largest advertising firms, law partnerships and, to a lesser degree, accountancy firms were concentrated in Toronto (Historical Atlas, vol. 3, plate 55).

Consumerism in Canada, postwar reconstruction in Europe, and American demand for steel during the Korean War created strong markets for Quebec natural resources, particularly iron ore, aluminum, and asbestos. The net value of production in the mining industry rose from $59 million in 1945 to over $246 million in 1960. The North Shore and other peripheral regions such as Abitibi developed rapidly after their severe suffering during the Depression. Company towns in northern Quebec like Schefferville and Gagnon developed around iron ore mines and were linked by the Iron Ore Company's railway to Sept-Iles. This port became one of Quebec's busiest, especially after 1957 when completion of the St. Lawrence Seaway gave improved access to midwestern markets.

Postwar prosperity kept unemployment rates low until the recession of the late 1950s. After oscillating around 4 to 5 percent (with a record low of 2.9 percent in 1951) unemployment rose to 8.8 percent in 1957 and peaked at over 10 percent in 1960 before dropping off.

At the end of the Second World War, Quebec's industrial structure gave clear evidence of the successive phases of industrialization. The oldest and still most important sectors of the economy—food, clothing, textile, leather, wood, and

Year	Total registrations	Family cars
1940	225 152	174 761
1960	1 096 053	820 152

Table 8.4   Motor Vehicle Registrations in Quebec

tobacco—continued to rely on cheap immigrant and rural labour. These industries accounted for 54.2 percent of Quebec's industrial labour force and 48.6 percent of the total value of industrial production in 1950 (Bernier et Boily, 1986). Industries created in the hydro-electric phase of Quebec's industrialization early in the century continued to have an important role; pulp-and-paper and chemicals were central to postwar industrial growth. Rapid growth also occurred in industries linked to growing consumer demands: petroleum and electronics. Quebec did not, however, benefit from automobile manufacturing. Ford, Chrysler, and General Motors built their Canadian plants in southern Ontario. The growing dominance of the tertiary sector (from 38.4 percent of Quebec's gross domestic product in 1941 to 51.1 percent in 1961) was the key element in Quebec's postwar economic development. Consumerism stimulated the expansion of retail outlets, consumer credit and insurance institutions, advertising, entertainment, and tourism and recreational industries. Motor vehicle registrations provide a good measure of consumer spending (Table 8.4).

WOMEN

Women's paid work continued to form a large labour reserve—useful in times of labour demand, dispensable when a labour surplus existed. Women were paid about half what men were and remained susceptible—both in their own thinking and in restrictions imposed on them—to an essentially maternal and domestic image. The struggle for suffrage revealed the strength of this ideology across Quebec society. Obtaining the vote in 1940 was the culmination of a three-decade struggle by feminists against the presumption that only men had access to the public arena. In the post-suffrage period, women's influence was felt in the character of certain universal programs and in changes to education law (Jean, 1988). Within the union, farm, and co-operative movements, however, women acceded to power only slowly as leaders persisted in a paternalistic ideology.

As jobs declined dramatically during the Depression, Quebec women were quickly reminded that they were merely reserve labour. Authorities like Cardinal

J.M. Rodrigue Villeneuve and Henri Bourassa told women of their primary duty in the home and of the importance of leaving the factory floor to male heads of families. Nor did demands for wage labour during the Second World War calm conservatives. Troubled by the strong presence of married women in war-time industrial work, Hervé Brunelle told the House of Commons that the "infiltration of women" into male preserves of the labour market would "create an overwhelming afterwar problem." For its part, the medical profession reinforced the "caring" role of women. "Maternity is the ultimate destiny of women," Dr. Ernest Couture wrote in *La mère canadienne et son enfant,* "and signifies the flowering of her existence" (Translated from citation in Lévesque, 1984a: 28).

The Second World War sharply transformed the labour market; in Montreal alone, there was a shortfall of 19 000 industrial workers in 1943 (Pierson, 1986: 31). With patriotic appeals, the federal government led in recruiting married women into war factories. A few mothers near the Cherrier munition factories were offered day-care services, and a 1943 amendment to the income tax act permitted husbands to claim a married-status exemption regardless of their wives' income (Figure 8.4). The number of married women in paid work doubled during the war; in 1945, 20 percent of women workers in Quebec were married (Education Committees of CSN and CEQ, 1987: 114). After the war, women were expected to cede their paid work to returning soldiers or male heads of families and only in the mid-1960s did women's participation in the paid work force return to war-time levels (Pierson, 1986: 215).

To gender must be added region, ethnicity, and social class as determinants in the education and work experience of Quebec women. Since there was no network of public secondary schools before 1954, Catholic girls attended private boarding institutions run by religious communities. During the nineteenth century, educational opportunities for boys expanded in classical colleges, commercial schools, and universities but it was only in 1908 that the first classical college for girls opened. Established by the cream of the female religious communities— the Ursulines in Trois-Rivières and Quebec City, the Congregation of Notre-Dame in Montreal, and the Grey Nuns in Hull—classical colleges for girls attracted 80 percent of their students from among the daughters of the elite (Dumont et Fahmy-Eid, 1986: 198–211). Female graduates of classical colleges had limited professional opportunities and most married into unpaid work in the family, the home, and in philanthropy. Some went to secretarial, nursing, or music schools. Others entered religious orders, where they exercised real power in education, social services, schools, and hospitals.

It took generations to regain the vote lost by women in the mid-nineteenth century. Through the 1920s and 1930s, leaders like Thérèse Casgrain and Idola Saint-Jean fought for the provincial vote in the press, in party conventions, before parliamentary committees, and in suffrage organizations like the Alliance canadienne pour le vote des femmes du Québec. Opposition to suffrage was

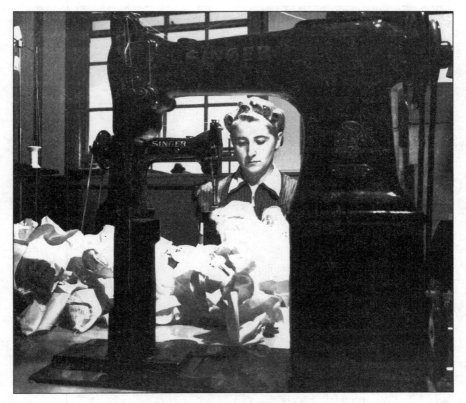

Figure 8.4 Woman working in the Cherrier war materials factory

anchored in the concept that the world of women was "private" and circumscribed by family and home; from this perspective, participation in juries or politics would subject women to passions antithetical to their nature. Not one of thirteen suffrage bills brought before the legislative assembly from 1919 to 1940 went beyond a second vote. Only in 1940 did the Godbout government grant women the right to vote and to hold public office (Table 8.5).

New Zealand	1883	**Quebec**	**1940**
U.S.S.R.	1917	France	1945
Canada (federal)	**1918**	Italy	1946
U.S.A.	1920	Belgium	1948
Great Britain	1928	Switzerland	1971
Spain	1931		

Table 8.5 Women's Franchise

Figure 8.5 A rural teacher. In 1936, Charlevoix native Laure Gaudreault founded the first rural women teachers' association and the following year the Fédération Catholique des institutrices rurales was created. Young girls from more prosperous rural families—those able to pay board for their daughters—attended normal schools. Huguette Tremblay, only daughter of a cheese maker, graduated in 1938 at age seventeen from the Baie St. Paul normal school. The school was run by the sisters (visible in the front row) of one of the oldest female teaching orders, the Congregation of Notre-Dame. Tremblay is in the second row behind the inspector and the chaplain.

Like most of her graduating class, Tremblay found work in a rural one-room schoolhouse, in her home parish of Saint-Philippe de Clermont near La Malbaie. In July 1941, she travelled across the St. Lawrence to attend the fifth annual convention of the female rural teachers' federation at Sainte-Anne-de-la-Pocatière. Travelling for the first time without parents or chaperone, Huguette, seen here (second from the left) on the ferry, made the most of it, writing home: "lots of participants and lots of fun. 2 a.m. and still not in bed." Marriage one month later signalled the end of her three-year career since married women were not allowed to continue teaching.

Figure 8.6 Madeleine Parent. The struggle for suffrage was only the most evident confrontation in women's efforts to gain access to the public arena. A student at McGill University in the 1930s, co-founder of a textile workers union in the 1950s, and a founding member of the National Action Committee on the Status of Women, feminist Madeleine Parent was in the union movement for over forty years.

> I first taught evening classes, with the Workers Educational Association, for trade unionists, women in the garment industry. We wanted one wage, one job and that issue was won in Quebec cotton mills, as a result of our 1946 strike. . . . Even though it was not written into the law or in the contract, we often won maternity leave in practice. Paid maternity leave is a different issue, but we won *de facto* maternity leave by united action on the shop floor (Parent, 1989: 13–36).

Suffrage did not bring political and legal equality (Figure 8.6). Two decades passed before a woman was elected to the Quebec legislative assembly; in 1961, Claire Kirkland (better known by her earlier married name as Kirkland-Casgrain), was elected. She became the first woman cabinet minister (1964), fought for women's rights, and was named the first female Provincial Court judge in Quebec (1973). Only in 1964 were women recognized as equals in Quebec civil law.

During the Depression and Second World War, the health and social service sector expanded rapidly and new female professional positions such as physiotherapist, nutritionist, and social worker appeared. The Université de Montréal established its public health program (Ecole d'hygiene social appliquée) in 1925 and its

School of Social Work in 1940. Between 1940 and 1960, the number of women enrolled in professional programs at the Université de Montréal increased from 90 to 2000. Here again in concert with the traditional institutional power of religious communities, the male medical profession assumed authority over emerging female professions (Cohen et Dagenais, 1987: 173).

Nor did unions and co-operative movements cede power to women easily. Unions often undercounted the number of their female members while echoing the dominant ideology that women's position in the paid workplace was secondary to their role in the home. As late as 1942 the CTCC congress (Confédération des travailleurs catholiques du Canada) called for the employment of men over women. Much of the discrimination was more subtle. In 1952, for example, the CTCC formed an all-female committee to examine the particular problems of working women but within the framework of their "condition particulière feminine" (Rouillard, 1981: 235).

LABOUR

Labour presents more evidence that Quebec society was less homogeneous and conservative than generally depicted. Labour institutions were marked by four phenomena. The first was steady growth in union membership. The number of unions tripled from 484 to 1435 between 1932 and 1957, while union membership multiplied sevenfold (Bernier et Boily, 1986: 302–3).

The second phenomenon was the challenge to craft unions—dominant in the Quebec labour movment with some two-thirds of unionized skilled workers—from industrial unions. Based on the principle of organizing all workers on a work site, both unskilled and artisans, these unions had great appeal in mass-production industries such as steel and mining. Most of them eventually became part of the Congress of Industrial Organization (CIO).

Third, Catholic unions (CTCC) continued to wield power with their blend of Catholic social principles, nationalism, and corporatism. These confessional unions expanded greatly across the period, showing flexibility in their methods of dealing with industrial unionism and their recruitment in expanding sectors such as the public service. The number of Catholic unions rose from 121 in 1931 to 338 in 1946 and 442 in 1960, and membership increased from 15 587 in 1931 to 62 960 in 1946 and 94 114 in 1960. From representing 21.6 percent of unionized workers in Quebec in 1931, Catholic unions rose to 33.1 percent in 1940 and remained around 30 percent of the unionized work force in the 1950s. (Rouillard, 1981: 113, 167, 218.) Particularly after 1943, Catholic unions were increasingly militant and prominent in strikes.

Figure 8.7   Montreal mounted police disperse strikers during the Radio-Canada strike of 1959.

Finally, Quebec labour became more socially conscious and more militant. The Fédération provinciale du travail, established in 1937, lobbied both the federal and provincial governments for social legislation and education programs. Strikes in Quebec declined during the Depression, rose in 1937, and peaked in 1942.

Labour was not docile in the Duplessis years, as the important strikes at Asbestos (1949), Louiseville (1952), and Murdochville (1957) testify. The state tried to suppress labour by appointing pro-employer mediators, by refusing accreditation to unions, by using the provincial police to escort scabs and intimidate strikers, and by using repressive legislation such as the Padlock Act to restrict free assembly.

Conflict between labour and authority meant that by the 1950s, strikes in Quebec were longer and more divisive than elsewhere in Canada. In 1957, for example, Quebec's forty strikes represented 16.1 percent of the strikes in Canada and 15.4 percent of striking workers; days lost, however, equalled 44.4 percent of the Canadian total (Table 8.6). The Radio-Canada producers' strike of 1959 was an important precursor of later labour action (Figure 8.7). It pitted a Québécois group against a federal crown corporation; it raised the spectre of white-collar labour relations; and it signalled the new profile and rising influence of intellectuals such as René Lévesque.

	Strikes and lockouts	Workers involved	Days lost
1937	46	24 419	359 024
1942	135	41 260	155 284
1947	51	20 070	236 733
1952	40	17 524	853 936
1957	40	14 047	725 401

Table 8.6   Strikes and Lockouts in Quebec, 1925–1958

(Statistical Year Book, Quebec, 1960, 567)

THE CHANGING ROLE OF THE STATE

Quebec in the period 1930–1960 is often characterized as rural and reactionary, with Duplessis in the saddle and authoritarian measures such as the Padlock Act as his whip (Figure 8.8). Examined closely, however, the period shows increasingly sharp social conflict and an emerging sense of democratic and universal rights among unions, women's groups, and farm organizations. Across the period can be detected clear signs of the weakening of conservatism and a decline of the church's real power. The church was challenged by youth, agricultural co-operatives, unions, and progressive clerics.

The period was marked by two distinct social policies from the two levels of government. Ottawa became increasingly interventionist as it established the pillars of the welfare state. For their part, the Duplessis governments remained sharply critical of government intervention in the social sector. In his 1959 budget speech, Minister of Finance J.S. Bourque described welfare state measures as "tending to replace savings by the popular classes [. . .] and to discourage private initiative, personal effort and the work ethic to the detriment of the nation's liberty and economic progress" (Translated from citation in Vaillancourt, 1988: 129]

In the 1930s the state—particularly the federal government and the municipalities—stepped in to provide social services for victims of the Depression. Rapid expansion of the technocratic and centralized state over the 1930–1960 period had many elements: the formation of federal corporations such as Central Mortgage and Housing (1946); war-time measures such as conscription and the recruitment of female labour; international agreements such as the GATT (1947), the Saint-Lawrence Seaway project, and defence agreements; and the institution of universal social security programs such as the family allowance and government pension plans.

Figure 8.8 Anti-Semitism in Quebec. In the Depression, Quebec nationalists moved away from a pan-Canadian perspective to focus on Quebec's specific problems. They waged campaigns to boycott anglophone (particularly Jewish) businesses. Although Jews in Lower Canada were granted full civil rights in 1832, anti-Semitism in Quebec can be dated from 1807–1809 with the attempt to stop Ezekiel Hart from taking his seat in the legislative assembly. In the 1920s and 1930s anti-Semitism in Quebec became virulent. The "achat chez nous" campaign illustrated in this cartoon is one example and Adrien Arcand's Nazi-type movement—attracting 700 members—is another. Despite the emphasis of writers such as Mordecai Richler on the intensity of francophone anti-Semitism, recurrent struggles between Jews and Montreal's Protestant school board, and the restrictive admissions policy at McGill University, are reminders that anti-Semitism was also rife amongst anglophones.

Much of this changing state power was federal; the number of federal civil servants increased from 45 581 in 1931 to 147 909 in 1959 (Urquhart and Buckley, 1965: 621). Using the Rowell-Sirois Royal Commission Report (1940) as an intellectual and economic rationale, the central government extended federal state power into family relations, work, family size, and education. Specifically, the Report called for a pan-Canadian unemployment insurance plan and assumption by the central government of all of the costs of old-age pensions. The advent of the welfare state was signalled in 1944 with Ottawa's introduction of the family allowance.

Throughout the postwar period, federal–provincial conflicts over jurisdiction were prominent political issues. Expansion of federal cost-sharing programs such as highway and university programs emphasized Ottawa's ambitions in social, regional, and educational sectors, prerogatives traditionally and constitutionally reserved for provincial authority. Federal power extended increasingly into culture. The 1929 federal Royal Commission on Radio Broadcasting proposed a national broadcasting service capable of "fostering a national spirit and interpreting national citizenship," and in 1936 a federal crown corporation, the Canadian Broadcasting Corporation/Société Radio-Canada was established. The creation of the National Film Board in 1939 reinforced the sense of federal expansionism. In 1951, the federal government further aroused Quebec nationalists' sensitivity to Ottawa's intrusion into culture and education by placing over $7 000 000 at the disposition of Quebec universities (Behiels, 1989: 335).

Federal intervention was difficult to resist because of the structure of government finances. In 1933, 47.7 percent of taxes in Quebec were collected by the federal government, 10 percent by the provincial government, and 42.3 percent by municipalities. By the end of the Second World War the federal government collected 82.8 percent of taxes in Quebec, the province received 7.3 percent, and the municipalities' share had plummeted to 9.9 percent (Linteau et al., 1986: 152).

Although the Duplessis government opposed social security, it was not hostile to the development of a public sector bureaucracy as a vehicle for patronage. To meet the increased demand for services, especially in health and education, Duplessis expanded the Quebec civil service: in 1933 there were 8072 civil servants (2.51 for every 1000 people in Quebec); by 1960 there was a total of 36 766 government employees (7.13 per 1000) (Bernier et Boily, 1986: 373).

THE DUPLESSIS PHENOMENON

In 1933, a coalition of social activists from the Ecole sociale populaire, the Catholic farmers union, and the Catholic labour unions published a reform program, "le programme de restauration sociale." Inspired by their experience in co-operatives, they agreed upon the need for increased state action: relief programs; break-up of the great electric trusts; and electoral, labour, and agricultural reforms. Progressive Liberals like Paul Gouin, son of the former premier, and nationalists such as Philippe Hamel and René Chalout were attracted to this program and in 1934 a new political group, the Action Libérale Nationale (ALN) was established.

In the same period the Conservative Party, out of power since 1897, was revitalized under Maurice Duplessis, who became its leader in 1933. Son of a Conservative politician, Duplessis was a Trois-Rivières lawyer whose forte was his understanding of rural and small-town Quebec. He was attentive to constituents' needs, familiar with local elites, and in harmony with a conservative ideology that emphasized agriculture, Catholicism, and traditional values. Although Gouin and the progressives were suspicious of Duplessis's reform credentials, the Action Libérale Nationale and the Conservative Party formed a common front, the Union Nationale.

The Taschereau government was weakened by charges of corruption, tired leadership, and complicity with monopolistic electrical trusts like Montreal Light, Heat and Power (Regehr, 1990). In the elections of November 1935, sixteen Conservative and twenty-six ALN members in the Union Nationale front were elected to face Taschereau's forty-eight Liberals. In the months that followed, Duplessis established his parliamentary dominance; in June 1936, he broke with Gouin and, as undisputed leader of the Union Nationale, forced an election in August. Duplessis understood the province's electoral map: some 63 percent of the members of the legislature were returned by rural areas although the rural population represented only 37 percent of the population (Quinn, 1963: 69). Campaigning for a break-up of the trusts and for rural electrification, Duplessis overwhelmed the Liberals and won a majority.

The Union Nationale quickly established its colours as a conservative party. Breaking with progressives who wanted to nationalize the electric trusts, Duplessis built up his political base in rural Quebec by extending agricultural credit, creating agricultural schools, bringing in rural electrification, and improving rural roads. Taking an anti-labour stance, he prohibited the closed shop, passed anti-labour bills, and sided with owners in the textile strike of 1937.

His sustained campaign against communism gained him conservative and clerical support. The Act Concerning Communist Propaganda (1937) was particularly repugnant to civil libertarians. Better known as the Padlock Act, this measure permitted the police to lock any building used for "Communism or Bolshevism." Taking advantage of this broad definition, political and police authorities used the act against unions, political groups, and religious minorities such as the Jehovah Witnesses. Despite decades of resistance by civil libertarians, the law was only declared unconstitutional by the Supreme Court of Canada in 1957 (Sarra-Bournet, 1986).

With the outbreak of war in 1939, Duplessis called an election on the issue of possible conscription. With support from Quebec ministers in Mackenzie King's Liberal government, who threatened to resign if Duplessis was re-elected, Adélard

Godbout and the Liberals were elected. Faced with the general crisis of war Godbout left centralized economic planning to the federal government. When Ottawa created the family allowance program in 1944, he did not fight vigorously to preserve exclusive provincial jurisdiction in social services.

On other fronts, however, Godbout did respond to demands for reform by intervening in social and economic matters. In 1940, Quebec women were finally granted the right to vote in provincial elections. Labour relations were regulated by a new law that recognized workers' right to join accredited unions and to nego-tiate collective agreements. Schooling was made mandatory in 1943 for children between the ages of six and fourteen. Finally, Hydro-Québec was established in 1944 by the nationalization of Montreal Light, Heat and Power.

Despite these measures, Godbout's Liberal government was defeated by Duplessis's effective use of nationalism and the conscription issue in the 1944 election. Godbout's association with federal Liberals played a significant part in his defeat. Since the conscription crisis of World War I, Quebec had consistently returned Liberal members to Ottawa and the province expected Prime Minister Mackenzie King to stand by his 1939 commitment against conscription for over-seas service. The prime minister, faced with war losses and pressure from other parts of Canada, announced a plebiscite, 27 April 1942, to release his govern-ment from its "no conscription" pledge. Canada divided sharply: Quebecers voted

Figure 8.9 A Union Nationale campaign placard. Duplessis's electoral strategy brandished the threat of assimilation and underscored his image as the staunch defender of provincial rights.

27 percent "no"; the other provinces voted 79 percent yes. Quebec reacted with anger and riots to Bill 80 which empowered the government to introduce con- scription (Quinn, 1963: 109). In the provincial election of 1944, Duplessis capi- talized on this resentment by portraying himself as a defender of provincial autonomy, language, and traditions (Figure 8.9).

THE ORIGINS OF THE QUIET REVOLUTION

The four-volume Tremblay Report (Quebec, 1956) gave ideological and statistical support to provincial autonomy and to the idea that the Quebec government was the primary defender of a threatened culture. The ideology of conservative nation- alists such as Esdras Minville and Jesuit Richard Arès dominated the Report, which interpreted Confederation in terms of provincial rights (the compact the- ory), arguing that it was the result of a pact between two founding peoples:

> The 1867 Constitution made the Province of Quebec, which was already his- torically its national focus, the French-Canadian centre *par excellence*, and the accredited guardian of French-Canadian civilization. It also applied indi- rectly, insofar as it constituted the cultural focus of the French minorities of the other provinces and to the extent that its influence was exerted on all- over Canadian policy. No other Canadian province is, as a political unit, charged with any such high and difficult mission (Quebec, 1956, 1: 66).

The commission maintained that provinces had the right to impose direct taxa- tion to finance programs within their exclusive jurisdiction. The Quebec govern- ment used the report's preliminary findings to justify the establishment of a provincial income tax in 1954.

By the 1930s, Quebec's intellectual and cultural life was increasingly rich and pluralistic. Older nationalists like Edouard Montpetit (1881–1954) continued to emphasize traditional values such as frugality, anti-consumerism, a rural way of life, and co-existence within Confederation (Faucher, 1970: 80–89). On the other hand, the Bloc Populaire (1942–1949)—an essentially urban movement that grew out of opposition to conscription and federal centralization—pressed for nationalization in areas tradionally dominated by the church, for an enlarged co- operative movement, and for long-term credit plans (Behiels, 1982; Comeau, 1982). Using radio, a weekly newspaper, and local meetings, the Bloc Populaire sought a middle road between socialism and capitalism, promoting the welfare state but attacking the monarchy, old-line parties, and Duplessisism. It elected four members in the provincial election of 1944 (15 percent of total vote) and two in the federal election of 1945 (12.8 percent of the Quebec vote) (Comeau, 1982: 335, 337).

By the end of the war, intellectuals were deeply divided between left and right, between liberal and conservative Catholicism, between Catholics and humanists, and between those who emphasized collective rights and those who insisted on the supremacy of individual rights. Working within a framework of social Catholicism and liberalism at the Laval University faculty of social sciences, intellectuals such as Jean-Charles Falardeau, Léon Dion, Fernand Dumont, and Georges-Henri Lévesque insisted that the work of social scientists be put, as Father Lévesque stated in 1951, "at the disposal of the people and that, whenever possible, they carry their scientific knowledge forward into social action, by entering into conflicts over questions of truth and justice" (Behiels, 1989: 333). In Montreal, Gérard Pelletier and Pierre Elliott Trudeau and the *Cité Libristes* attacked the clericalism, conservatism, and insularism of Quebec society (Behiels, 1985: 92). For Pelletier, the struggle against Duplessis lasted a generation:

> Maurice Duplessis's reign had coincided with our youth. We were emerging from adolescence when he came to power, and we were getting on for forty when he lost it. And during those twenty years it was not only occasional disagreements that found us in opposition to him, but an inevitable, deep and unrelenting rejection of his most cherished assumptions. [. . .] Our generation had realized that the collectivity of Quebec was behind the times, and that it must at all costs be brought up to date without delay, accelerating the process the war-time period had begun. But Duplessis and his cronies leaned hard with all their considerable weight on every available brake (Pelletier, 1984: 35).

Social struggle was not simply a battle of intellectuals. William D. Coleman has demonstrated how the urban working classes increasingly ignored traditional culture and institutions, particularly the church (Coleman, 1984: 26). In recounting his youth, Fernand Dumont has shown how the spirit of resistance was transmitted across the generations:

> when I recall my childhood lived far removed from books and the city, I seem to remember a drama. . . . I heard similar challenges to the old customs, to the old priests and politicians, but in a language different from that of the writers. Our fathers kicked and complained for centuries; they were not the docile sheep that have so often been described to us. . . . They bequeathed to their children a new scepticism, a radically critical attitude, and a passionate anger that had something in common with writers of the time. The centuries-old accumulation of bitterness among the working class burst like a ripe abcess. The words of an illiterate people began to penetrate the silence of generations (Dumont, 1971: 13).

This ferment emphasizes that the roots of the dramatic changes of the 1960s must be sought, as Guy Rocher has noted, in the preceding decades:

It is precisely because the stage for the Quiet Revolution was prepared for with a slow and laborious putting into question of ideas, ideologies, attitudes, and mentalities that it was first and foremost a cultural mutation. The Quiet Revolution did not engender important changes in the economic structure of Quebec, nor in its principal institutions; rather than a social revolution it was a cultural revolution. It provoked changes in mentality but few structural transformations (Translated from Coleman, 1984: 85).

RELIGION AND CULTURE

Conflict between conservatism and modernism is perhaps most evident in the fields of religion and culture. The power, influence, and numerical strength of the Roman Catholic church peaked in the 1950s. With over 8000 priests and some 50 000 members of religious communities, the church was a daily presence in the lives of Quebecers through its control over Catholic education and health care as well as parish life. Militant clerics such as abbé Groulx (Figure 8.10) and members of the Ecole sociale populaire ensured that Catholic ideology continued as a strong influence on nationalism and social mores. But despite this apparently secure position the church was vulnerable.

It was never monolithic and in the 1930s a significant number of clerics like frère Marie-Victorin (Figure 8.11) questioned church social policy and traditional values. The Dominicans, always a liberal community, founded two institutions that emphasized a scientific as opposed to a religious approach to knowledge: the Institut d'études mediévales at the Université de Montréal (1942), and the Ecole des sciences sociales at the Université Laval (1938) under Georges-Henri Lévesque. After the Second World War, new university departments were established that eluded control by theology faculties. The church hierarchy also felt the influence of new social forces. In Montreal in the early 1940s, Mgr Joseph Charbonneau pushed the church to respond to the needs of urban Catholics. In Sherbrooke, Bishop Phillipe-Servule Danserleau was another who reflected the deepening division over social principles among the Quebec episcopacy. "Capitalism," he declared in 1949, "is the cause of all our hurt. We have to work against it, not to transform it—since it is incorrigible—but to replace it" (Translated from Hamelin, 1984: 22–23).

The traditional dependence of Quebec publishers and booksellers such as Beauchemin, Granger, and Garneau on clerical patronage for textbook purchases and large volume sales added to the church's censorship clout. In 1933, Albert Pelletier's publication of *Un homme et son péché*, by Claude-Henri Grignon, marked the beginning of independent publishing in Quebec (Lemire, 1978–   ),

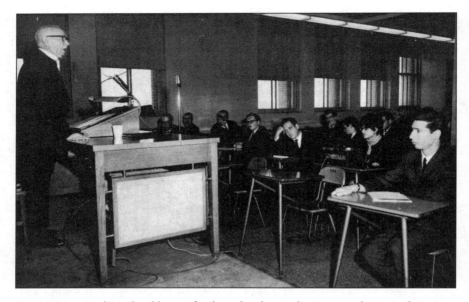

Figure 8.10 Lionel Groulx addressing faculty and students at the Université de Montréal. As a cleric, historian, and political and social activist, abbé Groulx (1878–1967) had a profound influence on Quebec intellectual life during the first half of the twentieth century. His passion for history developed as a teacher at the Valleyfield Classical College, where he discovered that students knew little of their heritage. Named to the Université de Montréal's newly created chair of Canadian history in 1915, he became French Canada's "national historian" encouraging a conservative nationalism based on French and Catholic roots. He founded a nationalist organization for youth called the Association catholique de la jeunesse canadienne-française (1903–1904), the *Action française* (1920), and the *Action nationale* (1929). The latter was xenophobic and blamed the Depression on industrialization and American capitalism. Initially, Groulx's nationalism followed that of Henri Bourassa; he wished to integrate French Canada into a larger Canadian federation stripped of imperial trappings. The influence of the French right and his own sense of religion and ethnicity, however, led him to focus increasingly on Quebec. Considered by many to be the spiritual father of modern Quebec nationalism, he traced the roots of French Canada's oppression to the British Conquest. Groulx is often considered the spiritual mentor of modern Quebec nationalism: "Our French state, we will have it; it will be young, radiant, and beautiful—a spiritual hearth and a dynamic pole for all of French America."

while the establishment of the Société des écrivains canadiens-français in 1935 symbolized a growing literary freedom and autonomy.

Until the Second World War, clerical censorship meant that Quebec publishers could not print books listed on the index, the list first issued by authorities in Rome in 1613 which itemized works that Roman Catholics were forbidden to read. With the fall of France in 1940, they started publishing French works and

Figure 8.11 Brother Marie-Victorin. As well as being one of Quebec's most important scientists in the interwar period, founder of the Montreal Botanical Gardens, and author of *La flore laurentienne*, Marie-Victorin was a freethinker troubled by the contradiction between his vows, his sexuality, important social issues such as birth control, and the church's official position. Writing to a younger female co-worker, he expressed his anxiety: "In the midst of social conventions and hypocrisy, in the midst of theological uncertainties and contradictions (over birth control etc.), I have tried—taking into account what biology has taught us—to construct for myself a moral system. . . . God in heaven judges souls by their intentions [. . .] rather than by their external conformism." (Translated from *L'Actualité*, 1 March 1990).

clerical control slipped (Lemire, 1978–   ). But already, Quebec literature no longer parroted the dominant conservative ideology. Between 1933 and 1945, the Quebec rural novel reached its apogée with the publication of Claude-Henri Grignon's *Un homme et son péché* (1933), Félix-Antoine Savard's *Menaud maître-draveur* (1938), *Trente arpents* (1938) by Ringuet (Philippe Panneton's pseudonym), and Germaine Guèvremont's *Le survenant* (1945). These novels moved away from the traditional idealization of rural life. Ringuet effectively illustrated the tensions between rural and urban values as well as the conflict between generations. Savard, the most conservative, used a rural setting to evoke strong nationalism:

> Menaud shook his fist. From his hoard of rebellion came bitterness against the weakness of his own kind. They had reached the point of no longer understanding what the voice of the dead was telling them. They were

betraying the sacred alliance with the land, letting themselves be plucked like a conquered people; consenting, in their own country, to the drudgery of servitude, even to selling their inheritance against the rights of their children and the duties of the past (Savard, 1976: 59).

Modernity in Quebec literature also had female voices. Jovette Bernier's *La chair décevante* (1931) and Medjé Vézina's *Chaque heure a son visage* (1934) illustrate challenges to traditional nationalism, duty, and patriarchy. Women writers of the 1930s introduced urban, bourgeois, and lay themes that were taken up by the postwar generation of writers such as Gabrielle Roy, André Langevin, Roger Lemelin, Gérard Bessette, and Anne Hébert (Robert, 1989: 198).

Opposition to intellectual repression climaxed in 1948 with Paul-Emile Borduas's manifesto, *Refus global*, which denounced the successive colonial regimes—those of Paris, London, and Rome—for having alienated Quebecers. Gérard Bessette's satirical novel *Le libraire* (1960) also showed hostility to church censorship. Resentment of patriarchy, authoritarianism, and the religious climate that prevailed in Quebec society burn in Claire Martin's autobiographical novels on her childhood. Her bitter portrayal of her father and mother say volumes about the idealization of traditional Quebec family life: "In July, Mother became pregnant with her fifth child. What can have been the state of mind of that poor woman, so gentle and frail, when she found herself on her way to producing yet another little misery, a part of whose life, as she well knew, would be abominable."

The most influential attack on traditional order came from Jean-Marie Desbiens who, under the pseudonym Frère Untel, published his famous *Insolences du frère Untel* in 1960. He attacked clerical control of education, particularly the anachronistic curriculum and the alienation of young people by the use of ultra-conservative Catholic authors in the teaching of French. With sales of over 100 000 copies in four months, *Les insolences du frère Untel* was an important factor in the intellectual turmoil of the 1960s.

Publishing in Quebec changed dramatically across the period. During the war, publishers flourished with new markets in railway stations, drugstores, and newsstands and with no competition from France. The postwar years brought a new period of crisis; competition from French magazines and American comic books and pocket books reduced the number of Quebec publishers from twenty-seven to four in the decade after the war (Robert, 1989: 136).

A rising standard of living, advertising and the media, and the advent of the automobile homogenized Quebec culture and weakened regional variations. Radio and television, for example, played an important role in the permeation of urban values into every corner of the province. Of particular importance was the establishment of the state-owned Canadian Broadcasting Corporation/Société Radio-Canada in 1936, which produced much of the popular entertainment first in radio and, after 1952, in television, and had a distinctively Montreal accent and flavour. The electronic media also widened Quebecers' horizons with programs such as René Lévesque's "Point de Mire," which analysed international events such as Algeria's war for independence from a Quebec perspective. For their part, anglophones lived in the same cultural universe as their American and Ontario neighbours and shared tastes for fast foods, for rock and roll, for American network television programs, and for Hollywood movies.

CONCLUSION

The decades before 1960 were characterized in Quebec by important changes. The growing significance of American capital and the expansion of war-time industries in Montreal and of resource industries in other regions were accompanied by new militancy in labour, a growing presence of women in activities outside the home, and a questioning of traditional structures by intellectuals. The conscription crisis, postwar immigration, linguistic tensions, important strikes at Asbestos in 1949 and at the Gaspé Copper Mines in Murdochville in 1957, and activist reform movement within the church were clear signs that, behind Duplessis conservatism, class and ethnic relations were simmering well before the Quiet Revolution of the 1960s.

FURTHER READING

For ideology across the period see Fernand Dumont and Jean Hamelin, *Les idéologies au Canada français, 1939–1974*. The Taschereau regime has been treated by Bernard Vigod, *Quebec before Duplessis. The Political Career of Louis-Alexandre Taschereau*, and a case study of his involvement with the trusts can be seen in T.D. Regehr, *The Beauharnois Scandal*. For unionism see Jacques Rouillard, *Histoire du syndicalisme québécois*. The Duplessis era has been treated by Herbert F. Quinn in *The Union Nationale. A Study in Quebec Nationalism*, and by Gérard Boismenu in *Le Duplessisme: politique economique et rapports de force, 1944–60*. An excellent analysis of the period is contained in Michael Behiels' *Prelude to Quebec's Quiet Revolution: Liberalism versus Neo-Nationalism, 1945–1960*, while his useful reader, *Quebec since 1945: Selected Readings* presents a variety of views. The *Tremblay Report* (Quebec, 1956) and the *Rowell-Sirois Report* (Canada, 1940) provide excellent documentation of the federal–provincial debate. Also of interest because of its emphasis on dependency theory is William D. Coleman's *The Independence Movement in Quebec, 1945–1980*. Like Coleman and Behiels, Jean-Louis Roy's *La marche des Québécois: le temps de ruptures (1945–60)* focuses on progressive elements present in the Duplessis era. For the impressions of a participant in the last Duplessis years, see Gérard Pelletier, *Years of Impatience 1950–60*. Relations between the family and the state are described in Dominique Jean, *Familles québécoises et politiques sociales touchant les enfants de 1940 à 1960*. The development of social programs and federal–provincial relations is examined in Yves Vaillancourt's *L'évolution des politiques sociales au Québec 1940–1960*. For women's political rights see Chantal Maillé, *Les Québécoises et la conquête du pouvoir politique*. An example of the rural cooperative movement is in Claude Beauchamp, *Agropur*. An interesting analysis of culture that emphasizes the importance of the period from 1920 to 1960 is Lucie Robert's *L'institution du littéraire au Québec*. For the electronic media see Gérard Laurence, "Le début des affaires publiques à la télévision québécoise" and André Couture's *Elements for a Social History of Television: Radio-Canada and Quebec Society, 1952–1960*.

Contemporary Quebec

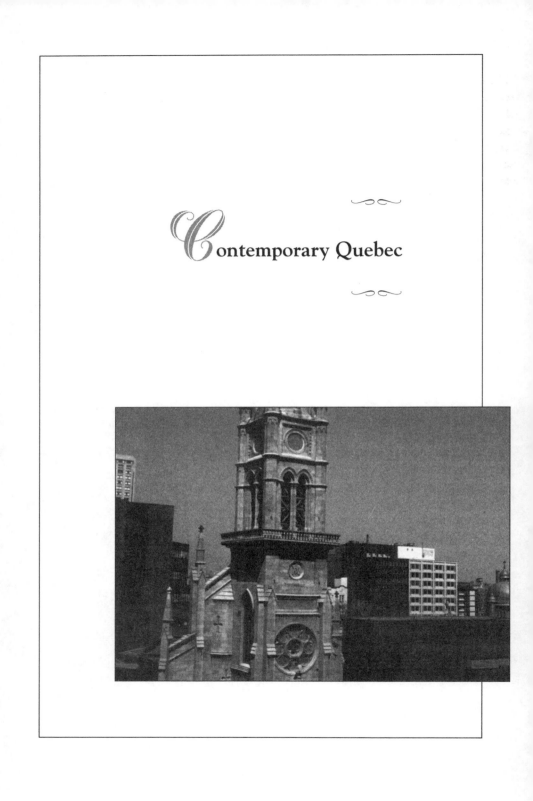

*𝒥*n the 1960s and 1970s intellectuals—or "the new bureaucratic middle class," as Posgate and McRoberts (1980: 99) describe them—succeeded to political power in both Ottawa and Quebec City. The product of classical college educations, these doctors, teachers, journalists, engineers, and public administrators rejected traditional Catholic values in favour of secularism and statism. They modernized, bureaucratized, and greatly increased the influence of the state, and built structures to cope with the demands of mass education and the welfare state. Language and nationalism became more important in the defence of Quebec society than the church and legal institutions.

A fundamental debate took place in both Pierre Elliott Trudeau's Ottawa and René Lévesque's Quebec City about nationalism, the role of the state, and the political future of Canada. From the federal Royal Commission on Bilingualism and Biculturalism in the late 1960s to the provincial Bélanger–Campeau Commission and the Liberal party's *Allaire Report* in 1991, Quebec's options have been examined from every perspective: the status quo in an ongoing federal structure, special status, sovereignty-association, and outright independence.

The national question has never been a simple issue of francophone versus anglophone; within Quebec, it has always had class implications. In the 1970s, radicals on the left attacked the co-opting of language and nationalism by the Parti Québécois:

> If the new PQ elite arrives in power, the Québécois language will find itself violently attacked by a [new middle-class] elite, which will cry out that we should speak French, that Quebec must be French, that the Québécois language is the oral excrement of ignorance and that we must speak the "French" of Jacques-Yvan Morin, just as this old-fashioned elite will tell us that we must develop a Québécois capitalism in order for our people to enter the world" (Léandre Bergeron, 1975, Cited in Posgate and McRoberts, 1980: 147; original French in *Chroniques* 3 (mars, 1975)).

In the 1960s and 70s, trade and farmers' unions, municipal reformers, and women and social-action groups pushed beyond the national question for political action on social issues ranging from housing, violence, education, and abortion. In its 1972 manifesto, for example, the teachers' union (the CEQ) described the school system as "a mirror image of a capitalist society which could not be maintained without the exploitation of the work of the majority by a minority which had expropriated the means of production and political power." Reform groups more and more frequently saw independence as essential to meeting their social goals.

The failure of the referendum in 1980, the shutting out of Quebec from the Constitution a year later, the resignation of Trudeau in 1984, and the defeat of the Parti Québécois in 1985 signalled an important shift in political direction. Since the mid-1980s, Quebec society has been characterized by greater conservatism, by a transfer of power from intellectuals to business, and by a decline in the importance of federal and provincial investment for francophone advancement.

As Montreal continued to cede pan-Canadian power to Toronto over the 1960–1990 period, Quebec's regional economy assumed greater importance for francophone entrepreneurship. Quebec focused increasingly on control of its own economy; francophone control of manufacturing in Quebec increased from 47 percent in 1961 to 60 percent in 1987 (Langlois et al., 1990: 411). While companies such as Bombardier heightened the perception that Quebec was moving steadily into international rather than Canadian markets, the international market was in fact more and more American. The percentage of Quebec exports—largely in semi-refined products—to the United States rose from 66 percent in 1968 to 77 percent in 1987. This helps to explain why Quebec was the most enthusiastic region in Canada over the 1988 Free Trade Agreement with the United States.

DEMOGRAPHY

Since 1960, Quebec's demographic evolution has been marked by four factors: a sharp decline in the birth rate; the aging of the population; the decline of the traditional family; and ethnic diversification. While these phenomena are common in the western world, the shifts in Quebec have been more dramatic.

Quebec's birth rate, once the highest in the western world, had dropped to one of the lowest by the 1980s. The effects of secularization and the birth-control pill were felt in Quebec in the second half of the 1960s as fecundity fell from 3.4 children per woman to 2.0 in 1970. In the following decades this trend continued, albeit at a slower rate, reaching an all-time low of 1.35 in 1987 (Perron, Lapierre-Adamcyk, et Morissette, 1987b). Although birth rates across Canada declined in the same period, the drop in Quebec has been more severe, resulting in a decline in Quebec's share of the Canadian population from 29 percent in the 1940s and 1950s to just over 25 percent in 1990.

The decline of the birth rate to below the natural replacement rate of 2.1 children per woman gave credence to fears that the francophone Quebec population would eventually disappear, and fostered both linguistic tension and pressure to force the integration of immigrants into the francophone majority. Since 1988 the Quebec government, strongly influenced by demographers like Jacques Henripin, has had an active pronatalist policy offering special bonuses beyond the family allowance program. By 1991, these bonuses had risen to $500 for the first child, $1000 for the second, and $7000 for the third child (Maroney, 1992: 26). While the effect of this policy is perhaps not clear, the birth rate rose in the early 1990s: the 95 423 babies born in 1990 represent a birth rate of 1.6, a significant increase.

Access to therapeutic abortions, a key demand of the feminist movement, has also affected the birth rate. During the 1970s an increasing number of abortions were performed in certain hospitals and government health clinics (Centres locaux de services communautaires). In 1971, there were only 1.4 therapeutic abortions for every 100 live births; by 1987 there were 18.5 and by 1990, 22.3. Of the 21 843 abortions performed in 1990 the largest number (6 449) occurred among those aged twenty to twenty-four. The use of other methods of birth control—vasectomies and ligatures—increased as well but mainly among men and women who remarried (Langlois, et al., 1990).

Despite a sharp decline in infant mortality from 31.5 per 1000 to around 7 per 1000 since 1960, the declining birth and stable adult mortality rates have contributed to an aging population (Figure 9.1). The median age of Quebecers has risen from twenty-four in 1961 to over thirty-two in 1990. The 1991 census revealed that the number of people aged fifteen to twenty-four had declined in Montreal by almost 11 percent since 1986 and was lower than the number aged forty to forty-nine. Male life expectancy increased from about sixty at the beginning of the Second World War to 73.2 in the 1990s; in the same period the rate for women increased from sixty-three to 80.5. There is an important ongoing class component to these mortality rates. In 1987, the life expectancy of Montrealers from well-off neighbourhoods exceeded by ten years the life expectancy of those from poor neighbourhoods.

This age profile has important implications. While the school-age population has decreased steadily since the 1960s and the number of young people entering

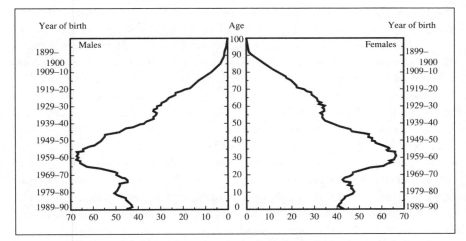

Figure 9.1   Age pyramids for Quebec, 1990. Note the decline in births during the Depression (50- to 59-year age groups) contrasted with the baby boom after the war. By the 1990s, the baby boomers were in their thirties and forties and were followed by a much smaller generation.

Figure 9.2 At the bowling alley. Better health care has enabled senior citizens to remain active. Although aging has had an important impact on the demand for manufactured goods, the service sector—and notably leisure activities—have benefited from the change.

the work force has slowed since the late 1970s, demand for health care and pensions has risen. Quebecers under fourteen years of age represented over a third of the population in 1961 but only one-fifth in 1987. During the same period, the number of citizens over sixty-five increased from 5.8 to 10 percent of the Quebec population (Figure 9.2). Although a higher standard of living has offset some of the negative effects of this evolution on demands for housing and consumer goods, Quebec's domestic market is shrinking, with deleterious effects on employment.

Changes in family structure are a striking feature of contemporary Quebec demographics. With the sharp decline in religious practice since 1960 and changes in moral attitudes, marriage is no longer the norm for many Quebecers. In 1986, 487 000 couples declared themselves to be living in common-law relationships in Quebec. The increase has been particularly important since 1980; in 1984, 27 percent of females aged twenty to twenty-four and 42 percent of those aged twenty-five to twenty-nine were living in common-law relationships. The phenomenon is particularly marked among educated francophones. A majority of women in common-law relationships express a wish to marry eventually.

Another demographic feature has been the tendency for people to live outside the traditional nuclear family structure—often alone or in single-parent families. In 1961, 4.9 percent of the population lived alone; by 1989 this had

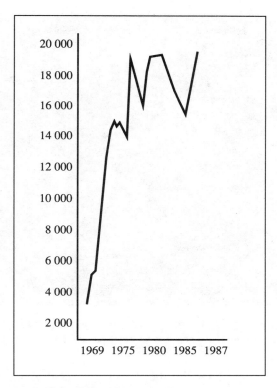

Figure 9.3 Divorces in Quebec, 1969–1987

risen to 24.5 percent. In 1961, only 8 percent of households with children were headed by single people—mostly widows—whereas by 1986 the percentage had jumped to almost 26 percent—usually single or divorced women. This is double the Canadian average. Divorce has been an important demographic fact since legislation in 1969 made it easier to obtain (Figure 9.3). In 1982, the number of marriages ended by death and divorce surpassed the number of new marriages (Langlois et al., 1990). The structure of the family changed for married couples as well. In 1961 the average size of a Quebec household was 4.53 people; by 1989 this had declined to 2.59 people. Of homebuyers in 1986, 42 percent did not have children in the home.

Family work strategies have also changed. With married women remaining in the labour force, day care has become a priority of the women's movement. Greater female participation in the paid labour force has also reduced their traditional function of caring for the aged. The Quebec government has created a network of residences for the elderly, who have the highest rate of institutionalization in North America.

Figure 9.4 A delicatessen along Montreal's "Main." Small ethnic shops along the Main, selling such traditional foods as smoked meat and bagels, are meeting places for the city's cultural communities.

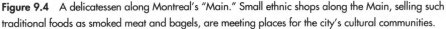

Immigration has contributed to the changing population profile (Figure 9.4). Heavy immigration into Quebec in the postwar years has given way since the mid-1960s to net emigration out of the province. Emigration climaxed following the election of the Parti Québécois government and emigrants outnumbered immigrants by more than 80 000 in the years 1977 through 1979. Between 1971 and 1986 a net of 198 274 anglophones left Quebec. The anglophone population stabilized between 1986 and 1991; in 1991, 759 000 people in Quebec declared English to be their first language.

The vast majority of immigrants settle in the Montreal region; in 1981, 87.3 percent of Quebecers with a mother language other than French or English lived on the Ile de Montréal. More than 90 percent of immigrants in 1987 opted for the Montreal area. At the same time the concentration of anglophones in the Montreal region has continued. The proportion of Quebec anglophones living on the Ile de Montréal rose from 70 to over 75 percent between 1961 and 1986. At the same time, the percentage of anglophones of British origin has dropped from 95 percent in 1931 to 60 percent in 1981 and barely 50 percent in 1991. It is also important to note that not all anglophones are part of the elite. Across Quebec in 1988, 17 percent of anglophones were living below the poverty line (Legault, 1992: 212, 214).

	1961	1986
French	4 241 354	5 240 250
English, Scottish, Welsh, Irish	567 057	465 750
German	39 457	28 425
Greek	19 390	47 450
Italian	108 552	163 880
Jewish	74 677	81 190
Polish	30 790	18 835
Asian	14 801	72 435
Carribean	—	12 980
Indian and Inuit	21 343	49 710

Table 9.1   The Ethnic Origin of the Population of Quebec, 1961–1986

Immigration to Canada has been declining since 1974 and Quebec's share of this immigration has been decreasing as well. The ethnic origin of immigrants to Quebec has changed dramatically: in the postwar years most immigrants were Europeans, but since 1975 most have come from the Caribbean, particularly Haiti, and from Southeast Asia (Table 9.1). In recent years many immigrants have come as refugees and, despite Quebec's policy of favouring francophones, many of these arrive speaking neither French nor English. The concentration of immigrants in Montreal neighbourhoods such as Côte des Neiges has resulted in racial tension, violence with the police, and difficulties in the schools.

Quebec's native populations have increased at a much faster pace than the general population. As well, census figures probably underestimate their total numbers since women who married whites were barred from tribal membership by the Indian Act (1876) and Métis descendants of these marriages had no Indian status. With the Canadian Charter of Rights and Freedoms (1982) and amendments to the Indian Act that prohibit such discrimination, many native women have returned to live on reserves. Since native territories in southern Quebec are limited and expansion is impossible, the inhabitants are overcrowded and lack economic opportunities.

⌒⌒

THE QUEBEC ECONOMY

As in other western countries, recent years have seen important shifts in the structure of the Quebec economy, with greater emphasis on the tertiary sector at the expense of resource extraction and industry (Table 9.2). This has strongly influenced regional development and the nature of employment. Behind

	Primary (agriculture, forestry, fishing, mining, etc.)	Secondary (manufacturing, construction)	Tertiary (transportation, communication, commerce, finance, public administration, service)
1961	12.4	35.9	51.7
1966	8.3	34.9	56.8
1971	6.4	31.7	61.9
1976	5.0	29.9	65.1
1981	4.6	26.3	69.1
1986	4.4	24.6	71.0

Table 9.2 Importance of Different Sectors in the Quebec economy, 1961–1986 (as percentages of the gross provincial product)

Quebec's conspicuous consumerism lie increasing disparities between rich and poor. While Montreal's relative importance in the Canadian economy has continued to decline, a new francophone business bourgeoisie has emerged to concentrate on local and international markets.

Quebec's industry has declined but its profile remains the same. Food, clothing, textile, leather, wood, and tobacco continue to be important and, as in the past, rely heavily on immigrant and female labour (Figure 9.5). This sector accounted for 43.1 percent of industrial labour and 35.7 percent of industrial output in 1983 (Bernier et Boily, 1986).

Quebec's privately owned electricity companies were nationalized in the 1960s. Huge power developments along the North Shore in the 1960s and in the James Bay drainage basin in the 1970s created thousands of jobs and a generating capacity that enabled Quebec to export electricity to New England. In the initial phases of this development public opinion supported Hydro's expansion. More recently, Quebec's honeymoon with the corporation has ended. The huge capital costs of new generating projects in the James and Hudson bays, environmental concerns, protests from native people, and aging and breakdowns in the delivery system have lead to increased public scrutiny.

Since Montreal area refineries used imported rather than Canadian crude, they were severely affected by the energy crises of the 1970s and 1980s. In contrast, the oil crisis benefited the aluminium industry as automobile manufacturers turned to lighter metals to improve fuel efficiency. Quebec's hydro-electric resources have helped the province to lead the world in aluminium production. It has also been a leader in rail and mass transit technology, where the Bombardier company has played an important part in international markets.

Figure 9.5 A downtown Montreal textile factory, 1987. Despite improvements to many work sites, conditions in the textile industry have hardly changed since the beginning of the century. Because of fierce competition from off-shore producers, wages remain low and most workers are female immigrants.

Although there are important General Motors and Hyundai plants in the Montreal region, automobile production remains centred in Ontario, as does the auto-parts industry. Despite the success of some projects—such as the Canadair water bomber and the Challenger executive jet—Montreal's aeronautics industry has not regained its war-time prominence. And despite the initial success of such companies as Ogivar, Quebec has not made its mark in the fields of high technology and computers.

The construction industry is the usual barometer of Quebec's economic health. After fifteen years of steady growth in the housing, retail, and office sectors before 1966, the industry slowed down. Large government-sponsored projects such as Expo '67 (1965–1967), hydro-electric developments on the North Shore (1962–1978) and in the James Bay drainage basin (1971–1980), the Olympic site (1974–1976), and Mirabel airport (1974–1977), and government-sponsored housing programs such as Quebec's "corvée habitation" or Montreal's "Opération 100 000 logements," have been largely responsible for maintaining the industry since the mid-1960s.

The growing dominance of the tertiary sector (from 51.7 percent of Quebec's gross provincial product in 1961 to over 70 percent since 1982) continued to be central to Quebec's postwar economic development. New state and bureaucratic services in health and education after 1960 enlarged the public service sector. In 1960, there were 7.13 provincial civil servants for every 100 people in Quebec; in 1985 the rate stood at 22.8 with a total of 150 333 civil servants (Bernier et Boily, 1986: 373). Expansion of the civil service helped to make metropolitan Quebec City the fastest growing urban centre in the province in the 1980s.

Most new jobs have been created in retailing and services. In the grocery sector there has been increasing concentration. Situated within shopping plazas, with their numerous services and large parking lots, supermarkets have come to dominate the sector. Supermarket chains—led by Provigo and Metro with their own canning, baking, and transportation networks—have used price wars to eliminate most of the small independent grocers. Government monopoly on the sale of beer and the right to sell certain Quebec bottled wines and lottery tickets kept small outlets in business as convenience stores. During the 1980s, however, the large chains were allowed to sell beer and wine, and set up affiliated chains of convenience stores. In other retail activities concentration is less clear. Although Eaton's and The Bay have consolidated their hold over large department store outlets, competition from small boutiques and catalogue counters has cut their share of the market.

Quebec's postwar growth was in good measure due to expansion of the natural-resource extraction industries. Since the 1970s, this sector has suffered. Recurrent recessions in the all-important American market, relocation of international corporations to the cheaper labour markets of Third World countries, and health hazards associated with asbestos fibres have led to the closure of iron, copper, and asbestos mines. During the 1950s and 1960s, the North Shore region's growth was fuelled by hydro-electric projects and iron mining. The boom was slowed with the completion in 1978 of several massive hydro-electric power plants (the Manic–Outardes complex) along the Manicouagan and Outardes rivers. The collapse of the iron-ore market after 1985 condemned the mining towns of Schefferville and Gagnon and severely curtailed Sept-Iles's shipping activity. The latter's population dropped from over 30 000 to 25 000 between 1976 and 1986.

Despite important regional differences—urban areas have usually fared better than peripheral areas such as the North Shore, Abitibi, and Asbestos regions— unemployment is a province-wide phenomenon. Although unemployment decreased to a low of 4.1 percent in 1966, it rose as the baby boomers entered the job market. Those born since 1955 faced unemployment rates of over 10 percent by 1977. Quebec's economy suffered severely in the recession of 1982, with unemployment reaching a peak of 13.9 percent in 1983. Despite economic growth during the period 1983–1990, unemployment remained high, decreasing only slowly to 9.3 percent in 1989. With the recession of 1990–1992, unemployment had risen to 12.1 percent by February 1991. The Montreal region was particularly hard hit; its rate topped 13 percent.

These economic cycles have particularly affected women, the most vulnerable sector of the labour market. Although women under twenty-five have been more likely than their male peers to find jobs, often in the low-paid and part-time tertiary sector, female unemployment has consistently surpassed that of males.

Part-time employment, an increasingly important feature of the Quebec labour market, has both a gender and an age dimension. Women represent 70 percent of workers in this category. Part-time employment affects both ends of the age scale but in different ways. More widespread company pension plans and government incentives to invest in retirement savings plans have allowed many men over 55 to leave the labour market progressively by working part-time (Langlois et al., 1990: 173). One-third of people under twenty-five, faced with the absence of full-time opportunities, are forced into part-time work in the tertiary sector. The flexibility offered by part-time work is welcomed by some young people, but it rarely compensates for the loss of security and career advancement. Contractual labour enables some small and medium-sized companies to survive, and also helps large corporations to restructure. More often than not, part-time work has benefited employers by giving them flexibility, reducing costs, and minimizing union strength in rapidly changing economic conditions.

Unemployment and part-time labour and the conservative fiscal policies of the Mulroney era have widened of the gap between rich and poor. Overall, Quebecers have become better off. The average family income has risen from $22 120 (in 1986 dollars) in 1961 to $37 282 in 1986. Much of the rise, however, has occurred because both partners now work in the paid labour force. Quebec has more low-income households than the national average and single people are three times more likely to meet the definition of low income. The economic position of single women and single-parent families headed by women has deteriorated more than any other group (Canada Year Book, 1990; Langlois et al., 1990).

As we saw in chapter 8, Montreal, until the Great Depression, was the metropolis of Canada, but its position has declined steadily since then. By the 1960s it was a regional metropolis as much as a pan-Canadian one (Kerr and Holdsworth, 1990: plate 55). The construction of the Saint-Lawrence Seaway hurt its port and rail traffic. The exodus of corporate head offices accelerated in the 1970s, undermining the city's financial position. It also lost air traffic to Toronto.

Montreal's changed status and government promotion of French in the workplace have nurtured a strong francophone business bourgeoisie. Paul Desmarais of Power Corporation and Pierre Péladeau of Quebecor exemplify the members of this new group. Francophone companies have risen to prominence in, for example, banking (National Bank), engineering (SNC), transportation (Bombardier), and food processing and distribution (Culinar), both in Canada and in international markets. Some important Quebec business enterprises, however—such as Lavelin (engineering) and Steinberg (food distribution)—were bankrupted by the recession of the late 1980s.

Although foreign capital remained important in the Canadian and Quebec economies throughout the postwar period, government policies and local capital have reduced the proportion of foreign capital in the economy from a high of 38 percent in 1968 to 26 percent in 1982. The influence of the Caisse de dépôt et de placement, which manages Quebec Pension Plan contributions, must not be underestimated, but credit for the trend away from foreign financing is also due to the expansion of the Mouvement Desjardins. By 1986, the Mouvement, a banking co-operative consisting of 1500 Caisses Populaires in Quebec, had assets of over $30 billion. This capital was of increasing importance in corporate financing in Quebec. The Quebec Stock Savings Plan was also an important vehicle to inject new capital into Quebec enterprises in the 1980s. Established in 1979, this Plan allowed income-tax reduction for provincial residents who invested in certain Quebec-based companies.

Despite the visibility of large corporations, the Quebec economy is still characterized by the strong presence of small and medium-sized companies of under fifty employees. In 1978, these companies employed 33.4 percent of the labour force, compared to 44.6 percent in 1988. Many of these jobs are very insecure because of the low level of capital involved, and companies in this category fail regularly. Concentrated in the domestic market, these firms are the backbone of the Quebec petite bourgeoisie.

The traditionally cautious Quebec business community became more politically active in the 1980s. More members began to favour some form of sovereignty. The economic policies of the federal government—notably maintaining high interest rates for the benefit of southern Ontario and to the detriment of Quebec, and abandoning regional development programs—contributed to disenchantment with federalism. As Montreal slipped from Canadian dominance, expansion into new markets became an important objective. Continued constitutional infighting with the rest of Canada over the future of Quebec prompted many business people to look to the United States both as a symbol of neoconservatism and as the means to free Quebec from Canadian control. Public opinion followed and although the provincial economy is still dependent on interprovincial trade Quebec offered the greatest support for the continentalism promised in the 1988 free trade agreement.

∽

AGRICULTURE

Quebec agriculture continues to be characterized by increasing productivity and declining employment. The reduction in the number of Quebec farms began before the First World War, speeded up in the 1950s and 1960s, and then accelerated sharply from 95 777 farms in 1961 to 41 448 in 1986. The abandonment of farming in peripheral areas and urban sprawl around Montreal and Quebec City provoked the Parti Québécois's 1978 "green" law, which protected rural lands from non-agricultural development. At the same time, family farms were consolidated into larger units; the average farm grew from 60 hectares in 1961 to 87.8 hectares in 1986. Larger size also means larger revenues. In 1981 only 8.6 percent of farms had total sales over $100 000 whereas over 22 percent of farms passed this figure in 1986.

The process of modernization began after the Second World War. Gains due to increased use of chemical fertilizers and specialization were offset, however, by the persistence of many small, unproductive units. Overall productivity stagnated between 1950 and 1965 before showing appreciable gains. In the period from 1971 to 1987, the value of agricultural production rose from $305 million to $3 billion.

Modernization had important consequences for the way that farming was financed. In 1961, the average Quebec farm had $18 606 invested in land, equipment, and livestock. This figure rose to $35 390 in 1971 and $197 594 in 1981. As capital requirements grew, large corporations entered the agricultural sector and an increasing percentage of farmers leased all or part of their land. In 1941, only 6.8 percent of farmers leased land compared to 21.8 percent in 1981. Greater capital requirements also caused debt loads to rise, making farmers vulnerable to price and interest rate fluctuations.

Under these conditions, marketing boards and accounting became increasingly important. At the same time, farmers used traditional co-operative methods to try to retain control over production, markets, and prices. Co-operatives prospered but, as they became large corporations, original democratic principles were often sacrificed to business-school principles of management. Like its labour counterpart, farm unionism became more radical. The Union catholique des cultivateurs (UCC) evolved into the Union des producteurs agricoles (UPA). Its collective strength was used to lobby government for marketing programs, subsidies, and quotas. Dairy farming, which accounts for over a third of Quebec agricultural revenue, has benefited substantially, obtaining 47 percent of Canadian milk quotas.

POLITICS: FROM MAITRES CHEZ NOUS TO SOVEREIGNTY

The 1960 defeat of the Union Nationale government by Jean Lesage's Liberals is usually cited as the beginning of the Quiet Revolution, a movement that radically changed Quebec society and politics. The period may have been less pivotal than it is often painted, however. Clerical influence was already on the decline by the Second World War, while in the 1930s the union movement was challenging both employers and the state. Government expenses rose sharply in the postwar period and even faster in the 1960s. Through the influence of radio and television, the automobile, and other elements of consumer society, the popular classes had long been undergoing a process of integrating American values into their culture.

Cabinet colleagues like Paul Gérin-Lajoie saw Jean Lesage as a pragmatic politician who assumed leadership of the Liberal Party leader in 1958

> with the particular intention of modernizing and rationalizing structures of government and of putting in place instruments useful for the collective development of Quebec. Shaped by the structures and operating techniques of an anglo-saxon (which is not meant in a pejorative sense) federal bureaucracy and inspired by the accepted Keynesian theories of the 1940s and 1950s, he exercised leadership in a very pragmatic sense, analyzing and adopting reform measures one by one in the light of circumstances (Comeau, 1989: 17).

Symbolized by the slogan "Maîtres chez nous"—"Masters in our own house"— the Lesage administration used government to effect change. "Québécois," according to Lesage, "have only one powerful institution: their government. And they now want to use this institution to build a new era to which they could not formerly aspire" (Gagnon, 1984: 46). Establishment of a ministry of education was a crucial act which took control of the curriculum away from the church and entrusted the socialization of children to lay intellectuals. Lesage's government actively intervened in the economy by nationalizing the remaining private electricity companies in 1963. With the construction of the Manic–Outardes project, Hydro-Québec became a symbol of francophone ability to control massive technological and capital projects (Figure 9.6).

Quebec economists and bureaucrats, well-trained at Harvard and the London School of Economics, understood the importance of capital. Established in 1965

Figure 9.6 Daniel Johnson Dam on the Manicouagan River. Part of the Manic–Outardes complex, this dam was the biggest in the world when it was inaugurated in 1968, and symbolized the economic power of the state for many Quebecers. It was also important proof of the skills of Quebec-trained engineers.

by the Quebec government, the Caisse de dépôt et de placement du Québec (Quebec Deposit and Investment Fund), acts as investor for the Quebec pension fund (Régie des rentes) and fifteen other public agencies in Quebec such as the state-run automobile insurance fund (la Société de l'assurance automobile). A large pool of capital and the Caisse's dual mandate of "achieving an optimum financial return" and of making a "sustained and durable contribution to the Quebec economy" has made it a strong participant in the Quebec and Canadian economy in sectors such as energy, transportation, and manufacturing. With major investments in important companies in Quebec like Noranda Mines, Gaz Métropolitain, Domtar, and Cascades Paper, the Caisse was the eighth largest financial institution in Canada, with assets of over $38 billion in 1991, and the largest investor in the Canadian stock market.

One of the most significant acts of the Lesage government was to initiate dramatic expansion of the public sector. In one session, it created offices of federal–provincial relations, cultural affairs, family and social welfare, and natural resources. The number of public-sector workers rose from 60 980 in 1961 to 141 468 in 1987; provincial revenues in the same period rose (in 1981 dollars) from $3 183 150 to $18 290 207 (Langlois et al., 1990: 327).

The late 1960s were characterized by fragmentation among reform and nationalist forces. In 1966, the Lesage government was defeated by a renewed Union Nationale which tried to balance reform with nationalism and rural fears of statism. With the slogan "égalité ou indépendance," Daniel Johnson's Union Nationale recognized the growing support for exclusive Quebec control over important fields of action. In the same period, another group of intellectuals opted for a federal vision. In 1965, Pierre Elliott Trudeau, union leader Jean Marchand, and journalist Gérard Pelletier joined the federal Liberal Party. Three years later, Trudeau replaced Lester Pearson as Liberal prime minister of Canada.

The final straw that broke the Lesage alliance was René Lévesque (1922–1987). To many nationalists, the Lesage government refused the logical implications of its own *maître chez nous* policy by remaining subordinate to foreign capital and by refusing to consider the option of independence. Within the Lesage government, Lévesque—the minister largely responsible for the nationalization of electricity— was the foremost doubter. Born in the Gaspé, Lévesque studied law and was a war correspondent and a popular television journalist before he entered politics in 1960. His effective political style and nationalist message captured the public's imagination.

> Everything we do in the near future must take into account two basic facts. First, French Canada is a genuine nation and contains all the elements essential to nationhood; its sense of unity, its human and material resources, equipment, and talent are comparable or superior to those of many other peoples around the world. Secondly, however, we are not a sovereign people, politically speaking. There's no point going into the question of whether we could or could not be: right now we aren't. We are therefore an authentic nation, but a nation without sovereignty. We must work with these realities and make these two poles our starting point (*Le Devoir*, 5 July 1963, Cited in Provencher, 1975: 201–2).

During the 1960s, the weak political and cultural position of francophones outside Quebec, ongoing federal intrusion into provincial jurisdiction, and the emergence of an expanding and ambitious francophone bourgeoisie within Quebec all contributed to the independence movement. The first parties committed to independence, the Ralliement National (RN) and the Rassemblement pour l'Indépendance Nationale (RIN), won 8 percent of the popular vote but no seats in the 1966 elections.

In 1968, when Lévesque left the Liberal party and formed the Mouvement Souveraineté Association, he was joined by RN and RIN members. Together they formed the Parti Québécois in 1969. Entering the 1970 general election with

Quebec independence as the banner that unified its diverse political elements, the Parti Québécois won 23.1 percent of the popular vote and seven seats in the Quebec national assembly.

Much of the independence movement was powered by the issue of language, which became far more crucial to the nationalist cause than religion or civil law. The inferior economic position of francophones in Canada and even within Quebec was clearly documented by the federal Royal Commission on Bilingualism and Biculturalism in the late 1960s and by the Gendron Commission in 1972. The former showed that unilingual anglophones in Quebec earned an average annual salary of $6049. This was more than bilingual anglophones ($5929) and much more than bilingual ($4523) or unilingual ($3107) francophones. The conclusions of the Gendron Commission drew attention to the low status of French in business. English predominated, particularly in Montreal, and was essential for management positions. The rapidly expanding state bureaucracy gave employment to francophone professionals. At Hydro-Québec in 1963, 190 out of 243 engineers were francophones, as were 85 percent of scientists employed by provincial and municipal governments. Yet there remained a sharp difference between the public and private sectors; only 14 percent of scientists employed in mining and manufacturing were francophones (Gagnon, 1984: 173). The difference in language policy between companies in the private sector and Quebec-owned enterprises was not lost on nationalists. During the 1960s there were growing demands for legislation to ensure the use of French in the workplace; unions fought for contracts written in French and mounted movements to boycott anglophone stores; and nationalists fought to transform McGill University into a French institution.

Conflict over language crystallized in the field of education. As the birth rate declined and statistics showed francophones being assimilated, Quebec nationalists became increasingly worried about the status of French. Immigrants had to be assimilated into francophone rather than anglophone society through education. A microcosm of the language and school crisis of the 1960s is found in the Montreal suburb of Saint-Léonard. With heavy Italian immigration into the north end of Montreal, francophones dropped from over 90 percent of the population of Saint-Léonard in 1960 to about 60 percent seven years later. In 1968, the local school board enraged the allophone and anglophone communities by proposing to replace bilingual classes with an early elementary education entirely in French. The proposal was challenged before the courts, private English classes were formed, and violence broke out between francophones and Italian Canadians. In response, the Union Nationale government of Jean-Jacques Bertrand passed Bill 63. While the act's official purpose was "to promote the French language in Quebec," it in fact guaranteed freedom of choice. That only 13.7 percent (1972) of immigrants opted for francophone schools under Bill 63 rekindled the worst demographic fears of nationalists (Plourde, 1988: 11, 15).

Although Robert Bourassa's Liberal government made French the official language of Quebec and tried to promote French in the workplace through Bill 22 (1974), nationalists bitterly attacked its decision to grant freedom of choice in the language of education. The election of the Parti Québécois in 1976 ended the ambiguity between French as official language and linguistic freedom of choice. The Charter of the French Language of 1977 (Bill 101) underscored that the French language "permitted the Quebec people to express their identity." To this end, French was to become the official language of the state and the "normal language of work, education, communications, and business." The act restricted English education to children whose parents were educated in English in Quebec, prohibited bilingual signs, and restricted the use of English in business and government (Figures 9.7 and 9.8).

The education and language laws have been consistently supported by a great majority of Quebecers; their effect on the language of education (Table 9.3) and of the workplace have been important. Some in the anglophone and allophone minority, however, have persistently tried to thwart the laws in the courts, in politics through pressure groups such as Alliance Quebec, and in acts of civil disobedience, particularly by registering allophone children illegally in English schools and by continuing to use bilingual or unilingual English signs. Prominent journalists like William Johnson of the Montreal *Gazette* (4 April 1990) have been unceasing in attacking the language legislation: "No one quarrels with promoting French. But it is newspeak to use the euphemism 'promote' when what is involved is the repression of English, even through the suspension of fundamental rights." More moderate, Alliance Québec has accepted that French is the predominant language of work in Quebec while retaining a vision of a pan-Canadian bilingualism: "Alliance Québec's National Language Issues Policy [1989] is

Language of instruction	Mother tongue			Total
	French	English	Other	
1971–1972				
French	98.1	9.7	15.0	84.5
English	1.9	90.3	85.0	15.5
1978–1979				
French	98.1	10.7	27.2	84.4
English	1.9	89.3	72.8	15.6
1989–1990				
French	99.0	16.0	70.2	90.2
English	1.0	84.0	29.8	9.8

Table 9.3   Public School Registration by Language of Instruction (in percentage)

Figures 9.7 and 9.8 Cultural communities in Quebec. Despite Bill 101, signs in languages other the English are tolerated and contribute to the cosmopolitan face of Montreal in the 1990s (9.7). While strongly insisting on the retention of their cultures, members of diverse cultural communities participate in traditional French-Canadian festivals. Figure 9.8, for example, illustrates signs of the Saint-Jean Baptiste celebration in Montreal's Chinatown (24 June 1992) with Hydro-Québec's headquarters visible in the background.

founded on the principle that Canada's linguistic duality is a cornerstone of this nation [. . .] Our commitment to this principle demands recognition of the right of English-speaking and French-speaking Canadians to feel at home across Canada" (Cited in Legault, 1992: 251).

While the primacy of the French language was being strengthened within Quebec, francophone minorities in the rest of Canada were undergoing assimilation. Nationalists like Henri Bourassa had sought to protect minorities at the beginning of the twentieth century but by 1960 there was a growing feeling that "outside Quebec there was no salvation."

Despite federal government efforts to provide services in both official languages throughout the country after 1969, official bilingualism is largely a myth. Growing numbers of anglophone children outside Quebec are enrolled in French immersion courses, but francophone minorities have had to fight (sometimes unsuccessfully) to obtain control of French schools, particularly in Ontario. The result is that outside northern New Brunswick and the Ontario counties bordering Quebec rapid assimilation is taking place. Outside Quebec in 1991, 35.1 percent of those whose mother tongue was French spoke English at home.

Revolutionary elements in the popular classes rejected the democratic process as a means to obtain independence. Embittered by unemployment, outside control of the Quebec economy, and conflicts over the language of education, many turned to Marxist ideologies and Third World national liberation models.

One of the leading marxist figures of the 1960s was Pierre Vallières. The product of a Montreal working-class family, he sought to politicize Québécois with his influential book *White Niggers of America* (1971) by comparing them to other colonized peoples. This ideology took practical form with the formation in 1963 of the Front de libération du Québec (FLQ). Committed to overthrowing "medieval Catholicism and capitalist oppression" through revolution, the FLQ took particular aim at the federal government and anglophone bourgeoisie, threatening to destroy:

a) all colonial symbols and institutions, in particular the RCMP and the armed forces;
b) all the information media in the colonial language that hold Québécois in contempt;
c) all commercial establishments and enterprises that practise discrimination against Québécois and that do not use French;
d) all plants and factories that discriminate against francophone workers.

Revolutionary activity through the 1960s culminated in the October Crisis of 1970. The kidnapping of British consular official James Cross was followed by that of Quebec Labour Minister Pierre Laporte. Pierre Elliott Trudeau's federal government reacted strongly. It quickly subordinated the Quebec government and, instituting the War Measures Act, suspended civil liberties. Hoping to crush the independence movement in Quebec, the Trudeau government dispatched the army. Hundreds of Quebec intellectuals, political activists, and labour leaders were imprisoned arbitrarily. Five days after passage of the War Measures Act, Quebec's three labour federations called for suspension of the Act. At first, the Quebec populace was divided. Many were attracted to the FLQ manifesto because of its powerful attacks on the church, corporate colonialism, and anglophone racism but the murder of Pierre Laporte discredited the revolutionary movement for independence.

Through the October Crisis and the early 1970s, the Parti Québécois remained strong. It distanced itself from radicals and built a political base on a program of independence and social democracy. Benefiting from a social climate poisoned by violent labour and linguistic disputes, the Parti Québécois took power in 1976. It moved quickly to institute its program, reinforcing earlier language legislation and making French the sole official language through Bill 101. Organized labour was given generous wage settlements and the labour code was reformed. Responding to social democratic demands for more state control, the government also created a provincial auto insurance plan.

These policies and a strong, popular cabinet formed the background to the 1980 referendum in which Quebecers were asked to allow the government to negotiate a sovereignty association. According to the wording on the referendum ballot, "this agreement would enable Quebec to acquire the exclusive power to make its laws, levy its taxes, and establish relations abroad—in other words, sovereignty—and at the same time, to maintain with Canada an economic association including a common currency."

Prime Minister Trudeau was a powerful force in the campaign. A wealthy Montreal intellectual from a mixed anglophone–francophone background, Trudeau had established reform credentials as a leader of the opposition to Duplessis. A strong believer in liberal democracy and federalism as protective forces for minorities, he was blunt in this 1958 assessment of both ethnic groups:

> Historically, French Canadians have not really believed in democracy for themselves; and English Canadians have not really wanted it for others. Such are the foundations upon which our two ethnic groups have absurdly pretended to be building democratic forms of government. No wonder the ensuing structure has turned out to be rather flimsy (Trudeau, 1980: 103).

As prime minister, Trudeau had implemented one recommendation of the Bilingualism and Biculturalism Commission: the Official Languages Act (1969) which made Canada officially bilingual. Through the 1970s, he fought to increase federal authority and involvement in the economies and cul regions of Canada. Trudeau actively campaigned for the "No" side, pointing to the federal government's important economic presence in Quebec, and he promised to revitalize Canadian federalism if the "Yes" vote was defeated. Although a majority of francophones supported the "Yes," non-francophone votes went overwhelmingly against and the referendum was defeated with 59.6 percent of voters opting for the "No."

Election of Brian Mulroney's conservative government in September 1984 with a massive majority in Quebec—thanks in large part to the support of local PQ riding associations—helped convince René Lévesque to take the "beau risque" of renewed federalism. Temporarily abandoning the independence option, the Parti Québécois under Lévesque and his successor Pierre-Marc Johnson sought a middle ground of compromise on the constitutional question. This led to factionalism within the Parti Québécois, which combined with fatigue in party ranks and the disenchantment of social democrats over the party's increasingly conservative social policy to bring about defeat at the hands of the Bourassa Liberals in the election of December 1985.

The sovereignty option seemed even more remote in the following years as Premier Bourassa encouraged a renewed federalism by announcing five conditions for adhering to the Canadian constitution of 1982:

1. recognition of Quebec as a distinct society;
2. additional Quebec powers over immigration;
3. limits to federal spending in Quebec;
4. a Quebec veto of constitutional changes or the right to opt out of them with compensation;
5. Quebec participation in the appointment of Supreme Court judges.

At Meech Lake in April 1987, the prime minister and ten premiers unanimously agreed on a text incorporating Quebec's conditions. The Meech Lake accord, if not ratified by the federal government and each of the provinces, was to expire on 23 June 1990, in accordance with the terms of the 1982 constitution.

In December 1988, the Supreme Court invalidated the sections of Quebec's language charter that imposed French-only commercial signs, deciding that they were a violati~   · Canadian Charter. This blew the lid off ethnic relations. Ang!-   d this decision as confirming individual rights as the cen-
nocracy. Francophones generally had a different perspec-
of language as a collective right, they saw the Court's
ational survival. Forced to respond by a revitalized
d scenes of thousands marching in Montreal, the
ked the notwithstanding clause of the Canadian
ns, which allowed provinces to circumvent charter

provisions. Passage of Bill 178 prohibiting non-French exterior signs acted as a catalyst for eighteen months of ethnic crisis culminating in the failure to ratify the Meech Lake accord. Three of the four anglophone ministers in the Bourassa cabinet resigned and in the months that followed the Equality Party was formed. The party was committed to freedom of language on commercial signs, freedom of access to English schools, and major revision of the Meech Lake accord. It elected four members in September 1989, two of whom were unilingual.

Opposition to the accord from anglophones within Quebec merged with larger suspicions already present in English Canada. The distinct-society clause roused latent feelings of francophobia as well as traditional constitutional fears that Quebec would have more power than other provinces. Social democrats expressed concern that the accord would weaken the central government's capacity to implement pan-Canadian social programs. On the right, a growing element centred in western Canada charged that the accord would impede senate reform. The free-trade debate in the 1988 federal election campaign had already heightened suspicion that Quebec could impose unpopular policies on English Canada.

As the June 1990 deadline for ratification approached, former prime minister Pierre Elliott Trudeau and Newfoundland premier Clyde Wells came to represent opposition to the Meech Lake accord; they underlined the danger—symbolized by Bill 178—that a Quebec "distinct society" posed for individual and minority rights. The accord then received a mortal blow from another quarter. Largely excluded from the constitutional process surrounding Meech Lake, native peoples had the final say when Manitoba M.L.A. Elijah Harper used parliamentary procedure to block the vote on ratification.

Failure to ratify the Meech Lake accord led to renewed Quebec nationalist demonstrations on Saint-Jean Baptiste day, 24 June 1990, and to the formation of the Bloc Québécois as a federal party. In September 1990, responding to nationalist pressure, the national assembly of Quebec unanimously established the Bélanger-Campeau commission to analyse the political status and constitution of Quebec and to formulate recommendations. Reporting over a period of five months, the commission received 607 submissions, including ones from the Société Saint-Jean Baptiste de Montréal, the Innutakuaikan Uashat Mak Mani-Utenam, and the League for Human Rights B'nai Brith Canada. The report leaned strongly in favour of sovereignty, and emphasized several characteristics of the Quebec reality:

> The English-speaking community has been historically part of Québec's reality. Its significant contribution to Québec's development must be stressed and continue to be recognized. As a linguistic minority in Québec, it is seeking, with French-speaking Quebecers who are themselves a minority in Canada, the development of respectful, harmonious relations, and this goal has largely been attained. A number of differences persist; both sides must endeavour to resolve

> them in a spirit of openness. With respect to the political and constitutional future of Québec, it is important to maintain, in collaboration with the English-speaking community, legal guarantees which ensure the complete protection of its rights and institutions, and its full participation in Québec society.
>
> . . . profound changes must be made to Québec's political and constitutional status. Regardless of the solutions adopted, they must promptly and permanently dissipate the uncertainty and instability resulting from the current stalemate.
>
> Two courses are open to Québec with respect to the redefinition of its status, i.e. a new, ultimate attempt to redefine its status within the federal regime, and the attainment of sovereignty.
>
> Should a final attempt to renew federalism fail, sovereignty would be the only course remaining (Quebec, 1991: 66–73).

For its part the constitutional committee of the Liberal Party of Quebec (Comité constitutionnel du Parti libéral du Québec) also responded to the collapse of the accord. Its Allaire Report called for a referendum on a restructured Quebec–Canada in which Quebec's power would be dramatically expanded by the patriation of all federal powers that influenced "l'identité québécoise." In addition to obvious areas affecting culture such as education and communications, these would include social affairs, employment, and regional development. While foreign policy, justice, immigration, and financial institutions would be shared, the federal government would be essentially restricted to defence, customs, and money (Parti libéral du Québec, 1991).

Despite the Spicer and Beaudoin-Dobie reports, the federal government of Brian Mulroney had trouble formulating a position acceptable to Canada's diverse constituencies, particularly Quebec, native peoples, women's groups, and westerners. The Charlottetown accord for constitutional renewal was unanimously agreed upon on 28 August 1992 by the eleven first ministers and representatives of other groups at the bargaining table. It was then subjected to a pan-Canadian referendum on 26 October 1992. The accord contained a complex series of compromises. Prominent was the recognition, within the "Canada clause," of Quebec as a "distinct society within Canada," a distinctiveness based on its French language, its unique culture, and its civil law tradition (Canada, *Our Future Together: An Agreement for Constitutional Renewal*, 1992: 2).

The proposed constitution also described a reformed Senate in which each province would be assigned six senators and each territory one, and additional seats would be added for aboriginal peoples. To compensate for Quebec's loss in a Senate that had expanded powers in blocking appointments, vetoing bills concerning tax policy changes related to natural resources, and delaying supply bills, Quebec was guaranteed one-quarter of the seats in an enlarged House of

Commons of 337 seats. In addition, three judges on the Supreme Court of Canada were to be drawn from the civil law tradition of Quebec.

1867 – British North America Act (Confederation)
1931 – Statute of Westminster
1940 – Rowell-Sirois Report (federal Royal Commission established to examine "the economic basis of Confederation and the distribution of legislative powers")
1954 – Tremblay Report (Quebec Royal Commission on Constitutional Problems)
1960 – Rassemblement pour l'Indépendance Nationale (RIN) formed
1963 – Front de libération du Québec (FLQ) formed
1965 – Jean Marchand, Gérard Pelletier, and Pierre Elliott Trudeau enter federal parliament
1966 – Ralliement National (RN) founded
1967 – French president Charles de Gaulle visits Quebec and declares, "Vive le Québec libre!"
     – René Lévesque founds Mouvement souveraineté association (MSA)
     – Estates-General of French Canada
1968 – Liberal Party re-elected; Pierre Elliott Trudeau becomes prime minister
     – Parti Québécois founded
1969 – Canadian Official Languages Act
     – Bill 63 adopted
1970 – FLQ crisis
1971 – Quebec vetoes "Victoria Charter"
1974 – Bill 22 passed
1976 – Parti Québécois elected; René Lévesque becomes premier
1977 – Charter of the French Language (Bill 101)
1980 – Referendum on sovereignty association
1981 – Quebec excluded from patriation of the Constitution
1982 – Canada Act patriates the Constitution and establishes the Canadian Charter of Rights and Freedoms
1983 – Quebec Charter of Rights and Freedoms implemented
1987 – tentative agreement reached on Meech Lake accord
1988 – Supreme Court invalidates section of Quebec's Charter of the French Language requiring French-only commercial signs in Quebec
     – Bill 178 passed by Quebec national assembly
1990 – Meech Lake constitutional accord collapses
     – Bloc Québécois established
1991 – Rapport Allaire (Rapport du comité constitutionnel du Parti Libéral)
     – Rapport Bélanger-Campeau (Rapport de la Commission sur l'avenir politique et constitutionnel du Québec)
1992 – Beaudoin-Dobie Report
     – defeat by referendum of Charlottetown accord on the Constitution

---

Table 9.4   A Constitutional Chronology

Figure 9.9 "At this price—It's No." The word "price" in this poster from the 1992 referendum campaign in Quebec appealed to broad and often ill-defined feelings as to the economic and cultural costs inherent in the renewed federalism of the Charlottetown Accord. The "No" in the slogan permitted a broad base of Quebecers to make a strong statement to Ottawa and anglophone Canada while remaining vague in their intentions concerning the independence of Quebec.

Also important in the proposed renewed federation were clauses recognizing the inherent rights of aboriginal peoples to self-government.

The proposed constitution was roundly defeated in Quebec—and in the rest of Canada. Some Quebecers felt that the accord did not recognize them adequately as one of the founding peoples of Canada, and contrary to the arrangement offered to aboriginals, placed Quebec on par with other provinces. Others rejected the accord because they believed that it inadequately protected the rights of Quebecers with respect to social programs, language, culture, education, and women's rights. In Quebec, 82.3 percent of eligible voters went to the polls and 56.63 voted No. This compared to a cross-Canada No vote of 54.4 percent. While Atlantic Canada generally supported the agreement, Ontario was sharply divided, and the western provinces rejected it. British Columbia's 67.9 percent for the No represented the strongest rejection in Canada (*Le Devoir* 28 October, 3 November 1992).

LABOUR

The 1960s were marked by the separation of the Quebec labour movement from its religious roots; in 1960 Catholic unions ended their religious affiliation and became the Confédération des syndicats nationaux (CSN). Although international unions were still the strongest in the 1960s they have since given way steadily to national and public sector unions. In 1962, 55.2 percent of unionized workers were in international unions, 39.1 percent in national unions, and 5.7 in public sector unions; in 1987, 25.9 percent of unionized workers were in international unions, 64.7 percent were in national unions and 9.4 percent in public sector unions. Women in 1987 represented 37.6 percent of unionized workers (Langlois et al., 1990: 344–45).

Along with a high level of unionization, Quebec was characterized by the militancy of its labour movements. The number, size, and duration of strikes peaked in the mid 1970s. Labour struggles in 1976, the year of the Parti Québécois victory, were particularly bitter; in 293 work stoppages, 376 123 workers lost 6 333 114 work days. The number of workers and time lost in 1989 represented about 10 percent of 1976 rates (Table 9.5).

The adoption of a new labour code in 1964 gave new guarantees to unions, ensured their financial independence, and, most important, gave public-sector employees the right to strike. Quebec unions with international affiliations became more nationalistic and obtained a greater degree of independence. Louis Laberge, leader of the Fédération des travailleurs du Québec (FTQ), 1964–92, became a prominent spokesman for the union movement and was deeply involved in politics through his support for both the Parti Québécois and the New Democratic Party.

	Work stoppages	Number of workers involved	Person days lost
1960	38	9 861	207 240
1965	98	38 826	606 820
1970	126	73 189	1 417 560
1975	362	135 765	3 204 930
1976	293	376 123	6 333 114
1980	344	157 272	4 008 659
1985	270	41 536	1 083 665
1989	202	36 499	662 317

Table 9.5   Work Stoppages in Quebec, 1960–1989

(Langlois et al., 1990: 268)

The CSN was the primary benefactor from growing unionization in the public sector, attracting many new members. Leaders like Marcel Pépin used union power to fight for fundamental social and economic change. Unlike the FTQ, which supported traditional political action and established political parties, the CSN adhered to a Marxist ideology of class struggle, integrating the union movement into a larger class and national struggle to control multinational corporations. The CSN program of 1971 had a nationalist appeal, seeing workers as part of a larger Quebec collectivity to capture power: "The one and only long term solution for the people of Quebec: stop counting on others for development and have faith only in our strength." The efforts of the CSN to transform nationalism from a conservative force into a vehicle for social reform were strongly supported by the teachers union. The Corporation des enseignants du Québec (CEQ) characterized the school system as "the spitting image of capitalist society."

Unions were in the forefront of political opposition in the early 1970s. They were prominent in the formation of Common Fronts in 1972 and 1975–1976, alliances that grouped all unionized workers in the public sector. The bitter Common Front strike of 1972 ended with government injunctions against the unions, a legislated settlement, and the jailing of union leaders Marcel Pépin, Louis Laberge, and Yvon Charbonneau.

Not all workers were enchanted with the left and in 1972 a new organization, the Centrale des syndicats démocratiques, protested the increasingly radical politics of the CSN. The destruction of a James Bay hydro project site, in which workers drove bulldozers through buildings before setting them on fire (Figure 9.10), and the disruption of essential services, especially in health care, alienated public opinion and tarnished the image of the union movement. In the late 1970s, union influence began to decline.

The election of the Parti Québécois in 1976 brought respite from the violent labour confrontations of the Bourassa years. At least initially, the Parti Québécois, which included important reformers such as Robert Burns, Claude Charron, Jacques Couture, and Pierre Marois, espoused certain social democratic goals. The labour code of 1977 was unique in outlawing strikebreaking. It also instituted the Rand formula for deducting union dues at source. Legislation in 1979 regulated working conditions in non-unionized sectors, allowing workers to refuse work that endangered their health and regulating minimum wages, maternity leave, and annual vacations. In 1984, 1 132 000 people in Quebec were unionized; this represented 43 percent of the paid labour force (Lipsig-Mummé et Roy, 1989: 125).

Torn between the conservative and social democratic tendencies that had always existed within the party under the umbrella of nationalism, the PQ opted for the right in the recession of 1981. The alliance between labour and the PQ ended a year later when the deficit-strapped government forced across-the-board

Figure 9.10 The destruction of LG2. In March 1974, union activists destroyed most of the camp that housed several thousand workers building the dam and generating station on the Grande River near James Bay. This, along with other violent labour conflicts such as that of Montreal fire fighters (during which dozens of buildings burned), and the 1971 strike at Montreal's most important francophone paper, *La Presse*, which left one person dead and hundreds injured, contributed to a lessening of public support for organized labour.

pay cuts on public-sector employees. Anti-strike and back-to-work legislation destabilized labour. In the late 1980s, the growing power of conservative and entrepreneurial forces in Quebec further weakened a labour movement hard hit by recession, layoffs, free trade, and deindustrialization. Labour in the early 1990s remains fragmented, unable to offer an alternative to the conservative nationalism offered by mainline political parties.

ᦔ

WOMEN

Gender relations in both the public and the private sphere have evolved dramatically since 1960. Women's role in the paid workplace has continued to expand in most sectors. The resulting economic autonomy—despite ongoing wage disparity—has increased the options for women (and often their financial responsibilities) in terms of marriage and parenting. With their public role no longer restricted to the convent or to philanthropic activities, women have achieved at least partial power in the unions, professions, and politics.

Feminist demands have been taken up only slowly in reform groups dominated by males. In the 1960 platform of the Liberal Party—a virtual manifesto of the Quiet Revolution—women's rights were addressed only in a short section on the legal status of the married women. Women's rights were also not a priority in the early years of the Parti Québécois. The highly influential FLQ Manifesto of 1970, while calling attention to the exploitation of native peoples, did not specifically mention women's rights either. The 1972 manifesto of the CEQ made the status of women a major political question by pointing out the treatment of female role models in textbooks and noting that twice as many girls as boys abandoned their studies at the end of secondary school. With a particular section entitled "The Inferiority of Women," it attacked the educational bias that directed girls to careers of unpaid maternal and wifely duties in the home (Latouche et Poliquin-Bourassa, 1979, 3: 161–66).

Despite the creation of the Quebec Council on the Status of Women (Conseil du statut de la femme) in 1974, women only obtained a specific voice in cabinet when television personality and playwright Lise Payette was named ministre d'État de la condition féminine in 1979. She expressed the viewpoint of Quebec feminists who saw political power as the major vehicle of achieving rights in both public and private domains:

> Long before 1976, I stated that, apart from completely transforming outlooks on gender relations, the solution to a significant number of problems related to the status of women could be found in parliamentary action: it was through the government in Quebec City that women could increase their autonomy by achieving equality in the workplace and by services such as day care and maternity-leave (Payette, 1982: 60).

By 1989, twenty-three women held 18 percent of the seats in the National Assembly of Quebec: the highest percentage of female members among the ten provincial legislatures. Thirteen of the province's seventy-five seats in the federal House of Commons were held by women (Maillé, 1990: 56).

Simon Langlois (1990) has argued that Quebec women have succeeded to executive power in Quebec faster in the private than in the public sector. They held 7.6 percent of the upper management positions in the Quebec civil service (1988), 5.7 percent of the judgeships (1988), 14.7 percent of the seats on the boards of crown corporations in Quebec (1988), and 20 percent of cabinet seats at the end of 1989 (Langlois et al., 1990: 121). On the other hand, women represent 25 percent of the management positions in the Caisses Populaires and 35 percent of the management positions in the Banque Nationale.

1964 – Married women receive the right to administer and dispose of their own property

1968 – Legalization of divorce in Quebec

1975 – Quebec Charter of Human Rights and Freedoms recognizes the equality of spouses in marriage

1977 – Civil code amended to replace the notion of "paternal authority" with that of "parental authority"

1989 – Civil code amended to favour the equal division of a family patrimony when a union ends by death, divorce, or separation

Table 9.6   The Legal Status of Women in Quebec

A network of women's organizations has played an important role in this partial access to power. The establishment in 1966 of the Fédération des femmes du Québec (FFQ), a non-confessional and multi-ethnic umbrella group, was the key to this network. By 1982, it represented more than 100 000 members from associations as diverse as the B'nai Brith Women's Council, the Club Wilfrid Laurier des femmes libérales, the Association de familles monoparentales du bas-Saguenay, and the Association des femmes diplômées des universités (Collectif Clio, 1982: 456). Although often divided over issues such as divorce and abortion, women's associations have been crucial in the struggle for maternity leave, day-care, shelters for battered women, changes in marriage law, and salary equality.

A first, important step in improving women's rights was Bill 16 (1964) which established the equality of men and women in marriage. It allowed women to leave the family home if they were physically threatened by their husbands and to exercise a profession different from that of their husbands. The federal Royal Commission on the Status of Women (Bird Commission) in 1970 played an important role in politicizing both women and men; it was particularly strong in showing the victimization of native women. The Quebec Charter of Rights (1975) established gender and wage equality and the equality of partners within marriage as fundamental rights: "Husband and wife have, in the marriage, the same rights, obligations and responsibilities. Together they provide the moral guidance and material support of the family and the education of their common offspring" (Article 47, Quebec Charter of Human Rights and Freedoms).

The autonomy of Quebec women over their bodies and individual lives has changed fundamentally since the 1960s. In that decade, the pill and family planning clinics, attacks on traditional religious and family values, and rising educational standards contributed to changing attitudes towards the family. Although abortion was only decriminalized by the Supreme Court in 1968 (Figure 9.11), it has become an important demographic and social phenomenon in Quebec. In 1971, as we saw earlier, 1.4 abortions were performed for every 100 live births; by

Figure 9.11 A demonstration in favour of legalizing abortions, 1970. Although Quebecers are often divided along linguistic lines, the women's movement has recruited support from both francophones and anglophones. While Quebec has been a leader among Western countries in providing free abortions, the system has been under persistent attack from Catholic conservatives, and throughout the 1970s abortion was a key issue. In the 1980s, day care, economic equality, pornography, and other violence against women became rallying points.

the second half of the 1980s, they had levelled off at 18 abortions for every 100 live births (Langlois et al., 1990: 151). Only 4 percent of births were by unmarried women in 1963; this proportion increased from 27 percent to 38 percent between 1986 and 1990 (Langlois et al., 1990: 135). The growing autonomy of Quebec women over their bodies has not passed unnoticed. In 1989, Jean-Guy Tremblay, determined to defend the rights of the father and of the unborn, took his companion Chantal Daigle to court in an attempt to block her from aborting. While the case, which she eventually won, was before the courts, Daigle had an abortion in the United States.

Violence against women is an ongoing historical problem in Quebec (Harvey, 1991). Some historians link fluctuations in violence to periods of economic

Figure 9.12 Commemorative plaque to the memory of the fourteen female victims of the massacre in December 1989 at l'Ecole Polytechnique, the Université de Montréal's engineering school. The event raised the issues of gun control and violence against women which later merged into a larger consciousness of violence in Quebec society with mass murders at Concordia University in the summer of 1992.

depression. Feminist historians attribute domestic violence to men's sense that their power is threatened by competition from women in the workplace and by the insistence of women in breaking away from traditional patriarchal control in the home.

Analysts are unsure whether conjugal violence and other forms of violence against women have changed, but it is certain that public awareness has increased (Figure 9.12). In the last decade, Quebec women have been increasingly ready to denounce domestic violence and more wives now leave their marriages for this reason within the first five years than previously did. Whereas women historically turned to family, friends, and church, there are now some eighty-five homes for women in difficulty. Each home shelters an average of 100 women a year who have an average of one child each. Domestic violence has also been dealt with more harshly by the courts since 1986. Only 18 percent of men charged with killing their wives, lovers, or children between 1982 and 1986 were convicted of murder; 66 percent were convicted of the lesser offence of manslaughter. In 1990, 65 percent were convicted of murder, 29 percent of manslaughter. Four-fifths of the cases involved women who had already left or who had threatened to leave their mates.

Although Canada signed the United Nations Declaration of the Rights of Man in 1948, Quebec women have had difficulty obtaining equality of salary and treatment in the workplace. Women form an increasing percentage of the paid labour force. Just 45 percent of women aged twenty-four to forty-four were active in the workforce in 1971, compared to 73.1 percent in 1986 (Maillé, 1990: 70). Despite some diversification and a greater presence in management positions, however, they remain concentrated in a limited number of traditional occupations (Table 9.7). Wage discrimination remains endemic in the Quebec work force. In 1971, salaries for full-time male employees were almost double those of their female counterparts and although the gap had narrowed by 1981, it still remained substantial (Table 9.8). During the 1980s the disparity remained fairly constant, with women earning two-thirds as much as men. Given the importance of part-time labour for women, the wage gap is even greater for the labour force as a whole.

Sector	1975	1980	1985
Managerial	3.2	4.0	7.4
Natural and social sciences	2.0	2.7	3.4
Teachers	8.4	7.1	6.8
Health	9.2	9.4	9.9
Arts and recreation	1.0	1.4	1.8
Office work	36.8	35.5	33.2
Commerce	8.0	9.0	8.4
Services	14.6	16.7	17.2
Manual work	14.4	12.0	9.7
Agriculture	2.1	1.7	1.8
Other	.3	.5	.4
Total	100.0	100.0	100.0

Table 9.7   Activities of Active Women over Age 15, 1975–1985 (in percentage of female work force)

(Langlois et al., 1990: 150)

Profession	1971		1981	
	Men	Women	Men	Women
Directors	14 802	8 184	29 068	18 599
Intellectual workers	10 888	6 816	26 887	20 016
Manual workers				
white collar	7 249	4 259	17 720	11 860
blue collar	6 631	3 609	17 504	10 188
Farmers	4 207	2 787	12 643	7 714
Army, police, fire	8 345	5 953	23 227	16 083
Quebec average	7 759	4 711	20 561	13 935

Table 9.8   Wage Spreads between Men and Women, 1971 and 1981 (in dollars)
(Brunelle et Drouilly, 1986: 282)

CULTURE

The strengthening and modernization of francophone culture have been important themes in recent decades. Religious domination of education and culture withered in the 1960s as Quebecers looked increasingly to the state as the defender of national life and francophone culture.

The Catholic church was transformed from within by Vatican II, 1962–1965, a reform process that emphasized ecumenicalism, religious liberty, the adaptation of the church to the modern world, and the role of lay people. Change dictated by Rome was not always acceptable, however, and while it did not go far enough for some, it alienated others who clung to traditional certainties. The crisis in the church is illustrated by sharp shifts in religious practice: holy days such as All Saints Day and the Immaculate Conception are no longer public holidays; confession and Friday fasting declined dramatically; the use of the rosary and the adoration of saints became practices unknown to the young; the number of Catholics who went to church at least twice a month dropped from 88 percent in 1965 to 46 percent in 1975, and to 38 percent in 1985 (Langlois et al., 1990: 352). Young people, affected by secular values, deserted the church almost en masse until only 12 to 15 percent were practising their religion. The struggle between progressives and traditionalists over liturgy, celibacy, and the church's social role in the aftermath of Vatican II prompted many clerics to leave the church. Ordinations dropped off dramatically, and the number of priests in Quebec fell from 8758 in 1966 to 6428 in 1988 (Figure 9.13). The number of nuns went from 34 571 in 1966 to 22 525 in 1988.

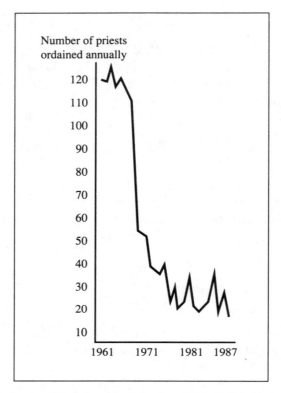

Figure 9.13 Ordination of Catholic priests in Quebec, 1961–1987. With the sharp decline in ordinations, the average age of the clergy rose dramatically. Although priests had fewer faithful to attend to, they were overworked. Abbé Jean-Guy Cadotte had an average weekly attendance in 1989 of about 500 people at his Sunday masses in the east-end Montreal church, La Nativité de la Saint-Vierge: "When I came here in 1969 between 2000 and 2500 people would come to mass every Sunday. In those days I had seven priests to help me. Now there's only one other priest beside myself and he is ill. . . . This is the civilization of leisure with an overabundance of material goods" (Montreal *Gazette*, 25 March 1989).

Accompanying the dramatic decrease in religious practice (Figure 9.14) was the state's progressive assumption of education and health care, beginning with the election of the Lesage government in 1960. The Université de Montréal's new charter in 1967 was symbolic of secularization. From the 1920 incorporation of the university on, the Catholic archbishop of Montreal had been appointed chancellor of the university. He would preside over all meetings of university bodies and had the right to cast the deciding vote. With the new charter, the rector became the chief administrative officer and the chancellor was relegated to a purely honorary role.

Figure 9.14 The Université du Québec à Montréal campus. Perhaps nothing is more symbolic of the decline of religious influence than this campus, where a church and a convent were torn down to build new university buildings. Parts of the church's façade were integrated into the new structure.

Decline in religious influence and expansion of American consumerism added a new dimension to the difficulty of retaining a francophone identity within North America. Catholicism and the idealization of rural values had offered some certainties. As these faded, francophones turned to new cultural defences. Although the 1962 Estates-General of French Canada, a bipartisan assembly, included representatives from francophone minorities of other provinces in an effort to define the status of French in Canada, many assumed that outside Quebec there was no hope of maintaining a vibrant francophone culture.

Quebec's artistic community had been at the forefront of demands for change since the 1930s. In the 1960s artists became leading voices of Quebec nationalism. Novelists such as Hubert Aquin, poets such as Gaston Miron, playwrights like Michel Tremblay, essayists like Pierre Vallières, and *chansonniers* such as Gilles Vigneault stirred up intense nationalist feeling by encouraging pride in being a Québécois.

Although some performers—Robert Charlebois and Diane Dufresne, for example—gave rock and roll a francophone flavour, the strongest impact came from the *chansonniers*. Félix Leclerc and Gilles Vigneault are examples of this type of singer, whose ballads stress the uniqueness of the Québécois identity. Popular singers such as Céline Dion, on the other hand, are much more prone to sing in English and to merge the Quebec and American markets. Emphasis on the distinct character of Quebec also influenced literature and theatre and fuelled a debate over *joual* (the language of Montreal's working classes) as a viable means of expression. Although *joual* did not have a lasting impact on prose, many playwrights like Michel Tremblay consider it necessary to express the true nature of Quebec.

The question of *joual* underlines the major theme of Quebec cultural consciousness in the post-1960 era: the primacy of the French language. Large anglophone corporations used English and it was also widespread in advertising and on many work sites. Pierre Vallières reflects the frustration felt by many young nationalists: "Spring 1951. I was soon going to leave . . . school for good. To go where? To the long, dark rooms of the Raymond canneries, to hull strawberries all day long? To the city streets to work as a drawer of water [. . .] or to be one of the unemployed? To the collège in Longueil, to study for a job as an office clerk—bilingual if possible?"

Nationalism was not the only theme in Quebec artistic production. Although social realism still permeated many works, the most widely recognized literary masterpieces—such as Marie-Claire Blais's *Une saison dans la vie d'Emanuelle* and *Manuscrits de Pauline Archange*, or Réjean Ducharme's *L'avalée des avalés*—were psychological portraits of characters, often adolescents, who questioned the world view of the older generation by attacking its basic institution, the family. The development of an indigenous movie industry (which moved quickly from soft-core pornography to quality productions) popularized important Quebec literary works such as Anne Hébert's *Kamouraska* even further. In the 1970s, literature also reflected a growing feminist voice within Quebec society through the works of Nicole Brossard.

Throughout the 1960s and 1970s, Quebec culture was extraordinarily dynamic in literature, theatre, and music. Pride in Quebec's national literature blossomed as Québécois authors replaced the traditional Catholic anthologies on the high school and CEGEP curriculum and universities made Quebec literature a distinct field of study from the undergraduate to the doctoral level. Quebec novelists published two to three times as many books in the 1960s as in the previous decade.

Although this number has continued to increase, print runs are growing smaller. People are faced with a greater choice of both books and magazines, and there has been a dramatic increase of photocopying by teaching establishments (Langlois et al., 1990). Literature also has stiffer competition from general interest magazines as local and imported French periodicals take up a growing share of the market (Figure 9.15).

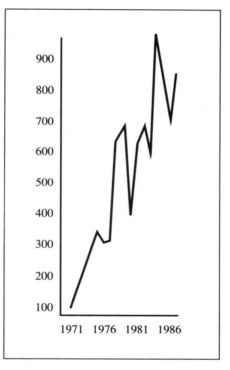

Figure 9.15 Increase in the value of periodials imported from France, 1971–1986

Cultural revival in Quebec was stimulated by expanding the sadly inadequate cultural infrastructure. In 1960, only 45 percent of the population had access to one of the seventy-one municipal libraries. Large, government-funded concert halls and auditoriums such as the Place des Arts in Montreal (1967) and the Grand Théâtre in Quebec City (1971), along with smaller regional cultural centres funded as part of the centennial celebrations in 1967, introduced classical music, opera, and theatre to wider audiences. The construction of regional high schools (polyvalentes) and CEGEPs (Collèges d'enseignement général et professionnel) also provided new cultural infrastructure. New galleries such as the Museum of Contemporary Art (1965) and the Saidye Bronfman Centre (1967), and the expansion of Montreal's Musée des beaux-arts, gave the visual arts new prominence. Alongside private historical museums such as the McCord Museum of Canadian History, the David M. Stewart Museum, Château Ramezay, and the dozens of museums run by local historical societies, the Quebec and federal governments have competed to present their interpretations of history. The provincial government established the Musée de la civilisation and the Canadian government opened Parks Canada interpretation centres and the Canadian Museum of Civilization.

Despite these improvements, many cultural activities were still the preserve of a small elite. A 1979 poll indicated that 77 percent of Quebecers never went to a public library, 50 percent never went to a bookstore, and 44 percent had not read a book or magazine in the previous year. In 1979–1980, the minister of cultural affairs initiated the development of libraries, museums, and concert halls. Within five years over a hundred new libraries were opened and within a decade floor space for cultural exhibitions had tripled. As a result, attendance at cultural events has soared.

Despite these developments, Americanization and internationalization of culture continue to concern nationalists. Many of the programs on French-language television are imitations or dubbed versions of popular American series and American pop stars draw huge crowds. Over a third of English radio stations' listeners are francophones and French stations include English-language songs in their programming. American films continue to dominate the Quebec market. In sports, baseball and hockey continue to be favourites but even in the latter the francophone presence has been diluted by expansion. Fast-food chains, fads for light and dry beers and specific wines which are shared with other western societies have undermined distinctive national characteristics.

NATIVE PEOPLES

The period since 1960 has seen a dramatic change in the aspirations of native peoples. A rapid increase of population has accentuated problems in economic development, housing, and social services on reserves. With a growing awareness of their distinct heritage, native groups are now pressing for the resolution of land claims, some of which have been outstanding since the end of the French regime. The politicization of native peoples has not been smooth, however, and community solidarity has been strained by the emergence of radical elements such as the Mohawk Warrior Society.

In Quebec, language is the usual indicator of cultural vitality. Among native peoples in Quebec, only the Huron have completely lost their language. The

Abenaki language, according to the Commissioner of Official Languages, is in on the verge of extinction and Micmac, Montagnais-Naskapi, and Mohawk are moderately endangered. Only the Cree and Inuktitut languages are considered to have excellent chances of survival. Native communities have increasingly encouraged their young people to learn their ancestral tongue. On the Kahnawake reserve near Montreal, for example, Mohawks established the Kahnawake Survival School in 1977. Run by natives themselves and separated from surrounding non-native school boards, its program is based on tribal tradition with emphasis on the Mohawk language, history and culture. At the same time it prepares native young people for integration into mainstream labour markets by offering courses in computing and science.

Language continues to be a barrier to intertribal relations since most Abenakis, Hurons, and Montagnais-Naskapis speak French, whereas Cree, Inuit, Micmacs, and Mohawks favour English as their first or second language.

In southern Quebec, native groups such as the Mohawk of Kahnawake and the Huron of Lorette have, for over a century, shared many of the same industrial work experiences as their white neighbours. Mohawks have specialized in high steel construction work; 75 percent of Kahnawake men worked in this trade in the 1960s and found their skills in demand at skyscraper and bridge construction sites across North America. The decline of this industry has severely affected Mohawk employment. United States regulations that allow native Americans to buy domestic and foreign tobacco products tax-free, high Canadian cigarette taxes, and strict gaming regulations in surrounding white communities have presented alternative economic opportunities. Mohawks at Akwesasne (which straddles the Canada–U.S. border) and Kahnawake have established a new local economy based on bingo and tax-free cigarettes. Both activities have been defined as illegal by Canadian and Quebec authorities and have led to persistent conflict, some of it armed.

In the North, hunting and trapping remained the main activities for the Algonquins, Montagnais, Cree, and Inuit until the 1960s and 1970s, when resource development (particularly hydro-electric developments such as the James Bay complexes) changed life in their homelands by flooding traditional trapping areas. Their livelihood has also been hurt by international campaigns against fur clothing. As in native communities farther south, reserves are having difficulty creating alternative local employment for their growing populations.

One of the main problems confronting Quebec's native people is the lack of economic control over traditional native territories. The James Bay agreement of 1975 was a landmark in Quebec native land claims. By this agreement the Cree received $137 million as compensation for allowing Hydro-Québec to develop the hydroelectric potential of the James Bay watershed. In the past, the federal Department of Indian Affairs usually managed the proceeds of such agreements but monies from the James Bay settlement are administered by a holding company, Cree Regional Economic Enterprises (CREECO), which is controlled by the Cree band council. Despite initial optimism, ongoing social problems and economic depression in the North continued. In the late 1980s, Hydro-Québec announced North America's largest, most expensive—and, its critics say, most environmentally destructive— power project at Grande Baleine. Native insistence on protecting their hunting and fishing territories has been strongly supported by environmentalists, who have successfully lobbied to block power sales in American markets. At the time of writing, the future of the project seems uncertain.

Most native people in Quebec continue to suffer from discrimination and unemployment; 60 percent live on unemployment insurance or welfare. In 1981, the average annual income of non-native Canadians was $13 100 compared to an average native income of $8600. Quebec, like other Canadian provinces, has failed to resolve deepening native poverty accompanied by disintegrating public health problems. Infant mortality rates are more than triple the Canadian average, suicide rates for people under twenty are six times higher, life expectancy is almost ten years lower, and alcoholism and drug abuse are widespread.

Although solutions to native land claims can be worked out for sparsely populated northern regions of the province, the continued existence of native communities alongside major urban centres in the South poses different problems, as the crisis at Oka and the blocking of the Mercier bridge in Kahnawake in 1990 clearly illustrated. Natives in southern Quebec never ceded their territorial rights by treaty and this was the fundamental issue at Kanesatake. The crisis revealed not only the bankruptcy of Ottawa's policy to native peoples but the divisions within Quebec society in adjusting to different cultures.

The immediate cause of events at Oka in July 1990 was the expansion of a golf club onto lands considered sacred by the Mohawk. Established on a reserve at Kanesatake (Oka) since 1721, native peoples have struggled over the centuries with the Sulpician proprietors of the seigneury and later with the Canadian government. Throughout this dispute Mohawk society has been divided; some have supported the recurrent violence while others have advocated negotiation.

In July, the local mayor called on the provincial police to remove native barricades blocking golf club expansion. The crisis escalated with the death of a Sureté du Québec officer, the blocking of the Mercier bridge at Kahnawake, the intervention of the army and a standoff that lasted through the summer.

Although many Quebecers supported the Mohawk in the early days of the conflict, tolerance decreased as the struggle dragged on. For residents inconvenienced by blockades and vandalism, racism took over. Most Quebecers, as in Riel's time, failed to grasp that native peoples had legitimate grievances.

Figure 9.16 The Oka crisis and the media. Violence at the outset of the Oka crisis resulted in the shooting of a Sûreté du Québec police officer. However, this well-publicized stand-off between a warrior and a soldier was more a media event than an actual confrontation. Massive media coverage enabled natives to voice their claims to the Canadian public without resorting to armed resistance.

Nationalists interpreted events as a plot to further subdue Quebec after the humiliation of Meech Lake. The Canadian government used tactics similar to those employed against the FLQ in 1970: military force and the psychological tool of branding the Warriors as common criminals.

Mohawk society was also deeply divided. The Warrior Society and the Longhouse vied for control with the elected band council. Traditional Mohawk values stress consensus but this was difficult to achieve and disagreement prolonged the crisis.

The Oka crisis put native affairs in the spotlight for a time. But with the disappearance of television crews, harassment of Mohawks by government authorities resumed, further alienating the native community from Quebec society. Questions of Mohawk authority on their own land have had far-reaching repercussions, in policing on the reserve, Hydro-Québec projects, and the judicial system. The bitterness and mistrust generated by the Oka crisis and its aftermath highlighted the province's difficulty in defining the place of native peoples within Quebec society.

CONCLUSION

During completion of this book in December 1992, the headlines have been dominated by the same social and economic questions that form the backbone of this history: employment; gender issues and violence; environmental questions, particularly the James Bay project; and the place of native peoples in Quebec society. After the referendum in October 1992, constitutional questions have been relegated to the backburner—at least for the moment.

To the historian, the public debate over these very real economic, human, and political questions is striking for its lack of historicity, the absence of an historical context that permits a larger understanding of issues.

For over three decades, Quebec has modernized, shaping institutions that have permitted it significant autonomy and control over its future. At the same time, a strong tension between past and present persists. In 1992, for example, Montreal organized a fête for its 350th anniversary; in the same year, Hydro-Québec celebrated its first thirty years. In its own way, the aging of Hydro-Québec illustrates the truism that the Quebec of the 1990s is not that of the 1960s and the Quiet Revolution. If church steeples and outside staircases persisted as the outsiders' image of Quebec despite the reforms and construction of the 1960s, now it is the landmarks of the Quiet Revolution that are dated. Postwar baby boomers who matured in the Quiet Revolution are now middle aged and as liable to be thinking of their pensions as of the reform heritage of 1968. If the Université du Québec served as a symbol of changing Quebec in the 1960s and 1970s, Nancy B., a paralyzed victim of Guillain-Barré syndrome and symbol of the "right to die" movement, was more central to philosophical debate in Quebec society in 1991.

Coincidental with modernization and the maturation process of the Quiet Revolution has been the subordination of national to global economies. The social programs of the welfare state in Quebec are being challenged by conservatives, by commercial partners, and by the fiscal realities of an indebted state. While entrepreneurs flourish, the gulf between rich and poor widens, weakening further the position of the vulnerable in Quebec, particularly women, the young, and the elderly.

The "national question" also seems to be at a crossroads; the future is unclear for the Bloc Québécois, the Parti Québécois, and federalist elements such as the Liberal Party. There are conflicting impressions of the health of Quebec culture. The vigour of French within Quebec seems to be confirming itself but at the same time new technologies of communication emphasize the vulnerability of culture to homogenization and American standards.

The referendum of October 1992, which gave an emphatic No across Canada to the constitutional reforms of the Charlottetown accord, has not resolved the national question. Fundamental issues remain: issues of economic orientation; of social policy; of the place of class, ethnicity, and language; and, in the deepest sense, of the nature of Quebec society—fodder enough for the historian and the reader interested in the fate of Quebec society.

FURTHER READING

For a precise chronology of contemporary Quebec, 1960–1988, see Alain Gagnon and Mary Beth Montcalm, *Quebec: Beyond the Quiet Revolution*. Of great use for its wealth of statistical information and analysis on demography, work, social relations, women, and education is Simon Langlois, Jean-Paul Baillargeon, Gary Caldwell, Guy Fréchet, Madeleine Gauthier, and Jean-Pierre Simard, *La société québécois en tendances 1960–1990*. For Quebec business see Yves Bélanger and Pierre Fournier, *L'Entreprise québécoise: développement historique et dynamique contemporaine*. The Caisse de dépôt is described in Mario Pelletier's *La Machine à milliards. L'histoire de la Caisse de dépôt et placement du Québec*.

LABOUR

For unions see Jacques Rouillard's several works and Carla Lipsig-Mummé and Rita Roy, "La population syndiquée au Québec." For the difficulties for labour in the 1990s of coping with conservatism and nationalism see Carla Lipsig-Mummé, "Future Conditional: Wars of Position in the Quebec Labour Movement." For a journal that incorporates much of the most recent work in Quebec labour history see the *Bulletin du Regroupement des chercheurs en histoire des travailleurs québécois* (UQAM). For the involvement of unions in the crisis of 1970 see Jean-François Cardin, *La crise d'octobre 1970 et le mouvement syndical québécois*. For manifestos and constitutions see Latouche and Poliquin-Bourassa, *Le Manuel de la Parole*.

WOMEN

For changes in the condition of women and particularly for declarations of Quebec women see Chantal Maillé, *Les Québécoises et la conquête du pouvoir politique*. Lise Payette's account, *Le pouvoir? Connais pas!*, is an important personal memoir, while the *Report of the Royal Commission on the Status of Women* (see Canada, 1970) is crucial in documenting women's place in Canadian society. An interesting analysis of public and autonomous lives of women is included in Diane Lamoureux, "Le mouvement des femmes: entre l'intégration et l'autonomie." For an interesting survey of the education of girls that includes an excellent bibliography see Micheline Dumont and Nadia Fahmy-Eid, "La pointe de l'iceberg: l'histoire de l'éducation et l'histoire de l'éducation des filles au

Québec." For feminism, see Heather Jon Maroney, "Contemporary Quebec Feminism: The Interrelation of Political and Ideological Development in Women's Organization, Trade Unions, Political Parties and State Policy, 1960–1980," along with her critique of demographers and pronatalists in, "Who Has the Baby? Nationalism, Pronatalism and the Construction of a "Demographic Crisis" in Quebec 1960–1988."

LITERATURE

For a treatment in English of Quebec women authors see Karen Gould, *Writing in the Feminine: Feminism and Experimental Writing in Quebec*. The best anthology of contemporary writing in Quebec is Lise Gauvin et Gaston Miron, *Ecrivains contemporains du Quebec depuis 1950*. Volumes 4 and 5 of Maurice Lemire's *Dictionnaire des oeuvres littéraires du Québec* are indispensable for literary production. For a personal description of the baby-boom generation of the Quiet Revolution, see François Ricard, *Le génération lyrique. Essai sur la vie et l'oeuvre des premiers-nés du baby-boom.*

THE QUIET REVOLUTION, FEDERALISM, AND INDEPENDENCE

For the Lesage period see Dale C. Thompson, *Jean Lesage and the Quiet Revolution* while the same author treats the De Gaulle visit in *Vive le Québec libre*. Trudeau's vision of Canada is best expressed in Trudeau, *Federalism and the French Canadians*. To compare Ottawa and Quebec visions of federalism see Canada, *Report of the Royal Commission on Bilingualism and Biculturalism* (1966) and Quebec, *Report of the Royal Commission of Inquiry on Constitutional Problems* (1956). The independence movement cannot be understood without reading Pierre Vallières's *White Niggers of America*; also useful on the subject are René Lévesque's *An Option for Quebec*, Pierre Bourgault's *Moi, je m'en souviens*, and Richard Jones, *Community in Crisis. French Canadian Nationalism in Perspective*. Particularly useful for their analyses of class and nationalism in the Quiet Revolution period are Dale Posgate and Kenneth McRoberts, *Quebec: Social Change and Political Crisis* and William D. Coleman, *The Independence Movement in Quebec 1945–1980*. An interesting collection of commentaries on the effects of the last thirty years can be found in Fernand Dumont, *La société québécoise après 30 ans de changement*. The role of the Catholic church in the Quiet Revolution is described in Jean Hamelin, *Histoire du catholicisme québécois: le XXe siècle. Tome 2, De 1940 à nos jours*. For the recent period see George Mathews, *Quiet Revolution: Quebec's Challenge to Canada*, while Meech Lake, abortion, and free trade are presented provocatively in Robert M. Campbell and Leslie A. Pal, *The Real Worlds of Canadian Politics: Cases in Process and Policy*.

Overall views of the language question are presented in Richard Joy's still useful *Languages in Conflict* and Michel Plourde's *La politique linguistique du Québec*

1977–1987; Quebec's view of the language question is presented in the *Gendron Report*. For francophones outside Quebec see the *Annual Report* of the Commissioner of Official Languages (Ottawa) and the poignant *The Heirs of Lord Durham: Manifesto of a Vanishing People* by the Fédération des francophones hors Québec. The language question in Montreal is treated in Marc Levine, *The Reconquest of Montreal: Language Policy and Social Change in a Bilingual City*. For a strong critique of the anglophone minority's position see Josée Legault, *L'invention d'une minorité. Les Anglo-Québécois*.

BIBLIOGRAPHY

This bibliography is weighted in favour of the socio-economic perspective of the text. For certain well-published authors such as Fernand Ouellet, Jean-Pierre Wallot, and others, only their most important works have been cited. The most extensive bibliography of Quebec history is Paul Aubin and Louise-Marie Coté's six-volume *Bibliographie de l'histoire du Québec et du Canada/Bibliography of the History of Quebec and Canada* (Québec: Institut québécois de recherche sur la culture, 1981–1987). Two recent bibliographies are of particular interest: Jacques Rouillard, ed. *Guide d'histoire du Québec du régime français à nos jours: bibliographie commentée* (Montréal: Meridien, 1992); and for Montreal, Joanne Burgess, Louise Dechêne, Paul-André Linteau, and Jean-Claude Robert, *Clés pour l'histoire de Montréal: bibliographie* (Montréal: Boréal Express, 1992). Also of importance both for their articles and for their bibliographical material are the *Revue d'histoire de l'Amérique française*, *Histoire sociale/Social History*, *Recherches sociographiques*, *Recherches amérindiennes au Québec*, *Labour/Le Travail*, and the *Urban History Review/ Revue d'histoire urbaine*. For a review of the state of Quebec historiography in the early 1990s, including criticism of the first edition of this work, see Ronald Rudin, Revisionism and the Search for a Normal Society: A Critique of Recent Quebec Historical Writing. *Canadian Historical Review* 73, 1 (March 1992): 30–61.

Abella, Irving. 1977. Portrait of a Jewish Professional Revolutionary: The Recollections of Joshua Gershman. *Labour/Le Travailleur* 2: 185–213.

Akenson, Donald. 1984. *The Irish in Ontario. A Study in Rural History*. Kingston and Montreal: McGill-Queen's University Press.

Allaire, Gratien. 1982. Les engagés de la fourrure, 1701–1745: une étude de leur motivation. Ph.D. diss., Concordia University, Montréal.

———. 1987. Officiers et marchands: les sociétés de commerce des fourrures, 1715–1760. *Revue d'histoire de l'Amérique française* 40 (3, hiver): 409–28.

Anctil, Pierre et Gary Caldwell. 1984. *Juifs et réalités juives au Québec*. Toronto: Gage.

Armstrong, Christopher and H.V. Nelles. 1986. *Monopoly's Moment: The Organization and Regulation of Canadian Utilities, 1830–1930*. Philadelphia: Temple University Press.

Armstrong, Robert. 1984. *Structure and Change: An Economic History of Quebec*. Toronto: Gage.

Association Générale des Etudiants de l'Université Laval. 1962. *Le Canada, Experience ratée . . . ou réussie?/The Canadian Experiment, Success or Failure?* Québec: Les Presses de l'Université Laval.

Audet, Louis-Philippe et Armand Gauthier. 1969. *Le système scolaire du Québec*. 2 vols. Montréal: Beauchemin.

Audet, Pierre. 1975. Apprenticeship in Early 19th Century Montreal, 1790–1812. M.A. thesis, Concordia University, Montreal.

Auger, Geneviève et Raymond Lamothe. 1982. *De la poêle à frire à la ligne de feu: la vie quotidienne des Québécoises pendant la guerre '39–45*. Montréal: Boréal Express.

Axtell, James. 1985. *The Invasion Within. The Contest of Cultures in Colonial North America*. New York: Oxford.

Baillargeon, Denyse. 1991. *Ménagères au temps de la crise*. Montréal: Les éditions du remue-ménage.

Baribeau, Claude. 1983. *Le seigneurie de la Petite-Nation, 1801–1854: le rôle économique et social du seigneur*. Hull: Asticou.

Barry, Francine. 1980. *Le travail de la femme au Québec: l'évolution de 1940 à 1970*. Québec: Les presses de l'Université du Québec.

Bates, Réal. 1986. Les conceptions prénuptiales dans la vallée du Saint-Laurent avant 1725. *Revue d'histoire de l'Amérique française* 40 (2, automne): 253–72.

Beauchamp, Claude. 1988. *Agropur*. Montréal: Boréal Express.

Bédard, Hélène. 1988. *Les Montagnais et la réserve de Betsiamites: 1850–1900*. Québec: Institut québécois de recherche sur la culture.

Behiels, Michael. 1982. The Bloc Populaire and the Origins of French-Canadian Nationalism, 1942–48. *Canadian Historical Review* 62 (4, December): 487–512.

———. 1985. *Prelude to Quebec's Quiet Revolution: Liberalism versus Neo-Nationalism, 1945–1960*. Kingston and Montreal: McGill-Queen's University Press.

———, ed. 1987. *Quebec since 1945: Selected Readings*. Toronto: Copp Clark Pitman.

———. 1989. Father Georges-Henri Lévesque and the Introduction of Social Sciences at Laval, 1938–55. In *Youth, University and Canadian Society: Essays in the Social History of Higher Education*, edited by Paul Axelrod and John Reid, 320–42. Kingston and Montreal: McGill Queen's University Press.

Bélanger, Jules, Marc Desjardins, et Yves Frenette. 1981. *Histoire de la Gaspésie*. Montréal: Boréal Express.

Bélanger, Réal. 1983. *Alfred Sévigny et les conservateurs fédéraux (1902–1918)*. Québec: Les Presses de l'Université Laval.

———. 1986. *Wilfrid Laurier. Quand la politique devient passion*. Québec: Les Presses de l'Université Laval.

Bélanger, Yves et Pierre Fournier. 1987. *L'entreprise québécoise: développement historique et dynamique contemporaine*. Montréal: Hurtubise HMH.

Belmessous, Saliha. 1990. La vision de l'autochtone canadien dans la correspondance officielle des gouverneurs-généraux de la Nouvelle-France, 1725–1753. M.A. thesis, Université de Lyon III, Lyon.

Bercuson, David J. and Barry Cooper. 1991. *Deconfederation: Canada without Quebec*. Toronto: Key Porter.

Bernard, André. 1977. *La politique au Canada et au Québec*. Sillery: Les Presses de l'Université du Québec.

Bernard, Jean-Paul. 1971. *Les Rouges: libéralisme, nationalisme et anticlericalisme au milieu de XIXe siècle*. Montréal: Les Presses de l'Université du Québec.

———. 1983. *Les rébellions de 1837–1838*. Montréal: Boréal Express.

Bernard, Jean-Paul, Paul-André Linteau, et Jean-Claude Robert. 1976. La structure professionnelle de Montréal en 1825. *Revue d'histoire de l'Amérique française* 30 (3, décembre): 383–415.

Bernier, Gérald et Robert Boily. 1986. *Le Québec en chiffres de 1850 à nos jours*. Montréal: Association canadienne-française pour l'avancement des sciences.

Bernier, Jacques. 1989. *La médecine au Québec: naissance et évolution d'une profession*. Québec: Les Presses de l'Université Laval.

Bilson, Geoffrey. 1980. *A Darkened House: Cholera in Nineteenth-Century Canada*. Toronto: University of Toronto Press.

Bischoff, Peter. 1990. Travelling the country "round": migrations et syndicalisme chez les mouleurs de l'Ontario et du Québec, membres de l'Iron Molders Union of North America, 1860 à 1892. *Journal of the Canadian Historical Association/Revue de la Société historique du Canada*, new series 1: 37–72.

Bischoff, Peter. 1992. Tensions et solidarité: la formation des traditions chez les mouleurs de Montréal, Hamilton et Toronto, 1851 à 1893. Ph.D diss., Université de Montréal, Montréal.

Bluteau, M-A., J-P. Charland, M. Thivierge, et N. Thivierge. 1980. *Les cordonniers, artisans du cuir*. Montréal/Ottawa: Boréal Express/Musée national de l'Homme.

Boismenu, Gérard. 1981. *Le Duplessisme: politique économique et rapports de force, 1944–1960*. Montréal: Les Presses de l'Université de Montréal.

Bonville, Jean de. 1989. *La Presse québécoise de 1884–1914. Genèse d'un media de masse*. Québec: Les Presses de l'Université Laval.

Bouchard, Gérard. 1977. Family Structures and Geographic Mobility of Laterrière, 1851–1935. *Journal of Family History* 2 (4, winter): 350–69.

———. 1991. Sur un démarrage raté: industrie laitière et co-intégration au Saguenay (1880–1940). *Revue d'histoire de l'Amérique française* 45 (1, été): 73–100.

————. 1992. Transmission of Family Property and the Cycle of Quebec Rural Society from the Seventeenth to the Twentieth Century. In *Canadian Family History: Selected Readings*, edited by Bettina Bradbury, 112–34. Toronto: Copp Clark Pitman.

Bourgault, Pierre. 1989. *Moi, je m'en souviens*. Montréal: Stanké.

Bradbury, Bettina. 1979. The Family Economy and Work in an Industrializing City: Montreal in the 1870s. Canadian Historical Association *Historical Papers*, 71–96.

————. 1982. The Fragmented Family: Family Strategies in the Face of Death, Illness and Poverty, Montreal, 1860–1885. In *Childhood and Family in Canadian History*, edited by Joy Parr, 109–28. Toronto: McClelland and Stewart.

————. 1984a. The Working Class Family Economy: Montreal, 1861–1881. Ph.D diss., Concordia University, Montreal.

————. 1984b. Women and Wage Labour in a Period of Transition: Montreal, 1861–81. *Histoire sociale/Social History* 17 (33, May): 115–32.

————. 1984c. Pigs, Cows and Boarders: Non-wage Forms of Survival among Montreal Families, 1861–91. *Labour/Le Travail* 14 (fall): 9–48.

————. 1989. Surviving as a Widow in 19th-Century Montreal. *Urban History Review* 17 (3, February): 148–61.

————. 1990. Devenir majeure, La lente conquête des droits. *Cap-aux-diaments* 21 (printemps): 35–38.

————, ed. 1992. *Canadian Family History: Selected Readings*. Toronto: Copp Clark Pitman.

Brandt, Gail Cuthbert. 1981. Weaving It Together: Life Cycle and the Industrial Experience of Female Cotton Workers in Quebec, 1910–1950. *Labour/Le Travail* 7 (spring): 113–25.

Brière, Jean-François. 1983. Pêche et politique à Terre-Neuve au XVIIIe siècle: la France véritable gagnante du traité d'Utrecht. *Canadian Historical Review* 64 (2, été): 168–87.

————. 1986. Le commerce triangulaire entre les ports Terre-Neuviers français, les pêcheries d'Amérique du Nord et Marseille au 18e siècle: nouvelles perspectives. *Revue d'histoire de l'Amérique française* 40 (2, automne): 193–214.

————. 1990. *La pêche française en Amérique du nord au XVIIe siècle*. Montréal: Fides.

Brierley, John. 1968. Quebec's Civil Law Codification Viewed and Reviewed. *McGill Law Journal* 14: 521–89.

Brunelle, Dorval et Pierre Drouilly. 1986. La structure socio-professionnelle de la main d'oeuvre. In *Le Québec en textes*. 2e éd., eds. Gérard Boismenu, Laurent Mailhot, et Jacques Rouillard. Montréal: Boréal Express.

Burgess, Joanne. 1977. L'industrie de la chaussure à Montréal: 1840–1870—le passage de l'artisanat à la fabrique. *Revue d'histoire de l'Amérique française* 31 (2, septembre): 187–210.

———. 1986. Work, Family, and Community: Montreal Leather Craftsmen, 1790–1831. Ph.D. diss., Université du Québec à Montréal, Montréal.

———. 1988. The Growth of a Craft Labour Force: Montréal Leather Artisans, 1815–1831. Canadian Historical Association *Historical Papers*, 48–62.

Cairns, John W. 1987. Employment in the Civil Code of Lower Canada: Tradition and Political Economy in Legal Classification and Reform. *McGill Law Journal* 32 (3, July): 673–711.

Caldwell, Gary and Eric Waddell. 1982. *The English of Québec: From Majority to Minority Status*. Québec: Institut québécois de recherche sur la culture.

Cameron, Christina. 1989. *Charles Baillargé: Architect and Engineer*. Kingston and Montreal: McGill-Queen's University Press.

Cameron, Elspeth. 1985. *Irving Layton: A Portrait*. Toronto: Stoddart.

Campbell, Robert M. and Leslie A. Pal. 1989. *The Real Worlds of Canadian Politics: Cases in Process and Policy*. Peterborough: Broadview Press.

Campeau, Lucien. 1975. *Les finances publiques de la Nouvelle-France sous les Cent-Associés, 1632–1665*. Montréal: Bellarmin.

———. 1987. *La mission des Jésuites chez les Hurons, 1634–1650*. Montréal: Bellarmin.

Canada. 1940. *Report of the Royal Commission on Dominion-Provincial Relations/Rapport de la Commission royale des relations entre le Dominion et les provinces. (Rowell-Sirois Report.)* 3 vols. Ottawa.

———. 1966, *Report of the Royal Commission on Bilingualism and Biculturalism*. Ottawa: Queen's Printer.

———. 1968. (Bird Commission). *Report of the Royal Commission on the Status of Women/Rapport de la Commission royale d'enquête sur la situation de la femme au Canada*. Ottawa: Queen's Printer.

———. 1980. *Québec, Canada: A New Deal*.

Canada Year Book. 1990. Ottawa: Statistics Canada.

Cardin, Jean-François. 1988. *La crise d'octobre 1970 et le mouvement syndical québécois*. Montréal: RCHTQ.

Cardin, Martine. 1987. Jean Leroux dit Provençal, marchand à Sorel au XVIIIe siècle. M.A. thesis, Université de Montréal, Montréal.

Careless, J.M.S. 1967. *The Union of the Canadas: The Growth of Canadian Institutions 1841–1857*. Toronto: McClelland and Stewart.

Casgrain, Thérèse. 1971. *Une femme chez les hommes*. Montréal: Editions du Jour.

Caulier, Brigitte. 1986. Les confréries de dévotion à Montréal du 17e au 19e siècles. Ph.D. diss., Université de Montréal, Montréal.

Cellard, André. 1991. *Histoire de la folie au Québec de 1600 à 1850*. Montréal: Boréal Express.

Chabot, Richard. 1975. *Le curé de campagne et la contestation locale au Québec de 1791 aux troubles de 1837–38*. Montréal: Hurtubise HMH.

Champagne, Lucie et Micheline Dumont. 1990. Le financement d'un seminaire diocesain: le Seminaire de Sherbrooke, 1915–1950. Comparison avec le financement des pensionnats de religieuses. *Historical Studies in Education/Revue d'histoire de l'Education* 2 (automne): 339–52.

Chapdelaine, Claude. 1989. *Le site Mandeville à Tracy. Variabilité culturelle des Iroquoiens du Saint-Laurent*. Montréal: Recherches amérindiennes au Québec.

Charbonneau, Hubert, ed. 1973. *La population du Québec: études rétrospectives*. Montréal: Boréal Express.

———. 1975. *Vie et mort de nos ancêtres*. Montréal: Les Presses de l'Université de Montréal.

———. 1985. Colonisation, climat et âge au baptême des Canadiens au XVIIe siècle. *Revue d'histoire de l'Amérique française* 38 (3, hiver): 341–56.

———, et al. 1987. *Naissance d'une population. Les Français établis au Canada au XVIIe siècle*. Montréal: Les Presses de l'Université de Montréal.

Charland, Jean-Pierre. 1982. *Histoire de l'enseignement technique et professionnel*. Québec: Institut québécois de recherche sur la culture.

———. 1987. Le réseau d'enseignement public bas-canadien, 1841–1867: une institution de l'Etat libéral. *Revue d'histoire de l'Amérique française* 40 (4, printemps): 505–36.

———. 1990. *Les pâtes et papiers au Québec, 1880–1980: technologies, travail et travailleurs*. Québec: Institut québécois de recherche sur la culture.

Charpentier, Alfred. 1971. *Les mémoires d'Alfred Charpentier*. Québec: Les Presses de l'Université Laval.

Chartrand, Luc, Raymond Duchesne, et Yves Gingras. 1987. *Histoire des sciences au Québec*. Montréal: Boréal Express.

Clement, Wallace. 1975. *The Canadian Corporate Elite: An Analysis of Economic Power*. Toronto: McClelland and Stewart.

Clermont, Norman. 1974. L'hiver et les indiens nomades du Québec à la fin de la préhistoire. *Revue de Géographie de Montréal* 29: 447–52.

Cliche, Marie-Aimée. 1978. Les attitudes devant la mort d'après les clauses testamentaires dans le gouvernement de Québec sous le Régime français. *Revue d'histoire de l'Amérique française* 32 (1, juin): 57–94.

———. 1985. La religion populaire dans le gouvernement de Québec sous le Régime français d'après la pratique des actes surérogataires. Ph.D. diss., Université Laval, Québec.

———. 1988. *Les pratiques de dévotion en Nouvelle-France.* Québec: Les Presses de l'Université Laval.

———. 1992. Unwed Mothers, Families and Society during the French Régime. In *Canadian Family History: Selected Readings,* edited by Bettina Bradbury, 33–65. Toronto: Copp Clark Pitman.

Clio Collective. 1992. *Quebec Women: A History.* Toronto: Women's Press.

Clippingdale, Richard. 1979. *Laurier: His Life and World.* Toronto: McGraw-Hill Ryerson.

Coates, Colin M. 1992. The Boundaries of Rural Society in Early Quebec: Batiscan and Sainte-Anne-de-la-Pérade to 1825. Ph.D. diss., York University, Toronto.

Codignola, Luca. 1989. The Rome-Paris-Quebec Connection in an Age of Revolutions, 1760–1820. In *Le Canada et la Révolution française,* edited by Pierre Boulle and Richard Lebrun, 115–32. Montréal: Centre interuniversitaires d'études européennes.

Cohen, Marjorie Griffin. 1984. The Decline of Women in Canadian Dairying. *Histoire sociale/Social History* 17 (34, November): 307–34.

———. 1986. *Women's Work, Markets and Economic Development in Nineteenth-Century Ontario.* Toronto: University of Toronto Press.

Cohen, Yolande. 1990. *Femmes de parole. L'histoire des cercles de fermières au Québec.* Montréal: Le Jour.

Cohen, Yolande et Michèle Dagenais. 1987. Le métier d'infirmière: savoirs féminins et reconnaissance professionnelle. *Revue d'histoire de l'Amérique française* 41 (2, automne): 205–32.

Coleman, William D. 1984. *The Independence Movement in Quebec 1945–1980.* Toronto: University of Toronto Press.

Collectif Clio. 1982. *L'histoire des femmes au Québec depuis quatre siècles.* Montréal: Les Quinze.

Collin, Jean-Pierre. 1987. Crise du logement et action catholique à Montréal, 1940–1960. *Revue d'histoire de l'Amérique française* 41 (2, automne): 179–204.

Collins, Anne. 1988. *In the Sleep Room: The Story of the CIA Brainwashing Experiments in Canada.* Toronto: Lester and Orpen Dennys.

Comeau, Paul-André. 1982. *Le Bloc Populaire 1942–1948*. Montréal: Québec/Amérique.

Comeau, Robert, ed. 1989. *Jean Lesage et l'éveil d'une nation*. Québec: Les Presses de l'Université du Québec.

Comeau, Robert et Bernard Dionne. 1980. *Les communistes au Québec (1936–1956)*. Montréal: Les Presses de l'Unité.

Cook, Ramsay. 1969. *French-Canadian Nationalism: An Anthology*. Toronto: Macmillan.

———. 1971. *The Maple Leaf Forever*. Toronto: Macmillan.

Copp, Terry. 1974. *The Anatomy of Poverty: The Condition of the Working Class in Montreal 1897–1929*. Toronto: McClelland and Stewart.

Courville, Serge. 1978. Un monde rural en mutation: le Bas-Canada dans la première moitié du XIXe siècle. *Histoire sociale/Social History* 20 (40 novembre): 237–58.

———. 1980. La rente agricole au Bas-Canada: éléments d'une reflexion géographique. *Cahiers de géographie du Québec* 24 (62–63, septembre-décembre): 193–223.

———. 1984. Esquisse du développement villageois au Québec: le cas de l'aire seigneuriale entre 1760 et 1854. *Cahiers de géographie du Québec* 28 (73–74, avril-septembre): 9–46.

———. 1990. *Entre ville et campagne*. Québec: Les Presses de l'Université Laval.

Courville, Serge and Normand Séguin. 1989. *Rural Life in Nineteenth-Century Quebec*. Ottawa: Canadian Historical Association.

Courville, Serge, Jean-Claude Robert, et Normand Séguin. 1990. Population et espace rural au Bas-Canada: l'exemple de l'axe laurentien dans la première moitié du XIX siècle. *Revue d'histoire de l'Amérique française* 44 (2, automne): 243–62.

Couture, André. 1989. Elements for a Social History of Television: Radio-Canada and Quebec Society, 1952–1960. M.A. thesis, McGill University, Montreal.

Couture, Claude. 1991. *Le mythe de la modernisation du Québec*. Montréal: Méridien.

Craig, Béatrice. 1991. La transmission des patrimoines fonciers dans le Haut-Saint-Jean au XIX siècle. *Revue d'histoire de l'Amérique française* 45 (2, automne): 207–28.

Craven, Paul and Tom Traves. 1983. Canadian Railways as Manufacturers, 1850–1880. Canadian Historical Association *Historical Papers*, 254–81.

Creighton, Donald. 1956. *The Empire of the St. Lawrence*. Toronto: Macmillan.

Cross, Michael. 1973. The Shiners' War. *Canadian Historical Review* 54 (1, March): 1–26.

Cross, Suzanne. 1973. The Neglected Majority: The Changing Role of Women in Nineteenth Century Montreal. *Histoire sociale/Social History* 6 (12, November): 202–23.

Crowley, Terence. "Thunder gusts": Popular Disturbances in Early French Canada. Canadian Historical Association *Historical Papers*, 11–32.

Dagenais, Michèle. 1989. Itineraires professionnels masculins et féminins en milieu bancaire: le cas de la Banque de Hochelaga, 1900–1929. *Labour/Le Travail* 24 (automne): 45–68.

Dales, John H. 1957. *Hydroelectricity and Industrial Development. Quebec 1898–1940.* Cambridge: Harvard University Press.

Danylewycz, Marta. 1987. *Taking the Veil: An Alternative to Marriage, Motherhood and Spinsterhood in Quebec, 1840–1920.* Toronto: McClelland and Stewart.

Danylewycz, Marta and Alison Prentice. 1986. Teachers' Work: Changing Patterns and Perceptions in the Emerging School Systems of Nineteenth and Early Twentieth Century Central Canada. *Labour/Le Travail* 17 (spring): 59–82.

Davis, Ralph. 1973. *The Rise of the Atlantic Economies.* London: Wiedenfeld and Nicolson.

Dechêne, Louise. 1971. L'évolution du régime seigneurial au Canada: le cas de Montréal aux XVIIe et XVIIIe siècles. *Recherches sociographiques* 12 (2, mai–août): 143–83.

———. 1976. William Price. In *Dictionary of Canadian Biography*, vol. 9, 638–43. Toronto: University of Toronto Press.

———. 1981. La rente du faubourg Saint-Roch à Québec, 1750–1850. *Revue d'histoire de l'Amérique française* 34 (4, mars): 569–96.

———. 1986. Observations sur l'agriculture du Bas-Canada au début du XIXe siècle. In *Evolution et éclatement du monde rural, France-Québec, XVIIe–XXe siècles*, edited by Joseph Goy and Jean-Pierre Wallot, 189–202. Montréal et Paris: Les Presses de l'Université de Montréal et l'Ecole des Hautes Etudes en Sciences Sociales.

———. 1992. *Habitants and Merchants in Seventeenth-Century Montreal.* Kingston and Montreal: McGill-Queen's University Press.

Dechêne, Louise et Jean-Claude Robert. 1979. Le choléra dans le Bas-Canada, mesure des inégalités devant la mort. In *Les grandes mortalités*, edited by Hubert Charbonneau and André Larose, 229–57. Liège: Ordena.

Delorme, Marie-Josée. 1991. Les rapports entre le pensionnat Sainte-Marie et la commission scolaire de Yamaskaville, 1930–1960. *Historical Studies in Education* 2 (1, spring): 49–74.

DeLottinville, Peter. 1981–1982. Joe Beef of Montreal: Working Class Culture and the Tavern, 1869–89. *Labour/Le Travail* 8–9: 9–40.

Denison, Merrill. 1955. *The Barley and the Stream: The Molson Story.* Toronto: McClelland and Stewart.

Dépatie, Sylvie. 1986. La structure agraire au Canada: le cas de l'île Jésus au XVIIIe siècle. Canadian Historical Association *Communications historiques,* 56–85.

————. 1990. La transmission du patrimoine dans les terroirs en expansion: un exemple canadien au XVIIIe siècle. *Revue d'histoire de l'Amérique française* 44 (2, automne): 171–98.

Dépatie, Sylvie, Christian Dessureault et Mario Lalancette. 1987. *Contributions à l'étude du régime seigneurial canadien.* Montréal: Hurtubise HMH.

Desbarats, Catherine. 1992. Agriculture within the Seigneurial Régime of Eighteenth-Century Canada: Some Thoughts on the Recent Literature. *Canadian Historical Review* 73 (1, March): 1–29.

Desbarats, Peter. 1977. *René: A Canadian in Search of a Country.* Toronto: Seal Books.

Desrosiers, Claude. 1984. L'analyse du livre de comptes (1794–1797) du marchand général Joseph Cartier: premiers résultats d'un traitement informatisé. M.A. thesis, Université de Montréal, Montréal.

Dessaulles, Henriette. 1971. *Hopes and Dreams: The Diary of Henriette Dessaulles, 1874–1881.* Toronto: Hounslow Press.

Dessureault, Christian. 1986. Les fondements de la hierarchie sociale au sein de la paysannerie: le cas de Saint-Hyacinthe, 1760–1815. Ph.D. diss., Université de Montréal, Montréal.

————. 1987. L'égalitarianisme paysan dans l'ancienne société rurale de la vallée du St-Laurent: éléments pour une re-interprétation. *Revue d'histoire de l'Amérique française* 40 (3, hiver): 373–408.

Dessureault, Christian and John Dickinson. 1992. Farm Implements and Husbandry in Colonial Quebec, 1740–1834. In *New England/New France, 1600–1850,* edited by Peter Benes, 110–21. Boston: Boston University.

Dever, Alan. 1976. Economic Development and the Lower Canadian Assembly, 1828–40. M.A. thesis, McGill University, Montreal.

De Vries, Jan. 1976. *The Economy of Europe in an Age of Crisis, 1600–1750.* Cambridge: Cambridge University Press.

Dickason, Olive Patricia. 1984. *The Myth of the Savage and the Beginnings of French Colonialism in the Americas.* Edmonton: University of Alberta Press.

Dickinson, John A. 1974a. Un aperçu de la vie culturelle en Nouvelle-France: l'examen de trois bibliothèques privées. *Revue de l'Université d'Ottawa* 44 (4, octobre-décembre): 453–66.

————. 1974b. La justice seigneuriale en Nouvelle-France: le cas de Notre-Dame-des-Anges. *Revue d'histoire de l'Amérique française* 28 (3, décembre): 323–46.

————. 1982a. La guerre iroquoise et la mortalité en Nouvelle-France, 1608–1666. *Revue d'histoire de l'Amérique française* 36 (1, juin): 31–54.

————. 1982b. *Justice et justiciables. La procédure civile à la Prévôté de Québec, 1667–1759.* Québec: Les Presses de l'Université Laval.

————. 1986a. Les Amérindiens et les débuts de la Nouvelle-France. In *Canada Ieri e Oggi*, 87–108. Bari: Schena editore.

————. 1986b. La législation et les travailleurs québécois, 1894–1914. *Relations Industrielles* 41 (2, juin): 357–80.

————. 1987. Réflexions sur la police en Nouvelle-France. *McGill Law Review* 32 (3, July): 496–522.

————. 1992. Law in New France. Canadian Legal History Project, Working Paper, Faculty of Law, University of Manitoba, Winnipeg.

Drolet, Antonio. 1965. *Les bibliothèques canadiennes, 1604–1960.* Ottawa: Cercle du livre de France.

Drummond, Anne. 1990. Gender, Profession, and Principals: The Teachers of Quebec Protestant Academies, 1875–1900. *Historical Studies in Education* 2 (1, spring): 59–72.

Dumas, Evelyn. 1975. *The Bitter Thirties in Québec.* Montreal: Black Rose Books.

Dumont, Fernand. 1971. *The Vigil of Quebec.* Toronto: University of Toronto Press.

————, ed. 1991. La société québécoise après 30 ans de changement. Québec: Institut québécois de recherches sur la culture.

Dumont, Fernand et Jean Hamelin. 1981. *Les idéologies au Canada français, 1939–1974.* Québec: Les Presses de l'Université Laval.

Dumont, Micheline. 1980. Des garderies au XIX siècle: les salles d'asile des Soeurs Grises à Montréal. *Revue d'histoire de l'Amérique française* 34 (1, juin): 127–56.

Dumont, Micheline et Nadia Fahmy-Eid. 1986. *Les couventines: l'éducation des filles au Québec dans les congrégations religieuses enseignantes 1840–1960.* Montréal: Boréal Express.

————. 1991. La pointe de l'iceberg: l'histoire de l'éducation et l'histoire de l'éducation des filles au Québec. *Historical Studies in Education* 3 (2, fall): 211–36.

Durocher, René et Michèle Jean. 1971. Duplessis et la Commission royale d'enquête sur les problèmes constitutionnels. *Revue d'histoire de l'Amérique française* 25 (3, décembre): 337–64.

Easterbrook, W.T. and M.H. Watkins. 1967. *Approaches to Canadian Economic History*. Toronto: McClelland and Stewart.

Eccles, William John. 1964. *Canada under Louis XIV*. Toronto: McClelland and Stewart.

————. 1969. *The Canadian Frontier*. New York: Holt, Rinehart and Winston.

————. 1971. The Social, Economic and Political Significance of the Military Establishment in New France. *Canadian Historical Review* 52 (1, March): 1–22.

————. 1979. A Belated Review of Harold Adams Innis's *The Fur Trade in Canada*. *Canadian Historical Review* 60 (4, December): 419–41.

Education Committees of the Confédération des syndicats nationaux and Centrale de l'enseignement du Québec. 1987. *The History of the Labour Movement in Québec*. Montreal: Black Rose Books.

L'Eglise de Montréal. See Litalien, Roland, ed.

Fahmy-Eid, Nadia. 1978. *Le clergé et le pouvoir politique au Québec: une analyse de l'idéologie ultramontaine au milieu du XIX siècle*. Montréal: Hurtubise HMH.

Fahmy-Eid, Nadia et Johanne Collin. 1989. Savoir et pouvoir dans l'univers des disciplines paramédicales: la formation en physiothérapie et en diététique à l'Université McGill, 1940–1970. *Histoire sociale/Social History* 22 (43, mai): 35–64.

Fahmy-Eid, Nadia et Micheline Dumont. 1983. *Maîtresses de maison, maîtresses d'école: femmes, famille et éducation dans l'histoire du Québec*. Montréal: Boréal Express.

————. 1986. See Dumont, Micheline et Nadia Fahmy-Eid.

Falardeau, Jean-Charles, ed. 1968. *Léon Gérin et l'habitant de Saint-Justin*. Montréal: Les Presses de l'Université de Montréal. See also Gérin, Léon. 1898.

Faucher, Albert. 1970. *Histoire économique et unité canadienne*. Montréal: Fides.

Fecteau, Jean-Marie. 1985. Régulation sociale et répression de la déviance au Bas-Canada au tournant du 19e siècle (1791–1815). *Revue d'histoire de l'Amérique française* 38 (4, printemps): 499–522.

————. 1986. Prolégomènes à une étude historique des rapports entre l'Etat et le droit dans la société québécoise, de la fin du XVIIIe siècle à la crise de 1929. *Sociologie et sociétés* 18 (1, avril): 129–38.

————. 1987. Mesures d'exception et règle de droit: les conditions d'application de la loi martiale au Québec lors des rébellions de 1837–1838. *McGill Law Journal* 32 (3, July): 465–95.

————. 1989. *Un nouvel ordre des choses: la pauvreté, le crime, l'Etat au Québec, de la fin du XVIIIe siècle à 1840*. Outremont: VLB Editeur.

Fédération des francophones hors Québec. 1978. *The Heirs of Lord Durham. Manifesto of a Vanishing People*. Toronto: Burns and MacEachern.

Ferland, Jacques. 1985. Evolution des rapports sociaux dans l'industrie canadienne du cuir au tournant du 20e siècle. Ph.D. diss., Université McGill, Montréal.

————. 1987. Syndicalisme "parcellaire" et syndicalisme "collectif": une interprétation socio-technique des conflits ouvriers dans deux industries québécoises (1880–1914). *Labour/Le Travail* 19 (spring): 49–88.

————. 1989. "In Search of the Unbound Promethia": A Comparative View of Women's Activism in Two Quebec Industries, 1869–1908. *Labour/Le Travail* 24 (autumn): 11–45.

Ferretti, Lucia. 1985. Mariage et cadre de vie familiale dans une paroisse ouvrière montréalaise: Sainte-Brigide. *Revue d'histoire de l'Amérique française* 39 (2, automne): 233–51.

————. 1992. *Entre voisins. La société paroissiale en milieu urbain: Saint-Pierre-Apôtre de Montréal, 1848–1930*. Montréal: Boréal Express.

Filteau, Gérard. 1975. *Histoire des patriotes*. Montréal: L'Aurore.

Francis, Daniel and Toby Morantz. 1983. *Partners in Furs. A History of the Fur Trade in Eastern James Bay, 1600–1870*. Kingston and Montreal: McGill-Queen's University Press.

Frégault, Guy. 1964. *Canadian Society in the French Regime*. Historical Booklet no. 3. Ottawa: Canadian Historical Association.

Frenette, Yves. 1988. La genèse d'une communauté canadienne-française en Nouvelle-Angleterre, Lewiston, Maine, 1800–1880. Ph.D. diss., Université Laval, Québec.

Fyson, Donald. 1989. Eating in the City: Diet and Provisioning in Early Nineteenth-Century Montreal. M.A. thesis, McGill University, Montreal.

Gadoury, Lorraine. 1988. Le comportement démographique et les alliances de la noblesse de la Nouvelle-France. Ph.D. diss., Université de Montréal, Montréal.

Gaffield, Chad. 1987. *Language, Schooling, and Cultural Conflict: The Origins of the French-language Controversy in Ontario.* Kingston and Montreal: McGill-Queen's University Press.

———. 1991. The New Regional History: Rethinking the History of the Outaouais. *Journal of Canadian Studies* 26 (1, spring): 64–81.

Gagnon, Alain-G. 1984. *Quebec: State and Society.* Toronto: Methuen.

Gagnon, Alain-G. and Mary Beth Montcalm. 1990. *Quebec: Beyond the Quiet Revolution.* Scarborough: Nelson.

Gagnon, France. 1988. Parenté et migration: le cas des Canadiens français à Montréal entre 1845 et 1875. Canadian Historical Association *Communications historiques*, 63–85.

Gagnon, France et Yves Otis. 1991. Les "enfants dispersés" de Mascouche. *Histoire sociale/Social History* 24 (48, novembre): 335–60.

Gagnon, Serge. 1966. Pour une conscience historique de la révolution québécoise. *Cité Libre* 16 (83): 4–16.

———. 1982. *Quebec and its Historians: 1840–1920.* Montreal: Harvest House.

———. 1987. *Mourir hier et aujourd'hui: de la mort chrétienne dans la campagne québécoise au XIXe siècle à la mort technisée dans la cité sans Dieu.* Québec: Les Presses de l'Université Laval.

———. 1990. *Plaisir d'amour et crainte de Dieu. Sexualité et confession au Bas-Canada.* Sainte-Foy: Les Presses de l'Université Laval.

Gagnon, Serge et René Hardy, eds. 1979. *L'église et le village au Québec 1850–1930.* Montréal: Leméac.

Gagnon, Serge et Louise Lebel-Gagnon. 1983. Le milieu d'origine du clergé québécois 1775–1840: mythes et réalités. *Revue d'histoire de l'Amérique française* 37 (3, décembre): 373–98.

Galarneau, Claude. 1978. *Les collèges classiques au Canada français.* Montréal: Fides.

Gauvin, Lise et Gaston Miron. 1989. *Ecrivains contemporains du Québec depuis 1950.* Paris: Seghers.

Gérin, Léon. 1898. L'Habitant de Saint-Justin. Mémoires de la Société royale du Canada, 2e série, 4 (mai): 139–216.

Germain, Annick. 1984. *Les mouvements de réforme urbaine à Montréal au tournant du siècle.* Montréal: Centre d'information et d'aide à la recherche, Département de sociologie, Université de Montréal.

Gervais, Gaetan. 1979. L'expansion du réseau ferroviaire québécois, 1875–1895. Ph.D. diss., Université d'Ottawa, Ottawa.

Gillett, Margaret. 1981. *We Walked Very Warily: A History of Women at McGill*. Montreal: Eden Press.

Gossage, Peter. 1983. Abandoned Children in Nineteenth-Century Montreal. M.A. thesis, McGill University, Montreal.

———. 1991a. Family and Population in a Manufacturing Town: Saint-Hyacinthe, 1854–1914. Ph.D. diss., Université du Québec à Montréal, Montréal.

———. 1991b. Family Formation and Age at Marriage in Saint-Hyacinthe, Quebec, 1854–1891. *Histoire sociale/Social History* 24 (47, mai): 61–84.

Gould, Karen. 1990. *Writing in the Feminine: Feminism and Experimental Writing in Quebec*. Carbondale, Illinois: Southern Illinois University Press.

Gourd, Benoît-Beaudry. 1975. La colonisation et le peuplement du Témiskamingue et de l'Abitibi, 1880–1950: Aperçu historique. In *L'Abitibi et le Témiskamingue hier et aujourd'hui*, edited by Maurice Asselin and Benoît-Beaudry Gourd. Cahiers du département d'histoire et de géographie, no. 2. Rouyn: Collège du Nord-ouest.

Gournay, Isabelle. 1990. *Ernest Cormier and the Université de Montréal*. Montréal: Canadian Centre for Architecture.

Government of Canada. See Canada.

Goy, Joseph and Jean-Pierre Wallot, eds. 1986. *Evolution et éclatement du monde rural, France-Québec, XVIIe–XXe siècles*. Montréal et Paris: Les Presses de l'Université de Montréal et l'Ecole des Hautes Etudes en Sciences Sociales.

Grant, Hugh M. 1981. One Step Forward, Two Steps Back: Innis, Eccles, and the Canadian Fur Trade. *Canadian Historical Review* 62 (3, September): 304–22.

Greenwood, Murray. 1984. The Chartrand Murder Trial: Rebellion and Repression in Lower Canada, 1837–1839. *Criminal Justice History* 5: 129–59.

Greer, Allan. 1978. The Pattern of Literacy in Quebec, 1745–1899. *Histoire sociale/Social History* 11 (22, November): 295–335.

———. 1984. Rebels and Prisoners: The Canadian Insurrections of 1837–8. *Acadiensis* 14 (1, autumn): 137–45.

———. 1985. *Peasant, Lord and Merchant. Rural Society in Three Quebec Parishes, 1740–1840*. Toronto: University of Toronto Press.

———. 1991. La république des hommes: les Patriotes de 1837 face aux femmes. *Revue d'histoire de l'Amérique française* 44 (4, printemps): 507–28.

Greer, Allan, and Ian Radforth, *Colonial Leviathan: State Formation in Mid-Nineteenth-Century Canada*. Toronto: University of Toronto Press.

Griffiths, Naomi. 1973. *The Acadians: Creation of a People*. Toronto: McGraw-Hill Ryerson.

———. 1992. *The Contexts of Acadian History*. Kingston and Montreal: McGill-Queen's University Press.

Groulx, Lionel. 1970. *Michel Barrin de la Galissonière*. Toronto: University of Toronto Press.

Groupe de Recherche sur la Mauricie. 1985. *Shawinigan: Genèse d'une croissance industrielle au début du XXe siècle*. Trois-Rivières: Université du Québec à Trois-Rivières.

Guindon, Hubert. 1988. *Quebec Society: Tradition, Modernity, and Nationhood*. Toronto: University of Toronto Press.

Hamelin, Jean. 1984. *Histoire de catholicisme québécois: le XXe siècle*. tome 2, *De 1940 à nos jours*. Montréal: Boréal Express.

Hamelin, Jean et Nicole Gagnon. 1984. *Histoire de catholicisme québécois: le XXe siècle*. tome 1, *1898–1940*. Montréal: Boréal Express.

Hamelin, Jean et Yves Roby. 1971. *Histoire économique du Québec, 1851–1896*. Montréal: Fides.

Hamelin, Jean et Jean Provencher. 1976. *Histoire du Québec*. Toulouse: Privat.

Hanna, David. 1977. The New Town of Montreal: Creation of an Upper Middle Class Suburb on the Slope of Mount Royal in the Mid-Nineteenth Century. M.A. thesis, University of Toronto, Toronto.

———. 1986. Montreal: A City Built by Small Builders, 1867–1880. Ph.D. diss., McGill University, Montreal.

Hardy, Jean-Pierre. 1987. Quelques aspects du niveau de richesse et de la vie matérielle des artisans de Québec et de Montréal, 1740–1755. *Revue d'histoire de l'Amérique française* 40 (3, hiver): 339–72.

Hardy, Jean-Pierre et David-Thiery Ruddel. 1977. *Les apprentis artisans à Québec, 1660–1815*. Montréal: Les Presses de l'Université du Québec.

Hardy, René. 1980. *Les Zouaves*. Montréal: Boréal Express.

Hardy, René et Normand Séguin. 1984. *Forêt et société en Mauricie*. Montréal: Boréal Express.

Hare, John, Marc Lafrance, et David-Thiery Ruddel. 1987. *Histoire de la ville de Québec (1608–1871)*. Montréal: Boréal Express.

Harney, Robert F. 1979. Montreal's King of Italian Labour: A Case Study of Padronism. *Labour/Le Travailleur* 4: 56–84.

Harris, Richard Colebrook. 1979. Of Poverty and Helplessness in Petite Nation. In *Canadian History before Confederation*, edited by J. Bumsted, 329–54. Georgetown: Irwin Dorsey.

———. 1984. *The Seigneurial System in Early Canada*. Kingston and Montreal: McGill-Queen's University Press.

————, dir. 1987. *Historical Atlas of Canada*. vol. 1, *Origins to 1800*. Toronto: University of Toronto Press.

Harris, Richard Colebrook and John Warkentin. 1974. *Canada before Confederation*. New York: Oxford University Press.

Harvey, Fernand. 1980. *Le mouvement ouvrier au Québec*. Montréal: Boréal Express.

Harvey, Kathryn. 1991. "To Love, Honour and Obey": Wife-battering in Working-class Montreal, 1869–1879. M.A. thesis, Université de Montréal, Montreal.

Heap, Margaret. 1977. La grève des charretiers à Montréal, 1865. *Revue d'histoire de l'Amérique française* 31 (3, décembre): 371–95.

Heap, Ruby. 1985. Urbanisation et éducation: la centralisation scolaire à Montréal au début du XXe siècle. Canadian Historical Association *Communications historiques*, 132–55.

————. 1987. L'église, l'Etat et l'enseignement primaire public catholique au Québec, 1897–1920. Ph.D. diss., Université de Montréal, Montréal.

Heidenreich, Conrad. 1971. *Huronia. A History and Geography of the Huron Indians, 1600–1650*. Toronto: McClelland and Stewart.

Helly, Denise. 1987. *Les chinois à Montréal, 1877–1951*. Québec: Institut québécois de recherche sur la culture.

Helm, June, ed. 1981. *Handbook of North American Indians*. vol. 6, *Subarctic*. Washington: Smithsonian Institution.

Henripin, Jacques. 1954. *La population canadienne au début du XVIIIe siécle*. Paris: Institut national d'études démographiques.

Heron, Craig. 1989. *The Canadian Labour Movement: A Short History*. Toronto: Lorimer.

Historical Atlas of Canada. See Harris, Richard Colebrook (vol. 1); Kerr, Donald and Deryck W. Holdsworth (vol. 3).

Hoskins, Ralph. 1987. Original Acquisition of Land in Montreal by the Grand Trunk Railway of Canada. Department of Geography, McGill University, *Shared Spaces* (7).

Howes, David. 1987. From Polyjurality to Monojurality: The Transformation of Quebec Law, 1875–1929. *McGill Law Journal* 32 (3, July): 523–58.

Hudon, Christine. 1990. Les curés du Richelieu-Yamaska, 1790–1840. Recrutement, vie matérielle et action pastorale. M.A. thesis, Université de Montréal, Montréal.

Hughes, Everett C. 1943. *French Canada in Transition*. Chicago: University of Chicago Press.

Igartua, José. 1974a. The Merchants and Négociants of Montréal, 1750–1775: A Study in Socio-Economic History. Ph.D. diss., Ann Arbor: Michigan State University.

———. 1974b. A Change in Climate: The Conquest and the Marchands of Montreal. Canadian Historical Association *Historical Papers*, 115–34.

———. 1989. Worker Persistence, Hiring Policies, and the Depression in the Aluminum Sector: The Saguenay Region, Québec, 1925–1940. *Histoire sociale/Social History* 22 (43, mai): 9–34.

Igartua, José et Marine de Fréminville. 1983. Les origines des travailleurs de l'Alcan au Saguenay, 1925–1939. *Revue d'histoire de l'Amérique française* 37 (2): 291–308.

Innis, Harold. 1956. *The Fur Trade in Canada*. Toronto: University of Toronto Press.

Jaenen, Cornelius. 1976a. *Friend and Foe: Aspects of French-Indian Cultural Contact in the Sixteenth and Seventeenth Centuries*. Toronto: McClelland and Stewart.

———. 1976b. *The Role of the Church in New France*. Toronto: McGraw-Hill Ryerson.

James, William C. 1985. *A Fur Trader's Photographs. A.A. Chesterfield in the District of Ungava, 1901–4*. Kingston and Montreal: McGill-Queen's University Press.

Jaumain, Serge. 1987. Contribution à l'histoire comparée: les colporteurs belge et québécois au XIXe siècle. *Histoire sociale/Social History* 20 (39, mai): 49–78.

Jean, Dominique. 1988. Familles québécoises et politiques sociales touchant les enfants, de 1940 à 1960: obligation scolaire, allocations familiales, travail juvénile. Ph.D. diss., Université de Montréal, Montréal.

———. 1989. Le recul du travail des enfants au Québec entre 1940 et 1960: une explication des conflits entre les familles pauvres et l'Etat providence. *Labour/Le Travail* 24 (automne): 91–130.

———. 1992. Family Allowances and Family Autonomy: Quebec Families Encounter the Welfare State, 1945–1955. In *Canadian Family History: Selected Readings*, edited by Bettina Bradbury, 401–37. Toronto: Copp Clark Pitman.

Johnston, Wendy. 1992. L'école primaire supérieure et le high school public à Montréal de 1920 à 1945. Ph.D. diss., Université de Montréal, Montréal.

Jones, Richard. 1972. *Community in Crisis. French Canadian Nationalism in Perspective*. Toronto: McClelland and Stewart.

———. 1983. *Duplessis and the Union Nationale Administration*. Ottawa: Canadian Historical Association.

Joy, Richard. 1972. *Languages in Conflict*. Toronto: McClelland and Stewart.

Kenneally, Rhona. 1983. The Montreal Maternity Hospital, 1843–1926. M.A. thesis, McGill University, Montreal.

Kerr, Donald and Deryck W. Holdsworth, eds. 1990. *Historical Atlas of Canada*. vol. 3, *Addressing the Twentieth Century*. Toronto: University of Toronto Press.

Kesteman, Jean-Pierre. 1985. Une bourgeoisie et son espace: industrialisation et développement du capitalisme dans le district de Saint-François (Québec), 1823–1879. Ph.D. diss., Université du Québec à Montréal, Montréal.

Kolish, Evelyn. 1980. Changements dans le droit privé au Québec/Bas-Canada entre 1760 et 1840: attitudes et réactions des contemporains. Ph.D. diss., Université de Montréal, Montréal.

——— . 1981. Le conseil législatif et les bureaux d'enregistrement (1836). *Revue d'histoire de l'Amérique française* 35 (2, septembre): 217–30.

——— . 1987. Imprisonment for Debt in Lower Canada, 1791–1840. *McGill Law Journal* 32 (3, July): 602–35.

Krech III, Shepard. 1981. *Indians, Animals and the Fur Trade*. Athens: University of Georgia Press.

Lacasse, Roger. 1988. *Joseph-Armand Bombardier: le rêve d'un inventeur*. Montréal: Libre Expression.

Lacelle, Claudette. 1987. *Urban Domestic Servants in 19th-Century Canada*. Ottawa: Parks Canada.

Lachance, André. 1978. *La justice criminelle du roi au Canada au XVIIIe siècle. Tribunaux et officiers*. Québec: Les Presses de l'Université Laval.

——— . 1984. *Crimes et criminels en Nouvelle-France*. Montréal: Boréal Express.

——— . 1987. *La vie urbaine en Nouvelle-France*. Montréal: Boréal Express.

Lacoursière, Jacques et Jacques Mathieu. 1991. *Les mémoires québécoises*. Québec: Les Presses de l'Université Laval.

Lacroix, Benoît et Jean Simard, eds. 1984. *Religion populaire, religion de clercs?* Québec: Institut québécois de recherche sur la culture.

Laforce, Hélène. 1985. *Histoire de la sage-femme dans la région de Québec*. Québec: Institut québécois de recherche sur la culture.

Laing Hogg, Grace. 1990. The Legal Rights of Masters, Mistresses, and Domestic Servants in Montreal, 1816–1829. M.A. thesis, McGill University, Montreal.

Lambert, Phyllis and Alan Stewart. 1992. *Opening the Gates of Eighteenth-Century Montreal*. Montreal: Canadian Centre for Architecture.

Lamonde, Yvan et Raymond Montpetit. 1986. *Le parc Sohmer de Montréal, 1889–1919. Un lieu de culture urbaine*. Québec: Institut québécois de recherche sur la culture.

Lamoureux, Diane. 1990. Le mouvement des femmes: entre l'intégration et l'autonomie. *Canadian Issues/Thèmes canadiennes* 12: 125–36.

Landry, Yves. 1992a. Gender Imbalance, Les Filles du Roi, and Choice of Spouse in New France. In *Canadian Family History: Selected Readings*, edited by Bettina Bradbury, 14–32. Toronto: Copp Clark Pitman.

———. 1992b. *Les filles du roi en Nouvelle-France: étude démographique.* Montréal: Leméac.

———. 1992c. *Pour le Christ et le Roi: la vie au temps des premiers Montréalais.* Montréal: Libre Expression/Art Global.

Langlois, Simon, Jean-Paul Baillargeon, Gary Caldwell, Guy Fréchet, Madeleine Gauthier, et Jean-Pierre Simard. 1990. *La société québécoise en tendances, 1960–1990.* Québec: Institut québécois de recherche sur la culture.

Lapointe-Roy, Huguette. 1987. *Charité bien ordonnée: le premier réseau de lutte contre la pauvreté à Montréal au 19e siècle.* Montréal: Boréal Express.

Latouche, Daniel et Diane Poliquin-Bourassa. 1979. *Le manuel de la parole. Manifestes québécois.* tome 3, 1960–1976. Montréal: Boréal Express.

Launay, Dominique. 1993. La banqueroute au Bas-Canada: une étude des années 1840–1849. M.A. thesis, McGill University, Montreal.

Laurence, Gérard. 1982. Le début des affaires publiques à la télévision québécoise. *Revue d'histoire de l'Amérique française* 36 (2): 213–37.

Lauzon, Gilles. 1987. Conditions économiques de la production et de l'usage des espaces d'habitation populaire et ouvrière en période d'industrialisation: le village St-Augustin (St-Henri), en périphérie de Montréal, 1850–1875. M.A. thesis, Université du Québec à Montréal, Montréal.

———. 1989. *Habitat ouvrier et révolution industrielle: le cas du village Saint-Augustin.* Montréal: Regroupement des chercheurs-chercheures en histoire des travailleurs et travailleuses du Québec.

Lauzon, Gilles et Lucie Ruelland. 1985. *1875/Saint Henri.* Montréal: Société historique de Saint-Henri.

Lavallée, Louis. 1992. *La Prairie en Nouvelle-France. Etude d'histoire sociale.* Kingston et Montréal: McGill-Queen's University Press.

Lavigne, Marie et Yolande Pinard. 1983. *Travailleuses et féministes: les femmes dans la société québécoise.* Montréal: Boréal Express.

Lavigne, Marie, Yolande Pinard, and Jennifer Stoddart. 1979. The Fédération Nationale Saint-Jean Baptiste and the Women's Movement in Quebec. In *A Not Unreasonable Claim: Women and Reform in Canada, 1880s–1920s,* edited by Linda Kealey, 71–88. Toronto: Women's Press.

Lavoie, Elzéar. 1971. L'évolution de la radio au Canada français avant 1940. *Recherches sociographiques* 12 (1): 17–49.

Lavoie, Yolande. 1972. *L'émigration des Canadiens aux Etats-Unis avant 1930.* Montréal: Les Presses de l'Université de Montréal.

Leacock, Eleanor. 1986. Montagnais Women and the Jesuit Program for Colonization. In *Rethinking Canada: The Promise of Women's History*, edited by Veronica Strong-Boag and Anita Clair Fellman, 7–22. Toronto: Copp Clark Pitman.

Lee, David. 1984. *The Robins in Gaspé, 1766 to 1825.* Toronto: Fitzhenry and Whiteside.

Legault, Josée. 1992. *L'invention d'une minorité. Les Anglo-Québécois.* Montréal: Boréal Express.

Legault, Roch. 1986. *Les aléas d'une carrière militaire pour les membres de la petite noblesse seigneuriale canadienne de la Révolution américaine à la guerre de 1812–1815.* Montréal: Mémoire de maîtrise, Université de Montréal.

———. 1991. L'organisation militaire sous le régime britannique et le rôle assigné à la gentilhommerie canadienne (1760–1815). *Revue d'histoire de l'Amérique française* 45 (2, automne): 229–49.

Lemieux, Denise et Lucie Mercier. 1989. *Les femmes au tournant du siècle, 1880–1940: âges de la vie, maternité et quotidienne.* Québec: Institut québécois de recherche sur la culture.

Lemieux, Lucien. 1968. *L'établissement de la première province ecclésiastique au Canada, 1783–1844.* Montréal: Fides.

Lemire, Maurice. 1978– . *Dictionnaire des oeuvres littéraires du Québec.* 5 vols. Montréal: Fides.

Lépine, Daniel. 1982. La domesticité juvénile à Montréal pendant la première moitié du XVIIIe siècle. M.A. thesis, Université de Sherbrooke, Sherbrooke.

Lévesque, Andrée. 1984a. Deviant Anonymous: Single Mothers at the Hôpital de la Miséricorde in Montreal, 1929–39. Canadian Historical Association *Historical Papers*, 168–84.

———. 1984b. *Virage à gauche interdit: les communistes, les socialistes et leurs ennemis au Québec, 1929–1939.* Montréal: Boréal Express.

———. 1989a. Eteindre le "Red Light": les réformateurs et la prostitution à Montréal, 1865–1925. *Urban History Review* 17 (3, February): 191–201.

———. 1989b. *La norme et les déviantes: des femmes au Québec pendant l'entre deux guerres.* Montréal: Les éditions du remue-ménage.

Lévesque, René. 1968. *An Option for Quebec.* Toronto: McClelland and Stewart.

Levine, Marc. 1990. *The Reconquest of Montreal: Language Policy and Social Change in a Bilingual City.* Philadelphia: Temple University Press.

Levitt, Joseph. 1972. *Henri Bourassa and the Golden Calf: The Social Program of the Nationalists of Québec (1900–1914)*. Ottawa: University of Ottawa Press.

———. 1976. *Henri Bourassa: Catholic Critic*. Ottawa: Canadian Historical Association.

Lewis, Robert D. 1990. Home Ownership Reassessed for Montreal in the 1840s. *The Canadian Geographer/Le Géographe canadien* 34 (2): 150–52.

Linteau, Paul-André. 1981. *Maisonneuve: Comment des promoteurs fabriquent une ville*. Montréal: Boréal Express.

———. 1992a. *Histoire de Montréal depuis la Confédération*. Montréal: Boréal Express.

———. 1992b. *Brève histoire de Montréal*. Montréal: Boréal Express.

Linteau, Paul-André and Jean-Claude Robert. 1977. Land Ownership and Society in Montreal: An Hypothesis. In *The Canadian City: Essays in Urban History*, edited by G. Stelter and A. Artibise, 17–36. Toronto: McClelland and Stewart.

Linteau, Paul-André, René Durocher, and Jean-Claude Robert. 1983. *A History of Contemporary Quebec, 1867–1930*. Toronto: Lorimer.

Linteau, Paul-André, René Durocher, Jean-Claude Robert, et François Ricard. 1989. *Histoire du Québec contemporain: le Québec depuis 1930*. Montréal: Boréal Express.

Lipsig-Mummé, Carla. 1991. Future Conditional: Wars of Position in the Quebec Labour Movement. *Studies in Political Economy* 36 (autumn): 73–108.

Lipsig-Mummé, Carla et Rita Roy. 1989. La population syndiquée au Québec. *Labour/Le Travail* 23 (spring): 119–57.

Litalien, Roland, ed. 1986. *L'église de Montréal. Aperçu d'hier et d'aujourd'hui*. Montréal: Fides.

Little, Jack. 1978. The Social and Economic Development of Settlers in Two Quebec Townships, 1851–1870. In *Canadian Papers in Rural History*, vol. 1, edited by Donald Akenson, 89–113. Gananoque: Langdale Press.

———. 1981. Colonization and Municipal Reform in Canada East. *Histoire sociale/Social History* 14 (27, May): 93–122.

———. 1982. Lewis Thomas Drummond. vol. 11, *Dictionary of Canadian Biography*, 281–83. Toronto: University of Toronto Press.

———. 1989a. *Nationalism, Capitalism, and Colonization in Nineteenth-Century Quebec: The Upper Saint-Francis District*. Kingston and Montreal: McGill-Queen's University Press.

———. 1989b. *Ethno-cultural Transition and Regional Identity in the Eastern Townships of Quebec*. Ottawa: Canadian Historical Association.

———. 1991. *Crofters and Habitants. Settler Society, Economy, and Culture in a Quebec Township, 1848–1881.* Kingston and Montreal: McGill-Queen's University Press.

Lord, Kathleen. 1981. Municipal and Industrial Development: Saint-Jean, Quebec, 1848–1914. M.A. thesis, Concordia University, Montreal.

Lowe, Graham. 1986. Mechanization, Feminization, and Managerial Control in the Early Twentieth-Century Office. In *On the Job: Confronting the Labour Process in Canada*, edited by C. Heron and R. Storey, 177–209. Kingston and Montreal: McGill-Queen's University Press.

———. 1987. *Women in the Administrative Revolution.* Toronto: University of Toronto Press.

McCallum, John. 1980. *Unequal Beginnings: Agriculture and Economic Development in Quebec and Ontario until 1870.* Toronto: University of Toronto Press.

McCann, L.D. 1982. *Heartland and Hinterland: A Geography of Canada.* Scarborough: Prentice Hall.

McGinnis, Janice P. Dickin. 1977. The Impact of Epidemic Influenza, Canada 1918–1919. Canadian Historical Association *Historical Papers*, 120–41.

McInnis, Marvin. 1982. A Reconsideration of the State of Agriculture in Lower Canada in the First Half of the Nineteenth Century. In *Canadian Papers in Rural History*, vol. 3, edited by Donald Akenson, 9–49. Gananoque: Langdale Press.

McInnis, Marvin and Frank Lewis. 1980. The Efficiency of the French Canadian Farmer in the Nineteenth Century. *Journal of Economic History* 40.

McNally, Larry. 1982. *Water Power on the Lachine Canal, 1846–1900.* Ottawa: Parks Canada.

Maillé, Chantal. 1990. *Les Québécoises et la conquête du pouvoir politique.* Montréal: Editions Saint-Martin.

Maroney, Heather Jon. 1988. Contemporary Quebec Feminism: The Interrelation of Political and Ideological Development in Women's Organization, Trade Unions, Political Parties and State Policy, 1960–1980. Ph.D. diss., McMaster University, Hamilton.

———. 1992. "Who Has the Baby?" Nationalism, Pronatalism, and the Construction of a "Demographic Crisis" in Quebec 1960–1988. *Studies in Political Economy* 39 (autumn): 7–36.

Martin, Calvin. 1978. *Keepers of the Game: Indian-Animal Relationships and the Fur Trade.* Berkeley: University of California Press.

Massicotte, Daniel. 1987. Le marché du logement locatif à Montréal de 1731 à 1741. M.A. thesis, Université de Montréal, Montréal.

Mathews, George. 1990. *Quiet Revolution: Quebec's Challenge to Canada.* Toronto: Summerhill Press.

Mathieu, Jacques. 1971. *La construction navale royale à Québec, 1739–1759.* Québec: Société historique de Québec.

———. 1981. *Le commerce entre la Nouvelle-France et les Antilles au XVIIIe siècle.* Montréal: Fides.

———. 1991. *La Nouvelle-France. Les Français en Amérique du Nord (XVIIe–XVIIIe siècles).* Québec: Les Presses de l'Université Laval.

Metcalfe, Alan. 1978. The Evolution of Organized Physical Recreation in Montreal, 1840–1895. *Histoire sociale/Social History* 11 (21, May): 144–66.

———. 1987. *Canada Learns to Play: The Emergence of Organized Sport, 1807–1914.* Toronto: McClelland and Stewart.

Michaud, Francine. 1985. Irma LeVasseur: pionnière, femme d'action, et fondatrice méconnue. *Cap-aux-Diamants* 2 (2, été): 3–6.

Michel, Louis. 1979. Un marchand rural en Nouvelle-France: François-Augustin Bailly de Messein, 1709–1771. *Revue d'histoire de l'Amérique française* 33 (2, septembre): 215–62.

———. 1986. Varennes et Verchères, des origines au milieu du XIXe siècle: état d'une enquête. In *Evolution et éclatement du monde rural, France-Québec, XVIIe–XXe siècles,* edited by Joseph Goy and Jean-Pierre Wallot, 325–40. Montréal et Paris: Les Presses de l'Université de Montréal et l'Ecole des Hautes Etudes en Sciences Sociales.

Miller, Pamela. 1992. *The McCord Family: A Passionate Vision.* Montreal: McCord Museum of Canadian History.

Miner, Horace. 1939. *St. Denis: A French-Canadian Parish.* Chicago: University of Chicago Press.

Miquelon, Dale. 1977. *Society and Conquest. The Debate on the Bourgeoisie and Social Change in French Canada, 1700–1850.* Toronto: Copp Clark.

———. 1978. *Dugard of Rouen. French Trade to Canada and the West Indies, 1729–1770.* Kingston and Montreal: McGill-Queen's University Press.

———. 1987. *New France, 1701–1744.* Toronto: McClelland and Stewart.

Monet, Jacques. 1969. *The Last Cannon Shot: A Study of French-Canadian Nationalism 1837–1840.* Toronto: University of Toronto Press.

Moogk, Peter. 1973. The Craftsmen of New France. Ph.D. diss., University of Toronto, Toronto.

———. 1979. "Thieving Buggers and Stupid Sluts": Insults and Popular Culture in New France. *William and Mary Quarterly* 3rd series (36): 524–47.

Morneau, Jocelyn. 1990. Louiseville en Mauricie au XIXe siècle: la croissance d'une aire villageoise. *Revue d'histoire de l'Amérique française* 44 (2, automne): 223–42.

Nahuet, Robert. 1984. Une experience canadienne de Taylorisme. Le cas des usines Angus du Canadien Pacifique. M.A. thesis, Université du Québec à Montréal, Montréal.

Neatby, H. Blair. 1973. *Laurier and a Liberal Quebec: A Study in Political Management*. Toronto: McClelland and Stewart.

Neatby, Hilda. 1966. *Québec: The Revolutionary Age 1760–1791*. Toronto: McClelland and Stewart.

Nelson, Wendie. 1989. The "Guerre des Eteignoirs": School Reform and Popular Resistance in Lower Canada, 1841–1850. M.A. thesis, Simon Fraser University, Burnaby.

Niosi, Jorge. 1975. La Laurentide (1887–1928): pionnière du papier journal au Canada. *Revue d'histoire de l'Amérique française* 29 (3, décembre): 375–415.

Nish, Cameron. 1966. *The French Canadians, 1759–1766: Conquered? Half-Conquered? Liberated?* Toronto: Copp Clark.

———. 1975. *François-Etienne Cugnet. Entrepreneur et entreprises en Nouvelle-France*. Montréal: Fides.

Noel, Françoise. 1988. *Competing for Souls. Missionary Activity and Settlement in the Eastern Townships, 1784–1851*. Sherbrooke: Université de Sherbrooke.

———. 1992. *The Christie Seigneuries: Estate Management and Settlement in the Upper Richelieu Valley, 1760–1854*. Kingston and Montreal: McGill-Queen's University Press.

Noel, Jan. 1986. New France: Les femmes favorisées. In *Rethinking Canada: The Promise of Women's History*, edited by Veronica Strong-Boag and Anita Clair Fellman, 23–44. Toronto: Copp Clark Pitman.

Ostola, Lawrence. 1989. The Seven Nations of Canada and the American Revolution, 1774–1783. M.A. thesis, Université de Montréal, Montréal.

Otis, Yves. 1991. La différenciation des producteurs laitiers et le marché de Montréal (1900–1930). *Revue d'histoire de l'Amérique française* 45 (1, été): 39–72.

Ouellet, Fernand. 1964. *Louis-Joseph Papineau: A Divided Soul*. Ottawa: Canadian Historical Association.

———. 1980. *Lower Canada, 1791–1840: Social Change and Nationalism*. Toronto: McClelland and Stewart.

———. 1981. *Economic and Social History of Quebec*. Toronto: Macmillan.

———. 1990. *Economy, Class, and Nation in Quebec: Interpretive Essays*. Toronto: Copp Clark Pitman.

Palmer, Bryan. 1992. *Working-class Experience: Rethinking the History of Canadian Labour, 1800–1991*. Toronto: McClelland and Stewart.

Paquet, Gilles et Jean-Pierre Wallot. 1973. *Patronage et pouvoir dans le Bas-Canada (1794–1812)*. Montréal: Les Presses de l'Université du Québec.

———. 1986. Stratégie foncière de l'habitant: Québec (1790–1835). *Revue d'histoire de l'Amérique française* 39 (4, printemps): 551–82.

Paquette, Lyne et Réal Bates. 1986. Les naissances illégitimes sur les rives du Saint-Laurent avant 1730. *Revue d'histoire de l'Amérique française* 40 (2, automne): 239–52.

Paquette, Pierre. 1984. Industries et politiques minières au Québec: une analyse économique 1896–1975. *Revue d'histoire de l'Amérique française* 37 (4, mars): 573–602.

Parent, Madeleine. 1989. Interview. *Studies in Political Economy* 30 (autumn): 13–36.

Parti libéral du Québec. 1991. *Un Québec libre de ses choix: rapport du Comité constitutionnel du Parti libéral du Québec. (Allaire Report)*. Québec: Publications du Québec.

Payette, Lise. 1982. *Le pouvoir? Connais pas!* Montréal: Editions Québec Amérique.

Pelletier, Gérard. 1984. *Years of Impatience, 1950–1960*. Toronto: Methuen.

Pelletier, Mario. 1989. *La Machine à milliards. L'histoire de la Caisse de dépôt et placement du Québec*. Montréal: Editions Québec Amérique.

Pendergast, James and Bruce Trigger. 1972. *Cartier's Hochelaga and the Dawson Site*. Kingston and Montreal: McGill-Queen's University Press.

Pentland, H.C. 1981. *Labour and Capital in Canada*. Toronto: Lorimer.

Perron, Yves, Evelyn Lapierre-Adamcyk, et Dennis Morrissette. 1987a. Le changement familial: aspects démographiques. *Recherches sociographiques* 28 (2–3): 317–39.

———. 1987b. Les répercussions des nouveaux comportements démographiques sur la vie familiale: la situation canadienne. *Revue internationale d'action communautaire/International Review of Community Development* 18 (58, automne): 57–66.

Petitat, André. 1989. *Les infirmières: de la vocation à la profession*. Montréal: Boréal Express.

Picard, Nathalie. 1992. Les femmes et le vote au Bas-Canada de 1792 à 1849. M.A. thesis, Université de Montréal.

Piédalue, Gilles. 1976. La bourgeoisie canadienne et le problème de la réalisation du profit au Canada, 1900–1930. Ph.D. diss., Université de Montréal, Montréal.

Pierson, Ruth Roach. 1986. *They're Still Women After All: The Second World War and Canadian Womanhood*. Toronto: McClelland and Stewart.

Plamondon, Lilianne. 1986. A Businesswoman in New France: Marie-Anne Barbel, the Widow Fornel. In *Rethinking Canada: The Promise of Women's History*, edited by Veronica Strong-Boag and Anita Clair Fellman, 45–58. Toronto: Copp Clark Pitman.

Plourde, Michel. 1988. *La politique linguistique du Québec 1977–1987*. Québec: Institut québécois de recherche sur la culture.

Pomfret, Richard. 1981. *The Economic Development of Canada*. Toronto: Methuen.

Posgate, Dale and Kenneth McRoberts. 1980. *Quebec: Social Change and Political Crisis*. Toronto: McClelland and Stewart.

Potvin, Damase. 1957. *La baie des HaHas*. Port Alfred: Chambre de commerce de la Baie des HaHas.

Poutanen, Mary Anne. 1985. For the Benefit of the Master: The Montreal Needle Trades during the Transition 1820–1842. M.A. thesis, McGill University, Montreal.

Pouyez, Christian et Yolande Lavoie. 1983. *Les Saguenayens: introduction à l'histoire des populations du Saguenay XVIe–XXe siècles*. Québec: Les Presses de l'Université du Québec.

Pritchard, James. 1976. The Pattern of French Colonial Shipping to Canada before 1760. *Revue française d'histoire d'outre-mer* 63 (231): 189–210.

Provencher, Jean. 1975. *René Lévesque: Portrait of a Québécois*. Toronto: Gage.

Quebec. 1956. *Report of the Royal Commission of Inquiry on Constitutional Problems/Rapport de la Commission royale d'enquête sur les problèmes constitutionnels. (Tremblay Report.)* 5 vols. Ottawa: Queen's Printer.

———. 1991. *Report of the Commission on the Political and Constitutional Future of Quebec. (Bélanger-Campeau Report)*. Québec: Publications du Québec.

Quinn, Herbert F. 1963. *The Union Nationale: A Study in Quebec Nationalism*. Toronto: University of Toronto Press.

Ramirez, Bruno. 1986. Brief Encounters: Italian Immigrant Workers and the CPR, 1900–30. *Labour/Le Travail* 17 (spring): 9–28.

———. 1991. *On the Move: French-Canadian and Italian Migrants in the North Atlantic Economy, 1860–1914*. Toronto: McClelland and Stewart.

Ramirez, Bruno and Michael Del Balso. 1980. *The Italians of Montreal: From Sojourning to Settlement*. Montreal: Editions du courant.

Ramsden, Peter G. 1981. Rich Man, Poor Man, Dead Man, Thief: The Dispersal of Wealth in 17th Century Huron Society. *Ontario Archaeology* 35: 35–40.

Regehr, T.D. 1990. *The Beauharnois Scandal: A Story of Canadian Entrepreneurship and Politics.* Toronto: University of Toronto Press.

Ricard, François. 1992. *La génération lyrique. Essai sur la vie et l'oeuvre des premiers-nés du baby-boom.* Montréal: Boréal Express.

Richler, Mordecai. 1992. *Oh Canada! Oh Quebec! Requiem for a Divided Country.* Toronto: Penguin.

Rioux, Marcel. 1961. *Belle-Anse.* Ottawa: National Museums of Canada.

Rioux, Marcel and Yves Martin. 1964. *French-Canadian Society.* Toronto: McClelland and Stewart.

Roback, Leo. 1985. Quebec Workers in the Twentieth Century. In *Lectures in Canadian Labour and Working-class History,* edited by W.J.C. Cherwinski and G.S. Kealey, 165–82. St. John's: Committee on Canadian Labour History.

Robert, Jean-Claude. 1972. Un seigneur entrepreneur, Barthélemy Joliette, et la fondation du village d'Industrie (Joliette). *Revue d'histoire de l'Amérique française* 26 (3, décembre): 375–96.

———. 1984. Aperçu sur les structures socio-professionnelles des villages de la région nord de Montréal durant la première moitié du XIXe siècle. *Cahiers de géographie du Québec* 28 (73–74, avril-septembre): 63–72.

———. 1988. The City of Wealth and Death: Urban Mortality in Montreal, 1821–1871. In *Essays in the History of Canadian Medicine,* edited by W. Mitchinson and J.D. McGinnis. Toronto: McClelland and Stewart.

Robert, Lucie. 1989. *L'institution du littéraire au Québec.* Québec: Les Presses de l'Université Laval.

Robichaud, Léon. 1989. *Le pouvoir, les paysans et la voirie au Bas-Canada à la fin du XVIIIe siècle.* Montréal: Mémoire de maîtrise, Université McGill.

Roby, Yves. 1964. *Alphonse Desjardins et les caisses populaires, 1854–1920.* Montréal: Fides.

———. 1976. *Les Québécois et les investissements américains (1918–1929).* Québec: Les Presses de l'Université Laval.

Rouillard, Jacques. 1979. *Les syndicats nationaux au Québec de 1900 à 1930.* Québec: Les Presses de l'Université Laval.

———. 1981. *Histoire de la CSN (1921–1981).* Montréal: Boréal Express.

———. 1983. Le militantisme des travailleurs au Québec et en Ontario, niveau de syndicalisation et mouvement de grève (1900–1980). *Revue d'histoire de l'Amérique française* 37 (2, septembre): 201–26.

———. 1989. *Histoire du syndicalisme québécois.* Montréal: Boréal Express.

————, ed. 1992. *Guide d'histoire du Québec du régime français à nos jours: bibliographie commentée.* Montréal: Méridien.

Rousseau, François. 1983. *L'oeuvre de chère en Nouvelle-France. Le régime des malades à l'Hôtel-Dieu de Québec.* Québec: Les Presses de l'Université Laval.

Rousseau, Louis. 1986. La conduite pascale dans la région montréalaise 1831–1865: un indice des mouvements de la ferveur religeuse. In *L'église de Montréal: Aperçus d'hier et d'aujourd'hui,* edited by Roland Litalien. Montréal: Fides.

Roy, Fernande. 1988. *Progrès, harmonie, liberté: le libéralisme des milieux d'affaires francophones à Montréal au tournant du siècle.* Montréal: Boréal Express.

Roy, Jean-Louis. 1976. *La marche des Québécois: le temps de ruptures (1945–60).* Montréal: Leméac.

Ruddel, David-Thiery. 1983. The Domestic Textile Industry in the Region and City of Quebec, 1792–1835. *Material History Bulletin* 17: 95–125.

Rudé, George. 1978. *Protest and Punishment: The Story of the Social and Political Protesters Transported to Australia, 1788–1868.* Oxford: Oxford University Press.

Rudin, Ronald. 1985a. *The Forgotten Quebecers: A History of English-speaking Quebec 1759–1980.* Québec: Institut québécois de recherche sur la culture.

————. 1985b. *Banking en français: The French Banks of Quebec, 1835–1925.* Toronto: University of Toronto Press.

————. 1986. Bankers' Hours: Life behind the Wicket at the Banque d'Hochelaga, 1901–1921. *Labour/Le Travail* 18 (fall): 63–76.

————. 1990. *In Whose Interest? Quebec's Caisses Populaires, 1900–1945.* Kingston and Montreal: McGill-Queen's University Press.

————. 1992. Revisionism and the Search for a Normal Society: A Critique of Recent Quebec Historical Writing. *Canadian Historical Review* 73, 1 (March 1992): 30–61.

Ryan, William. 1966. *The Clergy and Economic Growth in Quebec (1896–1914).* Québec: Les Presses de l'Université Laval.

Ryerson, Stanley. 1968. *Unequal Union: Confederation and the Roots of Conflict in the Canadas, 1815–1873.* Toronto: Progress Books.

Samson, Roch. 1986. Une industrie avant l'industrialisation: le cas des forges du Saint-Maurice. *Anthropologie et Sociétés* 10 (1): 85–107.

Sarra-Bournet, Michel. 1986. *L'affaire Roncarelli. Duplessis contre les Témoins de Jéhovah.* Québec: Institut québécois de recherche sur la culture.

Savard, Felix-Antoine. 1976. *Master of the River.* Montreal: Harvest House.

Savoie, Sylvie. 1986. Les couples en difficulté aux XVIIe et XVIIIe siécles: les demandes en séparation en Nouvelle-France. M.A. thesis, Université de Sherbrooke, Sherbrooke.

Schulze, David. 1984. Rural Manufacture in Lower Canada: Understanding Seigneurial Privilege and the Transition in the Countryside. *Alternate Routes* 7: 134–67.

Séguin, Maurice. 1968. *L'idée d'indépendance au Québec. Genèse historique.* Trois-Rivières: Boréal Express.

———. 1970. *La nation "canadienne" et l'agriculture (1760–1850).* Montréal: Boréal Express.

Séguin, Normand. 1977. *La conquête du sol au 19e siècle.* Montréal: Boréal Express.

———. 1980. *Agriculture et colonisation au Québec.* Montréal: Boréal Express.

Senior, Elinor Kyte. 1981. *British Regulars in Montreal: An Imperial Garrison, 1832–1854.* Kingston and Montreal: McGill-Queen's University Press.

———. 1985. *Redcoats and Patriotes: The Rebellions in Lower Canada, 1837–38.* Ottawa: Canada's Wings.

Sevigny, David. 1982. Le capitalisme et la politique dans une région québécoise de colonisation: le cas de Jacques Picard à Wotton, 1828–1905. M.A. thesis, Simon Fraser University, Burnaby.

Silver, A.I. 1982. *The French-Canadian Idea of Confederation.* Toronto: University of Toronto Press.

Smith, Françoise. 1975. The Establishment of Religion in the Eastern Townships, 1799–1851. M.A. thesis, McGill University, Montreal.

Snell, James and Frederick Vaughan. 1985. *The Supreme Court of Canada: History of the Institution.* Toronto: The Osgoode Society.

Steedman, Mercedes. 1986. Skill and Gender in the Canadian Clothing Industry, 1890–1940. In *On the Job: Confronting the Labour Process in Canada,* edited by C. Heron and R. Storey, 152–76. Kingston and Montreal: McGill-Queen's University Press.

Stevens, G.R. 1973. *History of the Canadian National Railways.* New York: Macmillan.

Stewart, Alan M. 1988. Settling an Eighteenth Century Faubourg: Property and Family in the Saint-Laurent Suburb, 1735–1810. M.A. thesis, McGill University, Montreal.

St-Georges, Lise. 1986. Commerce, crédit et transactions foncières: pratiques de la communauté marchande du bourg de l'Assomption, 1748–1791. *Revue d'histoire de l'Amérique française* 39 (2, automne): 323–43.

Stoddart, Jennifer. 1981. Quebec's Legal Elite Looks at Women's Rights: The Dorion Commission 1929–31. In *Essays in the History of Canadian Law*, vol. 1, edited by David Flaherty, 323–57. Toronto: University of Toronto Press.

Sweeny, Robert. 1978. *A Guide to the History and Records of Selected Montreal Businesses before 1947*. Montreal: Centre de recherche en histoire économique du Canada français.

——— . 1986. Internal Dynamics and the International Cycle: Questions of the Transition in Montreal, 1821–28. Ph.D. diss., McGill University, Montreal.

Sweeny, Robert, Grace Laing Hogg, et Richard Rice. 1988. *Les relations ville/campagne: le cas du bois du chauffage*. Montreal: Montreal Business History Project.

Tardival, Jules-Paul. 1975. *For My Country: "Pour la Patrie."* Toronto: University of Toronto Press.

Tétreault, Martin. 1983. Les maladies de la misère: aspects de la santé publique à Montréal 1880–1914. *Revue d'histoire de l'Amérique française* 36 (4, mars): 507–26.

Thivierge, Marîse. 1983. La syndicalisation des institutrices catholiques, 1900–1959. In *Maîtresses de maison, maîtresses d'école: femmes, famille et éducation dans l'histoire du Québec*, edited by N. Fahmy-Eid and M. Dumont, 171–89. Montréal: Boréal Express.

Thivierge, Nicole. 1982. *Ecoles ménagères et instituts familiaux: un modèle féminin traditionel*. Québec: Institut québécois de recherche sur la culture.

Thompson, Dale C. 1984. *Jean Lesage and the Quiet Revolution*. Toronto: Macmillan.

——— . 1988. *Vive le Québec libre*. Toronto: Deneau.

Thompson, John Herd and Allen Seager. 1985. *Canada 1922–1939: Decades of Discord*. Toronto: McClelland and Stewart.

Thwaites, Reuben Gold. 1896–1901. *The Jesuit Relations and Allied Documents*. 72 vols. Cleveland: Burrows Brothers.

Tousignant, Pierre. 1973. Problématique pour une nouvelle approche de la constitution de 1791. *Revue d'histoire de l'Amérique française* 27 (2): 181–234.

——— . 1979. The Integration of the Province of Quebec into the British Empire. vol. 4, *Dictionary of Canadian Biography*, xxxii–xlix. Toronto: University of Toronto Press.

Tremblay, Louise. 1981. La politique missionnaire des Sulpiciens au XVIIe et début du XVIIIe siècles. M.A. thesis, Université de Montréal, Montréal.

Tremblay, Robert. 1981–1982. Un aspect de la consolidation du pouvoir d'Etat de la bourgeoisie coloniale: la législation anti-ouvrière dans le Bas-Canada, 1800–1850. *Labour/Le Travailleur* 8/9 (automne/printemps).

————. 1983. La grève des ouvriers de la construction navale à Québec (1840). *Revue d'histoire de l'Amérique française* 37 (2, septembre): 227–40.

Trigger, Bruce. 1963. Order and Freedom in Huron Society. *Anthropologica* 5 (2): 151–69.

————. 1976. *The Children of Aataentsic. A History of the Huron People to 1660.* 2 vols. Kingston and Montreal: McGill-Queen's University Press.

————, ed. 1978a. *Handbook of North American Indians.* vol. 15, *Northeast.* Washington: Smithsonian Institute.

————. 1978b. *Indians and the "Heroic Age" of New France.* Historical Booklet no. 30. Ottawa: Canadian Historical Association.

————. 1985. *Natives and Newcomers. Canada's "Heroic Age" Reconsidered.* Kingston and Montreal: McGill-Queen's University Press.

Triggs, Stanley, Brian Young, Conrad Graham, and Gilles Lauzon. 1992. *Victoria Bridge: The Vital Link.* Montreal: McCord Museum of Canadian History.

Trofimenkoff, Susan Mann. 1975. Henri Bourassa and "The Woman Question." *Journal of Canadian Studies* 10: 3–11.

————. 1978a. *Abbé Groulx. Variations on a Nationalist Theme.* Toronto: Copp Clark.

————. 1978b. Les femmes dans l'oeuvre de Groulx. *Revue d'histoire de l'Amérique française* 32 (3, décembre): 385–98.

————. 1983. *The Dream of Nation: A Social and Intellectual History of Quebec.* Toronto: Gage.

————. 1985. Thérèse Casgrain and the CCF in Quebec. *Canadian Historical Review* 66 (2, June): 125–53.

Trudeau, Pierre Elliott. 1980. *Federalism and the French Canadians.* Toronto: Macmillan.

Trudel, Marcel. 1956. *The Seigneurial Regime.* Historical Booklet no. 6. Ottawa: Canadian Historical Association.

————. 1966–1983. *Histoire de la Nouvelle-France.* 4 vols. Montréal: Fides.

————. 1968. *An Initiation to New France.* Toronto: Holt, Rinehart and Winston.

————. 1973. *The Beginnings of New France, 1524–1663.* Toronto: McClelland and Stewart.

————. 1990. *Dictionnaire des esclaves et de leurs propriétaires au Canada français.* Montréal: Hurtubise HMH.

Tulchinsky, Gerald J.J. 1977. *The River Barons: Montreal Businessmen and the Growth of Industry and Transportation, 1837–53.* Toronto: University of Toronto Press.

————. 1984. The Third Solitude: A.M. Klein's Jewish Montreal, 1910–1950. *Journal of Canadian Studies* 19 (2, summer): 96–112.

————. 1992. *Taking Root: The Origins of the Canadian Jewish Community.* Toronto: Lester, 1992.

Turgeon, Laurier. 1981. Pour une histoire de la pêche: le marché de la morue à Marseille au XVIIIe siècle. *Histoire sociale/Social History* 14 (28, novembre): 295–322.

————. 1986. Pour redécouvrir notre 16e siècle: les pêches à Terre-Neuve d'après les archives notariales de Bordeaux. *Revue d'histoire de l'Amérique française* 39 (4, printemps): 523–49.

Urquhart, M.C. and K.A.H. Buckley. 1965. *Historical Statistics of Canada.* Toronto: Macmillan.

Vachon, André. 1969. The Administration of New France. vol. 2, *Dictionary of Canadian Biography*, xv–xxv. Toronto: University of Toronto Press.

Vaillancourt, Yves. 1988. *L'évolution des politiques sociales au Québec, 1940–1960.* Montréal: Les Presses de l'Université de Montréal.

Vallières, Marc. 1989. *Des mines et des hommes. Histoire de l'industrie minière québécoise des origines au début des années 1990.* Québec: Ministère des Communications.

Vallières, Pierre. 1971. *White Niggers of America.* Toronto: McClelland and Stewart.

Veilleux, Denis. 1992. Protectionisme et libéralisme: la lutte pour la libéralisation de la loi des brevets d'invention au Canada (1824–1872). M.A. thesis, Université du Québec à Montréal, Montréal.

Vigod, Bernard. 1978. Ideology and Institutions in Quebec. The Public Charities Controversy 1921–1926. *Histoire sociale/Social History* 11 (21, May): 167–82.

————. 1986. *Quebec before Duplessis. The Political Career of Louis-Alexandre Taschereau.* Kingston and Montreal: McGill-Queen's University Press.

Voisine, Nive. 1971. *Histoire de l'église catholique au Québec (1608–1970).* Montréal: Fides.

Wade, Mason. 1968. *The French Canadians 1760–1967.* 2 vols. Toronto: Macmillan.

Wallerstein, Immanuel. 1974. *The Modern World System. Capitalist Agriculture and the Origins of the European World Economy in the Sixteenth Century.* New York: Academic Press.

Wallot, Jean-Pierre. 1971. Religion and French-Canadian Mores in the Early Nineteenth Century. *Canadian Historical Review* 52 (1, March): 51–94.

————. 1973. *Un Québec qui bougeait: trame socio-politique au tournant du XIX siècle*. Trois-Rivières: Boréal Express.

Ward, Peter W. 1989. *A Love Story from 19th Century Quebec: The Diary of George Stephen Jones*. Peterborough: Broadview Press.

Weisz, George. 1987. Origines géographiques et lieux de pratique des diplômes en médecine au Québec de 1834 à 1939. In *Sciences et médecine au Québec: perspectives sociohistoriques*, edited by Marcel Fournier, Yves Gingras, and Othmar Keel, 129–70. Québec: Institut québécois de recherche sur la culture.

Wien, Thomas. 1988. Peasant Accumulation in a Context of Colonization. Rivière-du-Sud, Canada, 1720–1775. Ph.D. diss., McGill University, Montreal.

————. 1990a. Les travaux pressants: calendrier agricole, assolement et productivité au Canada au XVIIIe siècle. *Revue d'histoire de l'Amérique française* 43 (4, printemps): 535–58.

————. 1990b. Selling Beaver Skins in North America and Europe, 1720–1760: The Use of Fur-trade Imperialism. *Journal of the Canadian Historical Association/Revue de la Société historique du Canada.* 293–317.

Willis, John. 1987. *The Process of Hydraulic Industrialization on the Lachine Canal 1840–80: Origins, Rise and Fall*. Ottawa: Environment Canada.

Wright, J.V. 1980. *Quebec Prehistory*. Ottawa: National Museums of Canada.

————. 1981. *Ontario Prehistory: An Eleven Thousand Year Archaeological Outline*. Ottawa: National Museums of Canada.

Young, Brian. 1978. *Promoters and Politicians: The North-Shore Railways in the History of Quebec 1854–85*. Toronto: University of Toronto Press.

————. 1981. *George-Etienne Cartier: Montreal Bourgeois*. Kingston and Montreal: McGill-Queen's University Press.

————. 1986. *In Its Corporate Capacity: The Seminary of Montreal as a Business Institution, 1816–76*. Kingston and Montreal: McGill-Queen's University Press.

Zoltvany, Yves. 1971. Esquisse de la Coutume de Paris. *Revue d'histoire de l'Amérique française* 25 (3, décembre): 365–84.

————. 1974. *Philippe de Rigaud de Vaudreuil. Governor of New France, 1703–1725*. Toronto: McClelland and Stewart.

CREDITS

Fig. 1.2 Hudson's Bay Company Archives, HBCA Photograph Collection 1987/15 (A.A. Chesterfield, Album 14) (HBCA Copy Negative No. 83-87). Fig. 1.3 Illustration by Guy Lapointe, Recherches amérindiennes au Québec, 1986. Fig. 1.5 Detail from *Traité général des pêches de Duhamel du Monceau*, Paris, 1772. Fig. 1.6 Detail of Herman Moll's *Map of North America*, 1718, National Archives of Canada/C-3686. Fig. 1.7 *Indiens ouvrant une baleine*, *vers 1760*, Jesuit Relations, 1668, Melzack Collection, Université de Montréal. Fig. 1.10 Les Archives des Ursulines. Fig. 2.1 National Archives of Canada/C-155703. Fig. 2.2 B-962, Archives Nationales du Québec, 1688. Fig. 2.3 National Archives of Canada/C-355. Fig. 2.6 National Archives of Canada/C-352. Fig. 3.2 *Traversée du Lac des Moustiques*, 1863, Melzack Collection, Université de Montréal. Fig. 3.3 *Lake of Two Mountains* (Oka), Steel engraving originally drawn by W.H. Bartlett, McCord Museum of Canadian History. Fig. 3.4 Painting by Blanche Bolduc, McCord Museum of Canadian History. Fig. 3.5 *The Forges, River St. Maurice*, by J. Bouchette Jr., National Archives of Canada/C-4356. Fig. 3.6 *A View of the Chateau Richer*, Watercolour by Thomas Davies, National Gallery of Canada. Fig. 3.7 *Ploughing ca. 1830*, Melzack Collection. Fig. 3.8 *Ploughing, 1883*, T. Welch, Melzack Collection. Fig. 3.9 Detail from *Place Jacques-Cartier*, by R.A. Sproule, 1830, McCord Museum of Canadian History. Fig. 3.10 *Canadian Habitants Playing Cards*, by C. Krieghoff. Fig. 3.11 *Photo Livernois*, 1958, 4666, Ste-Anne de Beaupré Archives, Galerie d'art de la Basilique. Fig. 4.4 76310-I, Notman Photographic Archives, McCord Museum of Canadian History. Fig. 4.5 Lithograph by S. Russell, McCord Museum of Canadian History. Fig. 4.6 Courtesy of Redpath Sugar Museum. Fig. 4.7 Drawing by Trefflé Loisel, 1857, Collection Baby, Université de Montréal. Fig. 4.8 Painting by C. Krieghoff. Fig. 4.8 *Place d'Armes, Montréal*, by C. Krieghoff. Fig. 4.9 Archives du Séminaire de Trois-Rivières. Fig. 4.10 Courtesy of Missisquoi Historical Museum. Fig. 4.12 National Archives of Canada/C-4733. Fig. 4.13 9/90, Notman Photographic Archives, McCord Museum of Canadian History. Fig. 4.14 8/90, Notman Photographic Archives, McCord Museum of Canadian History. Fig. 4.15 Print by R.M.S. Bouchette in *British American Land Company: Views in Lower Canada*, London, 1836, Metro Toronto Public Library. Fig. 4.16 Société d'histoire régionale de Saint-Hyacinthe. Fig. 5.1 National Archives of Canada/C-15494. Fig. 5.2 National Archives of Canada/C-13392. Fig. 5.3 National Archives of Canada/C-40295. Fig. 5.4 Lithograph by William Lockwood, 1855, McCord Museum of Canadian History. Fig. 5.5 Private Collection. Fig. 5.6 21472-I, Notman Photographic Archives, McCord Museum of Canadian History. Fig. 5.7 1492-View, Notman Photographic Archives, McCord Museum of Canadian History. Fig. 5.10 24027-II, Notman Photographic Archives, McCord Museum of Canadian History. Fig. 5.11 *Burning of the Parliament Building in Montréal*, McCord Museum of Canadian History, M11588. Fig. 6.2 MP886(6), Notman Photographic Archives, McCord Museum of Canadian History. Fig. 6.5 Université du Québec à Trois-Rivières, Hydro-Québec. Fig. 6.6 National Archives of Canada/C-55787. Fig. 6.7 National Archives of Canada/C-30811. Fig. 6.8 National Archives of Canada/DND/PA-24439. Fig. 6.9 *Cap-Aux-Diamants*, vol. 1, no. 2 (Summer 1985). Fig. 6.10 *Cap-Aux-Diamants*, vol. 1, no. 2 (Summer 1985). Fig. 6.11 *La Presse*, 27 May 1916. Fig. 7.1 National Archives of Canada/PA-43304. Fig. 7.2 2698-View, Notman Photographic Archives, McCord Museum of Canadian History. Fig. 7.3 Archives de la ville de Montréal. Fig. 7.4 National Archives of Canada/C128063. Fig. 7.5 174471-Misc II, Notman Photographic Archives, McCord Museum of Canadian History. Fig. 7.6 Glenbow Archives, Calgary, Alberta. Fig. 7.7 Société des alcools du Québec. Fig. 7.8 Sisters of Miséricorde Archives. Fig. 7.9 National Archives of Canada/C-14394. Fig. 8.3 Archives de la ville de Montréal, Z-35. Fig. 8.4 National Archives of Canada/PA112815. Fig. 8.5 Author's private collection. John Dickinson. Fig. 8.6 Courtesy of Madeleine Parent. Fig. 8.7 Photo *La Presse*, Montréal. Fig. 8.8 Canadian Jewish Congress, Gilbert to H.M. Caiserman, June 30, 1937. Fig. 8.9 National Archives of Canada/C-87690. Fig. 8.10 Archives de l'Université de Montréal. Fig. 8.11 Archives du Jardin botanique, Montréal. Fig. 9.2 Alain Leloup, private collection. Fig. 9.4 Alain Leloup, private collection. Fig. 9.5 Alain Leloup, private collection. Fig. 9.6 Hydro-Québec Archives. Fig. 9.7 Author's private collection. Fig. 9.8 Author's private collection. Fig. 9.9 Referendum Poster, private collection. Fig. 9.10 Archives Hydro-Québec. Fig. 9.11 John Doggett/National Archives of Canada/PA-164027. Fig. 9.12 Author's private collection. Fig. 9.14 Université du Québec à Montréal. Fig. 9.16 Shaney Komulainen, Canapress.

INDEX